MINISTERS OF THE LAW

EMORY UNIVERSITY STUDIES IN LAW AND RELIGION

John Witte Jr., General Editor

BOOKS IN THE SERIES

Faith and Order: The Reconciliation of Law and Religion
Harold J. Berman

Rediscovering the Natural Law in Reformed Theological Ethics
Stephen J. Grabill

Lex Charitatis: A Juristic Disquisition on Law in the Theology of Martin Luther
Johannes Heckel

The Ten Commandments in History:
Mosaic Paradigms for a Well-Ordered Society
Paul Grimley Kuntz

Religious Liberty, Volume 1: Overviews and History
Douglas Laycock

Building Cultures of Trust
Martin E. Marty

Suing for America's Soul: John Whitehead, The Rutherford Institute, and
Conservative Christians in the Courts
R. Jonathan Moore

Theology of Law and Authority in the English Reformation
Joan Lockwood O'Donovan

Ministers of the Law: A Natural Law Theory of Legal Authority
Jean Porter

Power over the Body, Equality in the Family: Rights and Domestic Relations in
Medieval Canon Law
Charles J. Reid Jr.

Ministers of the Law

*A Natural Law Theory
of Legal Authority*

Jean Porter

WILLIAM B. EERDMANS PUBLISHING COMPANY
GRAND RAPIDS, MICHIGAN / CAMBRIDGE, U.K.

© 2010 Jean Porter
All rights reserved

Published 2010 by
Wm. B. Eerdmans Publishing Co.
2140 Oak Industrial Drive N.E., Grand Rapids, Michigan 49505 /
P.O. Box 163, Cambridge CB3 9PU U.K.

Printed and bound in Great Britain by
Marston Book Services Limited, Didcot

16 15 14 13 12 11 10   7 6 5 4 3 2 1

Library of Congress Cataloging-in-Publication Data

Porter, Jean, 1955-
Ministers of the law: a natural law theory of legal authority / Jean Porter.
  p.   cm. — (Emory University studies in law and religion)
      ISBN 978-0-8028-6563-2 (cloth: alk. paper)
1. Christianity and law. 2. Authority — Religious aspects — Christianity.
  3. Natural law — Religious aspects — Christianity.   I. Title.

BR115.L28P67   2010
261.5 — dc22

                                          2010022387

www.eerdmans.com

For Joseph Blenkinsopp

nemini quicquam debeatis nisi ut invicem diligatis
qui enim diligit proximum legem implevit (Rom. 13.8)

Contents

Acknowledgments

In the spring of 2005, I was invited by Professor John Witte, Director of the Emory Center for the Study of Law and Religion, to join a project sponsored by the Center on Christian jurisprudence. This book is the immediate result of my participation in that project, and I cannot adequately express how much I owe to Professor Witte, to my fellow participants, and to Mr. Alonzo McDonald, whose generous support made this initiative possible. I had been thinking about the questions I pursue here for some time, but not to much effect. The Center provided me with a framework for developing my inchoate thoughts, together with support, encouragement, and invaluable feedback from those far more knowledgeable on these issues than I am. This is by no means a perfect book, but it is incomparably better than it would have been, had I tried to write it on my own.

In the spring of 2008, I had the good fortune to hold a Richardson Fellowship at the University of Durham in the United Kingdom, during which period I wrote much of the first draft of this book. I want to thank the faculty of the Theology Department of Durham University for awarding me this fellowship, and for their generous hospitality and ongoing support during critical months of writing. Special thanks are owed to Christopher Insole for organizing a number of opportunities for me to discuss my work with like-minded colleagues, and for his own perceptive comments, suggestions, and criticisms.

I would also like to thank those who read and commented on portions of this manuscript, including Patrick Brennan and Robert Tuttle. Russell Hittinger not only read several sections, but also gave me the benefit of his own ongoing work and many invaluable conversations on matters of shared interest. I owe a special debt to Joseph Tomain, who read and commented at length on almost the entire text. John Tasioulas and Mary Ellen O'Connell offered helpful insights and saved me from many confusions in the course of conversations about issues discussed in this book. I am grateful also to Lindsey Esbensen, who provided research assistance, offered many useful stylistic and editorial suggestions, and prepared the bibliography and index. It is needless to say, but I will say nonetheless, that any remaining mistakes or infelicities are mine alone.

Finally, I want to express my ongoing gratitude to those whose support means the most — my parents, June and Henry Heidelberg, and my husband, Joseph Blenkinsopp. Joe's patience and encouragement have been unflagging, and mean more to me than I can say. I dedicate this book to him as a token of my love and gratitude.

Introduction

Western legal systems typically operate in accordance with their own internal structures, which function more or less independently of other institutions or wider social processes. The independence of the law is maintained through a range of characteristic institutional forms, including formal procedures for legislation and adjudication and the construction of a detailed, comprehensive system of legal precepts. What is more, the independence of law is closely tied to widely shared social values — that legislation and adjudication *should* be carried out without regard to extra-legal considerations, that the validity of these processes *does,* or at any rate *should* depend on authority or correct procedure and not on considerations of probity or intrinsic reasonableness, and that adjudication *should* be guided by authoritative laws, and not exclusively by general considerations of morality or expediency.

The high degree of independence of law characteristic of Western legal systems has generated — or at least sharpened — distinctive problems pertaining to the authority and the normative force of the laws. Almost no one today would be prepared to argue (as some early legal positivists did) that the law rests on arbitrary commands, backed by the threat of force. Yet what is the alternative? Most legal scholars would not accept the contrary view that positive law depends on and closely reflects the dictates of a pre-conventional moral or natural law. Law depends for its proper functioning on norms of due process and proper procedure that sometimes require us to bracket wider moral considerations. What is more, the independence of the laws apparently presupposes that the legal force of enactments does not depend on their moral soundness. Yet how can we offer a credible normative justification for legal authority itself, together with criteria for evaluating and reforming particular laws, without drawing on extra-legal considerations in such a way as to undermine the independence and integrity of the law?

We might suspect that the independence of the law, together with the normative commitments that it embodies, is a modern phenomenon stemming from the disenchantment of the natural world and the emergence of secular society. On the contrary, we find a high degree of independence in a number of pre-modern legal systems, including the various forms of ecclesiastical and civil law that emerged in western Europe during the twelfth and thirteenth centuries. Early scholastic jurists and theologians insisted that positive law depends on some kind of authoritative enactment, and they defended the right — indeed, the obligation — of judges and other public officials to act in accordance with recognized legal procedures, even when these require morally problematic courses of action (for example, ordering the punishment of someone whose innocence is known to the judge but cannot be legally established). The scholastic commitment to the independence and integrity of positive or human law suggests that this is not a distinctively secular phenomenon. Rather, it is at least consistent with, and perhaps promotes genuine theological commitments.

When we turn to the writings of early scholastic jurists and theologians, we find a rich and creative discourse on the origins, scope, and limitations of human law, clearly grounded in practical experience while also informed by a scripturally grounded, distinctively Christian concept of natural law. This concept, in turn, provided an analytic framework within which diverse senses of law could be related to one another in mutually illuminating and correcting ways — more specifically, within which human law could be related to God's providential ordering of the non-human natural world, on the one hand, and the ideal standards set by divine law on the other. Surprisingly, from our vantage point, the scholastics did not equate the natural law with a determinate, pre-conventional moral law. Rather, they identified it in its primary sense with fundamental rational and natural principles of operation, giving rise to objective values reflecting the optimum forms of human existence. In other words, like some contemporary anthropologists and cultural psychologists, they defended the existence of objective natural values, while also recognizing that these may legitimately be expressed through very diverse systems of social norms and institutional practices. Seen from this perspective, a legal system reflects one concrete construal of natural values, which stands alongside other such conventional normative systems without depending on these, or on a universal, rationally compelling moral law, for its validity.

In contrast to later scholastic and early modern natural lawyers, the early scholastics tended to explain and justify legal authority through appeal to the needs and claims of natural human existence, rather than grounding it in divine or human commands. For these early theorists, authority is a natural relation, which reflects God's will as a manifestation of God's creative wisdom and goodness. Thus, it can be understood, and must be justified and limited, by reference to the needs and values proper to human life. The authority of the law is not arbitrary — it is grounded in objective, natural values — yet it retains its own integrity as an expression of a particular complex of natural and political aims, which can only be safeguarded in this way. These natural aims include the sustenance of a communal life, calling for some kind of social coordination, and the protection of the weakest members of society and of the common peace. More specifically, positive law is justified as an integral expression of a distinctive kind of authority, namely the political authority appropriate to rule over free men and women. In contrast to the dominion of a master over a slave, legal authority does not undermine its subjects' freedom and equality precisely because it is impersonal in its operations, limited in its scope, and oriented towards public good rather than private advantage. As such, it ultimately reflects the capacities for free self-determination stemming from the status of humanity as the image of God, a status which was at this time also being understood as implying certain subjective human rights. Western notions of the independence of the laws and individual human rights thus begin to emerge together in this period, as correlative expressions of a specific set of normative and theological commitments to the freedom and security of the individual and the ideals appropriate to political community. Because they are ultimately grounded in the dignity of the human person as an image of God, these are commitments that the Christian, as such, has a stake in safeguarding and promoting. What is more, these commitments are particularly relevant to contemporary American society, in which the integrity of law, human rights, and norms of due process have recently been subjected to unprecedented challenges.

In this book, I offer a constructive account of legal authority as a natural relation, taking my starting points from early scholastic legal and political thought, and developing these in conversation with contemporary philosophy of law and political theology. My aim is twofold. I want, on the one hand, to address fellow Christians, making a case that as believers we have a stake in safeguarding and promoting ideals of due process and the integrity of the law, and reflecting on what this might mean, concretely, in contemporary societies. On the other hand, I want also to engage secular jurists and philosophers, arguing that a theologically informed account of legal authority can address questions that they themselves have posed, in terms that they can recognize as responsive to their concerns. I take my title from an expression recurring throughout early scholastic literature: the judge, these writers say, acts as "a minister of the law," in the name of and on behalf of the law itself rather than as a private individual.

I am writing in the United States at the end of the doleful first decade of the twenty-first century, a time and place where ideals of legal integrity and the rule of law have little purchase, and political processes more generally are on the verge of breakdown. I am well aware that many readers may be tempted to conclude that the theory of legal authority and political process that I offer is hopelessly idealistic. It is of course idealistic — any constructive normative theory will necessarily be idealistic, in the sense of setting forth ideals for conduct — but I refuse to believe that it is "hopelessly" so, that the ideas in question are altogether unrealistic. Even now, the rule of law and deliberative self-governance continue to operate, very often at local levels where they escape national and international attention. They have been instantiated more fully at national levels here and abroad, and I believe that they can be recovered at these levels today. Cynicism and despair about legal and political processes very often rest on self-fulfilling prophecies. In this book, I hope to persuade my fellow Christians, together with anyone else whose sympathies accord with ours, to embrace prophecies of a very different kind — grounded in a hope that we can recover ideals and practices that we have largely lost, and a faith that it is worth our while to try.

CHAPTER 1

The Paradox of Legal Authority

The ideal of a perfect law through which men and women might live in harmony with one another and the cosmic order has deep roots in the Hebrew and Christian scriptures and the theological traditions stemming from them. To take only one example, Psalm 19 begins with a celebration of the cosmic order and closes with a hymn in praise of God's law, the clear implication being that each mirrors the other. The psalm begins, "The heavens are telling the glory of God, and the firmament proclaims his handiwork. Day to day pours forth speech, and night to night declares knowledge. There is no speech, nor are there words; their voice is not heard; yet their voice goes out through all the earth, and their words to the end of the world."[1] This ancient poem calls to mind Immanuel Kant's often-quoted remark that "Two things fill the mind with ever new and increasing admiration and awe, the oftener and more steadily we reflect on them: the starry heavens above me and the moral law within me."[2] The similarity becomes more pronounced as the Psalmist continues, "The law of the Lord is perfect, reviving the soul; the decrees of the Lord are sure, making wise the simple; the precepts of the Lord are right, rejoicing the heart; the commandment of the Lord is clear, enlightening the eyes; the fear of the Lord is pure, enduring forever; the ordinances of the Lord are true and righteous altogether." Some commentators have suggested that the latter verses in praise of God's law, the Torah, were added to an earlier composition celebrating the cosmic order, in the style of ancient

1. Psalm 19:1-4 and (following the quotation from Kant) 7-9; I have quoted the NRSV, omitting the scansion breaks.
2. Immanuel Kant, *Critique of Practical Reason [1788]*, trans. Lewis White Beck (Indianapolis: Bobbs-Merrill, 1956, repr. 1981), 166.

1

wisdom traditions. Even if that is so, the psalm as it stands expresses what becomes a pervasive theme running through both Jewish and Christian thought, namely, the deep connections between law and cosmic order, considered as two expressions of God's wisdom and beneficence.

Formal law as we know it, the product of all too human processes of legislation and judicial interpretation, cannot answer to the ideal of a perfect law reflected in Kant, or in the Hebrew Scriptures before him. Even the (slightly) more modest ideal of a virtuous and enlightened regime, created and sustained through laws that reflect universal standards of reasonableness, decency and good conduct, has proven to be elusive. Yet lawyers and scholars of jurisprudence have not altogether given up on the biblical ideal of law, or its secular analogues. We see such an ideal reflected in the old adage that "the law works itself pure" — that is to say, that it comes ever closer to approximating standards of rationally informed justice through processes of adjudication, which can in turn be understood and assessed in terms of these emerging standards. Even those who believe this hope to be unrealistic — or, more seriously, misleading in its assumptions about the character of law — find it difficult to dispense altogether with some kind of normative standard, such as justice or equality or even efficiency, in which laws at their best might be grounded, and in terms of which laws at their worst can be reformed or even rejected. This should not surprise or trouble us. On the contrary, we would have real cause for alarm if our philosophers, and (even more) our legislators and judges, were to surrender any aspiration towards normative ideals to guide the all too imperfect processes of lawmaking and adjudication.

To a considerable degree this aspiration sets the agenda for the thriving discipline of the philosophy of law, at least as practiced in Western Europe and its former colonies. In the United Kingdom, a number of recent developments — including structural reforms of the British Parliament and the uneven processes of integration into the legal structures of the European Union — have given a new saliency to fundamental questions about the foundations and scope of law.[3] In the United States, and to a lesser extent the

---

3. Arguably, recent developments in British political and legal practices have amounted to an inadvertent, yet profound and probably irreversible change in the British constitution itself; see Anthony King, *The British Constitution* (Oxford: Oxford University Press, 2007), for an exhaustive and persuasive defense of this view. For illuminating remarks on the mutual influence between philosophy of law and the emergence of the European Union, from someone who has played a prominent role in both processes, see Neil MacCormick, *Rhetoric and the Rule of Law: A Theory of Legal Reasoning* (Oxford: Oxford University Press, 2005), 7-11.

United Kingdom, longstanding disputes over the proper scope of judicial interpretation, taken together with more recent controversies over the scope of judicial due process and the limits of executive authority, have placed the need for an accessible ideal of law on the public agenda.[4]

We might expect that theologians would have something to contribute to this agenda. After all, the topos of law is central to the sacred texts of the Abrahamic traditions, and theologians have had a great deal to say about the ways in which God's justice should be mirrored in human societies. Yet in recent times, Christian theologians have had surprisingly little to say about formal law as such; certainly, compared to the extensive body of theological writings on social justice, contributions to a theology of law have been meager and under-developed. To some extent, this relative inattention is understandable. Given the deeply entrenched separation of church and state in the United States and parts of Europe, it has been difficult for many theologians to see what they might contribute, precisely as theologians, to an understanding of contemporary secular legal systems. More importantly, modern Christian theology, especially but not only within Protestant traditions, has been informed by a keen sense of the ambiguity of law — a sense which is arguably as deeply rooted in Christian scripture and tradition as the idea of law itself.

As Peter Landau observes, scripturally grounded theologies of law and social order have been marked by a sense of the imperfections, not to say the downright sinfulness, of actual polities and their legal systems.[5] Thus, in his view, theologians have typically taken one of three approaches to political and legal systems. They have located the ideal law in an eschatological future, in which God's reign will be perfectly and comprehensively expressed; or, regarding civil society as sinful beyond redemption, even demonic, they have advocated withdrawal from the surrounding society, as far as possible; or finally, they have argued that actual polities and legal systems are grounded in an authoritative divine decree, through which God mercifully provides remedies for the worst effects of human sinfulness. This last approach, in contrast to the first two, acknowledges that legal systems play a legitimate role in most human societies. It emphasizes the ameliorative purpose of law and

---

4. Out of many possible examples of the literature generated by this debate, see the essays collected in Antonin Scalia et al., *A Matter of Interpretation: Federal Courts and the Law* (Princeton: Princeton University Press, 1997), and Ronald Dworkin, *Justice in Robes* (Cambridge, MA: Belknap Press/Harvard University Press, 2006).

5. Peter Landau, "Der biblische Sündenfall und die Legitimität des Rechts," in *Die Begründung des Rechts als historisches Problem,* ed. Dietmar Willoweit and Elisabeth Müller-Luckner (Munich: R. Oldenbourg, 2000), 203-14.

defends its authority by a more or less direct appeal to divine decree. Nonetheless, seen from this perspective, the law is at best an instrumental means towards the attainment of social justice and common utility, and it can as such be addressed in passing, or left to the care of those entrusted with putting the ideals of social justice into practice.

There are, however, other theological approaches to the law that emphasize the rational and even broadly natural origins of legal systems, and correlatively place less emphasis on the law's conventional and authoritative status. These tend to be formulated in terms of the ancient tradition of a natural law, pre-conventional, universal and unchanging, which functions as the originating principle and ultimate criterion for legal systems and social practices. The natural law tradition is of course pre-Christian in its origins, and today its most prominent defenders, at least among legal scholars, insist that the natural law does not depend on specific theological or broadly natural beliefs for its foundations or content.[6] Yet the natural law has been interpreted in other ways throughout the long history of Christian jurisprudence. In particular, when we turn to the work of scholastic jurists and theologians in the formative period for Western legal institutions — roughly, from the late eleventh through the thirteenth centuries — we find a very different approach to the natural law, one which is robustly scriptural and theological, while also drawing freely on rich classical traditions of reflection on human reason and the natural order. The natural law, thus understood, provided an analytic framework within which diverse senses of law can be related to one another in mutually illuminating and correcting ways — more specifically, within which human law can be related to God's providential ordering of the non-human natural world, on the one hand, and the ideal standards set by divine, that is to say, revealed law on the other. In this way, the scholastic concept of natural law offers a way to address the deep tensions over the value of law running through Christian scriptures and theological traditions. As we will see in more detail below, the concept of natural law, interpreted in the context of broader claims about the essential goodness of created nature, provides a touchstone for distinguishing those aspects of law which are valid and good from those which reflect the distortions of sinfulness. It thus opens up the possibility that formal law might be regarded as an intrinsically valuable component of natural hu-

6. This is the approach taken by the widely influential interpretation of a Thomistic natural law jurisprudence developed by John Finnis and others; see John Finnis, *Natural Law and Natural Rights* (Oxford: Clarendon, 1980), 23-58, and *Aquinas: Moral, Political, and Legal Theory* (Oxford: Oxford University Press, 1998), 304-12.

man life, imperfect and limited to be sure, and yet intelligible and authoritative considered on its own terms apart from a special divine decree.

This is the aspect of natural law jurisprudence that I hope to recover and to develop in this book. More specifically, I will offer a theological analysis of the authority of law, according to which legal authority is construed as a natural relation of authority, resting ultimately in God's wisdom as expressed in the free act constituting us as creatures of a specific kind. Thus understood, the authority and independence of the law are given their due, and at the same time, legal authority is both justified and delimited by reference to a distinctively human form of natural life. In developing this theory of legal authority, I will draw extensively on central strands of early scholastic theological and legal thought, developing and extending these in conversation with some important interlocutors in contemporary philosophy of law. However, I should make it clear from the outset that this is meant as a constructive theory of law, responsive to contemporary exigencies of legislation and judicial interpretation, particularly as these are experienced in the anglophone societies with which I am most familiar. My aim, in other words, is not to offer a historical interpretation of the scholastics' views on law, but rather to draw on their views as elements for a contemporary synthesis. My hope is that the resultant theory of legal authority will be responsive to a widely expressed need for normative standards by which laws might be evaluated and interpreted, while also doing justice to the independence and integrity of the law as it exists in modern Western societies.

It might seem that a theology of law would have little to offer to contemporary debates over lawmaking and legal interpretation, given the secular character of contemporary Western societies. I do not intend to challenge the civic ideal of religious neutrality informing most Western societies today, or to undermine the institutional arrangements through which that ideal is sustained. On the contrary, these arrangements appear to me to be, on the whole, both just and exigent, given the histories and circumstances of the societies in which they are embedded — which is not to say that secularity is an ideal towards which every society can or should aspire.[7] Nonetheless, it would be short-sighted to rule out the possibility that a theological account of law might be illuminating and fruitful, even for those who do not accept all of its

---

7. I am thus broadly in agreement with John Courtney Murray's defense of contemporary liberal secularism on natural law grounds, although my construal of the natural law tradition differs from his; see *We Hold These Truths: Catholic Reflections on the American Proposition* (New York: Doubleday, 1964), 17-142.

presuppositions. During the early and middle decades of the past century, theologians and church leaders played a central role in shaping public discourse and institutional life; Reinhold Niebuhr and Martin Luther King are perhaps the best known, but there are others, including John Courtney Murray and John Ryan ("Father New Deal"). We cannot say in advance whether, and in what ways, men and women might draw on theological perspectives in public deliberation — that will always depend on a complex set of convictions, sentiments, felt needs, and shared history.

At any rate, this book is primarily intended for Christians, together with others who share the theistic convictions of the Abrahamic traditions. I assume that we Christians can and should participate fully in civil society, including the institutions of law that give public expression, stability, and force to its central ideals. I hope to make the case that we can do so wholeheartedly, in the same way we enter into the practices of marriage, family life, and communal associations, celebrating these as aspects of the way of life we are naturally meant to enjoy. At the same time, systematic reflection on formal law turns out to offer more in the way of foundational theological insights than might initially have been expected. It provides a focal point for reflecting on the practical implications of natural law, and more specifically on the ways in which our practical formulations of a natural law emerge from and sustain the ideals and practices of particular communities. More fundamentally, it offers a way to interpret human legal and normative judgments in terms of their relation to God's eternal law, and thereby in relation to the natural order comprehensively considered. As we will see, this relation does not imply that moral (much less legal) norms share in the necessity and universal scope of God's providential wisdom. On the contrary — precisely because human deliberation and action are grounded in God's eternity, our formal legal systems and normative practices do not need to imitate the universality and necessity of God's law, nor do we need to save ourselves from the ambiguities of our own laws. We are free to be creatures in a finite world and to conduct our affairs accordingly. Or so I will argue in what follows.

Before doing so, however, I will identify a set of issues related to the necessary yet paradoxical interconnections among authority, normative criteria, and the independence of law in Western legal systems. I will do so by tracing one central trajectory in contemporary jurisprudence. Along the way I hope to clarify what I mean by critical jurisprudence and to begin to delineate key features of Western legal systems that any adequate jurisprudence, including a theological jurisprudence, would need to address. These will be the tasks of the first section.

1. Critical Jurisprudence and the Paradox of Authority

Preliminary Considerations

This book is intended as an essay in systematic theological jurisprudence. It is directed towards a critical and constructive account of actual legal practices developed along the same lines as the contemporary philosophical jurisprudence with which it is engaged. As such, it takes its starting point and immediate frame of reference from contemporary legal systems in Western societies, that is to say, the modern, post-industrial polities which trace their origins more or less directly to the nations and empires of early modern Europe.[8] These systems provide the initial "legal paradigms," in Ronald Dworkin's phrase, that is to say, "propositions of law like the traffic code that we take to be true if any are."[9] There is a good case to be made that all systematic intellectual inquiry will necessarily take its starting point from particular paradigms of this sort, setting the field of the inquiry and suggesting initial hypotheses. But in any case, contemporary philosophical jurisprudence and, *mutatis mutandis,* theological jurisprudence as well, should be tethered to actual legal practices, precisely because the point of this inquiry is to make sense of, and where appropriate to guide and direct, the practical activities of legislation and legal interpretation. As Neil MacCormick says, our aim is "rational reconstruction," through which we attempt to sort out the seemingly confused, disorderly, and incomplete legal systems governing our lives through "a new imagining and describing of the implicit order in potential disorder, based on some principles or values ascribed to the whole and its parts."[10] Thus, philosophical jurisprudence takes as its starting point attempts to "explain the nature of a certain kind of social institution" thereby illuminating "a concept entrenched in our society's self-understanding," as Joseph Raz puts

8. There is little to be gained by trying to define the boundaries of Western society too precisely. Western legal systems and traditions are practiced, and cherished, in many Asian and African societies, especially those that have been deeply shaped by interactions with a colonizing European state, such as India and Pakistan. As I hope will be apparent, I do not mean to imply the superiority or inevitability of Western legal traditions, vis-à-vis other ways of organizing legal practices.

9. Ronald Dworkin, *Law's Empire* (Cambridge, MA: Belknap Press/Harvard University Press, 1986), 91-92.

10. Neil MacCormick, *Rhetoric and the Rule of Law: A Theory of Legal Reasoning* (Oxford: Oxford University Press, 2005), 29. Although this book is focused, as the title indicates, on legal reasoning, MacCormick here generalizes his claim to include humanistic inquiries more generally.

it. The local and contingent context for systematic reflection on law may appear to be problematic, but as Raz goes on to show, legal theory properly moves from the parochial to the universal, leading towards a generally applicable concept of law.[11] Nonetheless, until we can make sense of our own legal practices as they actually are, we will not have the conceptual tools necessary to carry out an intelligent and critical assessment of those practices, much less to make sense of anyone else's legal practices.

We begin, therefore, with the law as it is practiced in contemporary Western societies in the early twenty-first century — the complex, confusing, largely invisible mass of statutes, institutions, and procedures structuring our day-to-day lives. We note, first of all, that the laws in question are rules governing human conduct, that is to say, normative propositions permitting, requiring, or forbidding an identifiable kind of action (or non-action), conditionally or categorically. Secondly, the systems of law constituted by these norms are relatively comprehensive in scope. No legal system takes account of every possible human action or concern, but the legal system governing a coherent political entity — say, the comprehensive law of the state of Indiana, or even more, the constitutional and federal law of the United States — does touch in some way on all the central aspects of human existence. So far, formal laws look a great deal like moral norms. Yet there is at least one critical difference between legal systems and morality, as the latter is generally understood in Western societies. That is, legal norms, in contrast to moral rules as commonly understood, are social conventions grounded in deliberate human actions.[12] Typically, they are the end results of formal processes of legislation and adjudication, although this need not be the case, since in at least some circumstances, customary practices have the force of law. But in either case, as Raz observes, "the law is posited, is made law by the activities of human beings."[13] No credible analytic jurisprudence can deny the conventional status of actual laws and practices, or fail to account for this as a proper and legitimate aspect of a legal system. This constraint does not necessarily rule out the possibility of analyzing legal systems

11. Joseph Raz, *Between Authority and Interpretation* (Oxford: Oxford University Press, 2009), 17-46; the phrases quoted are taken from 34.

12. At this point, I simply presuppose a broad understanding of social conventions seen as products of human artifice, in contrast to natural principles that play a constitutive role in all human activity and are in that sense prior to any actual practices or enactments. It will be one of the central tasks of this book to clarify and develop this rough idea.

13. Joseph Raz, *The Authority of Law: Essays on Law and Morality* (Oxford: Clarendon Press, 1979), 38.

in terms of the rational or natural principles they manifest (fortunately, since that is the aim of this book). But it does imply that any analysis of law in terms of its reasonableness or natural origins will need to explain the relation between the conventions of actual laws, and the fundamental principles that they embody, or express, or from which they emerge.

In his seminal book, *The Concept of Law*, H. L. A. Hart argues that law properly so called can best be understood as a set of socially sanctioned rules, comprising both what he describes as primary rules of obligation and secondary rules through which some of these are given legal force — "rules of recognition," which, whatever their origins or status, are embodied in social conventions.[14] Seen from another perspective, the law can be regarded as an ongoing activity, or in the words of Lon Fuller, as "the enterprise of subjecting human conduct to the governance of rules."[15] Fuller's way of characterizing the law, while not as precise as Hart's, has the advantage of keeping the ongoing, dynamic development of legal systems in view, and reminding us that analytic legal theories are themselves not only situated in, but also vital to the ongoing life of the law. And this brings us to a critical point.

The conventional status of law might seem to rule out the possibility of a genuinely interesting philosophy or theology of law, but this need not be the case. The processes of legislation and adjudication through which laws are made, interpreted, and obeyed are subject to rational constraints, arguably at least — and this point, as we will see, turns out to be central to Fuller's account of the law. What is more, these processes also call for judgments on a range of independently interesting questions, regarding, for example, the scope of human freedom and the contours of causality. Most fundamentally, if we — as legal professionals, legislators, or judges, or simply as citizens — are to take ownership of the law as a purposeful activity, we need

---

14. For a concise formulation, see the second edition of H. L. A. Hart, *The Concept of Law*, originally published in 1961 (Oxford: Clarendon Press, 1994), 94, quoted below. Recently, there has been some debate over whether the rules of recognition are genuinely conventional, but at least it seems clear that Hart regards them as necessarily embodied in social practices which are to some degree local and contingent — as, for that matter, are the primary rules of obligation. I agree with Andrei Marmor that there are rules of recognition, and these are best understood as constitutive conventions, that is to say, conventions determining what constitutes law, and setting internal norms for legal practices — even if this was not precisely Hart's own view. See Andrei Marmor, *Social Conventions: From Language to Law* (Princeton: Princeton University Press, 2009), 162-71.

15. Lon L. Fuller, *The Morality of Law*, revised edition (New Haven: Yale University Press, 1969), 106.

at some point to reflect intelligently on just what we take ourselves to be doing as we go about the processes of making, interpreting, and carrying out
laws. Practiced in this way, jurisprudence is a practical discipline, presupposing what Hart describes as the internal standpoint taken by those who regard the laws as placing them under obligations of various kinds — who regard them, in other words, as appropriate rational grounds for choice and
legitimate criteria for evaluating actions falling within their scope.[16] We can
offer more or less plausible accounts of legal systems from an external viewpoint, construing the law as nothing more than a summary of patterns of
behavior, or a set of predictions for what judges are likely to do, or a direct
expression of heterogeneous social and economic forces. But these kinds of
accounts, illuminating though they may be, cannot offer much guidance to
men and women who are actually engaged in some kind of legal practice,
and who hope to render explicit the rationale for what they are doing, in order to carry on in a more consistent and fruitful way.[17] Thus, precisely *because* formal law is a construct, the product of human activity, we need to reflect systematically and critically on the processes of legislation and legal
interpretation.

For that very reason, the characterizations of law offered so far — as the
activity of subjecting human conduct to the governance of rules, or alternatively, as the conventional norms which are the products of that activity —
are inadequate, or at least incomplete. We have occasion to regulate our activities through what are clearly conventional rules in many spheres of life,
for example, through the norms of etiquette, the codes of conduct binding
on a particular profession, or the rules of parliamentary procedure. Yet these
kinds of norms and practices would be regarded as distinct from law, properly so called. We seem to have little difficulty in distinguishing between legal activities and rules, and other kinds of conventional normative practices,
but what is the basis for this distinction? What are the characteristic features
of legal systems, in virtue of which we can so readily distinguish these from
other kinds of conventional systems?

The comparison between a legal system and the systematic rules of etiquette, parliamentary procedure, and the like, suggests that one distinguishing feature of the former would be its relative seriousness: the law matters,
and it obliges us to compliance, in a way that other, superficially similar nor-

16. *Concept of Law,* 89-91.
17. See *Concept of Law,* 83-84. In fact, I do not regard the various reductive accounts of law to
be terribly persuasive, except in limited ways.

mative systems do not. Failure to send a thank-you note or confusion between tabling a motion and postponing consideration may be regrettable, even reprehensible, but embezzlement is much worse — or so we assume. Yet on closer examination, this distinction breaks down. Some laws are trivial, and on the other side, some non-legal conventions can carry serious consequences for those who break them: marriages can be ruined, reputations and livelihood lost through failures to observe conventions of propriety, restraint, and good conduct. What is more, standards of etiquette, at least, do seem to be fully as comprehensive in scope as legal systems. Yet we do seem to attach distinctive importance to legal obligations, if only because we attach coercive sanctions to these laws. Someone who is rude can expect general contempt, but the lawbreaker can be thrown into prison. The coercive force of law also distinguishes it from the supposedly non-conventional rules of morality, even though the latter are widely regarded as carrying greater normative weight than legal systems; the moral guilt of murder is a terrible burden, but someone who is legally convicted of the crime of murder may well be killed herself, at least in some jurisdictions. None of this implies that coercive force is necessarily implied by the "very idea" of law, but at the very least, laws seem to differ from other kinds of social conventions insofar as they are regularly and normally attached to coercive sanctions of some kind.

Independence, Normative Constraint, and the Paradox of Authority

The distinctively coercive force of legal obligations provided the starting point for one of the dominant approaches to jurisprudence in the nineteenth and early twentieth centuries. On this view, developed most extensively by the nineteenth-century jurist John Austin, legal obligation is best understood as one example of the kind of coercion that depends for its force on the threat of unpleasant consequences — as seen, for example, in the classic phrase, "your money or your life." As Hart puts it, "To some it has seemed clear that in this situation where one person gives another an order backed by threats, and, in this sense of 'oblige,' obliges him to comply, we have the essence of law, or at least 'the key to the science of jurisprudence.'"[18] But this account of legal obligation does not stand up to analysis. As Hart goes on to argue, comprehensively and conclusively, a model of law as a sys-

---

18. *Concept of Law*, 6; the quotation is taken from John Austin, *The Province of Jurisprudence Determined* (London: J. Murray, 1832), Lecture I, 13.

tem of coercive orders cannot account for the most fundamental elements of ordinary legal systems, let alone, accommodate the perennial problem cases for modern jurisprudence, namely customary and international law.[19] This model is most persuasive in the context of criminal law, which does indeed consist primarily of prohibitions, together with attached sanctions. However, it cannot readily account for other centrally important forms of law, including those laws which establish the correct form for giving force to individual acts (for example, the proper form for a will) or those which confer rights or immunities, rather than forbidding actions. Even with respect to the criminal law, the model of coercive orders falls short, because it cannot capture the impersonal character and general scope of the rules of criminal law. The law against murder cannot plausibly be construed as if the State of Indiana, personified, were following me around, ordering me on every relevant occasion to refrain from killing this or that individual. It is a general rule, which applies to me as one member of a class, not as someone individually addressed by an actual or fictitious overlord.

Most importantly, the model of laws as coercive orders fails to take account of the distinctive normative force of the law, which is said to impose duties or obligations on those to whom it applies. As Hart explains, "the statement that a person was obliged to obey someone is, in the main, a psychological one referring to the beliefs and motives with which an action was done. But the statement that someone *had an obligation* to do something is of a very different type and there are many signs of this difference."[20] Hart thus calls attention to a distinction that is difficult to spell out in detail, yet intuitively persuasive and important — the distinction between being compelled by force or circumstance to do something and being obliged, bound to act, by what might be described as the intrinsic force of one's reasons for acting. These reasons may or may not include the obligations imposed by some legitimate authority, but Hart's point would be that authority can only impose a binding obligation by virtue of the reasons that justify its claims. Hart goes on to connect the obligatory force of the law with what he describes as the internal point of view of those who consider themselves to be bound by the laws, in such a way as to regard legal precepts as legitimate and normally decisive reasons for acting in one way or another.[21] His immediate

---

19. These arguments are set forth in *Concept of Law*, 18-49; the issues raised by international law are discussed at 212-37.

20. *Concept of Law*, 83; emphasis in the original.

21. *Concept of Law*, 89-91.

point is that the distinctive obligatory force of the law cannot be captured from an external standpoint, from which the laws may well seem to be nothing more than predictions about social behavior. At the same time, the distinction between external and internal viewpoints maps a still more fundamental distinction between acting in accordance with a general rule, and following a rule — that is to say, carrying out the relevant behavior knowingly, with the intent of enacting or respecting the rule. In order to follow a rule in the latter sense, the agent must grasp it as a rule, see its relevance to one's own prospective choices, and adopt it as one's own reason for acting, appropriating it into the internally held set of reasons governing one's deliberation and choice.

Of course, whenever anyone enters into any normative practice of any kind — even provisionally, or out of questionable motivations — she will necessarily regard the rules of that practice from an internal standpoint, so long as she is really engaged in the practice in question. I may not care in the least about parliamentary procedure, but so long as I am chairing a meeting in a certain kind of public forum, the motion to call the question constitutes a good and normally compelling reason for me to call for a vote to close debate. Nonetheless, I can choose to opt out of the activity altogether, in which case the rules of procedure exercise no binding force on me at all. In contrast, I would not normally consider myself free to opt out of the system of rules constituting the legal system of my polity; these constitute reasons for me, which I regard as such, even when it would be more pleasant or advantageous to disregard them. In this way, legal rules are unlike most other conventional sets of norms, but they are very much like norms of another kind, usually characterized in Western societies as the laws or rules of morality. These, too, are regarded as comprehensive in scope, supremely important, and inescapably obliging — even more so, on most accounts, than the norms of the law. How, then, are we to distinguish between legal and moral norms? Or should we perhaps regard legal norms as a sub-set of moral norms, dependent on these for their overall force on the moral considerations that they express?

Hart's reply to these questions is worth quoting at some length, because it will take us directly to one of the central features of the law as it is understood and practiced, not only in Western, but also in almost all large-scale human societies.

Rules are conceived and spoken of as imposing obligations when the general demand for conformity is insistent and the social pressure brought to bear upon those who deviate or threaten to deviate is great. . . . [He goes on to observe that this social pressure may take many forms, including] the operation of feelings of shame, remorse and guilt. When the pressure is of this last-mentioned kind we may be inclined to classify the rules as part of the morality of the social group and the obligation under the rules as moral obligation. Conversely, when physical sanctions are prominent or usual among the forms of pressure, even though they are neither closely defined nor administered by officials but are left to the community at large, we shall be inclined to classify the rules as a primitive or rudimentary form of law. . . . What is important is that the insistence on importance or *seriousness* of social pressure behind the rules is the primary factor determining whether they are thought of as giving rise to obligations. Two other characteristics of obligations go naturally together with this primary one. The rules supported by this serious pressure are thought important because they are believed to be necessary to the maintenance of social life or some highly prized feature of it. . . . Secondly, it is generally recognized that the conduct required by these rules may, while benefiting others, conflict with what the person who owes the duty may wish to do. Hence obligations and duties are thought of as characteristically involving sacrifice or renunciation.[22]

Hart refers to these as primary rules of obligation, noting that every human society is structured through rules of this kind. Within the context of small, homogeneous societies, such primary rules are not only necessary but sufficient to sustain the ongoing life of the community. But in larger or more complex communities, these primary rules of obligation prove to be insufficient. They cannot resolve uncertainties in cases of ambiguity or conflict; they cannot readily be modified in light of changing conditions since they are too static; and the procedures through which they are maintained are necessarily inefficient. In order to address these deficiencies, most societies have generated secondary rules, so called because, in Hart's words, "they are all *about* such rules."[23] The secondary rules presuppose primary rules of obligation, functioning in such a way as to determine how the primary rules are interpreted and applied in at least some recurring sets of circumstances. In order to remedy the uncertainty of the primary rules, societies introduce a rule of recognition, which interprets, qualifies, or specifies a subset of the primary rules as "conclusive affirmative indication[s]" that these reflect the

22. *Concept of Law,* 86-87; emphasis in the original.
23. *Concept of Law,* 94; emphasis in the original.

14

consensus of the community, as expressed through concerted social pressures to confirm to them.[24] In order to address the static character of the primary rules, societies typically introduce rules of change, through which some individual or body of persons is empowered to introduce new primary obligations and to modify or eliminate existing rules — in a word, to legislate. Finally, the inefficiency of the primary rules of obligation is addressed through secondary rules empowering individuals or bodies of persons to "make authoritative determinations of the question whether, on a particular occasion, a primary rule has been broken" — thus giving rise to at least the rudiments of a system of adjudication.[25] Significantly, Hart does not claim that the imposition of coercive sanctions is essential to a viable system of secondary rules, but he does go on to say most communities find it preferable to prohibit violent self-help and to specify some means for imposing sanctions on malefactors.[26]

According to Hart, these secondary rules, taken together with the primary rules of obligation that they mark out as having distinctive force, constitute at least a rudimentary legal system; thus, "law may most illuminatingly be characterized as a union of primary rules of obligation with such secondary rules."[27] By now, it should be apparent that Hart is not simply stipulating how the law should be understood, much less proposing a definition based on an analysis of an abstract concept of law.[28] Nonetheless, by now we begin to see in his analysis the main lines of a general theory of law, applicable across a wide range of social and historical contexts.[29] At the very least, Hart suggests that we can identify certain recurrent features of most social systems which can be properly and illuminatingly construed as legal systems, understood as such by analogy to the systems of formal law that we ourselves generate and use. In doing so, he relies on, and helps to explain, the common perception that most societies do indeed seem to have something recognizably analogous to our own legal system. In all but the simplest hu-

24. *Concept of Law*, 94.

25. *Concept of Law*, 96. The overall argument is set out in 94-99.

26. On this point, see *Concept of Law*, 97.

27. Peter Coss, *Concept of Law*, "Introduction," 1-16, 94.

28. Hart insists on this point, in response to Dworkin's claim that Hart proposes a theory of law based on an analysis of the meaning of the word "law"; see *Concept of Law*, 246-8. Raz argues, however, that Hart's analysis does imply a general theoretical statement of what the law is, even though it is tethered in actual legal institutions rather than a conceptual analysis of "law" taken in the abstract; see *Between Authority and Interpretation*, 17-46.

29. *Concept of Law*, 76-77.

man societies, we find some system of rules dedicated to what Chris Wick-ham calls "collectively sponsored redress"; furthermore, as Wickham goes on to say, "if a legal system was *only* a mirror of locally acceptable direct action, it would have no reason to exist as a separately organized sphere at all."[30] The boundaries between the "separately organized sphere" of the law may be open and permeable, or they may be well-defined and relatively fixed, but we can usually locate them through comparison with the differing functions of our own distinctive spheres of law, morality, norms of courtesy, and the like.

Thus understood, a legal system is embedded in, and yet distinct from, the wider framework of primary rules of obligation. The necessity here may not be strictly logical, in the sense of depending on a purely rational, abstract "concept of law," but it is conceptual, in the sense that we would have no criterion, and no motivation, for identifying something as a legal system unless it were marked out in this way. Hart himself refers to this as the independence of legal systems relative to other normative systems operative within the same society.[31] This attribute is also described, especially by legal historians and sociologists, as the autonomy of law, explained by the historian Peter Coss as follows: "In its crudest form, the notion of autonomy suggests that the law possesses internal structures which operate independently of the society within which it is situated."[32] The independence or autonomy of law cannot be absolute; as Hart himself demonstrates, the secondary rules which set up the rudiments of a legal system presuppose a wider context of primary rules of obligation. Further, as we will see, legal historians and so-

---

30. Both taken from *The Moral World of the Law*, ed. Peter Coss (Cambridge: Cambridge University Press, 2000), "Conclusion," 240-59, 242; emphasis in the original.

31. See *Concept of Law*, 24-25.

32. Peter Coss, "Introduction," 1-16 in *The Moral World of the Law*, 1. According to the sociologist Niklas Luhmann, the use of "autonomy" in reference to a kind of normative system can be traced to the biologist Francisco Varela, who introduced the term in 1979 in the context of explaining biological evolution; see his *Law as a Social System*, trans. Klaus A. Ziegert (Oxford: Oxford University Press, 2004), 95. Luhmann goes on to offer an exhaustive and illuminating development of this idea under the rubric of operational closure. On his view a legal system generates normative judgments based on its own, distinctive and self-justifying operative principles, albeit in such a way as to respond to its environment; see 76-141. For a most helpful guide through the work of this complex author, see the "Introduction" by Richard Nobles and David Schiff in *Law as a Social System*, 1-52. MacCormick takes Luhmann's work as the basis for his own nuanced account of the relation between law and politics, seen as two distinct yet mutually interactive systems; see *Institutions of Law: An Essay in Legal Theory* (Oxford: Oxford University Press, 2007), 171-85.

cial scientists have recently directed attention back to the many ways in which legal systems stem from and reinforce a wider set of cultural values and beliefs. Nonetheless, it would seem that legal systems come into being in response to the need for a delimited set of normative practices marked off as expressions of communal will through forceful social pressure and safeguarded through special procedures of various kinds. Correlatively, we could not intelligibly identify a set of norms as a legal system unless it functioned autonomously from other normative systems, at least to some degree.

At this point, we begin to see why legal authority strikes so many as problematic. A claim to legal authority implies legitimacy, acknowledged as such by those who regard themselves as normatively bound by the legal system in question. We recall that Hart identifies the failure to take account of the perceived legitimacy of legal norms as the fatal defect in earlier forms of legal positivism. Yet as he goes on to argue, legal authority is expressed in and through the generation and interpretation of a more or less closed system of precepts, which are recognized as valid legal rules in accordance with contingent, socially situated rules of recognition. This raises two interconnected, yet distinct questions. First, what are the normative grounds, if any, on the basis of which a claim to authority can be validated? We might worry that Hart's appeal to a communal rule implies that legal authority rests on nothing more than communal discretion — an improvement over the dominion of individuals, to be sure, but not obviously valid or just. In fact, Hart himself does not seem to regard a rule of recognition as conferring validity.[33] Rather, the rule of recognition, as we recall, is a normative practice or a complex set of interrelated practices through which the legitimacy of legislative and judicial agencies, and the legal force of specific enactments, are acknowledged and put into practice. As such, it indicates the community's judgments about validity without itself forming the ground for those judgments. Hart seems to me to be right on this point, but if so, this only heightens the problem of validity. What is the normative basis for the communal judgment expressed through the rule of recognition? Is it possible that it rests on no basis at all — that legal authority finally rests on sheer historical accidents and arbitrary choice?

Secondly, what are the normative constraints on the exercise of legal authority? That is, what are the internal normative criteria by which precepts within a legal system can be evaluated, not from some extraneous viewpoint,

---

33. This is unclear, but I agree with Raz that this was his original view, and makes the most sense in terms of his overall position; see *Between Authority and Interpretation*, 381.

but precisely as legal enactments? Hart himself does not seem to believe that there are any necessary normative criteria of this kind, beyond the system-specific norms determining the legal validity of specific enactments. He certainly believes that a legal system, taken as a whole, must be responsive to the general conditions and pervasive needs of human existence in order to be viable, and furthermore, he recognizes that moral standards can legitimately be incorporated into a legal system. Nonetheless, he rejects the view that conformity to moral standards (or presumably, any extra-legal normative standards) is a necessary condition for the legal validity of an enactment, leading him to embrace what he describes as a "soft positivism."[34] Even on his expansive view, therefore, we have to allow for the possibility that laws might be iniquitous or unjust, while nonetheless still carrying the full weight of legal authority. This would seem to imply that there are, at the end of the day, no internal limits to the scope of legal authority.

These questions are not always clearly distinguished, and yet they are distinct. The considerations justifying legal authority, in general or with reference to specific agencies bearing such authority, may or may not imply normative constraints on the proper exercise of that authority. These implications will of course depend on the kind of justification that is proffered; for example, the claim that kings enjoy authority by virtue of a divine authorizing decree may well imply that this authority is unlimited and unbounded in its proper force. Indeed, it can be misleading to frame the problem of internal criteria in terms of a question about the limits of legal authority, understood as authority exercised by someone or some agency. For one thing, not everyone agrees that legal systems are necessarily established by someone's authority. The sociologist Niklas Luhmann, for one, argues that they emerge spontaneously, through a process analogous to biological evolution. Yet on his account, the emergence of legal systems presupposes precisely the self-referential closure exhibited by autonomous normative systems of all kinds, including that of living organisms; otherwise, the system in question could not persist over time or reproduce itself as a distinct entity, independently of the environmental forces surrounding it.[35] This line of analysis suggests a more general point. The problem of internal criteria is generated by the independence of the law, its status as an autonomous, self-regulating sys-

34. Hart's overall analysis of the relation between law and morality is more subtle, and more open to the interconnections between legal and moral considerations, than is sometimes acknowledged; see *The Concept of Law*, 153-84. He introduces the term "soft positivism" in his Postscript, *Concept of Law*, 250-54.

35. This analogy is developed at some length in *Law as a Social System*, 230-73.

tem of precepts, within which non-legal normative criteria would seem to have no place. By the same token, a persuasive account of the normative criteria for legal validity would not necessarily cast light on the grounds of legal authority itself.

At the same time, however, these questions reflect the same broad worries about the reasonableness of legal authority. The contingency of the processes through which legal authority emerges, and the seemingly unconstrained paths along which it develops, raise the specter of arbitrariness — implying that legal authority, in its very existence and specific functions, cannot finally be justified in rational terms. Yet by Hart's own account, those who regard the law from the internal point of view must regard it as justified to some degree, if only because they adopt its precepts as normatively valid reasons for their own actions. When I pay my taxes to the state of Indiana, I do so because I regard the laws of this state as normatively binding on me: the state tax code, considered as a legal enactment, is as such a decisive reason for my action, and I regard it as such. How can I justify this (generally inconvenient) attitude, if the state of Indiana and its enactments rest on nothing more than sheer chance? By the same token, a theory of legal authority that both justifies such authority as valid and generates normative constraints on its exercise in terms of the same set of considerations would offer some clear advantages. Most importantly, it would enable us to offer a unified account in terms of which to identify criteria for evaluating the claims to exercise legal authority, while at the same time generating criteria for proper and improper uses of that authority. Without some such unifying account, it is difficult to see how we can do justice to our competing intuitions about legal systems — that they are marked off from other kinds of considerations through authoritative enactments and relative independence and yet that they also reflect a necessary and valuable aspect of human life, which can and should inform the deliberative judgments and choices of free, rational individuals.

The worry that legal authority might be arbitrary in some problematic way motivates the work of two of Hart's most powerful and influential critics, Lon Fuller and Ronald Dworkin. At the same time, each develops a constructive account of legal authority informed by wide-ranging considerations, which has generally, and deservedly, had wide influence on its own terms. Taken together with Hart's work, these accounts have largely set the agenda for philosophical jurisprudence, at least in the Anglophone world, since the middle decades of the last century.

Fuller's examination of legal authority is set out in *The Morality of Law*, which develops an analysis of normative constraints on the enactment and application of laws — constraints which, as the title implies, are properly and intrinsically legal, rather than imposed from some external vantage-point. More specifically, he takes his starting-point from the claim that the processes of legislation and judicial interpretation cannot function apart from a context of normative commitments stemming from the fundamental purposes of law itself, for example, generality, clarity, and consistency. These constitute, in his words, "the inner morality of law," without which a legal system could not function well, or at all. Hence, he adds, they may be said to comprise "the morality that makes law possible."[36] He does not hesitate to describe these in terms of the natural laws governing "the enterprise of subjecting human conduct to the existence of rules," so long as it is clear that the natural laws in question are not to be identified with a moral law *tout court*.[37] The norms comprising the internal morality of law are fundamentally procedural rather than substantive, and neutral with respect to specific moral aims:

> As a convenient (though not wholly satisfactory) way of describing the distinction being taken we may speak of a procedural, as distinguished from a substantive natural law. What I have called the internal morality of law is in this sense a procedural version of natural law, though to avoid misunderstanding the word "procedural" should be assigned a special and expanded sense so that it would include, for example, a substantive accord between official action and enacted law. The term "procedural" is, however, broadly appropriate as indicating that we are concerned, not with the substantive aims of legal rules, but with the ways in which a system of rules for governing human conduct must be constructed and administered if it is to be efficacious and at the same time remain what it purports to be.[38]

On this basis, Fuller develops a cogent analysis of what I described above as internal normative constraints on the exercise of legal authority, while at the same time preserving the independence of the law from extra-legal considerations. Yet this independence is no more absolute, on Fuller's view, than is the distinction between procedural norms and substantive aims. An ideal of proper legality presupposes respect for procedural norms,

36. Both phrases are taken from the second chapter of *The Morality of Law*, 33-94, *et passim*.
37. *Morality of Law*, 96.
38. *Morality of Law*, 96-97.

but these cannot be generated through the exigencies of practical reason, operating without reference to any substantive aims at all. On Fuller's own showing, they are also informed by political ideals, as manifested, for example, by consistency between "official action and enacted law." These ideals are properly legal, and yet they point beyond themselves towards a wider context of considerations, having to do with the kinds of social and political arrangements that the law is meant to express and preserve. This brings us to a fundamental point. According to Fuller, the institution of law itself can only be understood and evaluated in the light of its characteristic purpose, "the modest and sober one, that of subjecting human conduct to the guidance and control of general rules."[39] He anticipates that this suggestion will meet with skepticism; nonetheless, denying ourselves this "modest indulgence in teleology" will incur a heavy cost:

> The most significant element of that cost lies in the fact that we lose wholly any standard for defining legality. If law is simply a manifested fact of authority or social power, then, though we can still talk about the substantive justice or injustice of particular enactments, we can no longer talk the degree to which a legal system as a whole achieves the ideal of legality. . . . We can talk about contradictions in the law, but we have no standard for defining what a contradiction is. We may bemoan some kinds of retroactive laws, but we cannot even explain what would be wrong with a system of laws that were wholly retroactive. If we observe that the power of law normally expresses itself in the application of general rules, we can think of no better explanation for this than to say that the supreme legal power can hardly afford to post a subordinate at every street corner to tell people what to do.[40]

Procedural and substantive aims are thus interconnected through the exigencies generated by a particular kind of rational action, directed towards a specific purpose — the purpose, namely, of governing human conduct by rules, directly or as a willing participation in the system of rules thus generated. This is a critically important point. Like Hart, Fuller takes it as given that the law is a product of human activities. But precisely for that reason, it cannot be understood except by reference to the purposes informing those activities — purposes which Fuller rightly characterizes as general and widely applicable. For this reason, the analysis of formal law in terms of the

39. *Morality of Law*, 146.
40. *Morality of Law*, 147.

purposes it serves plays a fundamental role in the version of natural law jurisprudence to be developed in this book.

As it stands, Fuller's account of the purposes of law is underdeveloped. We noted above that we cannot fully account for formal law in his very general terms, as a system for governing human conduct by general rules.[41] Fuller himself apparently recognized that more needs to be said here. In his response to his critics, he admits that, to a considerable extent, the general rules constituting the inner morality of law would also emerge in what he describes as a managerial relationship, in which a superior directs the activities of a subordinate in such a way as to serve the superior's aims or the impersonal aims of the system as a whole. A managerial relationship of this kind cannot function efficiently over any length of time without "a tacit reciprocity of reasonableness and restraint," very similar to the reciprocity characteristic of a viable legal system. Yet "with a legal system the matter stands quite otherwise, for here the existence of a relatively stable reciprocity of expectations between lawgiver and subject is part of the very idea of a functioning legal order."[42] The key principle distinguishing a legal from a managerial system is that of congruence between official action and declared rule. As Fuller goes on to explain,

> The twin principles of generality and of faithful adherence by government to its own declared rules cannot be viewed as offering mere counsels of expediency. This follows from the basic difference between law and managerial direction; law is not, like management, a matter of directing other persons how to accomplish tasks set by a superior, but is basically a matter of providing the citizenry with a sound and stable framework for their interactions with one another, the role of government being that of standing as a guardian of the integrity of this system.[43]

Again, Fuller's point is underdeveloped, but critically important. That is, the purposes served by law cannot be grasped without some sense of the wider purposes animating a particular kind of human society, associated with what we will identify as a properly political authority appropriate to the governance of free men and women.

Fuller thus provides us with starting points for developing a cogent

---

41. Fuller does address this question directly, but in my view his response is not entirely satisfactory; see *Morality of Law*, 123-27.

42. *The Morality of Law*, 208.

43. *The Morality of Law*, 210.

analysis of the normative constraints on the exercise of legal authority, in virtue of which we can identify criteria for evaluating the enactments of a legal system in terms of the characteristic purposes served by the institution of law. He says considerably less about the justification of lawmaking authority itself. When he turns to this topic, he focuses on what he takes to be the profoundly mistaken view that a legal system owes its existence solely to the enactments of a recognized lawmaking authority. This view ignores two critical aspects of legal systems themselves: "the established authority which tells us what in law is itself the product of law," and moreover, "a formal structure of authority is itself usually dependent on human effort that is not required by any law or command."[44]

He goes on to direct our attention to the importance traditionally ascribed to custom in older theories of law.[45] As he observes, custom has never fit comfortably within the constraints of legal positivism, because on most such versions (as he interprets them), there is a vertical, one-way relation between legal authority and the specific enactments resting on that authority. Yet customs, if they are taken to have legal effect, would seem not to be imposed by anyone, or even to be imposed by the community on itself. Fuller claims that the efficacy and significance of customary law depend precisely on its "horizontal" dimension. Statutory law presupposes and depends for its functioning on a context of mostly tacit beliefs and commitments, as these are embodied in accepted practices. Custom is important precisely because it represents the point at which tacit commitments and unselfconscious practices come together with enacted law and the self-reflective observance and interpretation of the laws.

Again, these turn out to be critically important insights, but they sharpen, rather than resolving, the issues raised by the exercise of lawmaking authority. That is, formal lawmaking authority does in fact play a central role in the Western legal systems with which we are most familiar. Fuller is right that this is not a necessary feature of every legal system, but it is pervasive enough to suggest that it has not emerged by sheer chance. It would seem that the terms of Fuller's own analysis imply that we might fruitfully try to account for the emergence of legislative authority in terms of the broad purposes of law that he himself identifies, qualified perhaps by distinctive features of our own social and legal contexts. That, at least, is part of what I hope to do in what follows.

44. *The Morality of Law*, 148.
45. *The Morality of Law*, 233-36.

At this point, we need to consider an alternative attempt to ground the law in normative considerations and overall purposes, more radical and comprehensive than Fuller's account of the inner morality of the law — namely, Ronald Dworkin's account of law as the expression of an ideal political morality.

In his widely influential *Law's Empire,* Dworkin initially locates his own account of law and jurisprudence by contrasting it to what he takes to be the dominant view, expressed by Hart among others, that jurisprudence as a discipline presupposes some consensus about the meaning of the general term "law," on the basis of which meaningful arguments about the law can be formulated and pursued. As he explains, "I shall call the argument I have just described, which has caused such great mischief in legal philosophy, the semantic sting. People are its prey who hold a certain picture of what disagreement is like and when it is possible. They think we can argue sensibly with one another if, but only if, we all accept and follow the same criteria for deciding when our claims are sound, even if we cannot state exactly, as a philosopher might hope to do, what these criteria are."[46] Dworkin insists, on the contrary, that the actually existing laws of one's polity should be regarded as contingent yet indispensable starting points for interpretation:

> Law cannot flourish as an interpretative enterprise in any community unless there is enough initial agreement about what practices are legal practices so that lawyers argue about the best interpretation of roughly the same data. That is a practical requirement of any interpretative enterprise. . . . I do not mean that all lawyers everywhere and always must agree on exactly which practices should count as practices of law, but only that the lawyers of any culture where the interpretative attitude succeeds must largely agree at any one time. We all enter the history of an interpretative practice at a particular point; the necessary preinterpretative agreement is in that way contingent and local.[47]

So far, it might seem that Dworkin is making the relatively uncontroversial point that intellectual inquiry necessarily takes its starting points and

46. Ronald Dworkin, *Law's Empire* (Cambridge, MA: Belknap Press/Harvard University Press, 1986), 45. This remains the most developed comprehensive statement of Dworkin's theory of law, although it should, of course, be read in conjunction with his later work, especially his account of the substantive political morality he defends in *Sovereign Virtue: The Theory and Practice of Equality* (Cambridge, MA: Harvard University Press, 2000).

47. Ronald Dworkin, *Law's Empire,* 91.

criteria from our first, admittedly partial and confused knowledge and beliefs about whatever is the object of the inquiry. But he goes on to make a stronger claim, namely, that the interpretative inquiry in question is itself a part of the practice that is being interpreted. That is, "no firm line divides jurisprudence from adjudication or any other aspect of legal practice."[48] Properly understood, this discipline is not directed towards developing a general theory of law. Rather, the legal scholar is properly concerned with developing the best, most systematic and normatively satisfying account of an actual legal system. Moreover, "Any practical legal argument, no matter how detailed and limited, assumes the kind of abstract foundation jurisprudence offers, and when rival foundations compete, a legal argument assumes one and rejects others. So any judge's opinion is itself a piece of legal philosophy, even when the philosophy is hidden and the visible argument is dominated by citation and lists of facts. Jurisprudence is the general part of adjudication, silent prologue to any decision at law."[49]

Hart, for his part, protests that "It is not obvious why there should be or indeed could be any significant conflict between enterprises so different from my own and Dworkin's conceptions of legal theory."[50] He strongly rejects the charge that his work is meant to be a general theory derived from a semantic analysis of "law." "Nothing in my book or in anything else I have written supports such an account of my theory," he argues, insisting that he has simply set out a general, descriptive jurisprudence that offers an illuminating account of some recurring features of legal practice.[51]

Hart's objections to Dworkin's way of reading him seem to me to be justified. At any rate, he is certainly right to underscore the difference between Dworkin's conception of jurisprudence and his own. We can best bring out what is at stake between them by contrasting their accounts of interpretation and its place in legal practice. For Dworkin, jurisprudence *is* fundamentally the interpretation of actual laws. He has relatively little to say about legislation or about the operation of a legal system, considered as an institution, interacting with political and economic systems in a given polity.[52] In contrast, Hart presupposes that jurisprudential inquiry is properly concerned with a legal system taken as a whole. Yet he is well aware of the significance

48. *Law's Empire*, 90.

49. *Ibid.*

50. *Concept of Law*, 241.

51. *Concept of Law*, 246.

52. It is instructive to compare him in this respect with MacCormick's *Institutions of Law*, about a quarter of which is devoted to these and similar issues; see 171-242.

of legal interpretation for our overall understanding of the law, devoting a full chapter of *The Concept of Law* to this topic.

On Hart's view, the interpretation of laws will necessarily play a central role in any developed legal system, for reasons having to do with the logical limitations of normative standards and the language in which they are formulated. In order to act in accordance with a rule, we must first understand it sufficiently to recognize that it applies in a given case, and to know with some specificity what would count as complying with or breaking the rule. Normally, these judgments are unproblematic, but we can never rule out the possibility that we might confront a case in which the rule is genuinely indeterminate, in such a way that either its application or its practical implications can not be decisively settled. This is so, because rules are necessarily framed in general terms, and these display the open texture characteristic of all such terms in natural languages. That is to say, these terms can never be formulated so precisely and comprehensively as to rule out every possible doubt regarding their application in a specific instance. The relevant limitations apply as much to legal rules as to any other rules for action, since these will necessarily be framed in general terms. Even with respect to the most straightforward rules, there is always some possibility that we will be confronted with a genuinely ambiguous situation, in which we must finally just decide what the correct application of the general rule should be.

Nor does Hart regard this aspect of the rules as simply a regrettable limitation:

> It is however important to appreciate why, apart from this dependence on language as it actually is, with its characteristics of open texture, we should not cherish, even as an ideal, the conception of a rule so detailed that the question whether it applied or not to a particular case was always settled in advance, and never involved, at the point of actual application, a fresh choice between open alternatives. Put shortly, the reason is that the necessity for such choice is thrust upon us because we are men, not gods. It is a feature of the human predicament (and of the legislative one) that we labour under two connected handicaps whenever we seek to regulate, unambiguously and in advance, some sphere of conduct by means of general standards to be used without further official direction on particular occasions. The first handicap is our relative ignorance of fact: the second is our relative indeterminancy of aim. If the world in which we live were characterized only by a finite number of features, and these together with all the modes in which they could combine were known to us, then provi-

sion could be made in advance for every possibility. We could make rules, the application of which to particular cases never called for a further choice. Everything could be known, and for everything, since it could be known, something could be done and specified in advance by a rule. This would be a world fit for "mechanical" jurisprudence. Plainly this world is not our world; human legislators can have no such knowledge of all the possible combinations of circumstances which the future may bring.[53]

The open texture of legal rules thus provides judges with an ongoing opportunity to respond to unforeseen circumstances by extending or modifying legal rules, at least in those interstices at which the law is unclear or incomplete. This implies that judges sometimes interpret the law in such a way as to, in effect, create new law, by modifying the scope and force of a preceding rule or creating a new rule. And Hart does not hesitate to conclude just that. The open texture of legal rules implies that there will always be some possibility that we cannot say whether a given rule should apply to a specific case. "Such hard cases are not merely 'hard cases,' controversial in the sense that reasonable and informed lawyers may disagree about which answer is legally correct, but the law in such cases is fundamentally *incomplete;* it provides *no* answer to the questions at issue in such cases."[54] The resulting gaps can only be filled through judicial discretion, "by a choice, made by someone to whose choices in this matter authority is eventually accorded," namely, the judge, acting as the authoritative interpreter of established law.[55]

In contrast, Dworkin has little to say about the logical limitations of language, and he rejects Hart's claim that judicial interpretation necessarily involves an element of lawmaking to fill the gaps generated by the indeterminacy of legal rules. For Dworkin, the gap that renders judicial interpretation both necessary and potentially salutary is the gap between the ideal law and the law in its current state of formation, which may well be a congeries of incomplete and partially inconsistent enactments. The aim of the judge, in the process of interpreting the law, should be to discern what the ideal law implies in a given instance, and to interpret the relevant actual law accordingly,

---

53. *Concept of Law,* 128; I have omitted a paragraph break. MacCormick develops similar arguments at more length in *Rhetoric and the Rule of Law,* 12-31.

54. *Concept of Law,* 252; emphases in the original.

55. *Concept of Law,* 150. Hart is speaking here specifically with reference to the judge's interpretation of the rule of parliamentary sovereignty, but as his subsequent comments indicate, he would apply the observation to judicial activity generally.

in such a way as to bring the actual legal system into closer accord with what the law ideally should be.[56]

It is critically important to recall at this point that for Dworkin, the ideal law is always tethered to some actually existing legal system. For this reason, he insists that the standard governing judicial interpretation does not rely on a rational conception of the law as it necessarily must be, but follows, rather, from the ideals and commitments comprising a political morality expressed, albeit imperfectly, in the existing bodies of law. As he explains, "It would be a mistake — another lingering infection from the semantic sting — to think that we identify [legal] institutions through some shared and intellectually satisfying definition of what a legal system necessarily is and what institutions necessarily make it up."[57] Rather, "Interpretative theories are by their nature addressed to a particular legal culture, generally the culture to which their authors belong. Unless these theories are deeply skeptical, they will treat that legal system as a flourishing example of law, one that calls for and rewards the interpretative attitude."[58] The interpretative attitude consists in the readiness to construe something in the light of its purpose, as set by some ideal standard: "constructive interpretation is a matter of imposing purpose on an object or practice in order to make of it the best possible example of the form or genre to which it is taken to belong."[59]

In one way, Dworkin may be said to appropriate and extend Fuller's key insight, arguing that legal systems can only be understood on the basis of the wider purposes that they serve. But unlike Fuller, he does not identify the purpose of law with the maintenance of an ideal of proper legality, expressed and safeguarded through a system of open, transparent, and equitable enactments and procedures. Even this "inner morality of the law" would be too general and, by the same token, too far abstracted from the governing ideals of our actual legal system, to serve as an ideal political morality in Dworkin's sense. On Dworkin's view, the purpose of the law is more comprehensive and substantive — nothing less, in fact, than the expression and maintenance of a political morality centered on equality as "the sovereign virtue," interpreted as equal regard for the importance of each person's

---

56. Dworkin develops and extends his distinctive theory of legal interpretation throughout his career; for an early statement of his views, see Ronald Dworkin, *Taking Rights Seriously* (Cambridge: Harvard University Press, 1977), 14-80; for his most comprehensive treatment, see *Law's Empire*, 266-75.

57. *Ibid.*, 150.

58. *Law's Empire*, 102.

59. *Law's Empire*, 52.

life.[60] This ideal corresponds, in his view, to the actual commitments and ideals informing enactments and legal practices, at least within the contexts within which he works, and for that very reason, it reflects the community's sense of itself as a kind of moral community, bound together by the commitments and standards for public life towards which the community aspires.[61] Yet the ideal political morality reflected in the laws is just that, an ideal, and in the nature of things actual laws and practices will express it in imperfect and incomplete ways. It is the task of those entrusted with the interpretation and application of the laws — judges, first of all, but also public officials of all kinds — to articulate this political morality in such a way as to draw it out from its sometimes obscure expression in the laws as they actually exist, and to interpret and apply these in such a way as to bring them more fully into accordance with the ideals they represent. Thus, the ideal governing judicial interpretation is integrity, understood as a commitment to construe the laws in the best light possible — the best, seen by reference to what the law should be — in order to provide the best possible expression of the ideal political morality that it imperfectly expresses.

This is the sense in which judicial interpretation moves between the laws as they actually exist, and the law as it ideally should be: "Judges who accept the interpretive ideal of integrity decide hard cases by trying to find, in some coherent set of principles about people's rights and duties, the best constructive interpretation of the political structure and legal doctrine of their community. They try to make that complex structure and record the best that these can be."[62] In practice, judicial interpretation will always involve some measure of uncertainty, together with considerable scope for good-faith disagreements. Nonetheless, it is important to realize that for Dworkin, interpretative questions about the meaning of the law do have a uniquely right answer. They are determined by what the ideals informing the law would dictate in a particular instance. Here we see the key difference be-

---

60. The phrase is taken from Dworkin's *Sovereign Virtue: The Theory and Practice of Equality* (Cambridge, MA: Harvard University Press, 2000).

61. For Dworkin, this context is almost always the United States and, usually, debates over United States constitutional law. Most of what he says with respect to the substantive ideals of the political morality he defends could also be defended, with some qualifications, in the contexts of Western post-industrial nations generally, all of which share the same broad historical traditions and forms of political life. And as I note below, even though he insists on the contextual element of interpretative practice, Dworkin also seems to regard the idea of equality as a universally applicable normative ideal.

62. *Law's Empire*, 255.

tween his conception of interpretation and that of Hart. He altogether rejects the view that the judge necessarily and properly functions as a legislator, whose decrees are themselves the source of law. For Dworkin, the law is fundamentally discovered, not made, through the process of adjudication — or at least, that would be the case for an ideal judge, a Hercules of the law. There can be no gaps in the law, because, in one sense, the specifics of a legal system exist prior to their discovery and articulation — the sense, namely, in which the conclusions of an argument pre-exist in its premises.

Dworkin's account of legal interpretation thus does not leave much room, if any, for contingency and choice in the interpretation and application of enactments within a legal system. What is more, it is difficult to say how much genuine contingency he allows for the overall shape of the legal system itself — whether, in other words, he regards the actual, normatively substantive content of the laws, and the specific political commitments that they express, as matters left to legislative or communal discretion. Certainly, he insists that interpretation can only take place within a specific legal tradition, and in his earlier works especially he calls attention to the ways in which actual laws and precedents constrain interpretation.[63] Yet even in these earlier writings, Dworkin argues as if the core ideal of equality underlying our legal tradition is not simply part of the contingent tradition that we happen to inhabit; rather, he seems to regard this as an ideal that will necessarily be respected by, and reflected in, the laws of any legitimate polity. What is more, he apparently regards this as a substantive ideal, implying a fairly specific set of normative commitments. In his later writings, he makes this explicit: "No government is legitimate that does not show equal concern for the fate of all those citizens over whom it claims dominion and from whom it claims allegiance. Equal concern is the sovereign virtue of political community — without it government is only tyranny — and when a nation's wealth is very unequally distributed, as the wealth of even very prosperous nations now is, then its equal concern is suspect."[64]

If this is indeed the trajectory of his thought, then Dworkin in effect claims that there is an ideal law, grounded in the normative implications of a universally valid political ideal, in terms of which specific articulations of what the law requires — whether by a lawgiver or a judge — can be said truly to be the law, or else denied to be the law. Dworkin insists that legal interpretation is always bound by what he describes as the chain of law, com-

---

63. This point is central to his analysis of the ideal of integrity in *Law's Empire*, 245-75.
64. *Sovereign Virtue*, 1.

prised of the enactments and judgments that have been articulated so far. Yet in the process of interpretation, the judge is not bound to respect the intent of the lawgiver: "Law as integrity, then, begins in the present and pursues the past only so far as and in the way its contemporary focus dictates. It does not aim to recapture, even for present law, the ideals or practical purposes of the politicians who first created it. It aims rather to justify what they did . . . in an overall story worth telling now, a story with a complex claim: That present practice can be organized by and justified in principles sufficiently attractive to provide an honorable future."[65] Significantly, he says that the judge who aims to interpret statutory law should regard Congress as "an author earlier than himself in the chain of law," albeit one "with special powers and responsibilities different from his own," with whom the judge enters into a creative partnership, continuing to develop the statutory scheme in the light of whichever reading of the statute "shows the political history including and surrounding that statute in the better light."[66] Even the Constitution, which unlike statutory law is foundational of other law, is in the last analysis comprised of "issues of principle" that, on the construal of law as integrity, "constitute the constitutional law."[67] There is little sense here that the enactments of the legislator, as such, might carry a distinctive authoritative weight that the judge is bound to try to respect. By the same token, Dworkin's account of integrity and interpretation implies that, in the final analysis, the legislator too discovers the law rather than creating it. At one point, he remarks that "It is my view, in fact, that law is in large part philosophy" — and the truths of philosophy are uncovered through inquiry, not established through authoritative enactments.[68] We might say of both the judge and the legislator what Peirce said about the intellect in its speculative activities: they are distinguished by their imperfections and mistakes, and only united insofar as they arrive at the truth presented by the ideal set before them.[69]

What is more, the ideal in question is really a moral rather than a specifically legal ideal. In one of his most recent works, Dworkin remarks that

65. *Law's Empire*, 227-28.

66. *Law's Empire*, 313

67. *Law's Empire*, 380.

68. Ronald Dworkin, "Law, Philosophy and Interpretation," ARSP 80 (1994): 463-75, here 475.

69. Charles S. Peirce, "Questions Concerning Certain Faculties Claimed for Man" [1868], printed as 64-118 in *Charles S. Peirce: The Essential Writings*, ed. Edward Moore (New York: Harper and Row, 1972), 118.

even though we are accustomed to think of law and morality as comprising two fields of thought that are in principle distinct,

> I want now to suggest that this traditional understanding, which encourages us to claim relations between two different intellectual domains, is unsatisfactory. We might do better with a different intellectual topography: we might treat law not as separate from but as a department of morality. We understand political theory that way: as part of morality more generally understood but distinguished, with its own distinct substance, because applicable to distinct institutional structures. We might treat legal theory as a special part of political morality distinguished by a further refinement of institutional structures.[70]

Thus, the ideal law to which both judges and legislators aim is itself one expression of a more general moral ideal. Such a view clearly puts Dworkin at odds with Hart and with legal positivism more generally, on any plausible construal of that controversial term. More importantly, it also puts him at odds with the "modest and sober" version of natural law offered by Fuller, in spite of the important points of contact between the two. Fuller's ideal morality of law presupposes precisely the distinction that Dworkin rejects. That is, Fuller develops and defends the idea that the law is informed by distinctive ideals of proper legality and equity that are coherent, normatively significant, and valuable considered on their own terms. Dworkin would seem to deny that there are distinctively legal ideals of this kind, except perhaps as provisional or partial formulations of more general moral ideals of equal regard and respect. On this view, the autonomy of law, regarded as a more or less distinctive and self-contained normative system, can only be justified as a necessary concession to the current limitations and practical exigencies of our grasp of the ideal law.

By the same token, Dworkin has little to say about the justification and proper character of legal authority as such. He writes at length throughout his work about the conditions and implications of political legitimacy and the exigencies of life within a democratic community, but scarcely addresses legal authority and its relation to political life more generally.[71] It is difficult to see what he could say on this score, given his insistence that judicial interpretation should not take account of the actual ideals and practical purposes

---

70. *Justice in Robes*, 34-35.

71. See in particular *Law's Empire*, 186-224 and *Sovereign Virtue*, 184-210. It is also perhaps noteworthy that there is no entry for "authority" in the index of the more recent book.

of the legislator. He thus denies that legislative intent — and by implication, the authoritative decree of a lawgiver — plays any essential or independent role in determining what the law is. Most contemporary legal philosophers regard this as inadequate — hardly surprising, since the idea of legal authority is foundational to the discipline itself. So much the worse for the philosophy of law, Dworkin might reply, but there are deeper issues at stake. For one thing, very few philosophers today, legal or otherwise, are persuaded that there can be, even ideally, one and only one right interpretation of a proposition in a natural language. But more importantly, distinctively legal forms of authority have an integral part to play in actual legal systems, especially but not only in Western democracies. To the extent that Dworkin takes the law as it actually is to be the necessary context for judicial interpretation, it would seem that he is committed on his own terms to taking account of the distinctive force of authoritative enactments. Indeed, as we will see, legal authority expresses core values within the political community, including the value of equality that is central to Dworkin's own ideal political morality.

At this point, we are anticipating an argument that has yet to be developed. In order to move forward, we need to return to the set of issues generated by the autonomy of the law and legal authority — issues which, as we noted, can be distinguished in principle, but which are practically interconnected and would ideally be addressed in terms of one unifying account of authority and formal law. In their responses to Hart and the jurisprudential tradition that he represents, both Fuller and Dworkin concentrate on what we might describe, following Fuller, as the inner morality of the law, on those constraints on the exercise of legal authority that are in some way internal to a legal system itself. We will draw extensively on their work when we return to issues generated by the relatively high degree of autonomy of law exhibited by Western legal systems. But in order to move forward at this point, we need to turn our attention more directly to the concept of legal authority itself, its proper character and justification. That will be the focus of the next section.

2. The Paradox of Legal Authority: Contemporary and Medieval Perspectives

Recent Work on the Concept of Authority

What we need is an analytic account of legitimate legal authority which exhibits its intrinsic value and its distinctively rational character without reducing legal judgments to moral or reasonable judgments more comprehensively considered. The immediate difficulty is that authority entails the power to override the first-order rational judgments of those subject to it. If a policeman orders me to pull over after an accident and I say to myself that, all things considered, it would probably make sense to do so, then I have mistaken his orders for a kind of advice. Contrast this with a situation in which I pull over because someone in authority directs me to do so, even though, all things considered, it seems to me unwise (maybe I'll be holding up traffic at this particular spot). I act freely in the latter case — presumably, the policeman has not needed to hold a gun on me in order to get me to comply — but can I be said to act rationally?

In a widely influential essay, "Legitimate Authority," Joseph Raz frames the problem in this way:

> The paradoxes of authority can assume different forms, but all of them concern the alleged incompatibility of authority with reason or autonomy. To be subjected to authority, it is argued, is incompatible with reason, for reason requires submission even when one thinks that what is required is against reason. Therefore, submission to authority is irrational. Similarly the principle of autonomy entails action on one's own judgment on all moral questions. Since authority sometimes requires action against one's own judgment, it requires abandoning one's moral autonomy. Since all practical questions may involve moral considerations, all practical authority denies moral autonomy and is consequently immoral.[72]

In order to address these paradoxes, he goes on to say, we need an account of "authority [as] a practical concept. This means that questions of who has authority over whom are practical questions; they bear on what one ought to do. In other words statements that some persons have authority may serve as premises in practical inferences. The explanation of authority must explain the practical import of the concept. It must explain how it is capable of figuring in practical inferences."[73] Thus, we need to show that an authoritative claim is itself a reason for action, which can be put into practice without irrationality or a problematic surrender of autonomy.

Raz goes on to develop the requisite account by distinguishing two

---

72. *The Authority of Law,* 3. Raz has returned to this subject repeatedly throughout his career; see in particular *The Morality of Freedom* (Oxford: Clarendon Press, 1986), 21-69, and *Between Authority and Interpretation,* 126-65.

73. *Authority of Law,* 10.

kinds of reasons for action. First-order reasons, as he styles them, include any and every consideration that might count as a reason for or against a particular course of action — the ensemble of considerations that we bring together as we formulate judgments about the best course of action overall, all things considered. Raz's first imagined interlocutor would restrict practical reason to judgments at this level, insisting that it is irrational to act against the overall weight of reasons. But in reality, most of us do not formulate practical judgments in accordance with some overall assessment of every potentially relevant consideration. We give greater importance to some considerations than we do to others, while refusing to give others any weight at all. It may well be better, from the standpoint of an overall assessment of benefit and loss, if I were to ignore my deceased uncle's will, leaving his considerable fortune to his puppy, in order to take the money myself; I need it to finance my education, and I could do far more good as a doctor (let us say), than as a professional pet sitter. Nonetheless, I dismiss these considerations out of hand, because I promised to carry out my uncle's last wishes, or because I think it would be unseemly to take my own direct interests into account.

These are examples of what Raz calls second-order reasons for action, "the action concerned being acting for a reason and not acting for a reason."[74] Sometimes these are positive second-order reasons, in that they designate a reason for action which should override other considerations. "I promised my uncle to hold his money in trust for Solon (the dog)" is a positive reason. At other times, these are negative reasons, insofar as they are reasons to refrain from acting on some (otherwise sound) first-order reason: "I just cannot act in such a way as to enrich myself when dealing with another's money," would be a negative reason. Finally, some kinds of reasons are both positive and exclusionary: that is to say, they both enjoin that we act on the basis of some kinds of first-order reasons and require us to disregard any first-order reasons that would otherwise count against these.

According to Raz, authority is a certain kind of normative power, which he defines as the capacity either to set up protected reasons or to cancel those that would otherwise obtain in a given situation. Someone may be said to exercise this authority over his own future actions (as I presumably did when I promised my uncle to devote his estate to the care of his dog). However, the more fundamental concept is that of authority over persons, the normative power to change someone else's protected reasons in some way.

74. *Authority of Law*, 17.

Legal authority is a paradigmatic example (although not the only one) of this kind of authority over persons.[75] The state of Indiana exercises this kind of authority by requiring me to act in accordance with the provisions of a legitimate will, thus requiring me to act on my uncle's (strange) reasons, and forbidding me from acting in accordance with other, perhaps independently very good reasons.

As Raz goes on to say, a meaningful claim to authority implies, at a minimum, that an authoritative directive overrides the recipient's present desires to the contrary. Normally, one's acceptance of an authority as legitimate implies more: "There is a sense in which if one accepts the legitimacy of an authority one is committed to following it blindly. One can be very watchful that it shall not overstep its authority and be sensitive to the presence of non-excluded considerations. But barring these possibilities, one is to follow the authority regardless of one's view of the merits of the case (that is, blindly)."[76] In other words, an authority normally claims the power to set up exclusionary reasons, such as to rule out certain kinds of otherwise legitimate considerations. Thus, "accepting authority inevitably involves giving up one's right to act on one's judgement on the balance of reasons. It involves accepting an exclusionary reason."[77] Yet accepting authority need not be an unreasonable act: "since there could in principle be valid second-order reasons, there is nothing in the principle of autonomy that requires the rejection of all authority."[78]

There is therefore nothing necessarily irrational or irresponsible in the act of obedience, even though it involves some surrender of one's independent judgment. The second-order exclusionary reasons generated by authoritative decree are formally similar to the second-order exclusionary reasons widely accepted in moral reasoning. For example, it is often said that one's overall judgments about well-being are excluded by moral norms prohibiting certain kinds of intrinsically evil actions. Of course, such claims are contro-

---

75. According to Raz, the central case of authority, justified through what he calls the normal justification thesis, is that of one person exercising authority over another, and the authority of states and governments must be justified through some kind of extension of that thesis; see *The Morality of Freedom*, 70. This, it seems to me, gets it backward; political authority is conceptually paradigmatic for our conception of authority, and foundational for many, although not all, legitimate forms of authority. I believe that Raz has been misled here by his overly narrow service conception of authority, on which more below.

76. *Authority of Law*, 24.

77. *Authority of Law*, 26.

78. *Ibid.*, 27.

versial, but they cannot be ruled out of court on purely formal grounds; they stand or fall with the strength of the reasons adduced for accepting these kinds of normative boundaries. The same must be said about the rationality of obedience as Raz interprets it. We cannot rule obedience to authority out of court on formal grounds, but clearly, such an act can only be justified through some appeal to the rational considerations that lead one to accept authority in the first place. What kinds of considerations might these be?

In his later writings Raz devotes considerable attention to this question. His answer is developed under the rubric of what he describes as the service conception of authority, according to which "the role and primary normal function" of authorities "is to serve the governed."[79] As he further explains,

> The suggestion of the service conception is that the moral question is an-
> swered when two conditions are met, and regarding matters with respect
> to which they are met: First, that the subject would better conform to rea-
> sons that apply to him anyway (that is, to reasons other than the directives
> of the authority) if he intends to be guided by the authority's directives
> than if he does not (I will refer to it as the normal justification thesis or
> condition). Second, that the matters regarding which the first condition is
> met are such that with respect to them it is better to conform to reason
> than to decide for oneself, unaided by authority (I will refer to it as the in-
> dependence condition).[80]

Raz is surely right to insist that the qualified surrender of rational judgment implied by submission to authority can only be justified if the authority functions in some intelligible way to promote the rationality, or at least
the conformity to reasons, of those subject to its decrees. Thus, submission
to authority is rationally justified as a strategy for, or perhaps a necessary
condition or component of activities in accordance with reason. But as it
stands, the service conception of authority seems too narrow, even granting
Raz's admission that this represents the normal, but not the only possible,
way in which the claims of a given authority might be justified.[81] This becomes apparent when we try to think of specific examples of authorities that
would appropriately be justified in the "normal" way. I might accept the authority of a teacher, an experienced craftsman, a mentor, or a spiritual advisor because I recognize that she is better informed, wiser, more experienced,

79. *Morality of Freedom*, 56.
80. *Between Authority and Interpretation*, 136-37.
81. *The Morality of Freedom*, 70.

or more holy than I am myself. I choose to follow the directives of my guide because I realize that her judgments are likely to be superior to my own, even when I cannot understand why. Thus, by following her blindly, I improve my chances of conforming to reason here and now, as well as allowing my own rational capacities to mature and develop.[82] This kind of authority relation would indeed meet the normal justification thesis. But as Raz himself admits, we cannot fully justify governmental authority in these terms, and by the same token it is difficult to see how other forms of public authority, including legal authority, could be justified in this way.[83] We cannot plausibly claim that every government or public authority depends on the consent, actual or even implied, of those subject to it, as he subsequently — and in my view rightly — argues.[84] This being said, the questions raised by public authority, including the authority of law, remain to be addressed.

In the last section, we identified two issues raised by legal authority — its overall justification, and the constraints on its proper exercise. In contrast to the legal scholars examined in that section, Raz directly addresses the issue of justification. Yet he appears to have less to say about the internal constraints on the proper exercise of authority. Indeed, his use of the language of blind obedience, and his repeated claims that authoritative injunctions supersede or replace other reasons for action, can give the impression that he does not accept legitimate constraints on the exercise of a legitimate authority. In fact, this is not his overall view, but it is the case that he says less than we might expect about the ways in which authority remains bounded and provisional, in such a way as to qualify and direct rational obedience.

Why should this be a problem? If we are to justify authority in rational terms, we need to go beyond simply showing that compliance with legal authority can be rational. We also need to explain how compliance with the law can be carried out responsibly, that is to say, without a problematic surrender of responsibility. In order to exercise the requisite kind of autonomy, the individual needs to be able to identify those points at which the protected reasons set up by legal authority should not be regarded as overriding, and she also needs to be able to distinguish between legitimate and illegitimate expressions of legal authority itself. She needs, in other words, some sense of

82. Alasdair MacIntyre defends this conception of authority in order to make the case that acceptance of authority is not antithetical to rational inquiry and practice; see *Three Rival Versions of Moral Enquiry: Encyclopaedia, Genealogy, and Tradition* (Notre Dame: University of Notre Dame Press, 1990), 65-66.

83. Raz discusses this problem at some length in *Morality of Freedom*, 70-103.

84. *Morality of Freedom*, 80-94.

the rational constraints on the exercise of legal authority — those set by the competing demands of other kinds of normative systems, on the one hand, and those internal to the exercise of legal authority, on the other. Thus, the agent needs to be able to appreciate the rationality of particular laws, up to a point, in order to formulate responsible judgments to the effect that the demands of law should be set aside in a given case, or to reject putative laws as in some way illegitimate. These kinds of judgments, in turn, require some grasp of the ways in which the demands of law are themselves justified as such, and by implication, some appreciation of criteria in terms of which illegitimate demands can be recognized. So far, I have emphasized the importance of a responsible choice to comply with the law, or not, but it should be added that compliance itself will normally also call for some sense of the reasonableness of the laws. Without this, the agent will be unable to engage those capacities for discernment and spontaneous judgment that we associate with free activity, with the result that her obedience to law will be, at best, mechanical. In that case, it would be difficult at best for men and women to sustain what Hart describes as the internal viewpoint on the law, without which the rule of law degenerates into a series of commands.

While Raz does not raise this problem in precisely these terms, he does address it, at least in part, by distinguishing between the kinds of protected reasons that a given authority can set up, and those it cannot legitimately set up — the latter being those which fall outside the rationale for the authority itself. Once again, we are reminded that the rationality of legal authority is grounded in the purposes that it serves. We concluded that it is reasonable to accept legal authority, and to incorporate its directives into practical reason, because this authority serves purposes that a rational person can accept and identify as his own. And now it appears that obedience to legal authority can also be responsible, because it stems from purposes that constrain it and give it some definable contours. Because legal authority is reasonable, it cannot be absolute, and because it cannot be absolute, it can be obeyed as an act of responsible freedom.

None of this implies that legal enactments simply track the judgments of practical reason, in such a way that there would ideally be no differences between what the law prescribes and what the reasonable, plain person would prescribe for himself. The distinguishing characteristic of authority, we recall, is precisely that it establishes protected reasons that do not (necessarily) correspond to what a reasonable man or woman might judge to be the best course of action in a given set of circumstances. In this way, at least, authoritative enactments will necessarily be contingent — they are not necessitated by any set of reasons — and to that extent, arbitrary. Yet even the contingency of the laws does not render them rationally opaque. In order to see why not, we should recall Hart's claim (which was and remains widely shared) that our practical judgments are rule-governed, and yet the specific judgments that we make are not necessitated by the rules they express. He argues for this by appealing, rightly, to the indeterminacy of language, and as we will see, similar considerations apply to norms of every kind, including pre-linguistic principles of action as well as tacit and formulated precepts. Practical judgment always involves a contingent determination of a more general principle, and for that reason, it always involves an element of arbitrariness: we choose to act on this principle in this specific way, but there will almost always be some other rationally defensible course of action that we could have pursued instead.

The key phrase here is "rationally defensible." Even the contingency of practical judgments — including those practical judgments on the basis of which laws are enacted and applied — is a reasoned contingency, so to speak, which can be understood in terms of the rational principles from which it stems. The contingency of the laws does introduce a kind of arbitrariness, but it does not render them rationally opaque, nor does it rule out the exercise of responsible freedom on the part of those subject to them. It has sometimes been said that the indeterminacy of the laws, and the necessity for interpretation, undermines any efforts to identify rational constraints on the exercise of legal authority. But this claim is surely exaggerated. Just because we can interpret a rule or apply a normative principle in more than one defensible way, it does not follow that any way we choose is therefore defensible. There are some interpretations of a linguistic formulation that run so deeply contrary to any accepted usage that they simply cannot be rendered intelligible as interpretations of this proposition; it makes sense to say that abortion is murder (although I believe this proposition to be false), but it makes no sense to say that cutting one's hair is murder.

All this being said, Raz's central insight seems to me, nonetheless, to be sound. That is, if we are to regard obedience to authority as justified, and what is more, normatively exigent, we can best do so by showing that authority serves in some way to promote the overall rationality of those subject to its decrees — either directly, by facilitating rational judgment in some way, or at least indirectly, by enabling the agent to conform to the demands of rationality. What we need at this point is a fuller account of the way in which authority serves such a purpose. In developing this account, I will further assume that the paradigmatic forms of authority are public. Thus, any plausible justification of authority must be developed in such a way as to show that the authority of a community, or of some other collective agency, serves to promote the overall rationality of the individuals comprising it. If this line of analysis can be successfully developed, we will have good reason to believe that someone who follows authoritative directives is genuinely rational, in that he acts for practical reasons tethered to purposes that he shares, or at least plausibly could share.

Let us take stock of the argument so far. Claims to authority, including legal authority, would appear to rule out reasonable, responsibly free compliance with the laws. Yet we do regard at least some authorities as justifiable, in such a way that it is legitimate, and perhaps obligatory, for someone to submit to them. Otherwise, there would be no difference between submission to authority and a compliance elicited by coercion or self-interest. The paradoxical character of authority can be dissolved, however, through an adequate account of the purposes that it serves, purposes that a reasonable and responsibly free agent can recognize as (at least potentially) her own. In this way, we can explain how it is that authoritative enactments can serve as legitimate premises in the processes of practical reason, and we can also identify (at least some) constraints on the scope and the legitimate exercise of legal authority, and on the parameters for interpreting its enactments.

What we need, in order to move forward with this line of analysis, is a cogent account of the purposes of law, in terms of which we can make sense of legal systems as they exist and function in contemporary Western societies — that is to say, as relatively autonomous from other kinds of normative and social considerations — while at the same time providing a context within which processes of lawmaking and judicial interpretation can be rendered intelligible as expressions of a rational and purposive human activity. In the remainder of this book, I will attempt to develop such an account, taking my starting point from the scholastic conception of natural law and natural right. As I will argue in what follows, this conception provides the starting points for an account of practical rationality which ties it to more broadly natural purposes; correlatively, it suggests a justification for legal authority in positive terms, reflecting the natural goodness of social and political life. Thus, it contrasts with most modern and contemporary theories of the natural law in its more expansive understanding of human rationality and its relation to natural inclinations and values. As I hope to show, this conception opens the way to an attractive and cogent account of legal authority as a kind of natural relation, which can take many forms while still exhibiting a broadly intelligible structure.

Scholastic Perspectives on Authority, Power, and Political Freedom

I should emphasize once again that I will be offering my own constructive theory of legal authority, which is not meant to represent the views of any one scholastic thinker, much less a supposedly uniform approach to jurisprudence that they all share. Nonetheless, I do claim that the early scholastics offer distinctive and valuable perspectives on legal authority as we experience it today. For this reason, I develop my account through close readings and critical appropriations of the work of scholastic jurists and theologians, especially Aquinas, with the aim of bringing these medieval thinkers into conversation with our contemporaries.

This may seem like an unpromising approach. The medieval world seems so remote from our own, so different in its dominant ideals and way of life, that it is hard to see what we could learn from it. But in fact, the early scholastic period — running, roughly from the end of the eleventh century through the end of the thirteenth century — was much like our own in key respects.[85] Men and women of affairs were challenged by the demands of a social world that was shrinking and expanding at the same time; it was expanding in sheer numbers, in mobility, and in economic activity, and shrinking as previously scattered and disparate communities were once again brought into continual contact with one another through greatly expanded networks of transportation and communication. A region that had been thinly populated, agrarian, and dispersed was transformed with remarkable speed into a populous, increasingly urban society sustained by a vibrant market economy. The simultaneous expansion and contraction of medieval European society, in turn, both facilitated and eventually required

---

85. Although there would, of course, be very considerable debate over the best way to flesh out and to interpret the following account of European society in this period, I believe that in its main lines it would not be controversial. In my own approach to the historical context, I am especially indebted to Thomas N. Bisson, *The Crisis of the Twelfth Century: Power, Lordship, and the Origins of European Government* (Princeton: Princeton University Press, 2009); James A. Brundage, *The Medieval Origins of the Legal Profession: Canonists, Civilians, and Courts* (Chicago: University of Chicago Press, 2008); Giles Constable, *The Reformation of the Twelfth Century* (Cambridge: Cambridge University Press, 1996); Kenneth Pennington, *The Prince and the Law, 1200-1600: Sovereignty and Rights in the Western Legal Tradition* (Berkeley: University of California Press, 1993); R. W. Southern, *Scholastic Humanism and the Unification of Europe*, vol. 1: *Foundations* (Oxford: Blackwell, 1995); R. C. van Caenegem, "Government, Law and Society," 174-210 in *The Cambridge History of Medieval Political Thought, c. 350–c. 1450*, ed. J. H. Burns (Cambridge: Cambridge University Press, 1988), and his *An Historical Introduction to Western Constitutional Law* (Cambridge: Cambridge University Press, 1995).

centralized systems of governance, and correlatively, systems of formal law. That supposed hallmark of modernity, the dominance of bureaucratic systems of governance and administration structured through impersonal offices and functions, emerged in this period, as did the university system and some key elements of the modern nation-state system. In the words of R. C. Van Caenegem, "The period from the twelfth to the fifteenth century, sometimes called the Second Middle Ages, witnessed the foundation of the political structures of modern Europe."[86]

At the same time, and perhaps partially in response to these broad changes, the eleventh and twelfth centuries also experienced a troubling reassertion of claims to power, conceived in terms of personal dominion.[87] In order to appreciate the importance of this development, it is crucial to realize that it represented a reversion, deplored as such by those who experienced it. By the middle of the eleventh century, communities that had only recently been in a condition of dependence or outright servitude were beginning to enjoy a new independence and freedom, inspired in part through ideals of national community and political self-rule that had never been entirely lost. To a considerable extent, indeed, the reversion to exploitative forms of dominion was itself a by-product of the emergence of effective political institutions. The emerging governing authorities in Europe could only make their rule effective by means of subordinates, usually knights, commanding armed bands of fighting men, taking armed castles as their base of operations. These castellans, sometimes in collaboration with the governing authorities but very often not, took advantage of their position to impose their will on the populations subject to them, exploiting them for financial gain without even a pretense of justification. Ancient customs and authoritative decrees were simply set aside, to be replaced by customs and usages imposed by the overlord in control of a given area. Those unlucky enough to find themselves subject to one of these overlords found themselves reduced to servitude, which they protested, or regretfully accepted, in just these terms.

---

86. *Historical Introduction to Western Constitutional Law,* 72.

87. Bisson in particular regards this as one key factor leading to the emergence of political institutions as we know them — the latter being regarded by him as more or less deliberate and more or less effective attempts to counter the re-emergence of lordly power. The main lines of his argument are set out in his *Crisis of the Twelfth Century,* 1-83, and developed in considerable detail through the remainder of the book. Orlando Patterson develops a similar interpretation of this period, necessarily more briefly, at the end of *Freedom in the Making of Western Culture* (New York: Basic Books, 1991), 347-401.

This was particularly disturbing because this same period also saw the emergence of an ideal of freedom as a personal and Christian ideal. Now for the first time, the church began consistently to defend the right of men and women to marry the partners of their choice, or not to marry at all, even in the face of objections from family or overlords.[88] The right to move from less to more strict communities was enshrined in canon law, and beyond the law, the individual's right to pursue a distinctive path to holiness was generally respected.[89] As Orlando Patterson argues, it was the very experience of servitude, up until this point a pervasive feature of medieval life, which led men and women in this period to prize freedom so highly.[90] Men and women were not so inclined to submit meekly to the demands of power and conventional expectations, although of course many did. As a result of these developments, the rights — the *jura* — of individuals, mostly considered at this stage in terms of the claims attaching to traditional or innovative roles, emerged as a central point of contestation throughout society.

Given these circumstances, it is scarcely surprising that, beginning in the eleventh century, civic and church leaders throughout Europe began to undertake wide-ranging processes of reform and institutional innovation which were both informed and consolidated through the work of the newly emergent professional class of scholastic jurists and theologians.[91] These reforms took many forms, the most important of which, from our standpoint, were the reforms of legal institutions and practices, the recovery or creation of lawcodes, and correlatively, the emergence of jurisprudence as a systematic inquiry. In order fully to appreciate the significance of this development, it is important to realize that while the rule of law was a notable ideal even at this

88. On the right of those in a state of servitude to marry, see Antonia Bocarius Sahaydachcy, "The Marriage of Unfree Persons: Twelfth Century Decretals and Letters," in *De Jure Canonico Medii: Festschrift für Rudolf Weigand, Studia Gratiana* XXVII (1996), 483-506. As Sahaydachcy goes on to show, *Dignum est* was subsequently challenged, but the popes consistently upheld the validity of the marriages of unfree persons. Charles Reid offers a more comprehensive account of the rights pertaining to marriage and sexual functions in Charles J. Reid, Jr., *Power over the Body, Equality in the Family: Rights and Domestic Relations in Medieval Canon Law* (Grand Rapids: Eerdmans, 2004), 25-68.

89. Giles Constable provides an indispensable sense of the religious and broadly spiritual impetus behind the desire for freedom so pervasive in this period; see *Reformation of the Twelfth Century,* 257-93.

90. Orlando Patterson, *Freedom in the Making of Western Culture,* 402-6.

91. Southern argues for the centrality of the scholastics to the social and institutional developments in this period throughout *Scholastic Humanism;* see especially 134-62 and, with respect to the emergence of a scholastic jurisprudence, 235-318.

time, it was scarcely a reality, in part because of the widespread return of petty despots and violent exploitation. Van Caenegem observes that after the end of the Carolingian period in the late ninth century, there was "a period of more than two centuries in which the European Continent lived without legislation. Neither kings nor princes — nor popes for that matter — issued laws, edict or constitutions containing new legal norms for their subjects."[92] Such legal development as took place in this period occurred through the almost imperceptible evolution of customary law. This situation began to change in the late eleventh century, as the processes of expansion and centralization, and more immediately, the growing volume of claims generated by social mobility and conflict, rendered more formal legal processes both possible and necessary. Scholars of secular law, sometimes called civilians, took the lead here, but they were quickly followed by canon lawyers and then theologians, all of whom had much to say on the origins, scope, and force of positive law.

Initially, these efforts were not pursued through the wholesale enactment of new systems of law, as we might expect, but through the revival of a learned jurisprudence, focused on guiding the activities of the courts. When we take account of the historical context, this focus on adjudication is not so surprising as it might at first seem. For one thing, the courts, in all their civic and ecclesiastical varieties, were among the most stable and practically effective public institutions at the time. Even if princes could have been persuaded to undertake wholesale legal enactments at this time, they would scarcely have had the means to render their decrees effective. At the same time, Europeans in the late eleventh century did not give the same weight to legislative authority that we tend to do. They were more willing to acknowledge the legal force of customs, which were seen as conferring justifiable rights and privileges — so long as these were genuinely old customs and not the abusive new customs introduced by overlords and castellans.[93] This attitude reflected the realities of European society at this point; there were very few effective sources of centralized public authority, and societies were governed almost entirely through customary law, adjudicated and enforced through localized courts. It is thus hardly surprising that the earliest jurists were inclined towards an ideal of law as the direct expression of natural or rational norms. We find a striking example of this in an early-eleventh-century legal manual *Petri exceptiones,* intended as a practical guide for the

---

92. *History of Medieval Political Thought,* 181.

93. Bisson discusses these innovative "bad customs" at length; the index to *The Crisis of the Twelfth Century* lists about a dozen references, ending with "etc."

courtroom, in which the author coolly announces that "If anything useless, broken, or contrary to equity is found in the laws, we trample it under-foot."[94] What we find at the beginning of the scholastic period, therefore, is not so much a legal system, as an ongoing process of litigation based on tra-ditionally acknowledged customs, rights, and privileges, increasingly guided by those learned in legal traditions and forms of reasoning.

However, it was quickly apparent that this system was not adequate to the demands of an increasingly centralized and contentious society. The needs of such a society could not adequately be addressed through *ad hoc* adjudication, but called for laws that were generally acknowledged, stable, and more or less coherent — indeed, for a system of laws exhibiting the central virtues of Fuller's inner morality of the law. In short, they needed the kind of formalized legal systems that could only be established through deliberate authoritative enactment, extending beyond those laws embedded in immemorial customs or ideal principles. This is the point at which jurists begin to introduce a con-cept of authority, and to distinguish it from rational judgment *tout court*. We see clear examples of this process in the writings of two of the most influential jurists of the time, the secular jurist Irnerius and, shortly thereafter, the canon-ical jurist Gratian. In Irnerius's commentary on Justinian's *Digest*, written in the early decades of the twelfth century, he carefully distinguishes between the exercise of equity in the courtroom and the creation of law properly so called: "it is proper to equity simply to set forth that which is just. But it is proper to the law to set forth the same by an act of will, that is, relying on some author-ity."[95] Similarly, Gratian, whose *Decretum* was foundational for scholastic ju-risprudence in ecclesiastical contexts, insists that laws depend on authoritative promulgation, even though he gives considerable weight in different contexts to both natural and customary law (*Decretum* D.4 C.3).

We thus see that the scholastics, like ourselves, recognized the need for some acknowledged lawmaking authority if the legal system was to be ade-quate to the demands of the time. At the same time, authority was problematic for them, even more than for us, because they faced the urgent task of distin-guishing legitimate authority from then-current varieties of exploitative rule and petty tyranny. At the beginning of the scholastic period, many Christians, scholars and lay men and women alike, would have affirmed the Pauline view

94. Cited (in Latin) in Rudolf Weigand, *Die Naturrechtslehre der Legisten und Dekretisten von Irnerius bis Accursius und von Gratian bis Johannes Teutonicus* (Munich: Max Hueber, 1967), para. no. 21. All further references to primary texts cited by Weigand will be given by name and para-graph number.

95. Weigand, no. 20.

that human authority rests on a kind of divine authorization, conferred for the purpose of restraining the effects of sin. Yet this way of construing authority quickly came to be seen as inadequate, for much the same reasons that emerged in our analysis of contemporary accounts of authority. Certainly, if ruling authorities were established by God, then those subject to authority had reasons — the strongest imaginable reasons — for submitting themselves to these authorities. But it was difficult or impossible on this account to generate criteria on the basis of which to distinguish between legitimate and illegitimate uses of authoritative power or, by the same token, to distinguish between legitimate authorities and "bad lords," or "tyrants" who seek to "dominate" rather than to assume the burdens of the office of a ruler.[96]

Gradually, and with the help of key concepts in Roman law, scholastic jurists developed a workable account of the legislative and executive power of the prince, comprehending ecclesiastical as well as secular governing authorities. To us, the terms in which they formulated these accounts have an absolutist ring, particularly when, borrowing a phrase from Roman law, they claim that *princeps legibus solutus est* ("The prince is not bound by laws"). But as Kenneth Pennington has shown, they did not interpret this and similar phrases to mean that the power of the prince is altogether without limit. The prince is not bound by positive law, but the same may be said, with qualifications, of any recognized legislative authority; after all, legislative authority is precisely a legitimate claim to change existing law and to make new law. Nonetheless, this need not imply, and for the scholastics did not imply, that there are no normative constraints whatever on the exercise of legislative (or more generally, governing) authority. As Pennington observes, "Medieval and Renaissance jurists limited the prince's authority through natural law and by an amorphous concept that they called "status regni" or, in the Church, "status ecclesiae." They defined the state of the realm or the state of the Church as an inviolable body of law, custom, and tradition that was not subject to the authority of the prince."[97]

Pennington goes on to say that "Natural law was the kernel of medieval

---

96. These phrases are taken from John of Salisbury, quoted in Bisson, *Crisis of the Twelfth Century*, 281-82.

97. *Prince and the Law*, 278. This claim summarizes the case Pennington develops throughout his book; for his analysis of the early scholastic jurists with whom we are concerned here, see especially 38-164. In fact, Gratian does say that the lawgiver can overturn customs, but adds that customs of long standing should be respected, unless they are unreasonable or vicious. Given the proliferation of innovative "bad customs" then occurring, these qualifications are hardly surprising and in my view do not undermine Pennington's central point.

jurisprudence that sprouted into a coherent intellectual system harnessing the will of the prince."[98] Roman jurists had of course acknowledged the existence of a natural law, but for them the natural law was associated with the pre-rational, organic aspects of human existence, and as such it had little or no direct legal force. The scholastics, in contrast, developed ancient classical and Christian perspectives on the natural law into a natural law jurisprudence, yielding an account of natural rights and relations that the lawgiver is bound to respect.[99] They did not hold that the lawgiver can derive a comprehensive system of laws directly from natural law (or for that matter, from revealed divine law): from the time of Irnerius and Gratian forward, they are keenly aware that legal enactments must be formulated and promulgated by an authoritative act of will. Nonetheless, legislative authority operated within boundaries for them. By the same token, the authority of the courts was likewise limited by natural law principles, developed in this context into doctrines of due process. The judge was, in their view, a "minister of the law," someone whose actions were not, so to say, his own individual acts, but actions of the law itself.

Thus, the early scholastic conception of the natural law provided starting points for an account of normative constraints on the legitimate grounds of authority. The Roman republican tradition, mediated above all through Cicero, afforded the rudiments for an expanded account showing how it can be reasonable and praiseworthy to submit to authority at all.[100] With the full recovery of Aristotle's moral and political thought in the thirteenth century, the scholastics had the resources to go further; as Bisson says, "the very idea of political behaviour seems to have been new in the thirteenth century, being a revival of Aristotelian social theory together with the utilitarian precepts from Roman law and letters."[101] What Aristotle provided at this juncture was a cogent account of social life as an expression of our nature as social animals, which as such is good in itself, broadly intelligible in terms of natural principles, and normatively significant. On this basis, they began to develop an account of a properly political authority, legitimated by the necessary role that it plays in sustaining a common life.

98. *Ibid.*, 278.

99. This is still to some extent a controversial claim, but in my view it has been conclusively established by Brian Tierney in *The Idea of Natural Rights* (Atlanta: Scholars Press, 1997), 13-77.

100. Cary Nederman offers an invaluable analysis of Cicero's influence on early scholastic political thought in "Aristotelianism and the Origins of 'Political Science' in the Twelfth Century," *Journal of the History of Ideas* 52 (1991): 179-94.

101. *Crisis of the Twelfth Century*, 491.

Critically, the scholastics were able in this way to address the urgently practical need for a credible distinction between legitimate political authority, which does not compromise the free status of its subjects, and dominion, such as we see exercised over those in a state of servitude. This distinction is well expressed by Aquinas when, in the first part of the *Summa theologiae*, he considers whether authority and subordination would have existed in Paradise, if our first parents had never sinned. He addresses this question by drawing a distinction between two kinds of dominion. Understood in the first sense, dominion is exercised for the sake of the one holding power over another; this constitutes servitude, and it would never have arisen apart from sin. But there is another kind of dominion, grounded in human nature as such, which is not inconsistent with the free status of the subordinate:

> Someone exercises dominion over another as a free person, when he directs him to the proper good of the one being directed, or to the common good. And such dominion of a human person would have existed in a state of innocence, for two reasons. The first, because the human person is naturally a social animal; hence, human persons in a state of innocence would have lived in society. But the social life of a multitude is not possible unless someone is in charge, who aims at the common good, because a multitude as such aims at many things, whereas one aims at one thing. Hence the Philosopher says that whenever many are ordained to one thing, there is always found one as the principle and director. . . . Secondly, because if one person should be preeminent over another with respect to knowledge and justice, this would be inappropriate unless it were directed towards the well-being of the other. (ST I 96.4)

As Raz might say, the key distinction between political authority and dominion lies in the distinctive purpose of political authority, namely, to serve those subject to it. What is more, as we will see in more detail in the next chapter, political authority serves specifically to promote the well-being of its subjects precisely as rational agents — not in Raz's sense of enhancing their conformity to reasons, but in the still more fundamental sense of maintaining forms of social life that provide the necessary context for an individual's development and sustained functioning as a rational agent.

This conception of authority, in turn, determined the main lines of scholastic jurisprudence. Rational laws promulgated by legitimate authority were regarded as appropriate norms for the conduct of free men and women, and for that very reason they were effectively authoritative, as the commands of a master to his subjects could not have been. At the same time, however — as Fuller also recognized, albeit not in this context — the authoritative promulgation of specific laws in medieval European society presupposed that law, in some sense at least, was already in existence. The authority of the judge or lawgiver presupposed the existence of at least incipient or fragmentary systems for acquiring and exercising authority; what is more, adjudication and even legislation presupposed a basis of generally accepted norms and practices — the *status regni,* or *status ecclesiae* to which Pennington refers — to provide starting points and substance for new law.

None of this is as paradoxical as it sounds. We know, at least in general terms, how the processes of authoritative interpretation and promulgation of laws worked in medieval Europe.[102] Within the common law system taking shape in England at this time, legal procedures took shape through ongoing interactions among judges, lawyers, criminal defendants, litigants in civil suits, and juries — each taking advantage of the procedural resources of the law to carry out assigned functions or to advance his or her interests, in the process bringing tacit beliefs and commitments informing common practice to the level of explicit legal doctrine. Thus, for example, English juries faced in the twelfth century with the duty of assigning guilt or liability began to articulate, and thus to enshrine in legal doctrine, widespread assumptions about the nature, scope, and limits of freedom and responsibility — perspectives which, we may assume, had been operative all along, but which had not called for explicit and authoritative articulation under an older system of adjudication by ordeal.

In other jurisdictions, jurists drew on already existing bodies of laws — the canons of the church, or the newly revived *Digest* and other legal compilations of Justinian in the context of secular law on the Continent. But in neither case could these laws serve as a basis for contemporary legal practice without considerable interpretation and revision. The canons of the church were disorganized, incomplete, and partially inaccessible; church law could not begin to develop in a systematic way until Gratian placed what was available to him within a systematic framework of analysis, in terms of which existing laws could be assessed and placed in relation to one another, and new laws could be formulated. And of course, Justinian's codes were the laws of another polity, very different in structure and remote in time from early-twelfth-century Europe. In order to serve as a framework for the generation

---

102. For a good starting point, see S. F. C. Milsom, *A Natural History of the Common Law* (New York: Columbia University Press, 2003).

of effective contemporary laws, Roman law had to be interpreted and developed within the context of the very different assumptions and practices of medieval society. Of course, Roman law and the emerging principles and norms of canon law exercised a considerable mutual influence, in such a way that "the fusion of Roman, canon, and feudal law produced a *jus commune* and a common jurisprudence in Europe between 1100 and 1600."[103]

Thus, formal law emerged in this period through ongoing processes of specification and elaboration, through which implicit, fragmentary, or seemingly irrelevant norms for conduct were rendered explicit and relevant, while progressively being placed within a systematic framework. These processes were guided and informed by the practices of the community as a whole, or of the courts, or both in interaction with one another, all of which set constraints on the proper and effective power of lawgiver. Thus the articulation, interpretation and promulgation of positive law presupposed a context of customary practices, which conveyed the beliefs and normative commitments of the men and women for whom the law is intended. In this way, the considerations justifying a claim to authority were closely tethered to the constraints on the proper exercise of that authority, each being derived from the purpose of legislative authority, the promotion of the common good.

This brings us to a further point. It is sometimes said that the scholastics conflate natural law and formal enactments in such a way as to conclude that the precepts of the natural law have direct legal force. It should be apparent by now that this is not the case. They recognized the necessity for authoritative promulgation of formal laws, and they also saw that the formulation of laws required an element of contingent judgment, through which general principles can be given the necessary degree of concreteness and relevance. Thus, for them formal law is clearly on the conventional side of the ancient division between natural law and social conventions.

What is more, the scholastics do recognize — indeed, they insist on — what we would describe as the relative autonomy of legal systems, and they quickly begin to articulate norms of due process and proper legality embodying their respect for the independence of law.[104] This respect reflected their sense that political authority and the rule of law express the best possible safeguards for the genuine liberty of their subjects. It also reflects the complexity

103. *Prince and the Law,* 6. This is not to be confused with the common law of Great Britain, which remains in effect to this day in that country and its former colonies, including the United States.

104. See *Prince and the Law,* 148-164, and *Medieval Origins of the Legal Profession,* 126-63, 430-51 for details.

of European society and the contested claims in play at this time. Admittedly, these claims were lodged and adjudicated within a framework of shared convictions, including widely shared and deeply held theological commitments. Nonetheless, a shared allegiance to theological tenets could and did co-exist with very considerable conflicts over the competing claims of individuals and secular and ecclesiastical officials. Indeed, the presence of a shared theological framework sometimes made these conflicts worse, because it meant that very often the parties to a dispute would frame and justify their claims in the same theological terms — thus translating political fights into conflicts over fundamental principles. In this kind of situation, it becomes important to draw boundaries, both to sort out the competing claims of individuals and institutions, and even more importantly, to try to ensure as far as possible that fundamental convictions will be placed in question by social conflicts only very rarely, and in matters of genuinely far-reaching importance.

Thus, we should not be surprised that by the middle of the twelfth century, a "romano-canonical procedural system" began to emerge, in response to "a mounting deluge of legal actions."[105] This system exhibited the characteristics that we associate today with our own, markedly autonomous legal systems, including systems of formal law, reliance on formal roles and procedural norms, and the emergence of a specialized profession of legal advocates and scholars. As we have already noted, these systems were correlated with ideals of proper legality and due process, which were meant to guarantee impartial justice for all. As Brundage remarks, twelfth-century canon lawyers claimed that God himself established the foundations of canonical procedure in Paradise, "when he summoned Adam and Eve, questioned them about eating the forbidden fruit of the tree of the knowledge of good and evil, found their testimony inconsistent, their excuses unconvincing, and in consequence banished them from Paradise (Gen. 3:9-19)."[106] Of course, God already knew that Adam and Eve were guilty, but that was the point: rather than pronouncing summary judgment, he gave them their due, the opportunity to defend themselves in court, in accordance with impartial procedures. In a way, God himself acts as if bound by procedural constraints, independently of his own knowledge of the facts of the case. This high ideal works in both directions, and not always to happy effect; the scholastics are also prepared to say that a judge cannot save a condemned person from death on the basis of his own private knowledge of the innocence of

---

105. Both phrases are taken from *Medieval Origins of the Legal Profession*, 126.
106. *Medieval Origins of the Legal Profession*, 152.

the accused unless the judge can in some way establish the relevant facts through due processes of law. The judge, again, is the "minister of the law," for better or for worse, and the law operates in accordance with its own standards and procedures, in all courts human and divine.

From a very early stage, medieval jurisprudence, together with the practical problems and experiences on which it drew, are similar to our own in fundamental ways. Of course, they also differ in key respects, as we will see in more detail in the next chapter; otherwise, it would hardly be worth turning to this period to provide a fresh perspective on our own problems of legal authority. Nonetheless, we share enough in common with our forbears to introduce them once again into the ongoing conversations that constitute modern jurisprudence. By the same token, they open up unexpected possibilities for developing a cogent theology of authority which takes account of God's authority as well as our own. As we have seen, the scholastics do not hesitate to speak as if divine authority itself operates under certain constraints, set by the norms of proper legality and equitable procedures. Within the context of traditional Christian theism, this has an odd — not to say heretical — sound. How can God's authority be subject to constraints?

3. God's Authority and the Eternal Law

Christian theism has traditionally regarded God as the supreme authority over human affairs, and Raz's analysis of the concept of authority lends support and precision to this claim. God's acts *ad extra* are free and therefore reflect the contingency proper to authoritative decrees. God places claims on rational and intellectual creatures, enjoining them to act in ways that are sometimes contrary to their own considered judgments or desires. Given the source, these decrees nonetheless set up the strongest possible protected reasons, excluding these contrary desires and judgments from consideration. A rational agent can nevertheless accept God's authority and comply with its decrees without surrendering her autonomy in any problematic way. Willing obedience to God is reasonable and appropriate, because God is assumed to direct the agent to act in such a way as to conform to the demands of reason, as seen from the perspective of one who is supremely and uniquely qualified to make such a judgment. By doing so she also secures her own good — or so we may surmise, if we can assume that God is in some way friendly towards his creatures, actively concerned for our well-being in some practically effective way. Not every defense of divine authority would take this form; it is by no means obvious to everyone that God's decrees are necessarily directed towards our good, for example. Nonetheless, I think it is fair to say that historically, and even today, the majority view would be that God's activities towards us are directed to our ultimate happiness in some significant way, which may or may not be intelligible to us here and now. Traditional theism thus has no difficulty in establishing the legitimacy of God's authority in terms of Raz's service conception.

It is not so clear that we can construe God's authority in such a way as to address the second question emerging in contemporary jurisprudence regarding the normative constraints on the proper exercise of authority. Perhaps in this context we should not even try. After all, seen in the terms of traditional theism, God is the unconditional origin of all that exists apart from God, whose free creative act brings all delimited entities into existence and whose benevolent providence sustains their existence and their proper activities. God cannot be bound by constraints of practical reason because God determines these boundaries in the first place — or so the argument would go.

This line of analysis is problematic, however. In the first place, we cannot speak meaningfully of God's commands or decrees apart from some criteria for identifying these, in terms of whatever verbal or non-verbal formulations we expect them to take. These criteria, in turn, presuppose that we know something about who God is, enough at least to identify necessary or characteristic features of God's activities. And given the conception of God that we actually have, these criteria include, at a minimum, the expectation that God's activities are not malevolent or arbitrary. If we thought so, we would be confronted with a very different "god" and a different set of practical problems in the light of that deity's directives. So long as we construe something as an intelligible expression of God's commands, therefore, we can and must assume that what is enjoined is in some way congruent with normative criteria that we would apply to ourselves, given our own best ideals of consistency and benevolence.[107]

The difficulties in regarding God's exercise of authority as unbounded become still more acute when we consider the claim that human authority is in some way grounded in divine authorization. We are all too familiar with the long history of appeals to divine authority as a way of justifying what are manifestly authoritarian and arbitrary forms of rule. What is more, even in

107. I owe this insight to Robert Adams, "A Modified Divine Command Theory of Ethical Wrongness," in *The Virtue of Faith and Other Essays in Philosophical Theology* (Oxford: Oxford University Press, 1987), 97-122.

the best of circumstances such appeals would seem to place the intolerable weight of necessity and absoluteness on what are plainly contingent and limited constructions of human reason. The more we reflect self-consciously on lawmaking and legislative interpretation as human activities — as *our* activities — the less plausible an account of authority grounded directly in divine authorization becomes.

Given these difficulties, we might be tempted to say that God does not, after all, exercise authority over us in any proper sense. Yet this seems implausible, unless we are prepared to surrender a great deal in addition to this claim. After all, if God is in some irreducible way a personal agent, standing as such in a relationship with rational and intellectual creatures, then it is difficult to see how we can avoid construing this relation as being in some way a relation of authority. Fortunately, we need not deny either God's status as an agent or God's authoritative governance of creatures in order to address the problem just described. The key to understanding the relation between divine and human authority lies in the scholastics' conviction that the operations of authority are always structured and constrained by normative criteria. For them, relations of authority must always be understood in connection to some context out of which they emerge, and in terms of which they are both justified and limited. Thus, even though the scholastics occasionally use the language of absolute authority or power, they do not seem to understand even these forms of authority to be altogether unlimited, as Pennington argues at some length. Rather, the terms of their analysis indicate that they always presuppose some context, which delimits the scope and proper exercise of even the strongest forms of human authority.[108]

We may say the same about God's own authority. It too presupposes a context, in terms of which it is limited in scope and given a comprehensible shape. Admittedly, this claim goes beyond anything the scholastics explicitly say (although they do suggest it at some points, particularly in their discussions of whether, and in what ways, God can dispense with the norms of natural law).[109] Nonetheless, I believe that this way of construing God's author-

108. This is the overall point of *Prince and the Law;* see in particular the Epilogue, 269-90, and note: "We may, with some satisfaction, reflect that when we return to a conception of sovereignty that recognizes norms outside the state's positive law, we shall be returning to a system of thought that has deep roots in Western law" (290).

109. For further details, see Jean Porter, *Natural and Divine Law: Reclaiming the Tradition for Christian Ethics* (Grand Rapids: Eerdmans, 1999), 146-63. This same trajectory is further developed in the early Anglican tradition, as Christopher Insole observes; see *The Politics of Human Frailty: A Defense of Political Liberalism* (Notre Dame: University of Notre Dame Press, 2004), 73-74.

ity offers a legitimate and theologically defensible extension of the scholastics' general concept of authority. Of course, this construal invites the response that God's authority, unlike ours, is absolute and infinite. That, however, is just what I want to deny. God's authority, in contrast to those attributes proper to God's divinity as such (for example, God's simplicity or goodness) is, properly speaking, a function of the divine-human relation. Thus, God's authority over us is limited by conditions stemming from our intrinsic qualities and circumstances as creatures, and not by any limitations in God's own proper divinity.

The latter point should be underscored. The context within which God exercises authority over us is set by the contours of our condition as finite creatures standing in relation to an infinite God. Of course, we only exist as such because God willed to create us in the first place, and to sustain and direct our existence. Thus, the context limiting God's authority is itself a reflection of God's will, and more specifically, an expression of God's free self-limitation in entering into relations with a finite world. By the same token, this context expresses what we might regard as a different aspect of the divine reality — namely, the context set by divine intelligibility and goodness, as these are manifested in a created order displaying the same qualities in necessarily limited ways. In other words, God's own divinity, and the immediate manifestations of that divinity in creation, set the context for the more limited and, so to speak, personal relations in and through which God exercises authority over us. God's very self, considered as creator, is the ultimate context in and through which God as lawgiver and judge exercises authority over us.

Understood in this way, God's authority over us is limited, but only in ways that are congruent with other aspects of our relation to God as a personal force in human life — as redeemer, father, and friend. All these relations presuppose that we come to be and continue in existence, which is to say, they presuppose (logically, at any rate) God's creative and sustaining act. What is more, while we can and should affirm that God directly wills the initial and continuing existence of each and every individual creature, it is also the case that the paradigmatic act of creation is the act in and through which the cosmos as a whole comes to be and continues in existence. It is the cosmos as such, rather than any one creature, which most fully manifests God's intelligibility and goodness, and therefore it is the object in terms of which God's creative act is most properly grasped (to the extent that we can grasp it, of course).

This line of analysis implies a remote and impersonal relation to God —

but that is part of my point. As Oliver O'Donovan remarks, "The creation of the world by God and its redemption in Jesus Christ are the poles in relation to which Christians have consistently narrated the moral history of the world. . . . The narrative of creation and redemption has accompanied and disciplined Christian attempts to think about the moral dilemmas thrown up by every age."[110] The God who creates and the God who elects are one and the same, but we experience the one God in diverse ways, which from our standpoint stand in paradoxical tension with one another. Seen from the vantage point of our status as creatures, God appears to us in and through the natural forces which both sustain us and bear down and ultimately destroy us.[111] The beauty of the natural order, which the Psalmist rightly celebrates, is inextricably bound up with the processes through which individual entities emerge, flourish, and pass away, in relation to one another and inevitably at one another's expense. We celebrate the beauty of this order, all the while acknowledging that sooner or later we too will be destroyed by it.

At the same time, however, we as Christians believe that we have been invited into a personal relation with the God who knows us, and both judges and redeems us, as individual men and women. What is more — unless we are to embrace an ultimately nihilistic Gnosticism — the God whom we encounter as the impersonal ground of existence is one and the same as the God whom we embrace through personal love. This can appear to be intolerably paradoxical — the very same God both destroys us and saves us — but without this paradox there could be no Christianity. We cannot recognize and acknowledge the God who is revealed to us in Israel and in Christ *as* God, apart from grasping that there is a God who is in some more fundamental way the ground of our existence. Otherwise, the images of God conveyed in revelation quickly degenerate into symbolic reflections of broad cultural forces and our own fears and desires: God the Father becomes Santa Claus, the Lamb of God becomes the Easter Bunny. At the same time, once we see that the God who creates and the God who redeems are in fact one and the same, our view of cre-

---

110. Oliver O'Donovan, *Church in Crisis: The Gay Controversy and the Anglican Communion* (Eugene: Cascade Books, 2008), 86-87. More generally, my overall theological approach to creation and redemption is indebted to O'Donovan; see in particular *Resurrection and Moral Order: An Outline for Evangelical Ethics* (Grand Rapids: Eerdmans, 1986), 31-52.

111. I take this phrase from James Gustafson, *Ethics from a Theocentric Perspective, Volume I: Theology and Ethics* (Chicago: University of Chicago Press, 1981), 225; more generally, see 195-279. My interpretation of the ambiguities of the natural order as we perceive it is indebted to Gustafson, although I also affirm — as he does not — that God, as a personal reality, is ultimately concerned with, and well-disposed towards, us collectively and individually.

ation is itself radically transformed from an impersonal, albeit supremely beautiful cosmic order, to another expression of a supremely personal love, which cannot finally be hostile or even indifferent to us as individuals.

We may seem to have come some distance from the question of divine authority and the sources of law. In order to move to the next stage of the argument, we need to find a way to bring together the impersonal order of creation — considered as the context for God's authority — with the personal order of election and redemption, one aspect of which is God's authority over us. I propose to do so by drawing on Aquinas's claim that God's providential wisdom can itself be construed as a kind of law, the eternal law, understood as such by analogy to formal human law and comprehensible (in the limited way proper to theology) in terms of the purpose towards which it is directed:

> Now God through his wisdom is the founder of all things taken together, to which he is compared as artisan to artifacts. . . . He is also the governor of all the acts and motions which are found in individual creatures. . . . Hence, just as the rational principle of the divine wisdom, insofar as all created things are made through it, has the rational character of art or exemplar or idea, so the rational principle of the divine wisdom, moving all things to a due end, attains to the rational character of law. And thus, the eternal law is nothing other than the rational principle of divine wisdom, insofar as it directs all acts and motions. (*Summa theologiae* I-II 93.1)[112]

The eternal law is nothing other than the rational plan through which God governs the universe. It is comprehensive in scope, governing not only the activities of rational creatures, but also the acts and natural motions of every creature — each one of which, Aquinas insists, is governed individually through God's providence (ST I-II 93.5). The eternal law is therefore expressed through what we would call laws of nature in the scientific sense, as well as positive or moral laws, and it also governs random and unpredictable motion (if any such actually takes place). What is more, in contrast both to Augustine (his primary source here) and those few of his contemporaries

---

112. Hereafter cited as ST. For the patristic and medieval context, and for Aquinas's account of the eternal law, see Odon Lottin, "La Loi éternelle chez saint Thomas d'Aquin et ses prédécesseurs," in *Psychologie et Morale aux XII et XIII siècles*, 6 vols. (Louvain: Abbae du Mont César, 1942-1960), Vol. 2, 51-67. In my reading of Aquinas's own interpretation of this motif, I am indebted to Michel Bastit, *Naissance de la Loi Moderne: La Pensée de la Loi de Saint Thomas à Suarez* (Paris: Presses Universitaires de France, 1990), 77-82.

who discuss eternal law, Aquinas emphasizes its rational character, rather than its status as an act of authoritative will. The eternal law is promulgated through being uttered — otherwise, it would not count as a law according to Aquinas's definition as set forth in ST I-II 90.4 — but this takes place most fundamentally through the conception of the Word of God in the intellect of the Father (I-II 93.1 *ad* 2). The utterance of the Word can perhaps be construed as a kind of authoritative decree, but at any rate it is not primarily an authoritative decree directed towards human persons or any other creatures.

Aquinas's account of the eternal law construes it as an expression of comprehensive divine wisdom, expressed through what I have described as the impersonal, as well as the personal aspects of divinity as we experience it. By so doing, he provides a theologically informed and attractive way of construing the context within which divine authority is exercised. Seen from Aquinas's perspective, the eternal law comprises that context by constituting the intelligible order in and through which both the cosmos as a whole, and individual creatures exist and move through time. But we are looking for a way to connect this context with the exercise of God's authority over us as one who is personally related to us in some way. Does Aquinas's account suggest some way in which these two elements of the divine-human relation can be brought together?

It does, through his analysis of the way in which the natural law stems from the eternal law. As is well known, Aquinas holds that the natural law represents the distinctive way in which the rational creature participates in the eternal law:

> Hence, since all things which are subject to divine providence are governed and given measure by the eternal law, as is plain from what has been said, it is clear that all things participate in some way in the eternal law, insofar as they receive from it inclinations towards their own acts and ends. Among others, however, the rational creature is subjected to divine providence in a more excellent manner, insofar as he himself is also made a participant in providence, being provident for himself and others. Hence, in the rational creature there is also a participation in eternal reason, through which he has a natural inclination towards a due act and end. And this participation of the eternal law in the rational creature is called the natural law. (ST I-II 91.2)

This line of analysis offers two important insights. First, it makes it clear that even though the rational creature participates in the eternal law in a distinctive way, this participation can only be understood within the wider context set by the intelligible processes through which all creatures participate in appropriate ways in the eternal law. As Russell Hittinger observes, the natural law is thus an expression of divine providence, distinctive in form, but only theologically meaningful when seen in this wider context.[113] Secondly, it identifies what we might describe as the primary legislative moment in God's relation to human persons, the point at which God's wise plan for human existence is expressed in terms of an authoritative decree. The decree in question is nothing other than God's will to create a rational creature — which is to say, a kind of creature distinguished by the capacity to be "a participant in providence, being provident for himself and others." The authoritative decree through which God establishes human authority is thus, fundamentally, God's will that the rational creature exist and flourish, interpreted in light of the fact that the exercise of authority, in some form or other, is an intrinsic component of the natural life of the human creature, without which we cannot live as the rational, social creatures that we are.

It is important to note that this argument presupposes — it does not establish — that authority is in fact an intrinsic component of the natural life of the human creature, and establishes its goodness on that basis. So far, exactly the same line could be pursued with respect to marriage, or rational inquiry, or any other arguably natural aspect of human life. Can we extend this argument further to say something more about whether, and in what ways, the exercise of authority reflects the divine will in a distinctive way? The scholastics would seem to suggest that we can, if only because their conception of the natural law is consistently spelled out in the kind of legal terminology proper to a discourse of authority, subordination, and the rule of law. Aquinas himself, following a widely held patristic tradition, grounds the natural law in the human capacity for rational judgment and self-determination, which is in turn identified with the image of God properly so called. At the very least, this claim implies that the human person expresses the divine image in a distinctive and paradigmatic way through participation in those institutions of authority, subordination, and lawful conduct. If this is so, then it seems at least plausible that the contours of authority and law can and should express what we might call the contours of divinity, as reflected in the image of that divinity that constitutes human identity.

I believe that this is in fact the case, and this book represents an attempt

---

113. Russell Hittinger, *The First Grace: Rediscovering the Natural Law in a Post-Christian World* (Wilmington: ISI Books, 2003), 4-5.

to develop and defend this claim. That is to say, I will argue that formal law can best be understood, and correlatively evaluated, in the light of its grounding in natural and eternal law. It would be premature at this point to try to spell out in more detail just what this means, but let me attempt to forestall two misunderstandings. There is some tendency to speak of the eternal law as if it included a fairly specific set of precepts comprising the natural law, which can be accessed as such either through rational discernment or through divine illumination. Yet this is implausible on a number of grounds. For one thing, we do not have the necessary kind of access to God's knowledge of the created order. In addition, there is no good reason to assume that the natural law necessarily consists of specific precepts of the kind envisioned. Aquinas and his interlocutors did not in fact construe the natural law in this way. Rather, as we will see in the next chapter, they identified the natural law in the primary sense with capacities or general principles for rational judgment, which must be exercised or specified in more or less contingent ways in order to be practically effective. Similarly, I will not claim that human law represents an emanation from, or an approximation to, the eternal law, regarded as setting the template or criterion for all other kinds of laws. On the contrary, for Aquinas, the formal law with which we are most familiar provides, for us, the key paradigm for our concept of law, and every kind of proper law, including the eternal law, is understood as such by analogy to law as we properly understand it. Each kind of proper law perfectly expresses the essential marks of law, in accordance with its distinctive purpose, and can be understood in these terms without adverting to the eternal law as if it were a kind of Platonic Form of legality.[114]

These disclaimers may prompt the opposite thought, that human law is theologically significant simply because it is an expression of human reason and freedom, without any reference to the content of the laws in question, and that we therefore have no theological basis for evaluating some laws or practices as better or worse than others.[115] This, too, seems to me mistaken. The divine image is expressed through reason and freedom, to be sure, but these are not simply undifferentiated capacities; they stem from the intelligible natural structures of the human organism and human life, and can only be exercised and understood in terms of these structures. Human nature is always expressed in conventional forms — there is no one "natural" way of

114. I owe this point to Bastit, *Naissance de la Loi Moderne*, 48-49.
115. Hittinger offers an illuminating account of the origins and consequences of this mistake, at least in recent Catholic theology, in *First Grace*, 3-37.

life — yet we can discern its distinctive contours, and these do have a normative purchase on human conduct and the laws regulating that conduct. Just as the exigencies of God's activities as creator set the context for the exercise of God's authority, giving it definition and therefore boundaries, so the expression of God's creative act in the exigencies of human nature sets the most fundamental context for the exercise of human authority.

Understood in this way, the appeal to God's eternal law has real explanatory power, in that it provides the basis for a satisfactory explanation of the processes of legislation and legal interpretation and offers criteria for evaluating our efforts in these regards. This account does not presuppose that good legislators and judges must bring Christian or theistic beliefs to their activities — a manifestly absurd claim — but rather, that the activities of legislation and adjudication are grounded in, and find their context in a natural law, and thereby in the eternal law. It does not follow that human law as such reflects the eternity and perfection of God's wisdom, and yet nonetheless it draws on and is sustained by that wisdom, even in its contingency and imperfection. That is why human, formal law deserves respect on the part of all, and why we as Christians have a stake in promoting and extending an ideal of the rule of law. The Psalmist was not wrong to see something divine in the ideal of law.

CHAPTER 2

Authority and the Natural Law

The idea of a natural law is pre-Christian in origin, and we can trace a more or less continuous tradition of reflection on this idea from the Stoics to the early scholastic period (and beyond). As Gerard Watson remarks, "We might suspect a certain looseness in a term which has won such a variety of admiration," and yet, as he goes on to say, "the term survives."[1] It survives, I would suggest, precisely because the idea of natural law is not tied to any particular construal of nature or dependent on any one account of the relation between natural principles and social conventions. Rather, this long and diverse tradition is held together by the fundamental distinction between nature and convention — that is to say, between the practices of a given society and whatever innate principles may be said to generate or constrain them.

The relation between natural and conventional is sometimes construed as if the natural law were itself a set of normative precepts purified from all temporal and contingent elements, as if it comprised, as Watson puts it, as "a body of unchanging rules, somewhere at some time worked out and available for consultation in difficulties, a sort of secular version of the Ten Commandments."[2] On this view, the distinction between the natural law and the conventions of a well-ordered society tend to break down, and positive law comes to be regarded, in Lawrence Rosen's words, as itself "immanent, immune to human creation and manipulation notwithstanding the efforts of the shortsighted to the contrary."[3] This way of construing the natural law

---

1. Gerard Watson, "The Natural Law and Stoicism," in *Problems in Stoicism*, ed. A. A. Long (London: Athlone, 1971), 216-38, here 216.

2. "Natural Law and Stoicism," 217.

3. Lawrence Rosen, *Law as Culture: An Invitation* (Princeton: Princeton University Press, 2006), 184.

dominated natural law jurisprudence in the early modern period; as Rosen goes on to say, "Blackstone, in the eighteenth century, could argue that just as certain manifestations (Shakespeare's incomparable writing, for example) could seem so right as to be a force of nature, so too institutions that might seem to be of human creation fit so clearly with the unalterable features of God's own creation as to make laws themselves part of nature."[4] In its earliest stages, legal positivism offered a direct challenge to this unpromising approach, insisting that laws are social conventions, and as such contingent and changeable, in contrast to supposedly timeless and immutable natural laws. As Joseph Raz explains:

> In the most general terms the positivist social thesis is that what the law is and what it is not is a matter of social fact (that is, the variety of social theses supported by positivists are various refinements and elaborations of this crude formulation). Their moral thesis is that the moral value of law (both of a particular law and of a whole legal system) or the moral merit it has is a contingent matter dependent on the content of the law and the circumstances of the society to which it applies. The only semantic thesis which can be identified as common to most positivist theories is a negative one, namely, that terms like "rights" and "duties" cannot be used in the same meaning in legal and moral contexts.[5]

Given the conception of natural law exemplified by Blackstone, legal positivism in any of these forms would indeed stand in direct opposition to a natural law jurisprudence. Yet the capacious natural law tradition includes other ways of understanding the natural law and relating it to social conventions. We might take social conventions as specifications or manifestations of natural principles, while correlatively identifying natural principles through an analysis of the conventions that embody them in some way. Thus understood, the relation between the natural law and social conventions would not be construed as the relation between two sets of precepts, two codes, one subordinate to the other — in somewhat the way that the constitution and statutory laws of the State of Indiana are distinct from, and subordinated to, the Constitution of the United States. Rather, on this view the critical relation between natural principles and conventional norms is one of specification or exemplification. Thus, natural principles are identified by

4. *Law as Culture*, 184-85
5. Joseph Raz, *The Authority of Law: Essays on Law and Morality* (Oxford: Clarendon Press, 1979), 37-38.

reference to their conventional expressions, and correlatively, social conventions are identified and analyzed in terms of the principles rendering them intelligible as conventions of a certain kind.

Given that we can construe the natural law in this way, in terms of intelligible principles underlying social conventions, the conventional status of laws and legal systems is by no means necessarily inconsistent with a natural law jurisprudence. Raz himself makes this point. Immediately after setting out the three theses of positivism in the passage just quoted, he adds that "Of these the social thesis is the more fundamental" and neither the moral nor the semantic thesis necessarily follows from the social thesis.[6] He goes on to explain that

> The claim that what is law and what is not is purely a matter of social fact still leaves it an open question whether or not these social facts by which we identify the law or determine its existence do or do not endow it with moral merit. If they do, it has of necessity a moral character. But even if they do not, it is still an open question whether, given human nature and the general conditions of human existence, every legal system which is in fact the effective law of some society does of necessity conform to some moral values or ideals.[7]

Indeed, Raz continues, he himself is committed to a "moderate" version of legal positivism which does not necessarily rule out a natural law account of the relation between law and morality. As we saw in the last chapter, Fuller takes a similar line, and even Hart describes his position as a "soft positivism," which recognizes that the rule of recognition "may incorporate as criteria for legal validity conformity with moral principles or substantive values."[8] In the thirty years since Raz's essay first appeared, a number of other prominent legal scholars have taken a similar approach, so much so that in Anglophone circles at least, we are seeing an extensive revival of natural law jurisprudence, or at any rate a jurisprudence open to considerations of value and normative constraint. This revival does not reflect a rejection of legal positivism so much as the recognition that we are now in a position to move beyond earlier, overly simplistic divisions to incorporate what is best in both approaches. As Neil MacCormick says, speaking of his own most recent work:

6. *Authority of Law,* 38.
7. *Authority of Law,* 38-39.
8. H. L. A. Hart, *The Concept of Law, Second Edition* (Oxford: Clarendon Press, 1994), 250.

In its intellectual inheritance, and in the particular contrast drawn between the positive, institutional character of state law and the autonomous character of morality, this book belongs in the same tradition as those of Hart and Kelsen, and, I hope, represents an advance upon its predecessors. On the other hand, various contemporaries have pretty convincingly established that there is a need for improvement and correction to some of the tenets of Hartian or Kelsenian positivism. . . . It is better to reject the aforesaid dichotomy as based on a misleading account of the history of legal ideas than to trouble responding to the question: "Are you a positivist or a natural lawyer?" The question in what sense "human nature" or "the nature of things" can support arguments about good moral principles or sound legal foundations is one we have not had to pursue in the present work. The "natural" character of institutional normative order is not here in issue, though it is certainly natural at least in the sense of being neither miraculous nor unusual.[9]

As these remarks illustrate, secular legal scholars are once again open to considering natural law jurisprudence as a viable approach to legal theory, or at any rate as a resource for constructive insights into legal theory and practice. An attempt to recover and develop a pre-modern natural law jurisprudence would thus appear to be timely and potentially welcome. Yet among the many schools of natural law jurisprudence currently on offer, few draw on pre-modern natural lawyers to any considerable extent. Those theories that rely on Thomas Aquinas, including most notably the "new theory of the natural law" developed by Germain Grisez, John Finnis, and their many collaborators and students, are the one prominent exception.[10] Yet even these theories generally offer a truncated Aquinas, whose normative judgments do not depend in any substantive way on more broadly natural or

9. Neil MacCormick, *Institutions of Law: An Essay in Legal Theory* (Oxford: Oxford University Press, 2007), 278-79.

10. The main statements of the theory would include John Finnis, *Natural Law and Natural Rights* (Oxford: Clarendon Press, 1980), and *Aquinas: Founders of Modern Political and Social Thought* (Oxford: Oxford University Press, 1998); Germain Grisez, Joseph Boyle, and John Finnis, "Practical Principles, Moral Truth, and Ultimate Ends," *American Journal of Jurisprudence* 32 (1987): 99-151; and Germain Grisez, *The Way of the Lord Jesus 1: Christian Moral Principles* (Chicago: Franciscan Herald Press, 1983), and *The Way of the Lord Jesus 2: Living a Christian Life* (Chicago: Franciscan Herald Press, 1993). In addition, Robert George offers especially clear and helpful summaries of the theory in the course of defending it against various critics in the essays collected in *In Defense of Natural Law* (Oxford: Oxford University Press, 1999); see in particular 45-54 and 83-91.

metaphysical — let alone, theological — commitments. Whatever we may think of the theoretical merits of this kind of approach, it is clearly not Aquinas's own, and many of its leading proponents now recognize this.[11] Scholastic natural law thinkers prior to or contemporary with Aquinas are scarcely even mentioned by our own contemporaries, even though the early jurists, in particular, arguably had a greater impact on the development of jurisprudence and legal practices than did Aquinas himself.

In this book, I hope to show that the early scholastic conception of the natural law can offer a distinctive and valuable contribution to contemporary jurisprudence. In at least one fundamental respect, early medieval natural lawyers are closer to contemporary legal theorists than either would be to early modern natural lawyers. Yet in other respects they are different, and these differences represent the most challenging, but also the most fruitful starting points for constructive development.

The critical point of contact between the scholastics and ourselves concerns the relation between natural principles and social conventions. We observed that for modern natural lawyers, the laws and practices of a well-ordered society tend to be identified as natural principles without qualification. This is often assumed to be the medieval view as well, but in fact the early scholastics would have found such a view almost as uncongenial as do most of our contemporaries, albeit for a different reason; for them the natural law serves as a basis for the analysis of actually existing (or proposed) practices and laws, in terms of which these conventions may be justified, reformed, or rejected. If the natural law were simply identified with the conventions of a well-ordered society, this would leave insufficient space for it to illuminate social conventions, much less to provide a critical purchase on them. Of course, they might still have taken the line Watson suggests, identifying the natural law with God's ideal revealed law — the Ten Commandments themselves, together with whatever specifications are found in divine, that is to say, scripturally revealed law. But this approach too was ruled out for the scholastics, because — for better or for worse — their theology of progressive revelation, culminating in Christ, committed them to the view that the legal codes found in the Hebrew Scriptures represent the provisional laws of the Hebrew peoples of the time. The Decalogue itself is not similarly provisional, of course, but neither is it a fully articulated moral code or set of

---

11. So far as I know, John Finnis is the only leading defender of the "new natural law" who is still prepared to defend this as an accurate interpretation of Aquinas's own view; again, see his *Aquinas* for a recent, extended defense of this position.

legal prescriptions. As the scholastics recognize, its precepts are too general to serve as practical norms concrete enough to be readily applied to actual choices, apart from some further specification. Partially for this reason, they resist the suggestion that the natural law, understood in its most proper sense, can be identified with the precepts of the Decalogue, although these are regarded as necessary and immediate expressions or implications of the natural law.

As we will see, the scholastics attempted to preserve the generality and universality of the natural law by identifying it with the human capacity for rational judgment or with the most general and formal principles through which that capacity operates. This approach carried the opposite danger, that the natural law, far from being too closely identified with specifics, might be so abstract as to have almost no normative purchase on the practices it was meant to critique. For the early scholastics, however, this did not appear as a real possibility, because reason itself was thought to be grounded in natural principles informing human life and activity, seen as exemplifying the way of life proper to humankind as a kind of living organism. Seen from this perspective, human reason itself stems from these principles of intelligibility and flourishing, which structure its operations, and which it tracks more or less faithfully when it is functioning in good order. By implication, human laws stem from objective normative structures, which can be grasped as such and intelligently applied, even though these do not determine the structure of the laws in any one necessary or optimal way. And here, I want to argue, lies the greatest contribution that early scholastic natural law jurisprudence can make to contemporary thought.

Of course, this is also the point at which the scholastic approach differs most notably from our own. In contemporary Western societies, we can hardly understand the claim that at least some kinds of things exhibit objective normative structures, giving rise to values that we discover, as opposed to values created through our own judgments and desires. In contrast, natural law jurisprudence presupposes some account of the objective normative structures through which human nature is constituted. It is important to realize that these structures cannot be said either to comprise a moral law or to be identified with any one set of social arrangements. These natural principles under-determine the concrete conventions expressing them, including moral precepts as well as social norms, but they nonetheless comprise their basis, justification, and context for evaluation. As I hope to show, that is why it should matter to legal theory, even today, to take seriously the natural origins of our legal systems and practices.

The scholastic approach to the natural law is compatible with more than one specific theory of human nature and its normative significance, but it is not compatible with every such theory. It requires, at a minimum, an account of human nature that has enough content, as it were, to generate substantive interpretations of concrete norms and social conventions. Not only does the scholastic interpretation of reason imply as much — more fundamentally, the project of taking God's eternal law as the interpretative context for God's exercise of authority presupposes that nature is sufficiently intelligible to provide an independent touchstone for making sense of (putative?) divine injunctions. At the same time, the scholastic project of analyzing social conventions in terms of their origins in natural principles implies correlation and mutual dependence rather than a strict dichotomy between two distinct standards of conduct or (much less) two sets of specific precepts. This approach, in turn, implies a conception of human nature that is determinate, but not too determinate — in other words, a conception that opens up the possibility of interpreting the incommensurably distinct commitments and practices of different communities as comprising so many diverse expressions of natural right or law, construed in accordance with whatever is regarded as normative in human existence and its social and natural contexts. Otherwise, we would be forced to re-inscribe the sharp dichotomy between nature and convention that the scholastics reject, with the result that we would have no option but to evaluate human practices — and therefore positive law — in terms of standards that are not only distinct from, but exterior to those laws. And this would undercut any attempt to develop an account of positive laws which displays their *intrinsic* authority or (much less) displays their cogency and force as expressions, on the level of the contingent and human, of God's eternal law.

At the same time, if this account is to be at all persuasive, even on its own terms, it must be at least defensible in light of a range of objections, philosophical and scientific as well as theological. Ideally, it will be attractive, perhaps even compelling, to at least some who have no theological stake in embracing it. After all, a Christian theologian should at least hope to offer a true account of the world, and any such account should be broadly recognizable as such, at least at some points and within certain limits. What is more, it is important to keep sight of the overall aim of this project, namely, to contribute to a theological jurisprudence developed in conversation with contemporary philosophical jurisprudence and responsive to actual legal practices in modern Western societies. It would be difficult or impossible to set forth a credible theory of law on the basis of accounts of natural law and human nature that most legal practitioners within one's society could not accept at all.

My aim in this chapter is to set out the main lines of the conception of natural law that I will draw on through the remainder of the book. I will begin by outlining the concept of human nature presupposed by this account, paying particular attention to the ways in which a characteristically human form of life is expressed in, and may be identified through, the irreducible plurality of cultural forms. In this way, I will attempt to lay the groundwork for an account of the ways in which human nature and natural law come to be expressed in law properly so called, focusing on the role of practices and communal discernment as the mediating contexts within which this process takes place.

1. The Scholastic Conception of the Natural Law

Gratian: The Twofold Rule

The scholastics were no more inclined to uniformity than academics today, on the subject of the natural law or on any other significant topic.[12] Nonetheless, their debates over the natural law took place within the context of a shared tradition, classical in its origins but by this point deeply embedded in patristic thought. What is more, they entered into this tradition in conversation with one another, and especially, with key figures who set a trajectory for later work. In order to provide an entree into the broad conception of the natural law that emerged out of these processes, I will frame this section by considering two such key thinkers. The second of these, Thomas Aquinas, has of course determined the shape of much natural law thinking up to the present day. I begin, however, with an earlier author whose influence on subsequent reflection on the natural law, especially but not only in legal theory, can scarcely be exaggerated. The scholastic in question is known to us today

12. Throughout this section, I draw on and extend my earlier interpretations of the scholastic concept of the natural law and its contemporary significance: *Natural and Divine Law: Reclaiming the Tradition for Christian Ethics* (Grand Rapids: Eerdmans, 1999), and *Nature as Reason: A Thomistic Theory of the Natural Law* (Grand Rapids: Eerdmans, 2005); see in particular *Natural and Divine Law*, 268-83 and *Nature as Reason*, 342-78. In my treatment of Gratian, I also draw on and extend an interpretation first set forth in "Custom, Ordinance and Natural Right in Gratian's *Decretum*," in *The Nature of Customary Law: Legal, Historical and Philosophical Perspectives*, ed. Amanda Perreau-Saussine and James Bernard Murphy (Cambridge: Cambridge University Press, 2007), 79-100.

as Gratian; his legal thought comes to us through a single text, which seems to have first appeared sometime around 1140.[13]

This text, Gratian's *Harmony of Discordant Canons,* commonly known as the *Decretum,* has long been recognized by historians of law as foundational for modern Western jurisprudence.[14] Even though it presents many interpretative difficulties, having been almost certainly altered and expanded in a variety of ways, its main purpose is clear enough. It is, first of all, an attempt at a comprehensive collection of the laws, or canons, of the Roman Catholic church, as these existed in scattered conciliar decrees, papal pronouncements, and the like. The *Decretum* was not the first such compilation, but what set it apart was Gratian's further attempt to show how these diverse and seemingly inconsistent canons can be consistently interpreted and applied in the light of overall principles — in a word, harmonized. In accordance with this plan, Gratian devotes the first twenty distinctions of the *Decretum* to general principles governing the interpretation of laws. While these distinctions do not comprise a fully worked out theory of law, they do set forth a coherent conception of law developed in accordance with emerging scholastic methodologies, through the selection and interpretation of authoritative texts — here including copious citations from patristic sources and Isidore's *Etymologies* as well as legal texts properly so called. As

13. Gratian's *Decretum* is available in a number of editions; for reasons of convenience, I relied on the Rome edition of 1582. All translations of Gratian are my own. However, I checked my translations against Augustine Thompson's; see *Gratian: The Treatise on Laws (Decretum DD. 1-20), With the Ordinary Gloss* (Washington, DC: Catholic University of America Press, 1993). I also draw on Katherine Christensen's comprehensive introduction in this volume for general information on the background, overall purpose and structure of the *Decretum.*

All references to the *Decretum* are taken from the first part of the book, which consists of *distinctiones* comprising a series of texts *(capitula)* interspersed with Gratian's own comments *(dicta).* The citations follow the standard form for this part: *distinctiones* and *capitula* are cited by number, as for example, D.1, C.2, and Gratian's own dicta are cited by reference to the *capitulum* before or after which they appear, by *ante* or *post capitulum* (a.c. or p.c.). The *dicta* in the opening remarks of a *distinctio,* that is, *in principio,* are cited simply by pr, as in D.1 pr.

14. For two especially helpful discussions of Gratian's context and overall significance, see R. W. Southern, *Scholastic Humanism and the Unification of Europe,* vol. 1: *Foundations* (Oxford: Blackwell, 1995), 274-318, and James A. Brundage, *The Medieval Origins of the Legal Profession: Canonists, Civilians, and Courts* (Chicago: University of Chicago Press, 2008), 96-105. Peter Landau argues that Gratian exemplifies, but does not initiate, a turn to patristic sources and a focus on sacramental theology in early canonical jurisprudence; see "Wandel und Kontinuität im kanonischen Recht bei Gratian," 215-33 in *Sozialer Wandel im Mittelalter: Wahrnehmungsformen, Erklärungsmuster, Regelungsmechanismem,* ed. Jürgen Miethke and Klaus Schreiner (Stuttgart: Jan Thorbecke, 1994).

such, the *Decretum* offers one of the earliest free-standing treatises on juris-prudence, analyzing and setting forth the principles of law independently of commentary on any one text.

The *Decretum* begins as follows:

> The human race is ruled by a twofold rule, namely, natural law and prac-tices. Natural law is that which is contained in the law and the Gospel, by which each person is commanded to do to others what he would wish to be done to himself, and forbidden to render to others that which he would not have done to himself. Hence, Christ says in the Gospel, "All things whatever that you would wish other people to do to you, do the same also to them. For this is the law and the prophets." (*Decretum* D.1 pr)

Gratian thus begins with the claim that all laws can be understood as expressions of what is natural (we are ruled by *natura jure*, "natural right") or conventional (by *moribus*, "practices") in human society.[15] He goes on to interpret what is natural in terms of revelation, apparently equating natural law with the Golden Rule in both negative and positive formulations de-rived from Scripture. These remarks have received a considerable amount of scholarly attention, much of it unfavorable. As I have argued elsewhere, Gratian's point becomes clearer when we place his remarks within the con-text of the contemporaneous revival of Roman law.[16] Seen in this context,

---

15. Gratian says that we are ruled by "natura . . . jure," usually translated as "natural law" on the assumption that the English terms "law" and "right" can be used interchangeably as transla-tions for *jus* unless the context clearly indicates one or the other. Until recently, I shared this view, but I have become persuaded that the distinction between *jus* and *lex* ("law") as used by the scho-lastics should ideally be reflected in translation. For one thing, the scholastics themselves consis-tently distinguish between the two, although the exact terms in which they do so vary — a fact that, in itself, suggests that the distinction was widely acknowledged and not dependent on the specifics of any one author's approach. Secondly, it seems to me that whatever the specifics of their views, the scholastics consistently regard *jus* as basis for a juridical (or quasi-juridical) judg-ment; this idea is better captured by "right" than by "law." Nonetheless, in order to forestall unnec-essary confusions, I have translated *jus* by "law" in most of the contexts in which it would nor-mally be thus translated.

16. In *Natural and Divine Law*, 129-31. I am still persuaded by this reading, even granting An-ders Winroth's argument that the reception of Roman law and the emergence of the *jus commune* occurred almost simultaneously with the first recension of the *Decretum*, and not (as is more commonly believed) during the end of the tenth and the beginning of the eleventh century; see Anders Winroth, *The Making of Gratian's Decretum* (Cambridge: Cambridge University Press, 2000), 146-74. As Winroth notes, the Gratian of the first recension quotes the *Digest* four times, and very likely used the Justinianic *corpus* at first hand (151).

the opening words of the *Decretum* stand in pointed contrast to Justinian's *Digest,* which also begins (or very nearly so) with a definition of natural law, drawn in this instance from the second-century jurist Ulpian, according to which the natural law is "that which nature teaches all animals" (*Dig.* I 1, 1.3). By setting a theological definition, clearly indebted to Hugh of St. Victor, at the beginning of his *Decretum,* Gratian endorses Hugh's position that natural law, at least as seen from the perspective of canon law, can only adequately be understood through Scripture.[17] By implication, the civilians' understanding of natural law derived from Roman law does not provide a suitable starting point for a properly theological understanding of law.[18]

Yet this approach does not imply that the civilians' conception of natural law is incorrect, or even that it has no place within ecclesiastical jurisprudence. On the contrary, Gratian goes on to incorporate the key elements of a Roman conception of natural law as mediated through Isidore, whose own sources clearly overlap with those of the *Digest.*[19] He also endorses other conceptions of natural law, including the long-standing equation between natural law and reason. At least, he suggests as much by following statements that customs and ordinances are subordinate to natural law with texts asserting that these forms of law are subordinate to reason, or even to considerations of intelligibility and appropriateness. Thus, in the distinction devoted to the relation between natural law and customs, he first states that no one is permitted to act contrary to natural law (D.8, a.c. 2), and then goes on to cite texts saying that no one may act against God's command (D.8, C.2) or against reason and truth (D.8, C.4-9). Similarly, in

17. See Hugh of St. Victor, *De sacramentis* I 11.7, for the relevant text. Peter Landau argues that one of the distinctive features of the *Decretum* is the way in which it brings together the sacramental and the juridical aspects of church life; see "Wandel und Kontinuität im kanonischen Recht bei Gratian," 229-30. This line of interpretation lends further support to the view that Gratian's appeal to Hugh's influential treatise on the sacraments represents an attempt to establish a theologically sound alternative conception of natural law.

18. Experts in Roman law in this period are commonly referred to as "civilians," that is to say, scholars and practitioners of civil, as opposed to canon law.

19. Gratian's attitude to Roman law has long been disputed. Chodorow claims that Gratian deliberately excludes Roman law from consideration; see Stanley Chodorow, *Christian Political Theory and Church Politics in the Mid-Twelfth Century* (Berkeley: University of California Press, 1972), 60-64. In my view, however, the prominence that Gratian gives to Isidore's treatment of Roman law makes this line of interpretation unlikely (see D.1, C.7-12 and D.2 in particular). And if Winroth is correct, Gratian's limited use of Roman legal materials may also reflect a later reception of the latter than we have assumed (see note 13).

D.9 he develops the same point with respect to written laws, defending the claim that written laws yield to natural law (D.9, pr) by citing texts that assert the priority of Scripture (D.9, C.3), sound judgment (D.9, C.4), or sound reasoning (D.9, C.11).

The implication is clear: Scripture, reason, truth and sound judgment can all be considered as pre-conventional principles setting criteria for evaluating both customary practices and formal laws. This line of analysis does not imply that every scriptural norm can be taken as an expression of natural law (D.6, p.c. 3). Gratian's point is, rather, that any principle that can be regarded as a kind of pre-conventional natural law should also be considered as an expression of divine wisdom and will, which therefore stands in the same authoritative relation to human law as does Scripture itself. This is a critical move, especially given the fact that Gratian is dealing with canon law, which could well be given a quasi-divine status. Gratian will have none of this. Not only are the canons of the church to be evaluated in light of Scripture and rejected if they are contrary to its precepts; they are also to be interpreted, and if necessary rejected, in light of their congruity or otherwise with natural law: "whatever is regarded as yielding to the divine will, or to canonical Scripture, or to divine laws, natural law is also to be given precedence over it. Therefore, ordinances, whether ecclesiastical or civil, if they are shown to be contrary to natural law, are to be altogether excluded" (D.9, p.c. 11).

The relative and provisional status of human practices is also expressed in terms of a distinction of origins, drawn from Isidore: "Divine laws are established by nature, human laws are established by practices" (D.1, C.1.1). As the text goes on to explain, this accounts for the variability of the latter, since "different things seem good to different people." The same distinction can likewise be expressed in terms of a division between what is naturally permissible or legitimate, and the restrictions introduced by formal law: "What is permissible is divine law; the right is human law" (D.1, C.1.2). This observation leads on to a *dictum* further qualifying the distinction between divine and human laws: "For everything that is permissible is included in the term divine or natural law; by the term human laws, is understood practices put in writing and handed down as law" (D.1, p.c. 1).

These remarks imply what Gratian goes on to say, namely that both custom and written law are subordinate to natural law, in such a way that the former cannot contradict the standards set by the latter. Here, however, he is making a more basic point. That is, natural law is a basis for legitimation, permissive in force, in addition to providing criteria for limitation and restriction. Indeed, if placement is our guide, the permissive force of natural law is more fundamental than its restrictive force, which is discussed later (specifically, in D.8 and D.9). Certainly, the universally applicable scriptural norms, considered as revealed formulations of natural law, place stringent restrictions on human activity (D.13 pr). Outside these parameters, however, it would seem to be human conventions, rather than natural law as such, which limit and restrain the sphere of permissible human activity. That is why Gratian endorses Isidore's remark that "the right is human law" — because outside the sphere set by revealed laws, it is human laws rather than natural law which immediately determine juridical rights, that is to say, claims that can be asserted and defended in a court of law.

This may be a surprising conclusion, given the modern view according to which the natural law in some way provides (or supposedly provides) clear, accessible criteria in terms of which formal law can be evaluated, and even perhaps abrogated. Isn't that the point of the dictum that an unjust enactment does not bind? It is certainly the case that natural law, comprehensively understood, serves as the supreme criterion for interpreting human law, whether customary or written. Gratian repeatedly underscores the relative status of all human laws — written as well as customary, ecclesiastical as well as secular; the distinctions among these different kinds of laws are less important than their shared characteristics as derivative and provisional expressions of a natural law.

At the same time, however, natural law as such has no direct juridical force. For Gratian and the other scholastics, as for Raz, there is no necessary inconsistency between analyzing formal laws as expressions of natural principles and affirming the conventional status of the laws themselves. The basic principles of reason, truth, and justice must be formulated — and therefore restricted in scope, made determinate — in order to serve as a basis for adjudication. Of course, revealed law itself offers one such set of formulations, but even these precepts leave much undetermined (as Aquinas will later make clear; ST I-II 91.3, 99.3 *ad* 2, 99.4). The indeterminacy of natural law opens up a space for the permissible, the *fas,* within which human practices, including both custom and written law, provide the specific determinations necessary to give practical meaning and force to natural law. The subordination of practices to natural law is thus qualified and balanced by the indeterminacy of natural law apart from the specifics of human practices, and custom and written law can be considered together as two alternative and (ideally) complementary ways of giving expression to natural law. This fundamental parity is clearly expressed early on: "'Right' is a general name, whereas 'law' is a kind of right. Furthermore, 'right' [*jus*] is so called because it is just [*justum*]. Now right is determined by laws and practices" (D.1, C.2).

Gratian sets the trajectory for subsequent work on the natural law in a number of ways. Most fundamentally, he identifies natural law with a set of scriptural norms — not the moral laws of the Decalogue, as we would expect, but the very general principles of the love commandments — in the process mediating between his patristic forebears, whose approach he here appropriates, and his own contemporaries and followers. In this way, he vindicates the existence of a natural law as an originating principle for customary and formal law, while at the same time forestalling any identification of the natural law with specific precepts or social arrangements. By implication, he locates the natural law at the intersection of two distinct yet complementary points of access to God's creative wisdom and providential care: nature, understood as comprising the fundamental principles of order and causality structuring created existence, and Scripture, which attests to the existence of a natural law and draws out its practical implications.

Rational Judgment, Contingency, and Authority in Scholastic Thought

The natural law thus understood can accommodate a very wide range of considerations, since whatever can be construed as a pre-conventional principle for human action — including fundamental metaphysical principles of causality, the inclinations we share with other living creatures, sensual desires and even (in a qualified sense) revelation itself — can be identified as a principle of natural law. Over many centuries of reflection, just about all of these were thus identified, and it is scarcely surprising that the earliest commentators on Gratian identified multiple senses for the term "natural law," or else spoke in terms of a plurality of natural laws.[20] But the scholastics' penchant for analysis and systematization quickly led them to identify one interpretation of the natural law as the primary sense of the term, to which other legitimate senses were in some way related. They were well aware that natural principles can only be expressed in actual norms and practices through a mediating process of rational reflection, and partially for this reason (as I believe) the scholastics quickly settled on reason itself as the focal meaning for the terms "natural law," or "natural right." More specifically, they identified the natural law in its primary sense either with rational ca-

20. For details, see *Natural and Divine Law*, 76-85.

pacities for practical judgment or with the foundational principles through which practical judgment operates.

At the same time, the scholastics had a still more decisive reason to identify the natural law with a capacity for rational judgment. The scriptural texts which attest to a natural law, at least as they read them, did so in terms that strongly imply just such an interpretation. Thus, the Golden Rule to which Gratian appeals is understood as a principle or procedure for moral discernment, through which men and women can arrive at concrete precepts governing our interactions with one another. However, the text that did more than any other to confirm the identification between natural law and human rational capacity was Paul's remark, in Romans 2:14, that the Gentiles, who do not have the law, nonetheless have an inner law of conscience. Patristic commentary on this passage, summarized for the scholastics in the scriptural commentary known as the Ordinary Gloss, explicitly identifies the inner law to which Paul refers with the natural law, while construing both together as a power of discernment: "Even if one does not have the written law, one nonetheless has the natural law, by which one understands and is inwardly conscious of what is good and what is evil, what is vice insofar as it is contrary to nature, which in any case grace heals." Still following the main lines of patristic thought, the Gloss goes on to identify the natural law, thus understood, with the image of God, in which the human person is created, and which therefore cannot be altogether lost.[21] In this way, the scholastics affirm classical views that the natural law is universal, unchangeable and permanent, without identifying any one set of precepts or social arrangements with the unchanging natural law.

The scholastic identification of the natural law in its primary sense with rational capacities for discernment and self-direction is significant in another way that might easily be overlooked. As Brian Tierney notes, this was a genuine innovation with far-reaching effects: "If we are to find an earlier origin for natural rights theories we need to look for patterns of language in which *jus naturale* meant not only natural law or cosmic harmony, but also a faculty or ability or power of individual persons, associated with reason and moral discernment, defining an area of liberty where the individual was free to act as he pleased, leading on to specific claims and powers of humans qua

---

21. I take this from Migne's *Patrologiae Cursus Completus* (1852), vol. 114, 475-76; I also checked the facsimile text published as the *Biblia Latina cum Glossa Ordinaria*, Tomus IV (Turnhout: Brepols, 1992). The Ordinary Gloss later came to be attributed, wrongly, to Walafrid Strabo (d. 849), and is published under his name in Migne.

humans."[22] The identification of the natural law in its primary sense with an innate power of reasoned judgment — an identification grounded squarely in the received patristic interpretation of Paul's "unwritten law" of the Gentiles — represented just such a move. Now for the first time, the natural law is identified directly with a subjective faculty of reason rather than with an objective normative order discerned through reason.

We can track the effects of this innovation through the very language within which the scholastics appropriate the natural law tradition. In order to appreciate this, we must observe that Latin draws a distinction that English obscures, between the law understood as a more or less explicitly formulated precept or body of such precepts *(lex)* and the law understood as roughly equivalent to the right, or a right, understood as a just or equitable state of affairs, or as an individual claim that calls for some kind of recognition *(jus)*. Both Cicero and Augustine refer to the natural law in terms of *lex,* and the Vulgate similarly refers to "law" as *lex* in almost every context. Given the weight of these usages, it is noteworthy that the majority of scholastics who discuss the natural law speak of it as a *jus;* even those who prefer to speak in terms of the *lex naturalis,* including most notably Aquinas, also speak of a natural *jus* (for him, the object of the virtue of justice; ST II-II 57.1). What is more, the distinction between *lex* and *jus* is clearly marked and consistently maintained among the scholastics we are considering. Certainly, the focus on *jura,* or as we would say, rights or fundamental claims, reflects the situation of the late eleventh and early twelfth centuries, which as we saw in the last chapter were marked by a resurgence of claims to personal dominion, countered by claims to freedom and political authority. In such a situation, it was vitally necessary to establish that some *jura,* some rights or claims, are grounded in considerations of reasonableness or natural principles, and therefore cannot be usurped through force or lost in the midst of changing communal practices. In subsequent chapters, we will consider the further implications of this distinction in more detail. At this point, we should simply note that while this usage is not equivalent to a doctrine of subjective rights, the effect of speaking in terms of a natural *jus* is nonetheless to underscore the idea that some kinds of claims are grounded in the pre-conventional nature of things — and therefore part of the "law beyond the law" that both grounds and constrains human law.

The scholastics' tendency to interpret natural law in terms of basic principles or capacities was correlated with a reluctance to identify it too closely

22. Brian Tierney, *The Idea of Natural Rights* (Atlanta: Scholars Press, 1997), 54.

with specific precepts.[23] But for this very reason, the constitutive operations or first principles of the natural law must be specified in order to be put into practice. These specifications take the form of more or less concrete precepts, comprising more or less coherent bodies of laws, which can be understood as such by reference to the natural law from which they stem. Both Albert the Great and Aquinas set out analytic taxonomies displaying the relation of more specific kinds of law to natural law.[24] Although these differ in some details, they broadly agree that the natural law is specified in one of two primary ways, through the revealed laws of Scripture or through human positive law. It is noteworthy that neither mentions the moral law as a distinct division of laws, and apparently morality, understood in the distinctively modern fashion — that is to say, a coherent body of norms which can be discerned apart from revelation — is not included as a separate way of specifying the natural law. So far as I have been able to determine, this (to us surprising) omission reflects a more general approach.[25] Certainly, the scholastics do distinguish between moral and non-moral considerations, precepts, or virtues, the former having to do with the overall human good or general considerations of reasonableness and appropriateness, the latter pertaining to considerations that are in some way conditional or limited in scope. But they do not appear to have any concept of, or any need for, a self-

23. One exception to this general tendency is found in the anonymous canonical *Summa "Tractaturus magister,"* written about 1185, according to which "it seems rather that reason uses the natural law, than that it is itself the natural law, all the more so since according to some, reason is nothing other than free judgment. Hence, it should be said that according to this understanding, the natural law is a collection of precepts, prohibitions and indications placed in the human mind by God." Cited in Rudolf Weigand, *Die Naturrechtslehre der Legisten und Dekretisten von Irnerius bis Accursius und von Gratian bis Johannes Teutonicus* (Munich: Max Hueber, 1967), para. no. 319. Nonetheless, a later gloss which is found immediately after this passage reflects uneasiness with this straightforward identification: "I do not say [that it is] the collection itself, but a certain quality arising in the soul from these things collected, just as knowledge is not said to be the things known themselves, but a quality arising from them" (*Die Naturrechtslehre* no. 320).

24. Albert identifies four kinds of *lex*, or law: namely, the natural law; the law of Moses; the law of grace; and the law of the members, i.e., our innate tendencies to sin; see *De bono* V 2.2. Albert does refer to moral laws as comprising one kind of Mosaic law, but this is a standard and specialized usage which does not appear to be generalized (see V 2.2 *ad* 11, V.2.3, *solutio*). Aquinas's taxonomy as set out in the *Summa theologiae* I-II 91 includes the eternal law, the natural law, human law, divine law, and the law of sin.

25. For further details, see Jean Porter, "Christian Ethics and the Concept of Morality: A Historical Inquiry," *Journal of the Society of Christian Ethics* 26.2 (2006): 3-21.

contained, systematic moral law, specific enough to be put into practice and accessible apart from revelation.

Be that as it may, the scholastics recognize that human practices and laws are conventional and not (immediately, directly) natural. To borrow terms from Andrei Marmor's illuminating analysis, these practices and laws are constitutive conventions: they constitute the interlocking systems of rules through which the vital activities of human life can be carried out; correlatively, they set the normative standards in terms of which these activities are evaluated. As such, they comprise mediating structures of activity, through which the needs and activities necessary to human life can be pursued and expressed in concrete, orderly ways. This does not imply, of course, that human law is only conventional, without any tethering in preconventional principles of nature and reason. On the contrary, conventions can only be understood in terms of the rational or natural principles that they express. Nonetheless, as Marmor notes, "the needs, functions or values that such conventions respond to, radically *underdetermine* the content of the rules that constitute the relevant social practice."[26] In this sense, social conventions, like authoritative decrees, are arbitrary — not in the sense of being irrational or unjustified, but simply insofar as they overreach, as it were, the rational considerations in terms of which they are justified.

We should also note that the scholastics do not limit themselves to an analysis of natural law precepts in terms of general criteria for rational judgment, such as consistency, impartiality, and the like. The natural law in its primary sense is identified with reason (or with the general principles through which reason operates), but reason itself cannot be understood, nor can it be appropriately exercised in practical operations, except as informed by a more comprehensive set of natural principles and aims which structure the natural existence of the human creature. The scholastics agree that human practices and laws stem from natural principles, and unlike some contemporary natural law thinkers, they assume that we have some significant grasp of these principles, prior to and independently of their expression in moral norms. Thus, for the scholastics our knowledge of human nature can and should inform practical judgments in foundational and pervasive ways.

26. Andrei Marmor, *Social Conventions: From Language to Law* (Princeton: Princeton University Press, 2009), 41, emphasis in the original; see 31-57 for his overall account of constitutive conventions. It is worth noting that these are not, by and large, coordinating conventions, which as the term implies serve the specific function of coordinating the activities of large populations. As Marmor points out, legal philosophers have tended to underestimate the importance of conventions because they have identified these narrowly with coordinating conventions.

Nonetheless, it does not follow for them that the laws and practices structuring human society reflect organic, relatively fixed expressions of these natural principles. On the contrary, the scholastics interpret the relation between human law and the natural principles from which it stems in terms that acknowledge the indeterminacy of natural principles and allow room for considerable variation and flexibility at the level of specific expressions of those principles. As Cary Nederman has shown, the dominant approach to the natural law among the early scholastics is more Ciceronian than Aristotelian in this specific respect, even though their overall approach to natural philosophy is predominantly Aristotelian, especially in the thirteenth century.[27] That is to say, rather than regarding social conventions as more or less direct and unchangeable expressions of human nature, they emphasize the need for processes of rational, communally shared deliberation, in order to move from natural principles to their conventional formulations. Not only do they acknowledge the conventional status of human laws, they also interpret these in such a way as to emphasize the role of rational judgment and communal deliberation in moving from natural principles to social conventions.

In the last chapter, we saw that, beginning in the late eleventh century, scholars of both civil and canon law began to distinguish between judgments of practical reasonableness or equity and authoritative decree. At this point, we can more fully appreciate why the scholastics found this distinction to be both necessary and defensible, given their overall conception of the natural law as comprising fundamental rational principles, together with the intelligible structures of human nature from which they stem. These general principles are accessible to reflective judgment, and yet they remain relatively indeterminate, in such a way that they are not sufficient to govern conduct or to provide adequate structures for social activities. Seen in this context, relations of authority appear as appropriate and sometimes necessary elements in the social life of rational animals. The rational principles of natural law must be specified in order to be put into practice, and yet these specifications cannot be left to individual judgments; they must be generally accepted in order to provide a framework for social activities, and that means at least that they must be public and relatively stable. This kind of specification will always involve some element of contingency, since it represents only one possible construal of general rational considerations — and for that reason, it must be imposed in some way if it is to yield a cogent

27. Cary J. Nederman, "Nature, Sin and the Origins of Society: The Ciceronian Tradition in Medieval Political Thought," *The Journal of the History of Ideas* 49 (1988): 3-26.

claim, having binding force within a context of human relations. In this sense, a properly authoritative specification of the natural law will always rest in some way on an arbitrary determination of will, although not necessarily on the will of any one individual. At the same time, the specification in question must be intelligible and justifiable as *one* defensible construal of natural law principles, in order for the enactment or judgment to count as a rational precept, appropriately serving as a premise of practical reasoning for free and responsible agents.

This is one point at which the scholastic conception of the natural law can contribute to a contemporary analysis of legal authority. As I indicated in the first chapter, the overall aim of this book is to develop an account of authority as a natural human relation, stemming from natural purposes proper to human existence, in terms of which legal authority can be understood and justified as one specific and delimited response to these purposes. We now see more clearly just what the purposes in question are. That is, authority serves to bring a relatively final, public, and generally acceptable specificity to indeterminate rational and natural principles in such a way as to create a framework for shared activities of diverse kinds. As such, it addresses one of the pervasive needs of human life, since without a whole range of shared activities, we as rational, social animals could not live — fully, or perhaps at all — in the way characteristic to us as a specific kind of living creature.

At this point, it will be apparent that the line of analysis presupposes that we really can identify natural purposes, intrinsic to our activities as living creatures of a specific kind, in terms of which we can analyze recurring features of our communal life. These are by no means widely shared presuppositions. Nonetheless, I believe that they can be defended, in the terms of the broadly Aristotelian philosophy of nature that came to prominence in thirteenth-century scholastic thought. In pursuing these claims, we will eventually turn to the second of our medieval interlocutors, Thomas Aquinas. But first, it will be necessary to lay out the broad parameters of the Aristotelian philosophy of nature on which he drew in articulating his own conception of the natural law.

2. The Natural Law and the Intelligibility of Nature

Life, Form, and Purpose in an Aristotelian Perspective

In an earlier book, I defended a conception of human nature that is (I believe) an extension of Aquinas's Aristotelian conception, developed in conversation with contemporary moral philosophy and philosophical reflections on the biological sciences.[28] I argued that human nature, thus understood, is structured in accordance with natural purposes which are properly normative, and therefore imply norms for conduct, albeit not the complete, determinate and universally valid moral law that is often associated with the natural law. In this book, I will take this conception as the basis for an analysis of legal authority as a kind of natural relation, which is both justified and constrained by reference to the natural purposes that it serves. At this point, I want to begin to lay the foundations for a natural law analysis of authority by setting forth, necessarily in summary terms, what I take to be a defensible Aristotelian conception of human nature, focusing especially on the possibilities — and just as importantly, the limits — for normative appeals to a natural law.

It might seem that this excursus into metaphysics would take us some distance from the distinctive concerns of contemporary philosophical jurisprudence. But as I hope to show, just the opposite is true. The scholastics' distinctive and centrally important contributions to contemporary jurisprudence depend on the claim that human life and activity are informed by objective values, aspects of human goodness and flourishing that we discover and shape, but do not create. On this view, human nature itself is the ultimate principle of both customs and formal enactments, and of normative precepts and ideals more generally, although the concrete forms that these take will reflect the inevitable contingency introduced through the processes of specifying natural principles through local practices and reflective judgments. An Aristotelian philosophy of nature offers the most satisfactory way to understand the principles of practical reasoning inherent in human nature itself and to draw the needed distinctions with some degree of precision.

Those who are familiar with recent natural law jurisprudence will realize that this is the point at which I part company with most earlier attempts to develop an account of the natural law from broadly Thomistic starting points. This is especially true of the "new natural law" defended by Germain Grisez, John Finnis, and those who follow their lead, all of whom reject any appeal to human nature, broadly construed, as a starting point for ethical reflection. More generally, the approach that I will take would have been rejected out of hand by most philosophers until recently, for a number of reasons ranging from logical considerations to the then-current state of the

---

28. *Nature as Reason*, 53-140; I focus on the specifically Aristotelian presuppositions of the overall account of human nature at 82-103.

philosophy of science. More recently, however, a broadly Aristotelian approach to the philosophy of science and moral philosophy is once again gaining credence. Recent work in the philosophy of biology makes a strong case that an Aristotelian approach need not be incompatible with our best understandings of the evolutionary process, and moral philosophers are once again turning to an Aristotelian teleology as a starting point for a theory of the virtues.[29] In previous work, I have defended a broadly Aristotelian approach to normative reflection in some detail, and here I will necessarily presuppose a great deal. Accordingly, in the first part of this section, I will explain what I take the Aristotelian approach to be, in the process indicating its plausibility and explanatory power.

Let me begin by laying out some basic parameters. The concept of human nature that I propose is developed within the framework of an Aristotelian/Thomistic metaphysics and, more specifically, with the analysis of causation in terms of substantial kinds central to that metaphysics. This approach takes its starting points from the categories in terms of which we classify and distinguish different kinds of entities, and it presupposes that at

29. Among philosophers of science, the pioneering work of Marjorie Grene has played a key role in restoring the credibility of an Aristotelian philosophy of nature, especially as it pertains to living organisms; out of a very extensive body of work, see "Hierarchies in Biology," *American Scientist* 75 (1987): 504-9, and *The Philosophy of Biology: An Episodic History*, with David Depew (Cambridge: Cambridge University Press, 2004), 1-34. For an overview of relevant debates in contemporary philosophy of biology, see André Ariew, "Teleology," 160-81 in *The Cambridge Companion to the Philosophy of Biology*, ed. David L. Hull and Michael Ruse (Cambridge: Cambridge University Press, 2007). In this piece, Ariew argues that while many forms of teleological explanation are incompatible with contemporary evolutionary biology, this need not be the case with respect to an Aristotelian version. For a similar argument, developed without explicit relevance to Aristotle, see Lenny Moss, "Representational Preformationism to the Epigenesis of Openness to the World? Reflections on a New Vision of the Organism," *From Epigenesis to Epigenetics*, Volume 981 of the *Annals of the New York Academy of Sciences* (December, 2002), 21–230, and more generally, *What Genes Can't Do* (Cambridge, MA: MIT Press, 2003), 51-73.

There are a growing number of moral philosophers who defend an Aristotelian approach, including most notably James Wallace, *Virtues and Vices* (Ithaca: Cornell University Press, 1978), Philippa Foot, whose program is set forth most recently in *Natural Goodness* (Oxford: Oxford University Press, 2001), and Rosalind Hursthouse, *On Virtue Ethics* (Oxford: Oxford University Press, 1999). Alasdair MacIntyre begins a recent book on the virtues by observing that "I now judge that I was in error in supposing an ethics independent of biology to be possible," and goes on to develop an Aristotelian/Thomistic account of the virtues that reckons "not only with our animal condition, but also with the need to acknowledge our consequent vulnerability and dependence." See *Dependent Rational Animals: Why Human Beings Need the Virtues* (Peru, IL: Carus/Open Court, 1999), x-xi.

least some of these reflect essential qualities or aspects of the things in question, considered as representative of some specific natural kind. It presupposes, in other words, that it is in some way meaningful to speak of the essential forms of things, identifying them in terms of the kinds of things that they are. By the same token, this view presupposes that the forms of things can be grasped through concepts, albeit imperfectly, and moreover that these concepts are genuinely explanatory, that is to say, they help us to make sense of the operations of natural things in ways that would otherwise be inaccessible to us.

For both Aristotle and Aquinas, "what something is" can only adequately be understood in terms of the causal principles through which a creature of a given kind exists and carries out its characteristic kinds of operations in directed and intelligible ways. To the extent that we grasp what it is to be a creature of this kind, we understand what it means for it to come into existence, to interact with other entities in its typical environment, and to pass away. That is, we possess criteria for determining the identity and persistence of substances undergoing change over time. What is more, we apprehend all this concretely, in such a way that we can track the persistence and dissolution of substances in and through our observations of the world. Thus, we can not only offer a formal definition of a cat, we can also see that this particular kitten, that mature, healthy cat, and our neighbor's old, feeble tabby are all exemplifications of the same kind, whereas neither a stuffed toy kitten nor a dead cat counts as a cat (although the latter is, so to say, an ex-cat). In the Aristotelian terms that I am retrieving, these sorts of explanations would be described as appeals to the formal cause, but it is important not to be misled by this expression.[30] In this context, the language of "cause" does not necessarily imply efficient causality, but refers more broadly to any principle of intelligibility and explanation. More specifically, the forms of living creatures do not exist over against the creatures in such a way as to exercise efficient causality on them. As James Lennox puts it, referring specifically to Aristotle's conception of form, "the form of a living thing is its soul,

---

30. As Robert Pasnau points out, for Aquinas the intelligibility of a given kind of thing stems from its form, which (together with the matter, where appropriate) is captured by its proper definition; hence, the "formal cause" refers to the principle of explanation in terms of which something is identified as the kind of creature that it is. In the case of non-artificial substances, the formal and final causes are identical, since natural operations are directed towards sustaining or communicating some form. For further particulars, see *Thomas Aquinas on Human Nature: A Philosophical Study of Summa Theologiae Ia 75-89* (Cambridge: Cambridge University Press, 2002), 7-10, 21-22, 89-95. Grene and Depew make a similar point; see *The Philosophy of Biology,* 314.

and Aristotle considers soul to be a unified set of goal-ordered capacities — nutritive, reproductive, locomotive, and cognitive."[31]

I take the example of a living creature advisedly, because it seems to me that these are the kinds of natural objects which exemplify individual substances most robustly and clearly.[32] By the same token, these are the examples which most clearly indicate what it means to say that nature is normative, reflecting objective natural teleologies. There can be no doubt that any appeal to a natural teleology asks a great deal of any contemporary interlocutor. At the very least, such an appeal presupposes willingness to consider the logical coherence, to say nothing of the possible truth, of a claim that natural functions presuppose purposes which are genuinely such, and yet are not immediately and directly anybody's purposes — that is, purposes bestowed or pursued by an agent acting on some distinct object as an instrument or artifact of external aims. On this account, the purposes for which a living creature acts are inseparable from the intelligible principles giving structure and coherence to its development and activities. In this sense, the creature's natural purposes are necessary to its existence as a creature of a specific kind, not contingent to it, and therefore, they cannot be bestowed, as it were, by some external agency or impersonal force, including God. This point should be underscored. We should not conflate an Aristotelian/ Thomistic teleology with modern and contemporary arguments from design, according to which God imposes orderly functioning on inert matter, in much the way that an engineer contrives against gravity and entropy to design a workable bridge. More generally, a teleological explanation of this kind carries no implications about the causal trajectory leading to the emergence of a creature of the relevant kind, and therefore does not imply, *inter alia,* that the processes of evolution have in some way been guided or directed towards the production of specific kinds of creatures.[33] On the Aristotelian/Thomistic view, in contrast, teleological explanations are always tethered to some conception of what it means for a specific kind of creature

31. James Lennox, *Aristotle's Philosophy of Biology* (Cambridge: Cambridge University Press, 2001), 128; see more generally 127-30.

32. Although I may be pressing beyond what he intends, I take this point from E. J. Lowe, *The Possibility of Metaphysics: Substance, Identity, and Time* (Oxford: Clarendon Press, 1998), 154-73. Living creatures are not the only kinds of substances, for him or for me — artifacts are also substances — but living creatures are paradigmatic, precisely because their unity and persistence are sustained through internal principles of causality.

33. Grene and Depew make this point, as does Ariew; see *The Philosophy of Biology,* 313-21, and "Teleology," 179-81, respectively.

to live, to grow and develop normally, to flourish and reproduce, and finally to age and die, in accordance with the intrinsic principles animating a material object of this specific kind.

Teleological explanation shares many of the same characteristics as does an explanation in terms of formal causality. And this is hardly surprising. For Aristotle himself and for those who follow his lead, formal causes and teleological explanations — explanations in terms of final causes — are inextricably linked. The proper form of a given kind of living creature can only be adequately understood by reference to some idea of a paradigmatic instance of the form, that is to say, a healthy and mature individual of the kind in question. It is only by reference to this paradigm that we are able to identify immature, sick or defective individuals of this kind, that is to say, as genuine representatives of the kind that nonetheless fall short of its optimum states in specifiable ways. By the same token, appeals to formal and final causality provide a framework within which to develop and test hypotheses about the functions of the characteristic organs and operations of a given kind of creature, and to explain them in terms of their contributions to the functioning of the organism considered as a whole.

Teleology understood in this sense fits well with many of our attitudes and intuitions about the living things around us, and while this consideration is not probative, it does lend credence to the overall view. This is by no means a new observation, nor is it unfamiliar to contemporary jurisprudence. Hart observes that "This mode of thinking about nature seems strange when stated abstractly. It may appear less fantastic if we recall some of the ways in which even now we refer at least to living things, for a teleological view is still reflected in common ways of describing their development."[34] To begin with the most basic point of all, some distinction between living and non-living creatures appears to be basic to human (and indeed, animal) functioning. This rough distinction, in turn, is invariably fleshed out through a set of ideas concerning what it means to be a healthy, functioning, flourishing creature of a certain kind. We can tell a scrawny puppy from a robust puppy, a sick horse from a healthy horse, a dying ficus from a happy ficus. We cannot avoid making these discriminations if we are to function in a world of living creatures, even in our urban, post-modern society, and it would be absurd to regard them as cultural constructs without remainder.

This brings us to a fundamental point. Everything that has just been said about living creatures more generally can also be applied to human be-

34. *The Concept of Law,* 189.

ings. We too are a kind of living creature; it is possible to form a concept of the kind of creature that we are; and this concept is intrinsically teleological, in the way just indicated. That is to say, it traces the typical trajectory of a human life, in such a way as to provide an account of what it is to come into existence as a human being, to mature and to thrive, to suffer illness or dissolution, and to cease to exist. On this basis, we can form judgments about what counts as human well-being, what kinds of life best exemplify a fully flourishing human existence, and correlatively, what counts as immaturity, deficiency, or illness for a human being. Of course, such judgments as applied to human beings will invariably be more complex, if only because human life is capable of assuming a far greater variety of forms than we find among any non-rational species. Yet these are not altogether unlimited. There are constraints on human well-being, and perhaps more importantly, there are recurring components of human existence which will form the basis for well-being for almost all persons.

In fact, we do know quite a bit about characteristically human capacities, needs, and modes of functioning, both through the general fund of knowledge that anyone needs in order to function in society, and through systematic scientific inquiry and analysis. If we take Aristotle's own standards for inquiry as our guide, this information does not in itself amount to a complete concept of human nature; that is, it does not provide us with a comprehensive grasp of the intelligible principles characteristic of human functioning, in terms of which we can establish criteria for identity and persistence through change for an individual substance of the relevant kind.[35] At this stage, our empirical knowledge about human life in all its aspects is too extensive, it is expanding too quickly, and remains too contested to permit a complete systematic analysis of all the relevant data. Nonetheless, we do have conceptions of human nature that are relatively comprehensive, informed by a wide range of empirical data, and theoretically cogent. Given a defensible conception of human nature, we can indicate in a preliminary way how diverse aspects of human existence and functioning fit together to make up the "ordered set of goal-directed capacities" proper to human existence as such.

---

35. This is not the place to enter into a lengthy analysis of the Aristotelian ideal of scientific inquiry; I will simply say that on this point, I follow Alasdair MacIntyre, *First Principles, Final Ends and Contemporary Philosophical Issues* (Milwaukee: Marquette University Press, 1990), and David Charles, *Aristotle on Meaning and Essence* (Oxford: Oxford University Press, 2000), 221-309.

Thomas Aquinas and the Natural Structures of Reason

At this point, we turn to Aquinas, whose theory of the natural law implies just such a conception of human nature. While this conception is necessarily abstract, it is sufficiently rich to provide the needed starting points for practical judgments. Indeed, Aquinas lays out his conception of human nature in the course of developing an analysis of reason in its practical operations — his point being that practical reason is properly structured by, and responsive to, the natural purposes which inform our activities as creatures of a certain kind.

More perhaps than any of his predecessors or contemporaries, Aquinas attends to the diverse ways in which reason in its practical operations is structured and directed by more broadly natural principles, which are teleological in structure. The proper operations of practical reason thus include a necessary element of ordering and comparative judgments, through which diverse aims and goods are related to some comprehensive end: "this pertains to right reason, that one should make use of those things which lead to an end in accordance with the measure which is appropriate to the end" (ST II-II 152.2). These judgments are necessarily contingent to some degree, given the necessary indeterminacy of our broad teleological and normative concepts, and they will also incorporate a legitimate element of preferential choice. Nonetheless, reason in its practical operations does not proceed in complete independence from naturally given principles and purposes. Not only do these provide, as it were, the necessary substance for reason's practical operations; they are also reflected in the very structures of the faculty of reason.

Nor should this surprise us. Certainly, the eternal law can in no way be said to exist apart from or exterior to God. It is an order grounded in God's own wisdom, informing God's free creative act. Nonetheless, even God's own actions *ad extra* are to some degree structured and delimited by the providential ordering of the eternal law. We should not expect human reason in its practical operations to be freer, in the sense of independence from the constraints of some sapiential ordering, than God's own freedom. Aquinas suggests that we should carry this line of thought one step further — that is, we can and should understand human reasonableness and freedom through analogy to divine wisdom and will, because the human capacity for practical reasoning and judgment, understood as the natural law, is itself a participation in God's eternal law. That is to say, the natural law properly so called is the rational creature's active participation in the processes through which God providentially governs the world. As such, it represents both a point of continuity with, and a distinguishing difference from, every other kind of creature:

> since all things which are subject to divine providence are given rule and due measure from the eternal law . . . it is plain that all things participate in some way in the eternal law, namely, insofar as from its impress they have inclinations to their proper acts and ends. Among these others, however, the rational creature is subject to divine providence in a more excellent way, insofar as it is itself made a participant in providence, being provident for itself and others. Whence it also participates in eternal reason, through which it has a natural inclination to its due act and end. And such participation of the eternal law in the rational creature is called natural law. (ST I-II 91.2)

He goes on to say that the natural law in its most proper sense is "something constituted through reason," namely, the first indemonstrable principles, comprising the necessary structures through which reason operates practically (ST I-II 94.1). It is somewhat puzzling to read that the first principles are constituted through reason, but this claim is clarified through his subsequent comparison of the first principles of speculative and practical reason (I-II 94.2). Whenever reason operates speculatively, it necessarily does so within the structure set up by the principle of non-contradiction. Otherwise, whatever processes are going on would not lead to a determinate resolution, of a kind that might intelligibly be described as a reasoned conclusion. In this sense, reason constitutes the principle of non-contradiction in and through operating speculatively in any way whatever, even though this principle may only be identified and formulated after the fact through processes of reflective analysis.

Similarly, reason in its practical operations is structured through, and by its operations constitutes, its own first principle: "good is to be sought and done, and evil is to be avoided" (ST I-II 94.2). Like the principle of non-contradiction, to which it is explicitly compared, this principle must be engaged in some way if the mental processes are to count as practical reasoning, that is to say, reasoning directed at action. In order for an operation to count as an action it must be in some way intentional, which is to say at least that it is intelligibly directed towards attaining some end-state, which the agent regards as desirable and attainable through her own activities. Thus, the structure of rationality as manifest in practical operations will display an intrinsic orientation towards the attainment of some end, and since the end of an active power has the rational character of the good, Aquinas goes on to justify the formulation of the first principle of practical reason in these terms.[36]

Aquinas develops this line of thought in the rest of ST I-II 94.2, which takes up the question, "Whether the natural law contains many precepts, or only one?" The central issue engaging him in this article is the unity of the natural law, and by implication, its coherence as an overarching criterion for human action. He addresses this issue by elaborating further on the way in which the practical operations of reason are structured by the intelligible principles and the overarching order of human existence. More specifically, reason in its practical operations is directed towards the attainment of the necessities and proper activities of human life, each of which is naturally apprehended as being in some way good and worthy of pursuit, thus bringing some substance, as well as a rough structure, to the operations of the first principle of practical reason. What is more, these inclinations are themselves ordered in such a way as to incorporate both more universal and foundational inclinations (towards existence, and for animals, towards nutrition and reproduction), and more particular and species-specific inclinations (including in our case all those presupposing rationality, most notably political life and worship of a divine being). The former are more fundamental or exigent, while the latter are more directly expressive of the perfection of the human person in accordance with distinctively rational modalities of functioning. Taken together as dynamic interconnected inclinations towards a properly human form of life, they add a further level of structure to the operation of the first principle.

As Germain Grisez rightly insists, the first principle is not in itself a moral principle. It is engaged in every operation of practical reasoning, including those operations directed towards sinful acts.[37] Yet it would be a mistake to conclude that it is purely formal in such a way as to carry no specific normative implications at all. We should bear in mind that Aquinas's analysis of reason and its relation to goodness presupposes a broadly Aristotelian philosophy of nature, according to which the natural principles of activity are intrinsically directed to the continued existence and well-being of the entity, in accordance with its specific modality of existence — in other words, its specific kind. How does this general philosophical framework bear

36. I am grateful to David Elliot for helping me to see the significance of this point.
37. See "The First Principle of Practical Reason: A Commentary on the *Summa theologiae*, 1-2, Question 94, Article 2," 168-201 in *Natural Law Forum* 10 (1965).

on the issue at hand? At the least, it implies that the distinctively human operations of reasoning and action reflect the same kind of directed and ordered orientation towards specific kinds of goods that characterize the natural operations of all creatures — those goods, namely, which are necessary to, or constitutive of, the existence and fully developed activity of a creature of a specific kind. Thus understood, the desire for the good, in human beings as in every other kind of creature, is not targeted on any kind of desideratum whatever. Rather, it represents the creature's natural orientation towards its own existence, including the fullest possible exercise of its proper causal powers. Correlatively, the operations through which anything can be said to pursue the good are not only means towards the attainment of an end; they are also themselves intrinsic constituents of that end, that is to say, the dynamic, active development and expression of the creature's natural capacities and powers.

Reading further, it becomes apparent that Aquinas's analysis of the inclinations does indeed presuppose a conception of human nature, understood in Aristotelian terms as a form of life, constituted by an orderly ensemble of processes and activities. Aquinas's approach follows from his basic metaphysical and theological principles. He locates diverse human inclinations within a framework set by an analysis of the levels of created existence, beginning with the most basic level of simple existence, and proceeding through ever more comprehensive levels of engagement with one's environment and world, that is to say, life, sentience, and rationality.

That is precisely why the inclinations can be said to bring order to the precepts of the natural law; they themselves are ordered in accordance with the intelligible principles of activity structuring the life of creatures of our kind. Continuing with the analysis of ST I-II 94.2, we note that the first and most fundamental thing to be said about the human person is that she exists, a creature among other kinds of creatures, and as such, naturally desires continued existence. This most basic inclination underlies and informs the orientation towards the good which, in Aquinas's view, represents the fundamental active dynamism of every creature. For the human person, as for every other kind of creature, this orientation is expressed through orderly processes of development and sustenance, directed towards one's own specific form of goodness. For the human person, it takes the form of an orientation to exist as a human being, and to enjoy the fullest and most complete form of human existence available to it. This orientation is expressed, most fundamentally, in the natural desire to enjoy unimpeded functioning in accordance with one's basic capacities for action.

Turning to a second level of analysis, the human person is not only a creature, but a creature of a particular kind — that is to say, a living creature, and more specifically an animal. This means that for the human creature, the inclination to exist and to develop in accordance with one's specific ideal of perfection is at the same time an inclination to stay alive — for the living creature, existence *is* life — and to do so in a way appropriate to an animal, that is to say, attaining sustenance and security through an active engagement with one's environment. Hence, for the human creature, the inclination to exist will normally be expressed through natural desires to eat, drink, stay warm, and the like, desires which we share with the other animals, and to some extent with plants as well. In addition, we also share a further desire with the higher animals, which can be analyzed as a further expression of the fundamental desire to exist and to exercise one's distinctive forms of causality. This is of course the inclination to reproduce one's kind, which for us, as with many other animals, typically takes the form of a desire to mate and to reproduce sexually. At the same time, human reproduction goes beyond physical procreation to include the education and socialization of one's children. This aspect of human existence does not, in itself, distinguish us from other highly developed mammals, although Aquinas and his contemporaries probably would have thought so. At any rate, he goes on to consider a third level, reflecting distinctively rational and human inclinations, including most notably the inclinations to live in society, to seek the truth and to worship God.

Aquinas is sometimes taken to task for failing to spell out the practical consequences of the first principle of practical reason. His analysis of the operative principle in terms of inclinations is seen as helping, but only a little, since taken on Aquinas's own terms, the inclinations do not yield concrete precepts enjoining or forbidding recognizable kinds of actions. But such criticisms miss the point that Aquinas is making here. His analysis of the first principle of practical reason in terms of natural inclinations is meant to show that reason in its practical operations is a structured faculty, operating in such a way as to track the intelligible structures of human nature more broadly construed. Precisely because this analysis is meant to apply to all operations of practical reason, it cannot be framed in such a way as to imply that these operations always yield actions that are good in the comprehensive, morally salient sense. The inclinations can be pursued, and their characteristic targets attained, through actions which are in some way inappropriate, harmful to the overall well-being of the agent, or unfair to others — morally bad ways, in short. The structures of practical reason themselves give us the needed conceptual framework for formulating these options, but by themselves they do not provide the substantive judgments necessary to give it substance.

The interconnections and proper ordering of the specific inclinations thus make it plain that these do not yield normative precepts, taken separately. It is less apparent that the ordered ensemble of the inclinations does not yield determinate precepts, either. Yet on reflection, it is difficult to know how the broad ordering imposed by the necessities and exigencies of life, on the one hand, and distinctively human activities and enjoyments on the other, can be translated into normative judgments specific enough to yield a determinate course of action. I have to stay alive in order to engage in any other kind of activity, but which is the best way for me to do so? Should I sustain my life under any and all conditions, or may I legitimately forego, let us say, life-prolonging medical treatments? Reproduction is more directly and broadly expressive of my nature, considered as a certain kind of animal, but does this imply that I should give it priority over more distinctively human forms of activities? Is it necessarily irrational to forego reproductive activities altogether, in order to devote myself to a life of scholarship, or to preserve an ideal of physical beauty for as long as possible? So far, nothing has been said about the ways in which the claims of others, and my relation to wider orders of existence and goodness, can or should constrain my pursuit of my own good, and yet I should surely try to take these into account, since I am by nature a social animal and, like all creatures, naturally oriented to love God and the overall cosmic goodness of God's creation more than myself.

Aquinas is well aware that these kinds of questions need to be addressed, in order to determine what it means to pursue natural human inclinations in a fully rational, which is to say, a virtuous way. In contrast with nonrational creatures, we cannot attain natural perfection through the spontaneous unfolding and development of innate inclinations. In order to count as rational, our acts must be elicited and informed by an intelligent grasp of the end we seek, considered as in some way desirable and worth pursuing, together with some deliberative judgment to the effect that we can attain this end through the exercise of our causal powers. Of course, the objects of the inclinations are natural objects of the will, and the human person spontaneously desires and pursues them, even before she is capable of mature rational reflection and action (ST I-II 10.1, 2). The desire for and voluntary pursuit of the objects of the inclinations does not presuppose any kind of overall judgments concerning one's overall good, but that is at least partly because at this level, desire and voluntary activity have not yet risen to the level of fully rational human action. We are here in the realm of infants, children, and (perhaps) immature and unreflective adults. In order to attain a capacity for fully rational action, an individual must arrive at some kind of account concerning the proper end of human life, and of his or her life in particular (ST I-II 89.6). To the extent that our various aims and activities are rational, they will in some way stem from, or at least reflect, an overarching conception of this kind.

The Happy Life, the Virtues, and the Natural Law

This is the point at which Aquinas joins with another ancient tradition of normative reflection, namely, the classical and patristic tradition of reflection on happiness, considered as the final end of human action.[38] Aquinas explicitly endorses the consensus view that every individual necessarily desires his or her own happiness, and directs all actions towards the attainment or the secure possession of that end. This may appear as a shocking bit of ethical egoism, but when we place it within the broader metaphysical context, it takes on a different connotation. Early in the *Summa theologiae,* in connection with an extended discussion of the angelic intellect, Aquinas states that happiness (or beatitude) represents the form of perfection proper to the rational or intellectual creature: "by the name of happiness is understood the ultimate perfection of a rational or intellectual nature; and hence it is that it is naturally desired, since everything naturally desires its own perfection" (ST I 62.1). When he turns specifically to human happiness, he accordingly analyzes the universal desire for happiness in terms of the individual's necessary orientation towards perfection, which is to say, the full development and expression of his or her active potentialities as a creature of a given kind (I-II I.7, 8; I-II 3.2). This line of analysis has far-reaching consequences, as we will see, but its significance at this point lies in the immediate implication that the universal orientation of practical reason towards goodness is first of all an orientation towards the agent's own existence, full development, and perfection, in accordance with its natural principles of operation.

The key word at this point is "natural." The universal desire for good-

38. In my discussion of Aquinas's conception of happiness and its connection to the life of virtue, I rely on an interpretation developed at more length in *Nature as Reason,* 141-230. For the classical background to Aquinas's thought, including a cogent analysis of the issues at stake, see Julia Annas, *The Morality of Happiness* (Oxford: Oxford University Press, 1993), 3-46.

ness in accordance with one's specific form of perfection is tethered to natural principles in such a way as to bring substance and order to the relevant operations through which a creature aims at its own perfection — in the case of the human person, to his processes of rational deliberation and action. It does not follow that everyone necessarily desires and pursues happiness in the same way; people can and do pursue false and perverted ideals of happiness, and Aquinas at least suggests the possibility of legitimately diverse ideals as well. Nonetheless, ideals of happiness, false and true, cannot intelligibly be formulated in any terms whatever. They must in some way make sense as positive developments of our natural capabilities, or at any rate, as something other than their deliberate neglect or perversion. This implies that every functional agent has at least some grasp of the kinds of reasons that count, or can or should count, when evaluating a particular state of affairs as a credible human aim, and correlatively, some sense of what it would mean to suffer oneself, or to harm another, in pursuit of these goals. What is more, these basic apprehensions are tethered in the agent's own active inclinations towards existence and activity, and this implies that they reflect an orderly structure, just as the inclinations themselves do.

Aquinas's overarching account of goodness, perfection, and happiness points back to the eternal law and forward to a fuller consideration of the natural law. I observed earlier that Aquinas's identification of the natural law as a participation in God's eternal law underscores the similarities between rational agents and other kinds of creatures, as well as identifying what is distinctive about the human mode of participation. We can now specify the relevant similarities more clearly. Recall that on Aquinas's view, God governs all creatures through the inclinations towards naturally specific forms of activity, which stem from the natural principles constituting anything as a creature of this or that specific kind. As he elsewhere explains, each kind of creature reflects God's wisdom and goodness in and through its own proper form of existence and, in that sense, in seeking its own perfectly developed existence, each creature seeks the divine goodness in the way that is proper to it. Thus, Aquinas can say that each creature naturally loves God more than itself, and all creatures, ourselves included, share in the same last end, the attainment of divine goodness, in and through the full development of a way of life which is a similitude of God's own incomprehensible life (ST I-II 1.7, 8; I-II 109.3).

Of course, the human person participates in this order, and correlatively pursues her own naturally specific form of perfection, in a distinctive way — which is to say, in and through a rationally informed and intentional pursuit of those activities which she regards as enjoyable, fitting, decent, upright, or appropriate. In other words, she knowingly pursues what Aquinas and his forebears would style her happiness or perfection as a creature of a specific kind, an ideal that may well include (as Aquinas thinks it properly should) a due regard for the well-being and proper claims of others. Her practical judgments are thus informed by general beliefs about the kinds of things that are necessary for, or at least conducive towards, human existence, and they take shape through discriminating judgments about the ways in which these diverse goods fit together, in relation to one another and in relation to whatever overarching aims or ideals she seeks. In this way, she, like every other creature, is governed by the inclinations, which are nothing other than dynamic tendencies towards attaining one's fully developed existence as a representative of a natural kind. We are reminded once again that the natural law represents the distinctively human mode of participation in the eternal law, which as we have seen operates in and through the natural inclinations of all creatures.

Thus, even though the first principle of practical reason is structured by the diverse inclinations, it is not subsumed by them.[39] Unless the agent has some more or less concrete idea of what it would mean to integrate these inclinations into an overall way of life, directed towards some ideal of human existence, rational reflection on the inclinations, taken together or seriatim, will not provide an adequate rule for rational activity. By the same token, the inclinations, even taken together, can appropriately be pursued in more than one way. Aquinas claims that there is in fact only one true end of human life, which formally speaking is tantamount to perfection in accordance with the intrinsic active principles of human existence, namely, the fullest possible development and expression of characteristically human capacities for intellectual contemplation and rational activity (ST I-II 3.2). Thus understood, happiness can be attained at both the supernatural and natural levels. Connatural happiness, which is of course the kind that concerns us here, consists in a life of virtuous activity, through which the individual achieves the fullest possible development and expression of her powers as a rational agent (I-II 5.5). But clearly, the life of virtue is consistent with more than one specific way of life, and considered as an ideal, offers no clear basis for choosing among these. (Would I have been more virtuous, or less, if I had chosen the life of a farm wife, as opposed to that of a college professor?)

39. I thus disagree with John Finnis, who equates happiness with the unlimited and unrestricted enjoyment of the objects of the natural inclinations; see most recently *Aquinas*, 103-10.

The Universal and the Contingent in the Natural Law

This brings us back to the conclusion of the last section. A natural law comprised of the most general principles of practical reasonableness cannot be expressed without some degree of contingency and corresponding variation at the level of concrete specification. Even if we accept Aquinas's claim that the true end of human life consists in the ongoing practice of the virtues — as we should — that still leaves a high degree of indeterminacy. Probably we can all agree that (for example) courage is good and wanton killing is bad, but no individual, and especially no society, can live and function at this level of generality. In order to be put into practice, norms and ideals must be formulated in terms of the paradigmatic kinds of actions that would count as either instantiations or transgressions (or most typically, both) of the norms or ideals in question. A general agreement that courage is a good thing and killing is bad can hide deep disagreements over what counts as courage or what kinds of killing (if any) are strictly impermissible. It might be said that these kinds of disagreements reflect nothing more than the inevitable uncertainties that arise when we attempt to apply broad practical norms to a complex and difficult world. But this response overlooks the fact that what is at stake here are publicly accessible, social norms. Hence, the need for specification, with its attendant variability at the level of practice, is a communal necessity. General ideals and norms must be formulated through processes of communal discernment and mutual persuasion before they can be appropriated and put into practice by individuals. Thus, the indeterminacy of normative ideals will inevitably introduce a level of contingency into the processes of communal norm-formation, as well as generating some uncertainty at the level of individual judgment.

And yet, is the natural law quite so formal and open-ended as all that? There do seem to be real and important, albeit very general points of convergence among the ideals and normative precepts accepted among different societies, and it is asking a great deal of coincidence to explain them all. Is it just a matter of chance that every society admires and promotes some kinds of courage, and prohibits, or at least penalizes, some kinds of killing? At the very least, there is enough convergence to enable us to recognize, even in societies very different from ours, a set of normative ideals and practices sufficiently similar to our own to justify comparing these as two variants of what is fundamentally the same kind of thing. Thus, even if we reject strong claims for a universal, substantive normative law, this does not mean that we are driven to an unqualified relativism. Normative codes (legal and otherwise) do seem to reflect certain widely shared commitments and constraints, too general to guide action, but not just empty and not theoretically irrelevant. At the very least, these shared commitments and constraints suggest that the wide range of normative ideals and practices that we observe manifest something more fundamental than the contingencies of particular historical trajectories and the exigencies of specific social and environmental forces.

It will be clear by now where I am going with this line of argument. I want to claim that this "something" grounding the diverse ideals and practices is nothing other than human nature itself, expressed in and through the operative structures of practical reason. This is the point, I would claim, at which a theory of natural law is properly grounded in a kind of realism — a realism, that is to say, about the existence of human nature in this strong sense and about our capacities to know, admittedly in a partial and revisable way, what its characteristic principles are. This kind of realism is by no means incompatible with the recognition that rational inquiry and knowledge are always situated, in one way or another, in the context of specific traditions of inquiry, or more specifically with the acknowledgment that human nature can be expressed in an indefinite variety of ways in different societies. Indeed, the comparison of these different modes of expressing human nature offers us one of the best — I am inclined to say, *the* best — means of access to genuine knowledge of human nature that we possess.

This approach to the natural law opens up a fruitful way of thinking about the relation between human nature and the practical norms stemming from that nature. Recall that the human person, together with every other living creature, comes into being, pursues the activities characteristic of its specific kind, and finally passes away — all in accordance with natural principles of action. These natural principles are intrinsically intelligible, and the form of existence constituted by them is naturally good. By the same token, these principles can be regarded as normative principles, albeit in a carefully qualified sense. That is, these principles are not rules (or laws) in the primary sense of norms that are grasped as such through rational apprehension and carried out through deliberate choice. Yet they represent something more than statistical regularities or contingent conjunctions of events. They are intelligible components of a form of life, and they are intrinsically good and valuable insofar as they reflect (actually or potentially) the fullest possible development of that natural form. Given this, it is not inappropriate to refer to these principles as expressions or forms of a natural law, albeit in a secondary sense — secondary, because operations at this level do not presuppose rational comprehension and choice.

The natural law, properly so called, operates in and through rational reflection, including both speculative and practical reflection operating in tandem. These are the processes through which individuals and communities formulate substantive ideals and norms, which can be acknowledged, observed, and pursued precisely as rational norms for action. At the same time, however, these processes of rational reflection do not, so to say, emerge from the noumenal void. The natural law in its primary sense operates in tandem with natural law in a range of secondary senses — or to put it another way, rational reflection always operates within a context of pre-rational norms which stem from the natural life of the creature. It is of course possible to detach rational reflection from this context — generations of moral philosophers have done so — but only at the cost of detaching it from the only context that can give it objective direction or criteria for adequacy.

At this level, the norms generated by the natural law properly so called stem from the broad structures of human life, their exigencies, and their characteristic trajectories of development and completion. Initially, these norms will emerge through ongoing processes of reflection and articulation, through which men and women become aware of the natural patterns of activity structuring their lives, and begin to guide their lives in accordance with these structures — which is to say, they begin to formulate and affirm these precisely as rational norms for activity. The intelligibility inherent in these processes makes the relevant intellectual discernment possible, and the natural orientation of the human organism towards its own existence and perfection motivates it and gives it normative force. Initially, these reflections will move between specific paradigms for praiseworthy or forbidden acts and the very general, yet not empty ideals of virtue and basic practical norms in terms of which men and women can make sense of these paradigms. We would expect general ideals of the virtues to play a central role at this level, because the virtues are themselves perfections of the distinctive capacities of the human person. That is to say, they are constitutive components of the flourishing existence towards which the human person is naturally oriented. Similarly, this is the context within which broad norms of non-maleficence, more or less parallel to the neighbor-regarding precepts of the Decalogue, begin to be formulated. Even though these kinds of norms do not directly reflect human perfection in the same way as do ideals of the virtues, they do begin to establish the framework for mutual restraint and cooperation that is a necessary condition for communal life.[40]

40. For a fuller discussion of the relation between ideals of virtue and norms of non-

Yet — once again — ideals and norms formulated at this level of generality are not sufficient to guide communal or individual behavior. In order to specify these norms in the requisite ways, it will be necessary to offer some account of the kinds of actions that count as following or transgressing them, and this, typically, will be done through processes of shared deliberation and persuasion. At this point, there is no one story to be told, because the specific trajectories traced by the development of these norms will be shaped by all kinds of contingencies — the community's particular history, its specific needs and opportunities, its relations with its neighbors, and the like. It is worth noting, however, that any normative tradition emerging out of the process of ongoing specification can legitimately be described as a natural morality, that is, as an expression of human nature as it emerges in a particular time and place. Correlatively, we should not expect to find a clear division between natural law precepts and conventions within this system of norms. Because the substantive norms emerging through these processes reflect natural principles as expressed under specific circumstances, they will combine natural and conventional elements and can be analyzed accordingly.[41]

So far, this theory of the natural law can account for the emergence of practical norms through a process of rational reflection on the intelligible structures of human life. Thus, assuming that the above sketch can be adequately developed, this theory offers a strategy for analyzing these norms by distinguishing between their natural and conventional components, that is, by construing them as expressions of human nature, drawing on the most adequate and comprehensive concept of human nature that we have so far attained, and then on that basis identifying those elements that are more clearly contingent and conventional. This line of analysis can tell us a great

---

maleficence, see Alasdair MacIntyre, *After Virtue,* second edition (Notre Dame: University of Notre Dame Press, 1984), 165-80.

41. For this reason, I would go well beyond Marmor in defending the conventional status of any actual moral system; cf. *Social Conventions,* 131-54. Certainly, I would agree that "there is nothing conventional about the idea . . . that murder, rape, and torture are morally wrong and ought to be avoided. At least the basic or fundamental moral requirements or principles are not conventions" (131). However, what counts as (for example) murder, rape, or torture will always involve some — admittedly often quite limited — element of conventional specification, and the way in which these concepts are embedded in an overall framework of obligations and prohibitions will require further levels of conventions. I do not at all mean to deny that a legitimate moral system will include certain key prohibitions, nor do I believe that the scope for legitimate disagreement over some key moral concepts (especially rape and torture) is great. But we can acknowledge constraints while at the same time recognizing that these underdetermine the moral concepts — and even more, the moral systems — which express these constraints.

deal. Precisely because it acknowledges a natural basis for human practices, while also presuming that these are expressed in conventional terms, this approach offers a corrective to the assumption that social practices are determined by nature (or indeed, by natural reason) in such a way that they cannot be changed or reformed. At the same time, it offers a way of expanding and developing our grasp of human nature itself, in and through the process of explaining how the principles of human nature have come to be expressed in this particular set of contingent circumstances. In the next section, I will attempt to develop and defend these claims.

3. Natural Principles and Cultural Practices

The Human Difference: Human Reason and Natural Principles

Before moving forward, it will be helpful to summarize what has so far been established. If the above analysis is tenable, then we have begun to identify the broad outlines of a plausible concept of human nature, formulated in terms of the intelligible principles structuring human activity seen on a descending scale of generality, from the level of our existence as creatures to that of our existence as members of a distinctive kind, that is, as rational animals. This schema, in turn, offers a framework within which to interpret those paradigmatically human activities that go to make up the natural history of this kind of living thing — the trajectory through which a developmentally normal human being comes into existence, matures into healthy adulthood, and reproduces itself through offspring before entering into inevitable processes of decay and death. Like every other concept of a kind of living creature, this is an intrinsically normative concept, insofar as it is formulated in terms of development, maturity, flourishing, and correlatively, immaturity and decay.

Yet taken by itself, this concept of human nature does not yield practical precepts that could be meaningfully formulated in terms of the paradigmatic kinds of actions targeted by a given precept. It does yield a substantively meaningful criterion for human action, tethered in a conception of human happiness as the practice of the virtues, but while this ideal is not purely formal, it can be interpreted in such a way as to yield in an indefinite plurality of plausible candidates for an admirable and desirable way of life. This may appear an unsatisfactory conclusion, but it follows from the distinctive character of reason itself and, by implication, from those characteristics which distinguish human activity from the activities of other kinds of animals. As we saw in the preceding section, the natural inclinations of the human person do not spontaneously emerge and operate in such a way as to lead inevitably to his full development as a creature of a specific kind. For them to do so, the inclinations must be carried out in and through intentional actions, guided by a reflective conception of what it means to live a fully human life. In this way, the agent is able to interpret, order, and evaluate a whole range of naturally desirable activities in terms of an overarching conception of the good, and more specifically, of what is comprehensively good for a human being. Far from being a deficiency, the relative indeterminacy of human practical reasoning is the precondition for the distinctively human ensemble of capacities enabling the human person to be provident for others as well as herself. Because the human person acts in accordance with a conceptual grasp of what is good, a concept that can be detached from its immediate context of desires and aversions, she can formulate and reformulate a whole range of conceptions of the good and guide her actions accordingly.

This may appear to be a hopelessly dated way into the distinctive difference generated by human rationality. But on closer examination, Aquinas's approach is not so different from that taken by a number of philosophers, social scientists, primatologists, and others. Among philosophers, John McDowell offers a particularly illuminating way of getting at what is distinctive about human rationality through his analysis of the relation between what he describes as the receptivity and the spontaneity of reason, both of which need to be affirmed and held together if we are to maintain some version of epistemic realism.[42] Without receptivity, our thought would not be subject to constraints from the extra-mental world and therefore could not

42. John McDowell, *Mind and World* (Cambridge, MA: Harvard University Press, 1994), 3-23, 66-86. Unsurprisingly, I agree with McDowell up to this point, but he then goes on to develop the idea of the naturalness of reason in terms of what I think is an unhelpful appeal to Aristotle's idea of "second nature," which understands it in Wittgensteinian terms as formation in a form of life. This, it seems to me, simply re-introduces McDowell's problem at the level of communal formulations. It would be better, on McDowell's own terms, to retrieve the scholastic (and classical) insight that the capacities of the human mind are informed by the intelligibilities structuring the natural world as a whole, in such a way as to track these intelligibilities through their proper operations. In other words, our most basic processes of perception and reasoning attain reality because the natural operations of the mind are isomorphic with the fundamental metaphysical structures of reality. Janet Coleman makes this point with respect to Aquinas in "MacIntyre and Aquinas," in *After MacIntyre: Critical Perspectives on the Work of Alasdair MacIntyre*, ed. John Horton and Susan Mendes (Notre Dame: University of Notre Dame Press, 1994), 65-90.

relate it to us in any systematic, illuminating way. Yet these constraints must not function in such a way as to deprive human thought of some element of spontaneity. Otherwise, our perceptions of, and responses to, situations and events would remain locked into their immediate context, in such a way as to preclude us from abstracting general concepts and principles from our direct experiences and applying these in distinct and unfamiliar circumstances. Finally, he argues that we can only hold receptivity and spontaneity together in the needed way by affirming the naturalness of human reason, in virtue of which it is tethered and directed by extra-mental constraints, while at the same time it exhibits capacities for self-reflective detachment and abstraction from those constraints.

Admittedly, McDowell is more Aristotelian than many contemporary philosophers in his overall approach. Yet his central distinction between the receptivity and the spontaneity of reason recurs, of course in varying formulations, among primatologists and others who attempt systematic comparisons among the different forms of life exhibited among the higher primates (and sometimes, other animal species). Michael Tomasello summarizes recent work in this area as follows:

> The conclusion is thus that nonhuman primates have many cognitive skills involving physical objects and events . . . but they do not perceive or understand underlying causes as mediating the dynamic relations among these objects and events. They thus do not show the kind of flexibility of behavior and understanding of general causal principles characteristic of human children, from a very young age, as they try to solve physical problems. Nonhuman primates understand many antecedent-consequent relations in the world, but they do not seem to understand causal forces as mediating these relations.[43]

In McDowell's terms, human cognition is characterized by the spontaneity reflected in the capacity to understand sequences of antecedent and consequent events as instantiating some kind of intentional or causal relation — the capacity, in other words, to step back from the immediately perceived sequencing of events, to identify them in terms of abstract categories of intention or causation, and to explain them accordingly. Yet this spontaneity is grounded in, and remains constrained and directed by, the paradigmatic examples in terms of which intentional and causal relations are

43. Michael Tomasello, *The Cultural Origins of Human Cognition* (Cambridge, MA: Harvard University Press, 1999), 22.

grasped. Aquinas would say that the proper object of the intellect is the abstract form of some concrete reality, understood as such in and through the act of understanding this particular as an instance of a general concept. McDowell would say that reason in its spontaneity retains its character as reason because it remains tethered to something outside the intellect, and thus cannot degenerate into sheer play.

This dialectic between spontaneity and receptivity characterizes not only individual cognition, but the formation of a distinctively human form of culture. It is sometimes said that discrete populations among certain species of higher primates exhibit distinctive cultures. If we understand culture in a broad sense to consist in contingent patterns of activity — different ways of collecting food, for example — this would seem to be established beyond doubt. Human culture is distinctive, however, because it exhibits not only the stability conferred by imitation, but also the development over time brought about by reflective appropriation and innovation. As Tomasello explains,

> In general, then, human cultural traditions may be most readily distinguished from chimpanzee cultural traditions — as well as the few other instances of culture observed in other primate species — precisely by the fact that they accumulate modifications over time, that is to say, they have cultural "histories." They accumulate modifications and have histories because the cultural learning processes that support them are especially powerful. These cultural learning processes are especially powerful because they are supported by the uniquely human cognitive adaptation for understanding others as intentional beings like the self — which creates forms of social learning that act as a ratchet by faithfully preserving newly innovated strategies in the social group until there is another innovation to replace them.[44]

As McDowell might say, sustaining a culturally specific way of life involves not only a moment of receptivity, as distinctive practices and perceptions emerge in response to environmental pressures, but also a moment of spontaneity, in which men and women reflect on their practices, pass them on through active imitation and teaching, and develop them through deliberate innovation. This process, in turn, leads to the formation of a distinctive structure of practices, beliefs, and ideals identified by social scientists as a fully developed human culture.

The individual's rational faculties for receptivity and spontaneity, in

44. *Ibid.*, 40; for a full defense and development of these claims, see 13-55.

turn, depend on the child's receptivity to the examples and instruction of others, together with his spontaneous grasp that these shared activities are meaningful, in categories that go beyond the immediacies of particular experiences.[45] Although there would be some debate over the exact way in which a child is socialized into a rational adult, almost everyone would agree that the distinctively human ensemble of cognitive capacities can only emerge within the context of an ongoing social life, broadly similar to the kinds of interactions that we see among other sophisticated social animals. Hence, the distinctively human capacities for empathy, linguistic mastery, and ultimately responsible freedom all presuppose a way of functioning, natural to us as a kind of animal and pre-rational in its broad contours. Our most distinctive rational capacities thus presuppose a degree of receptivity to the natural going beyond what the scholastics themselves recognized, and as we will see, this receptivity shapes the laws, just as it shapes every other aspect of our social lives. Yet if the scholastics underestimate the extent to which the social character of rationality connects us to other kinds of animals, we tend to overlook the ways in which our rational social life is distinctively human, in such a way as to point to a powerful ideal for human existence at the individual and social levels. As Tomasello says, speaking for himself and colleagues at the Max Planck Institute of Evolutionary Anthropology, "We propose that the crucial difference between human cognition and that of other species is the ability to participate with others in collaborative activities with shared goals and intentions" — thus, "human beings, and only human beings, are biologically adapted for participating in collaborative activities involving shared goals and socially coordinated action-plans (joint intentions)."[46] Participation in collaborative activities, in pursuit of shared goals and intentions: these are the hallmarks of properly political relationships, in which men and women jointly pursue aims that are in some sense their own, as well as being shared with others jointly pursuing socially coordinated activities. In this way, the social life natural to us as advanced primates, to which practical reason is naturally receptive, is transformed through the spontaneity of reason into a distinctively political way of life.

Understood in these terms, human existence as such does have a recognizable, distinctive shape, which can be identified in part through compari-

45. Again, Tomasello provides a cogent and illuminating review and interpretation of the relevant data; see *the Cultural Origins of Human Cognition*, 56-93.

46. Michael Tomasello, et al., "Understanding and Sharing Intentions: The Origins of Cultural Cognition," *Behavioral and Brain Sciences* 28 (2005): 675-735, 675, 676.

sons with the ways of life proper to other kinds of animals. In most respects, we resemble the other higher primates fairly closely. At the same time, however, the forms that our social life take are far more complex, and vary more widely than anything that we find among our nearest evolutionary kin, reflecting a distinctive capacity to detach from the immediacies of our desires and perceptions, and to form practices, in part, through intentional reflection. We are, in other words, rational animals. As such, our nature as social animals under-determines the forms that our social existence can take. We do not have any basis for regarding any one of these variant forms as clearly superior to the others, or much less as the only genuine expression of human nature; they are in that sense incommensurable. And yet, they are all recognizably variant ways of sustaining a distinctive way of life — structures within which to sustain animal existence, to support the extended activities of procreation and child rearing, and to form the extended communities within which these more fundamental inclinations can be pursued.

This brings us to a critical point. The diversity of cultures, each with its attendant ideals of human happiness or excellence and its distinctive range of alternative ways of living, is sometimes said to count decisively against natural law or Aristotelian defenses of the normative significance of human nature. This criticism would indeed be decisive if a claim for the normative significance of human nature necessarily implied that the normative or ideal specification of human nature must take one determinate form, equivalent in its specificity to the ideals and practices associated with some actual set of social arrangements. Yet as we have just seen, this is by no means the case. It is possible to defend a conception of human nature implying broad normative guidelines — mostly, as we will see, positive and legitimating rather than directly implying prohibitions — which nonetheless remains sufficiently indeterminate to allow for a diversity of concrete formulations, each offering plausible and attractive ideals of human existence, which are nonetheless deeply incompatible with one another.

Indeed, a general conception of human nature is not only compatible with the reality of irreducible cultural diversity — we can only recognize this diversity for what it is, and begin to make sense of it, because we presuppose a general conception of human nature. When we say that two accounts (explanations, theories, or the like) are incommensurable, we presuppose that these are being applied to one and the same objects or fields of inquiry, which all participants can recognize as such, however differently they may describe and interpret it. This is a familiar problem in the philosophy of science, generally approached by means of an explanation of how it is that the interlocutors can come to agree on identifying targets for an explanation — agreeing that they disagree about *this,* this kind of object or event or process. (We could not regard Aristotelian and Newtonian explanations of motion as incommensurable, unless proponents of these two views agreed broadly on what counts as motion.) But if the norms and ideals of different societies are generated by nothing other than what we might call their collective intentionalites, how can these be said to represent incommensurable accounts of anything?[47]

Here is another point at which the Aristotelian/Thomistic conception of human nature can contribute to a contemporary debate, by offering a plausible account of the shared field of inquiry — or better, reflective practice — in virtue of which incommensurable systems of primary and secondary rules can be identified as incommensurable construals of what is recognizably the same field of concern. That field, more specifically, is constituted by our species-specific way of life, for which this conception offers at least a plausible account. What is common to us all does not stand over against our communal particularities, but is revealed in and through reflection on those particularities.

Culture as Product and Presupposition of Reason

We find unexpected confirmation of this approach from the relatively new field of cultural psychology, a relatively new discipline that has emerged in close conjunction with primatology, evolutionary theories of social life, and anthropology. These diverse lines of inquiry are held together by a renewed interest in the idea of culture, understood broadly to include the fullest possible range of beliefs, ideals, and practices informing human societies. A formulation and defense of the idea of culture has been proposed, discredited, revived, critiqued, and revived yet again since the early 1950s — and yet, as

---

47. This is by no means merely a theoretical or hypothetical problem. We have by now accumulated several centuries' experience of dealing practically with cultural diversity, but as Anthony Padgen points out, early encounters between native American and European (mostly Spanish) peoples raised genuine questions, on both sides, about how to make sense of seemingly pointless or perverse behaviors as intelligibly human practices. Ultimately, the Europeans did so through a retrieval of the early scholastic conception of the natural law — an approach that had practical consequences, insofar as it laid the foundations for a defense of the claims of the native American peoples, over against the Spanish crown. See Padgen, *The Fall of Natural Man: The American Indian and the Origins of Comparative Ethnology* (Cambridge: Cambridge University Press, 1982), 10-14 for a summary of the argument.

Richard Shweder observes, the concept of culture "not only survives; it thrives."[48] Drawing on a variety of accounts put forward over the course of these debates, he summarizes what he describes as the standard view among cultural anthropologists as follows:

> culture refers to community-specific ideas about what is true, good, beautiful, and efficient. To be cultural, those ideas about truth, goodness, beauty, and efficiency must be socially inherited and customary. To be cultural, those socially inherited and customary ideas must be embodied or enacted meanings; they must be constitutive of (and thereby revealed in) a way of life. Alternatively stated, the standard North American anthropological view of culture refers to what the British philosopher Isaiah Berlin called "goals, values and picture of the world" that are made manifest in the speech, laws, and routine practices of some self-monitoring and self-perpetuating group.[49]

As Shweder's summary implies, cultural psychology attempts to make sense of the diversity of ways of life in terms of broad, generally instantiated ideals, principles, and practices. More specifically, this field emerged out of attempts to mediate between two strikingly different perspectives on human nature which dominated different branches of the social sciences throughout much of the preceding century. Following the historian and philosopher G. E. R. Lloyd, we might describe these as relativism and universalism. By relativism, he refers to the view of those who hold that "the diversity of humankind goes all the way down," which came to dominate the field of cultural anthropology in the early twentieth century.[50] In contrast, highly influential voices in other fields, including linguistics, psychology, and more recently, evolutionary psychology have defended variants of universalism, that is to say, the view that "the processes that characterize the working of the human mind are the same everywhere."[51] Thus, for example, many linguists claim that they can identify invariant grammatical structures shared by all languages, which in their view were "hard-wired" into the human psyche. Cognitive scientists often claim to identify categories of thought and

48. Richard Shweder, *Why Do Men Barbecue? Recipes for Cultural Psychology* (Cambridge, MA: Harvard University Press, 2003), 9.
49. *Why Do Men Barbecue?* 11; for his summary of the checkered fortunes of the idea of culture, see 7-27.
50. G. E. R. Lloyd, *Cognitive Variations: Reflections on the Unity and Diversity of the Human Mind* (Oxford: Clarendon Press, 2007), 3; his overall argument is summarized at 1-7.
51. *Cognitive Variations*, 2; he is quoting M. E. Spiro.

structures of perception and inference common to all, however much differences of belief and judgment may initially obscure these. Developmental psychologists, who attempt to map out the trajectory of maturation from infancy to adulthood, frequently conclude that all children go through the same stages of cognitive development, which cannot only be recognized as such but unfold in an orderly and invariant practice.

The field of cultural psychology emerged out of ongoing engagements over these and similar issues between anthropologists and developmental psychologists in particular, although perspectives from the other disciplines mentioned have also shaped this field. Cultural psychologists (and those who work along the same general lines) emphasize pluralism and diversity and resist any claim that Western modes of development, perception, and cognition are universally instantiated. Nonetheless, this approach does presuppose that at least some aspects of human psychic functioning are universal. Indeed, this assumption is foundational, because cultural psychology takes its task to be the analysis and articulation of cultural diversity in terms of plural expressions of shared modes of psychic functioning. As Shweder explains,

> Cultural psychology attempts to spell out the implicit meanings that give shape to psychological processes, to examine the distribution of those meanings across ethnic groups and temporal-spatial regions of the world, and to identify the manner of their social acquisition. A related goal is to reassess the principle of psychic unity or uniformity and to develop a credible theory of psychological diversity or pluralism. Cultural psychology looks at how the human mind can be transformed and made functional in different ways that are not equally distributed across ethnic and cultural communities around the world. Hence the slogan, popular among some cultural psychologists, "one mind, but many mentalities: universalism without the uniformity," which expresses that pluralistic emphasis.[52]

And what are these unities, which constitute the "one mind" characteristic of human nature as such? Cultural psychologists do not attempt to identify these in advance; rather, they emerge through the processes of comparison and analysis of differences that are central to their discipline. Thus, we can arrive at credible accounts of human universals by identifying those commonalities that best make sense of a range of diverse cultural forms of cognition and ways of life — in other words, by articulating our best sense of what it is that these diverse forms are expressing.

52. *Why Do Men Barbecue?* 135.

One of these emergent commonalities is particularly relevant to our project, namely, the formation of what Shweder describes as moral evaluations, that is, "judgments about actions and practices that are classified as loathsome, outrageous, shameful, evil, or wrong." He goes on to say that ethnographic research has established a number of things about these judgments, including, first of all, that "Moral judgments are ubiquitous. Members of every cultural community assume that they are parties to an agreement to uphold a certain way of life, praise or permit certain kinds of actions and practices, and condemn and prohibit others. In this regard, Emile Durkheim was right. The social order is a moral order vigilantly and incessantly sustained by small and large judgments about right and wrong, good and bad, virtue and vice."[53]

It might seem that we have now found what has so far eluded us, namely, the starting points for a universally valid natural law morality. But this conclusion would be too quick, because as Shweder adds, ethnographic research has also established that "Moral judgments do not spontaneously converge over time. Actions and practices that are a source of moral approbation in one community are frequently the source of moral opprobrium in another, and moral disagreements can persist over generations, if not centuries." And why should this be the case? Because "the imagined truths or goods asserted in deliberative moral judgments around the world are many, not one." He adds, several proposals have been advanced in the social sciences for classifying these goods into a smaller set, such as the three ethics of "autonomy, community, and divinity" — a clear example of analyzing diversity in terms of a set of universal categories or modes of functioning.[54]

If we can plausibly identify universal categories of human goods underlying the diversity of ethical systems to be found among all peoples, why can't we take these as the basis for a universally valid ethical system? Simply because, as we have already seen, the values intrinsic to human life must be specified through contingent cultural processes in order to be translated into concrete practical norms. Steven Parish makes this point in the context of his ethnographic work on the Hindu Newar society of Nepal:

53. *Why Do Men Barbecue?* 35-36.
54. *Why Do Men Barbecue?* 36-38. For a detailed and persuasive analysis of the ways in which Western moral assumptions, and more especially the norms associated with Catholic moral theology, might be appropriated and thereby transformed in an African context, see Bénézet Bujo, *Foundations of an African Ethic: Beyond the Universal Claims of Western Morality*, trans. Brian McNeil (New York: Crossroad, 2001).

Arguably, each human culture gives its own distinctive signature to the moral; moral knowing is in part transcultural, drawing on universal moral ideas. Yet always, these universals enter into culture, are reshaped and redirected. Dharma is perhaps one of these culturally transfigured universals; it carries within it the idea of transcendent objective standards of immutable "natural law." The paradox of dharma is, then, that it is known subjectively, by individual men and women, and given meaning that reflects their place in society.[55]

Thus, he adds, "in cultural terms, Western minds and Newar minds are different historical and cultural phenomena. While both grow out of whatever innate powers of thought that human beings possess, minds absorbed in culture construe experience differently, drawing on different cultural presuppositions to bring forth different conclusions about moral life, different visions of moral order."[56]

More specifically, these natural (and related or derivative) goods are not always compatible, and must be ranked, or otherwise brought together through acts of judgment, in order to be translated into concrete practical norms. As Shweder goes on to say:

> Notice in this regard that a stance of moral pluralism is not opposed to universalism. . . . I am a universalist, but the type of universalism to which I subscribe is universalism without the uniformity, which is what makes me a pluralist. In other words, there are universally binding values, just too many of them. Those objectively valuable ends of life are diverse, heterogeneous, irreducible to some common denominator such as "utility" or "pleasure," and inherently in conflict with each other. All the good things in life cannot be simultaneously maximized. When it comes to implementing true values, there are always trade-offs, which is why there are different traditions of values (cultures) and why no one cultural tradition has ever been able to honor everything that is good.[57]

Once again, we come up against the limitations of practical reason operating within a field of disparate and potentially incompatible goods. We can consider and assess these disparate goods in practical deliberation, proceed-

---

55. Steven A. Parish, *Moral Knowing in a Hindu Sacred City: An Exploration of Mind, Emotion, and Self* (New York: Columbia University Press, 1994), 117-18.

56. *Moral Knowing in a Hindu Sacred City*, 119.

57. *Why Do Men Barbecue?* 38.

ing in well-grounded, reasonable ways, which we can defend as such; we do so every day. And yet, the final judgment may well remain contingent in some significant way. We *could* defensibly have reached another, very different conclusion, which could also be justified as a reasonable ranking and application of diverse goods. At the level of individual deliberation and choice, this indeterminacy goes a long way towards explaining why practical reason cannot, in principle, constitute the basis for a true science. At the level of communal norm-formation, it opens the door to the emergence of profoundly different practices and ideals of life, constituting incommensurable moral traditions which can all nonetheless be recognized as defensible construals of what it is to exist and to flourish as a human being. The Thomist would only add that these diverse goods are best understood under a common rubric, that is to say, diverse forms of perfections proper to human nature. But this construal taken by itself does not obviate the necessity for contingent judgments, since the question at hand is precisely what it means to attain perfection, comprehensively considered: through which concatenation of goods attained, in what proportions, and in what ways? An appeal to the formal Aristotelian ideal of perfection in accordance with a substantive form, taken by itself, cannot answer this question in any definitive way.

Given these limitations, can a natural law analysis offer any second-order normative judgments, on the basis of which to evaluate and perhaps to reform specific ways of life — our own, or (more problematically) those of other societies? Like Shweder, I am a value pluralist — I do not believe that there is a basis on which to decisively resolve every normative conflict, even — especially! — those concerned with fundamental issues. Ethical systems will remain to some degree ineradicably, incommensurably different, whatever progress we make towards shared values and normative commitments. And yet we have good reason to believe that we can make progress, both in self-critique and agreement on some norms of practice with those who disagree with us on matters of fundamental importance.

In earlier work, I argued that the natural law, properly understood, generates substantive norms in the form of ideals of virtue and broad categories of harm.[58] These are not sufficiently determinate to secure agreement at the level of concrete norms, but neither are they purely formal. At least, they have enough substantive content to provide a basis on which to engage in processes of rational self-scrutiny and persuasive advocacy. As we will see, ideals of virtue are politically and legally significant, albeit in unexpected ways, and

58. *Nature as Reason,* 241-30, 288-308.

we will have occasion to explore these issues further. At this point, I want to focus on a different, although related point. That is, the account of the natural law that I propose offers a methodology for identifying broad, pervasive aspects of human life in terms of the natural purposes they serve and promises both conceptual clarification and a shared framework for deliberation.

This may not seem like much of a contribution to normative reflection, but that is only because we presuppose that analytic judgments and normative evaluations must necessarily be distinct. The methodological and substantive implications of the natural law as I understand it are closely interconnected, both in their theoretical justification and in practice. This is what we should by now expect, given the broadly Thomistic/Aristotelian framework within which both are developed. An analysis of authority developed within this framework will be informed by an account of the natural purposes served by relations of authority, which account will offer a starting point for evaluating actual institutions and practices. What is more, any such account will presuppose the way of life and the forms of functioning proper to human existence, including, critically, the exigencies of a distinctively rational mode of activity. This means that the terms of a natural law analysis of authority must show it to be informed and bounded by the considerations stemming from the purposes it serves, by the general conditions of human life, and by requirements that these be defensible through rational processes of deliberation and persuasion.

4. The Practical Purchase of the Natural Law: Methodological Implications

A Teleological Analysis of Social Conventions

On an Aristotelian view, systematic inquiry into the proper nature of a given kind of living thing is aimed at developing an account of its characteristic processes and functions, showing how these fit together in such a way as to promote the typical aims of a living creature — existence, growth and development, mature health and reproductive success.[59] Evaluative judgments and analytic formulations develop in tandem through inquiries moving between preliminary observations and evaluations, and an analysis of the

---

59. Lennox defends this as an interpretation of Aristotle's own program in *Aristotle's Philosophy of Biology*, 1-109; see in particular 98-109.

forms of existence and agency proper to this kind of thing. (As we reflect on what it means to be a cat, we consider the relevant differences among kittens, mangy cats, deformed cats, sleek, sassy cats, and the like — all with the aim of grasping what it means to be a fully normal, healthy, mature cat.) It would be profoundly misleading to approach this process in the spirit of the philosopher who said that anything whatever can be valued — even a saucer of mud — the implication being that we bestow value from without on neutral facts.[60] (We like mangy cats, thank you — and will build a natural history of the cat around that preference.) On the contrary — normative analysis of this kind presupposes a realism that takes the existence and intrinsic intelligibility of objective reality seriously. Because living creatures (at least) embody natural goals and values in their characteristic functioning, a realistic conception of such creatures calls for a teleological analysis.

Up to a point, a natural law analysis of human practices will follow this general procedure. Only up to a point, however, because in this case the starting points for analysis are not natural functions as such, but the conventions through which these are expressed. Again, human nature is always mediated through its conventional expressions; we do not otherwise have access to human processes and activities, except perhaps at the most basic level of spontaneous organic functions such as growth and nutrition. If we overlook this point, we risk identifying natural principles too closely with the local and contingent forms that they take. From this point, any conception of human nature that we develop would invariably be narrow and distorted. What is more, it would not take due account of the distinctive role that conventions themselves play in natural human functioning. As James Wallace observes, "The conventional aspect of human life is a natural phenomenon. It is essential to *human* life"[61] — precisely because we are rational animals, whose social lives are structured, in key part at least, through the knowing and self-reflective observance of conventional norms.

By the same token, every conventional practice is grounded, more or less directly and immediately, in natural principles, that is to say, in the distinctive forms of functioning characteristic of human life, insofar as we are living creatures, social primates, and distinctively rational. In some instances — with respect to marriage, for example — the practice in question is clearly grounded in one of the essential functions of human existence, so

---

60. I take this example from Elizabeth Anscombe, who offers it (appropriately) as a *reductio ad absurdum;* see *Intention* (Ithaca: Cornell University Press, 1957), 70.

61. *Virtues and Vices,* 34-35, emphasis in the original.

much so that we need to pay attention to the conventional aspects of its expression in this or that particular society. In other instances, the conventional elements of a practice will be most apparent; it is difficult to connect the functioning of contemporary economic systems to natural processes of production and consumption, which indeed turns out to be one weakness of these systems. Nonetheless, even these latter kinds of practices have some tethering in natural principles. They come about in response to pervasive human needs and desires, and they develop and function through the proper natural principle of human operations, namely, reason.

A natural law analysis thus understood is not aimed immediately and directly at moral judgments, understood in terms of concrete normative precepts enjoining or forbidding certain kinds of actions. The focus initially is understanding and comprehension of social practices as one expression of natural principles, sometimes with the further aim of making sense of the conventions of different societies as variant expressions of the same natural principles. Of course, this kind of natural law analysis does carry normative implications; that, after all, is why we engage in it. But at least initially, these emerge out of our ongoing efforts to place ourselves, within and across communal boundaries, within the twofold context of a shared, dynamic human nature and the diverse, partially contingent and perpetually changing practices and institutions that challenge and divide us. In the ongoing processes of defending or reforming our own practices, we draw on our best insights into the limits and possibilities of human existence in this time and place. At the same time, and in much the same ways, we attempt to justify our way of life to those whose social perspectives are very different — or perhaps we would like to learn from them ourselves. At any rate, we hope to open spaces for mutual understanding, or failing that, enough sympathetic tolerance to interact on some basis other than outright hostility.

A natural law analysis will therefore typically take its starting points from some conventional practice or institution, sufficiently pervasive and well established to play a significant role in our individual and collective lives, which has nonetheless become problematic in some way.[62] To general-

---

62. At this point, a terminological clarification is in order. By "institution," I mean a self-sustaining system of roles, practices, and expectations through which some activity is structured and regulated. By "practice," I mean a recurring form of human activity which can be identified as such by reference to its overall aim, and which is governed (in part) by normative considerations intrinsic to the pursuit of that aim. Practices are typically instantiated in a range of institutional forms. Thus, marriage is an institution; promising is a practice that plays a role in marriage, family relationships, professional life, legal contexts, and unspecified day to day interactions.

ize Dworkin's point in the last chapter, we do not begin with a well-formulated, comprehensive concept of the convention in question. We can, however, normally and non-problematically identify at least the basic institutions of society, marriage for example, and by implication, we can identify a range of paradigmatic kinds of activities associated with married life — activities that would generally be associated with entering into marriage, the kinds of things that husband and wife typically do and expect from one another, and the like. Without at least this much in the way of preliminary observations and evaluations, further analysis could not get off the ground. Given that we have this much in place, however, we can begin to raise questions about the scope, the proper structure, and as we might say, the true meaning of the institution. Should informal but long-term alliances count as instances of marriage? What about a union between sexual partners who have no intent to form a family or to participate in a wider kinship network? Must marriage be limited to two partners only? Two partners of different sexes? We as a society can disagree about these questions because we agree on so much else — and we have a stake in doing so because the institution of marriage matters to us, and to the extent possible, we want to preserve and enhance, rather than to undermine, those features that give value to the practice in the first place.[63]

But what purposes are these? Here we come to the key point. A natural law analysis is directed towards identifying the natural purposes served by a conventional practice or institution, with the aim, in the first instance, of rendering this practice intelligible as one aspect of the "unified set of goal-ordered capacities" that jointly inform human existence. Certainly, many of our contemporaries would regard this as an unpromising approach, but I nonetheless believe that it expresses what we actually do, typically if not always, in processes of public deliberation and debate. In support of this claim I offer an observation and assumption, neither controversial in itself, which taken together indicate that much of our actual popular and political discourse over disputed practices and institutional forms does follow the overall lines of a natural law analysis of this kind.

63. These questions have a special salience in the United States due to the widespread movement for the recognition of gay unions as marriages; for a summary of the recent debate, with a cogent analysis of the issues at stake, see David Cole, "The Same-Sex Future," *New York Review of Books* 56.11, July 2, 2009, 12-16.

Natural Law Analysis and Conceptual Clarification

The observation is simply that we do in fact identify certain broad kinds of practices, institutional arrangements, and kinds of relationships as being variant expressions of some one kind of thing, even when these are expressed in very different ways over a historical trajectory of development or across a range of culturally diverse societies. Or at any rate, we think we can do so, and it would call for a very considerable level of skepticism to deny that this confidence has no grounding in reality at all. At the very least, it makes sense to describe extended polygamous families, and dyads enmeshed in a complex web of wider relations, and relatively free-standing dyads, and perhaps even transitional sexual alliances, as variant forms of one institution, marriage. We can make sense of these diverse practices by regarding them as varying forms of marriage, and thus it serves a range of purposes — explanatory as well as practical — to construe them in this way. We may find ourselves confronted by novel or problematic kinds of unions, and these may provoke sharp disagreements over whether, for example, gay unions can count as a form of marriage. But even in these cases, we have some sense of what is at stake in these debates, some rough idea of the categories in terms of which we attempt to place a contested practice.

The assumption is that from the outset these processes of identification, distinction and classification presuppose a set of background beliefs about the normal course and the typical patterns of activity characterizing human life. To put the same point in the language of cultural anthropology, in our reflections on marriage, we start with a set of schemata for marriage, in terms of which we identify what a marriage is, what it ideally should be, and what can be regarded as acceptable, if not ideal.[64] This claim does not of course imply that we bring anything like a well-worked out, systematic framework to our initial judgments, on this or any other topic. Nonetheless, it does seem to be the case that even the most tentative inquiries will neces-

---

64. For a good overview on recent work on the significance of schemata in cognitive anthropology, with explicit attention to contemporary Western schemata pertaining to marriage, see Roy D'Andrade, "Cognitive Anthropology," in *New Directions in Psychological Anthropology*, ed. Theodore Schwartz, Geoffrey M. White, and Catherine A. Lutz (Cambridge: Cambridge University Press, 1992), 47-58. The volume as a whole provides numerous examples of the ways in which internalized schemata of this kind serve both to maintain the culture and way of life of a self-sustaining community, and provide alternatives and an overarching framework for developing a plurality of options within the overall culture, including some which open up possibilities for critique and development.

sarily presuppose some working framework of beliefs and judgments, of the kind sometimes described (in this context) as "folk psychology." Otherwise, we would not be able even to begin to identify patterns, commonalities, relevant points of resemblance or diversity. In short, we could not generate general categories, without which reflective inquiry cannot even begin. The theory-laden character of intellectual inquiry is of course a commonplace among social scientists and philosophers of science, most of whom would agree that this quality, in itself, does not rule out genuine knowledge and intelligible discourse about the extra-mental world. In the case at hand — with respect to identifying essential similarities and salient differences among patterns of human activity — we begin with a set of assumptions and beliefs about what is normal, typical, or characteristic about human existence, and correlatively, what is problematic in such a way as to call for some kind of explanation or justification.

We move now to a further observation, which may be more controversial but which is, in my view, likewise confirmed by experience. That is, our starting assumptions about what is typical, normative, or characteristic, however more precisely these are spelled out, will at least imply that we can in some way make sense of the activities involved as fitting together in some coherent way, suggesting an underlying structure of capacities and functions which expresses itself in recognizable patterns. We simply cannot make sense of random vocalizations and uncontrolled hand-waving as a part of a practice; on the contrary, this kind of behavior is more likely to be regarded as pathological. Nor can our tentative judgments about what is characteristic of human life be reduced to observed statistical regularities. Consider, again, the example of marriage. Our initial judgments about what counts as a normal marriage may or may not reflect our observations about what always or usually happens. We celebrate the durable, stable union of a man and woman who clearly have loved each other for many years, through which they have raised happy children in a life of decent prosperity. We celebrate these unions all the more fervently, because we know, even without much reflection, that they represent a difficult and relatively rare achievement. By the same token, we may want to claim that other kinds of relatively rare unions — same-sex unions, or arranged marriages, or plural marriages — should really count as marriages as well. Whatever we think may support our judgments in such cases, frequencies of occurrence in themselves do not.

But in that case, what kinds of considerations do count for or against our initial assumptions about normal, characteristic human practices? The teleological structure of human existence, understood in a broadly Aristotelian way, implies that one such set of considerations stems from judgments about the natural purposes served by the practice. That is to say, as we reflect on the meaning of marriage, to continue the example at hand, we will want to ask what purposes this practice serves, given what we grasp about the teleological structures displayed by living creatures generally, taken together with what we regard as distinctive about human life. It is critically important to keep in mind that this line of inquiry does not imply that social practices are set up to serve somebody's purposes — as if every such practice represented a legal enactment, or traced its origins to a kind of social contract or to the more or less conscious dominion of one category of persons by another. The former two claims have been widely discredited, and the last now seems unpromising as a general explanation for social dynamics. Nor do these practices reflect God's own purposes, except in the sense that God wills to create diverse kinds of creatures, each of which lives in accordance with its own proper principles of activity. Once again, we should recall that an Aristotelian teleological analysis presupposes that the ongoing activities of living creatures are directed towards purposes, but the purposes in question are not anybody's purposes, in the sense that they have been bestowed on the creature by some external agency. By implication, when we speak of the purposes served by a human practice, we are asking how this practice fits within an overarching structure of capabilities and activities in such a way as to sustain the ongoing lives of individuals and communities.

By this point, the main lines of a natural law analysis should be clear. This kind of analysis aims towards interpreting conventional practices as expressions of the forms of existence and functioning proper to human existence as such. Since the dynamic functions of human life cannot be rendered intelligible apart from some sense of the natural purposes that they serve, such analysis focuses above all on identifying the natural purposes served by the convention under consideration. Of course, human practices are complex; they generally serve diverse purposes, and include many elements which no longer serve much of anything, except perhaps to affirm social solidarity and ongoing tradition. Nonetheless, we can and do identify central natural purposes served by the conventions structuring our social life — marriage, property, civic life, religious practices. Once we have done so, we can then move on to analyze divergent practices in terms of the natural purposes that they serve, in this way identifying the odd practices of other societies, or the even stranger variants exemplified by our own past, as variants of the same convention, serving the same natural purposes.

The immediate outcome of a successful natural law analysis will thus be conceptual clarification. Through reflection on the natural practices served by an institution, as displayed over a range of examples within and (perhaps) outside our society, we begin to formulate a concept with significant explanatory power. That is to say, we arrive at a concept that accounts for most of what we regard as the paradigmatic activities of the practice in question in terms of the natural purposes that they (more or less directly) serve, and which correlatively allows us to make principled judgments about the status of supposed instances of the practice which are in some way problematic. It would be a mistake to assume that even a successful concept of this kind would yield a universally valid ideal form of the practice, or allow for formulation in terms of necessary and sufficient conditions for its instantiation.[65] At the same time, our practical concepts will set limits on what we can intelligibly describe as variant instances of the same practice, in our own society or in other societies. Through dialectical processes of reflection on problematic activities, we expand and refine our concept of a given practice, seen in terms of diverse expressions of one coherent set of natural purposes and functions. To the extent that the expanded conception seems sufficiently substantive, broad, and supple to enable us to identify and explain diverse practices across a wide range of contexts, we have reason to be confident that this concept reflects a real grasp of the intelligible structures of human nature as exemplified in diverse conventional forms in many times and places.

To continue with the example of marriage, it seems reasonable to say that whatever other purposes this institution serves, it facilitates the processes of reproduction. In making this claim, we do not rely on supposed observations that all marriages do in fact result in offspring, or that people always marry with the intent of having children, or that there are no other ways to have them — all demonstrably false. Rather, the claim that marriage

---

65. I think Raz is right that a fully developed theory of law would yield some necessary truths — otherwise, we could not identify instantiations of the concept of a legal system in any way that would allow for rational analysis; see Joseph Raz, *Between Authority and Interpretation* (Oxford: Oxford University Press, 2009), 17-90. However, the character of legal systems as partially contingent determinations of universal human practices implies that even though a well-developed theory will yield some necessary truths about these systems, the varieties of credible legal systems will always, so to speak, outrun our conceptual schemes. A fully developed natural law analysis of the core institutions and practices of human life would yield a concept of human nature meeting the Aristotelian ideal of necessary and sufficient conditions; however, it hardly needs saying that any such ideal is out of reach, although it remains as a touchstone for rational inquiry in the biological and social sciences.

serves the natural purpose of reproduction takes its starting point from the much simpler observation that in most of its forms, marriage is understood by the participants themselves, and by society at large, to serve this purpose. Of course, in itself this consensus might reflect some kind of confusion or bad faith, but two further considerations render it credible. Reproduction is a natural purpose, reflecting the inclination of a kind of living creature to maintain its existence over time — and the various forms of marriage that we identify do, by and large, promote this purpose in comprehensible ways, for example, by creating institutional forms conferring public recognition and legitimacy on sexual unions, providing a stable family environment, facilitating the acquisition of sufficient means to raise children, and the like. What is more, the institution of marriage expresses and serves the natural purpose of marriage in a distinctively rational way. It sets up a context in which men and women can deliberate and choose with respect to reproduction — for themselves, or for their dependents. Even more significantly, it provides the necessary framework for the formation of children as recognized participants in a kinship structure, which confers on them the social identity necessary to their full development as rational agents and participants in a shared way of life.

The Natural Law as Grounds for Legitimation

Thus understood, the relatively isolated husband-wife dyad that we often take to represent "traditional" marriage, and dyads embedded in extended kinship networks, and polygamous associations of sexual partners, would all count as variant forms of marriage so long as they function within their context as a framework for bringing forth the next generation in an intentional, socially acknowledged way. It might seem that by the same token, unions which are in some way characteristically non-procreative cannot count as marriages. In our own immediate history, this issue arises most sharply in the context of debates over the possibility of same-sex marital unions. But it arises in other guises in other societies. There was a lively debate in the medieval period over whether a celibate union should count as a genuine marriage or not, and African Christians today are engaged in debate over whether plural marriages are acceptable from a Christian standpoint.[66] It might seem that a natural law

66. For an extended account of these debates, see Dyan Elliott, *Spiritual Marriage: Sexual Abstinence in Medieval Wedlock* (Princeton: Princeton University Press, 1993). Bénézet Bujo offers a

analysis developed along the lines just indicated would require us to rule out both kinds of unions as forms of marriage.

But this would be too quick. The central, comprehensive institutions of human life have developed in complex ways over a very long history, in such a way as to incorporate other purposes in addition to the primary purpose served by the institution. These will characteristically bear some relation to that primary purpose, for example by facilitating it indirectly, or expressing a community's values with respect to some aspect of the practice. In the case of marriage, these associated purposes will include making provision for the decent regulation and expression of sexual desire and maintaining a network of social relations. In addition, and as one expression of the latter purpose, marriage provides a framework for establishing claims for mutual support, personal and financial, and for securing society's recognition of these claims — by enforcing demands for care and sustenance, recognizing that each spouse has a primary right to make health-care decisions for the other, and the like. Finally, marriage serves what many today would regard as the centrally important function of providing a framework for the public expression and support of interpersonal love, yielding what is sometimes described as an ideal of companionate marriage. All these are themselves recognizably natural purposes, even though they will be evaluated and expressed differently in diverse societies. While these purposes are not necessarily connected to marriage as such, we can readily comprehend why a given society would pursue them through the institution of marriage, which inevitably directs and regulates interpersonal sexual relationships anyway, and which can readily be expanded in such a way as to serve a broader range of natural purposes emerging in sexual relationships and other kinds of interpersonal unions. On this view, both same-sex unions and celibate unions can intelligibly be regarded as variant forms of marriage, insofar as both represent novel ways of expanding the natural purposes and potentialities that inform marriage in a given time and place.

This brings us to an important point. Those who engage in natural law discourse, especially within religious contexts, sometimes argue as if the naturalness of a specific institution or practice somehow both validates it and rules out alternatives. As we will see, the analysis of a practice in terms of the natural purposes it expresses does legitimate it, although only in part and provisionally. But this analysis does not imply that alternative arrangements

---

nuanced consideration of the theological issues raised by polygamy as practiced and experienced in some African societies, in *Foundations of an African Ethic,* 34-39.

are unnatural in a pejorative sense. We have already observed that natural principles under-determine the conventional forms through which they are expressed, and this implies that the intrinsic purposes of human life can be expressed through a variety of forms, none of which can be ruled out as contrary to nature. To continue with the example of marriage, it seems clear that this practice serves the purpose of giving some cohesive structure for the stable pursuit of a very basic human function, namely, the reproduction of the species. But that does not imply that our particular construal of this structure is the only one possible. On the contrary, if we started with that assumption, we would be at a loss to identify divergent forms of marriage as all representing variants of one pervasive institutional practice. Nor could we make sense of — or even see — the very considerable changes in our own understanding and practice of marriage over the years, or, more serious still, contemplate reforms of the problematic aspects of the practice. The point of analysis of an institution in these terms is precisely to bring some flexibility to the analysis of conventional practices in natural law terms, so as to enable an appropriate spontaneity with respect to these practices.

At the same time, an analysis of a conventional practice in natural law terms serves one basic yet critical evaluative function, even at this preliminary stage. That is to say, it legitimates the practice in question by construing it as an expression of the innate goodness of human existence itself and an expression of the goods and values intrinsic to our characteristic way of life. By itself, this judgment remains provisional. And yet in certain contexts, we do need to affirm, if only in a provisional way, that a given conventional practice is in itself legitimate, good, and worthy of respect. This is especially so in the contexts of medieval and contemporary theological debates over the significance and value of political and legal institutions. Let me explain.

There seems to be some tendency among serious Christians in every age to identify especially salient forms of sinfulness, which seem so pervasive in human society as to call for principled withdrawal or wholesale condemnation on the part of faithful Christians. In the medieval period, as is well known, the intelligentsia were acutely conscious of the potentially corrupt and sinful possibilities in human sexual experience, so much so that a number of the early scholastic jurists and theologians regarded all sexual activity as at least venially sinful.[67] Since sexual activity is necessary to reproduction, this implies that human existence is in itself and in principle corrupt, and not merely distorted by sin. Leaving all other considerations aside, such a

---

67. For details, see *Natural and Divine Law*, 188-99.

conclusion was felt to be problematic because it is heretical. This realization prompted a re-evaluation of the place of sexual activity, in itself and as pursued within the framework of the institutional norms of marriage, leading to the conclusion that both are legitimate expressions of the innate goodness of human existence, and therefore valid and valuable components of an authentically Christian life.

For many serious Christians in Western societies today, the sinful possibilities inherent in political processes have the kind of salience that the potential corruptions of sex had for our medieval forebears. This contrast should not be over-drawn; men and women in the twelfth century were acutely aware of the potentially corrupting effects of power, and many contemporary Christians remain quite conscious of the ambiguities of sex. Nonetheless, this broad contrast offers a historical perspective on the deep suspicion of political processes and legal institutions that we find among so many thoughtful Christians today. The modern nation-state claims to have a monopoly on the legitimate use of violent coercion, and for many within the churches, that in itself is enough to undermine any claim to legitimacy that it might otherwise possess. I think it is fair to say that most Christians would allow for legitimate uses of coercive violence, given the harsh necessities of life within a society of sinners. Yet many theologians who accept this stance nonetheless regard political institutions and the rule of law as good only in a conditional sense, as serving what we might describe as the ameliorative purposes of preserving peace and rendering justice, to the extent possible in a fallen world. Thus, Oliver O'Donovan claims that since the triumph of the kingdom in Jesus' death and resurrection,

> secular authorities are no longer in the fullest sense mediators of the rule of God. They mediate his judgements only. The power that they exercise in defeating their enemies, the national possessions they safeguard, these are now rendered irrelevant by Christ's triumph. . . . No government has a right to exist, no nation has a right to defend itself. Such claims are overwhelmed by the immediate claim of the Kingdom. There remains simply the rump of political authority which cannot be dispensed with yet, the exercise of judgement.[68]

This stance towards secular political life, associated historically with Augustine and today, in variant forms, with Augustinian theology, pacifism, or

68. Oliver O'Donovan, *The Desire of the Nations: Rediscovering the Roots of Political Theology* (Cambridge: Cambridge University Press, 1996), 151.

Christian realism, is only one strand of thought, but it is today widely influential. Given this context, it is particularly important to affirm, on theological as well as more generally rational grounds, that political life and the rule of law are in themselves legitimate, valid, and worthy of respect, insofar as they serve natural purposes and express the intrinsic goodness of our created nature. Certainly, political institutions and the legal system also serve ameliorative functions as correctives for human sin, which are tethered to natural purposes at one remove, so to speak. Any theological analysis will need to take account of these functions. But I want nonetheless to argue that the ameliorative functions of law and political life generally do not represent their only or their most fundamental justification. They also directly express positive values of human life, serving purposes intrinsic to our created nature. To return to the central argument of the book, the natural relation of authority, considered within and beyond legal contexts, expresses positive human values in a direct way, in addition to its undoubted ameliorative functions in human societies as we know them.

Of course, even at this first level of provisional justification, it is not enough to say that a given social convention is legitimate because it serves natural purposes in some way or other. We presuppose that all social conventions are good in the basic sense that they serve to express some aspect of natural human life. But unless we can specify the purposes served by a given practice more exactly, the bare claim that it is good in this qualified sense cannot provide much of a basis for informed participation and support, to say nothing of social reforms. By the same token, once we do have a plausible account of the specific purposes served by a given social convention, we have the necessary starting points for the kind of comprehensive normative analysis needed in order to argue reasonably that a convention is worthy or acceptable, that it calls for reforms in some ways, or that it represents an unjustified, inequitable, or iniquitous expression of natural principles.

Thus, a natural law analysis offers a framework within which to assess a conventional practice, taken in its concrete forms in a particular society, as a more or less adequate or appropriate expression of the purposes from which this convention stems — multiple purposes, as we noted, which need to be weighed and combined through processes of deliberative judgment. To continue with the example of marriage, we concluded that this institution serves a range of purposes including the obvious one of facilitating reproduction. Which of these is most central or exigent, given the overall structures and the pervasive conditions of human life? How should the others be related to its central purposes (if any) and to one another? Do we risk undermining the central aims of the institution through excessive or inappropriate expression of the other purposes it serves? We can readily understand why modern Western societies, which give a high priority to the personal and erotic elements of the marital relationship, would regard the relation between two independent individuals, who freely enter into marriage and can if necessary leave it, as the ideal form of marriage. By the same token, we are disposed towards tolerance regarding a wide range of non-traditional dyadic arrangements, but we have little tolerance for arrangements which give greater weight to an extended family, and almost none for plural or arranged marriages.

It will be apparent by now why a natural law analysis of a social convention cannot by itself resolve the normative questions that it raises. Even at this level, focused as we are on the diverse purposes served by a specific social convention, we need to engage in processes of comparative assessments and theoretical formulation in order to express these purposes in some concrete, defensible way. These processes will inevitably call for some degree of contingent judgments regarding the relative value and urgency of these diverse purposes. The realism of the Aristotelian account of human nature implies that this contingency will not be unlimited; some natural purposes are more central than others, if the life of the organism and the way of life proper to the species are to be maintained. But even so, a great deal remains undecided, open to resolution by deliberative choice.

What is more, no social convention operates in complete independence of others, or of the overall way of life that these jointly comprise. Each expresses a distinctive, yet partially overlapping configuration of natural purposes, and all are framed by the ideals and commitments that jointly constitute a culture, a dynamic and yet coherent way of life. In order to evaluate our actual practices of marriage in a satisfactory way, much less to reform or develop these, we need to take these wider contexts into account. There is no doubt that marriage in most Western societies once played a greater role in systems of production and consolidation of wealth than it now does. This development has opened up possibilities for personal freedom that few of us would want to surrender, but it also partially stems from, and in turn fosters, broader economic forces that undermine the stability of marriage. Are we satisfied with the trade-offs that we have in fact made, and if not, how should we recalibrate them? More specifically, we give priority to personal choice in marriage because the political morality informing most Western societies gives priority to autonomy and the free pursuit of one's overall happiness.[69] Is this a priority that we want to affirm without qualifications, accepting the tradeoffs with ideals of stability and permanence that we will inevitably have to accept? How should we negotiate the tensions between the freedom of individual partners, and the interests and needs of others, including first of all children, but arguably extending to the family circle and the community as a whole?

Questions are not in themselves arguments, but these serve to illustrate a further point. That is, in our ongoing efforts to assess and to reform our own social conventions, we as a society will inevitably find ourselves making (at least) partially contingent judgments regarding the relative urgency, significance, and concrete realization of diverse natural purposes, seen in the context of the complex affairs of human life. These processes of comparative assessment and formulation, in turn, presuppose some more comprehensive judgment regarding central ideals and the bounds of acceptable behavior, in order to provide a basis for ranking these diverse values and expressing them within a set of acceptable parameters. This is tantamount to saying that deliberative processes presuppose some overall conception of what it means to live a good human life, a life worthy of the kinds of creatures that we are, within bounds set by our commitments to ourselves and to one another. To the extent that we presuppose such an ideal, we will find ourselves articulating it through the processes of assessment and reform of our major social conventions. And to the extent that we lack such an ideal, we will need to develop one, in order to continue deliberating in a principled, reasonable way.

The processes of practical reasoning, on the communal as well as the individual levels, thus move by their own logic towards the formation of some overarching ideal, or at least some sense of the general and expected course of a typical human life, in order to provide a basis for orderly, reasonably coordinated and meaningful choices. Without some such broad organizing standard, at some point it becomes impossible to bring together the diverse aims and activities that inform both individual and communal existence in any sort of principled, coherent way. Admittedly, many men and women go through life without reflecting on its overall structure and point, but individuals can evade this kind of inquiry only because society carries it out on their behalf, providing a complex web of social relations, rewards and expec-

---

69. This point is frequently made; for a clear and sympathetic, yet also critical assessment of the ways in which ideals of individual freedom and personal love have shaped contemporary Western views of marriage, see Don Browning, *Marriage and Modernization* (Grand Rapids: Eerdmans, 2003), 1-54, 155-85.

tations comprising ready-made ideals for human existence. Yet these kinds of pre-fabricated ideal do not work for many individuals, and when the social order itself is in flux, they do not work well for anyone.

At any rate, even if individuals can evade these larger questions, society cannot. We, collectively, need defensible and workable ideals for living if we are to function as a society of reasonable creatures at all. These ideals will themselves be closely tethered to our specific practices and institutions, which provide much of our fund of paradigms for human activities of all kinds, and which already have certain preferences and judgments, as it were, built in. To that extent, these ideals will be local and contingent — our ideals, not the ideals for humanity taken as a whole. Again, we can recognize the contingency of our own cultural ideals without necessarily concluding that they are contingent all the way down. We have already noted that certain ideals of key virtues and social practices, together with broad parameters for acceptable behavior, seem to be cultural universals. What is more, we do have the resources we need to carry out rational self-critique, and to arrive at a broad cross-cultural consensus on at least the outer boundaries of acceptable behavior within the international context — or so I will argue in the next chapter.

Yet important though these kinds of judgments are, they do not amount to a comprehensive and concrete ideal of human existence, which can only be formulated through processes of comparative judgment and valuation with respect to the indefinite possibilities of human life. These kinds of ideals presuppose processes of communal judgment, which are expressed through a community's distinctive culture. These processes are themselves rational, and yet they necessarily involve an element of contingency — they yield what are defensibly construals of human good, but not the only such construals. The formation of culture thus reflects the distinctive hallmarks of authority itself, and that is the key to the analysis of authority as a natural relation. In the next section, I will set out the main outlines of that analysis, in order to indicate in a preliminary way how political and legal authority stem from, and are both justified and constrained by, the natural purposes that they serve.

5. Authority as a Natural Relation: A First Formulation

Authority and the Exigencies of Reason

Both the scholastics and our own contemporaries recognize that an authoritative claim cannot plausibly be equated with either a peremptory order, backed up solely by threats of coercive force, or simply good advice. Someone who exerts authority can be said to compel obedience, but only in somewhat the same way that a moral imperative or overwhelming practical considerations compel action. Yet the one subject to an authoritative decree does not simply give himself the moral law, nor does he follow his own best practical judgments. In this instance, he acts as he does because he has been authoritatively enjoined to do so, even though he may be aware of independent considerations that would have led him to act in a similar way, were he not constrained by some authority.[70]

If we are to develop a persuasive account of authority, we need therefore to explain how it is that some kinds of authoritative relations generate normative power, of such a kind as to bring it about that someone subject to authority ought to act (or refrain from acting) in given ways.[71] This consideration suggests a tentative definition, which can serve to focus our inquiry: Authority is a normative power, through which one agent legitimately requires some performance or forbearance from another, in such a way that the authoritative demand itself constitutes a (normally) sufficient reason for the subject's action. Thus, when someone (or some impersonal agency) places an authoritative demand on another, she determines what the subject ought to do, in such a way that the range of normatively acceptable choices open to him is limited or expanded in a way that would otherwise not be the case. Thus understood, an authoritative decree is always to some extent contingent; an authoritative agent could always have required something different than he actually does. At the same time, the contingent character of an authoritative decree does not imply that it is unjustified. On the contrary, by stipulating that the one subject to authority ought to act in the ways it determines, we imply that these demands can be justified to her as a rational and responsible agent — not necessarily on their own terms, but at a minimum, through offering reasons why she should recognize this agency as authoritative over her in the relevant ways.

In what follows, I will set forth a preliminary analysis of authority as a

---

70. In Raz's terms, an authoritative claim sets up exclusionary and protected reasons — considerations that cannot be overridden, except in limited circumstances; see *The Authority of Law*, 16-19. I prefer this to his subsequent formulation that authority sets up a preemptive reason, that is to say, a reason that not only overrides but replaces relevant considerations, including those which would (otherwise) count in favor of the prescribed course of action. However, in his recent work he qualifies this analysis in such a way as to render it more plausible; see *Between Authority and Interpretation*, 142-47.

71. I take the concept of a normative power from Raz; see *The Authority of Law*, 16-19.

natural relationship, to be developed and defended in the following two chapters. In doing so, I do not mean to imply (what would be clearly absurd) that authority is ever expressed apart from some conventional form. On the contrary, I presuppose that authoritative relationships are always expressed through conventions of some kind. What is more, I presuppose that there would be general consensus on a range of paradigmatic examples of the conventions in question which provide starting points and shared context for further analysis. The state of Indiana has authority over my activities as someone who drives a car, the chair of my department has authority over the courses I teach, my mother has the authority to demand that I provide for her care in some way: as all these examples illustrate, authoritative claims typically emerge within conventionally structured relationships. By the same token, it is apparent that authority is a kind of relationship that is exemplified in many different ways, implying that authority itself may be said to serve pervasive natural purposes which can be identified in many distinct spheres of life, in terms of which it can therefore be analyzed and justified. These are the terms in which I hope to analyze authority generally, and political and legal authority more specifically, in what follows here and in the next two chapters.

This brings us to the question that, as we have just seen, is the starting point for a natural law analysis of any kind of convention. That is to say, what are the natural purposes that this convention — or in this case, this kind of relation, exemplified in diverse kinds of conventions — serves to promote, directly or as a corrective to recurring needs and limitations? Given our reflections so far, especially seen in the light of the kinds of examples just mentioned, it is at least clear that authority emerges out of the exigencies of joint activity and relational actions, as these take shape through the interaction of rational, social animals. That is, authoritative relationships typically emerge in contexts of shared activity, or in contexts in which one's individual acts need to be directed or constrained, in view of the effect that they might have on other individuals or on the community as a whole. The purposes promoted by authority are thus central to our existence as the kind of creature that we most distinctively are, that is to say, agents who characteristically act together, through participation in shared activities and interrelationships structured through rationally intelligible conventions.

It may not be apparent why the exigencies of joint activity and acts carried out in relation to others would, in themselves, generate a need for relations of authority. After all, in very many instances we participate in shared activities, or act in relation to one another, without anyone taking charge to direct and coordinate these activities. No one is in charge in the performances of a good jazz band, and neither my husband nor I exercise authority over the other with respect to joint decisions about the disposition of our income. Yet even in instances such as these, shared activities and interrelationships do presuppose a kind of authoritative determination, if not a formal decree — not on the part of any individual or agency but on the part of the community itself, which has determined the conventional forms within which we act through its customary practices and distinctive culture. These conventions themselves express natural purposes in an indefinite range of ways, but they do so in a contingent way — a jazz band is very different from an orchestra, and the claims and expectations generated by marriage today look very different from the common law practices of coverture.

This brings us to a critical point. That is, some kind of authoritative determination is necessary in every aspect of human life, precisely because the natural principles informing our existence under-determine the practical norms that give them expression. Just as the individual cannot function as a rational agent without some formation in the *habitus* of the moral and intellectual virtues, so the community cannot sustain any kind of shared common life except through processes generating determinate conventions in a reasonable and yet contingent way. In the actual exercise of their active capacities, both individuals and communities will need to make further determinations, in order to apply the mid-level practical norms generated by social conventions or ideals of virtue to specific acts. These kinds of determinations do not always require an exercise of authority, at least not at the level of cooperative activities among individual participants. But the relative indeterminacy of natural and rational principles does open up the needed conceptual space within which authoritative relations are both possible and necessary. If the weight of reasons, taken by itself, could yield one determinate course of action, then we would not necessarily need authoritative decrees, even to coordinate joint activities. In some situations, men and women would simply see what needs to be done, and would do it. Admittedly, we would still need something like relations of authority in order to compel the wicked and to shepherd the young and the hapless, but these relations would not play the pervasive role in our lives that our actual relationships of authority do, nor in all probability would they look much like these.

Authority thus serves the fundamental natural purpose of determining or specifying the principles and reasons informing human action, in ways and contexts within which individuals cannot do so, or cannot effectively do so, either by themselves or through simple agreements. Because this need for specification is so pervasive, and at the same time so integrally tied to characteristically human forms of functioning, we may take this to be the central natural purpose in terms of which authoritative relations are to be analyzed and justified. Thus understood, authority and practical reason, rather than standing in paradoxical tension, turn out to be closely connected and mutually interdependent.

This brings us to a further point. We remarked above that the compelling force of authoritative decrees cannot simply be equated with the kind of force we associate with overwhelming moral or broadly practical considerations. But it now turns out that the force of authority cannot be separated from these kinds of considerations, either. Even though specific authoritative decrees are by definition contingent, and therefore would not be compelling except for the authority behind them, nonetheless authority itself, in some form or other, is necessary if individuals and communities are to attain anything like a fully developed, desirable, and praiseworthy way of life. Authority thus shares in the goodness, the attractive power, and the rational cogency proper to human life as such. That is the only justification that authority as such has, or requires. Men and women spontaneously see that some kinds of authoritative relationships are necessary and desirable, and are drawn to these as integral components of any naturally attractive and satisfying way of life. Of course, the natural value and attractiveness of authoritative relations as such need not extend to particular authorities or their decrees, which may well be onerous, inefficient, corrupt, or just not to someone's tastes. Nonetheless, we naturally recognize the value of having some kinds of authoritative structures — just as we spontaneously realize that marriage in some form or another is a necessary and attractive arrangement, even though we may have reservations about this or that specific form of marriage.

By the same token, it is one thing to acknowledge that authority as such plays a necessary and legitimate role in human life, but something else to acknowledge that some agency legitimately holds authority over me, here and now. Our analysis of authority so far implies that just as authority itself is rationally legitimated, so any specific claim to legitimate authority must be backed by reasons that its putative subjects can and should accept. As we saw in the preceding chapter, Raz dissolves the paradox of authority and responsibility, in part, through the strategy of showing that claims to authority are indeed both grounded in, and in their exercise informed by, broad rational considerations. In later work, he expands on this idea in terms of what he describes as the normal justification thesis, which "claims that the normal way to establish that a person has authority over another person involves show-ing that the alleged subject is likely better to comply with reasons which ap-ply to him (other than the alleged authoritative directives) if he accepts the directives of the alleged authority as authoritatively binding and tries to fol-low them, rather than by trying to follow the reasons which apply to him di-rectly."[72]

Raz is right to call attention to the way in which authoritative decrees are normally formulated in terms of considerations and aims that are in some way reasonably defensible to those subject to the decrees, in terms of beliefs, values, and goals that they already share. This is one of the hallmarks of political authority, which is the paradigmatic instance of an authoritative relationship. Nonetheless, as stated, Raz's normal justification thesis is in one way misleading. It implies that men and women encounter authoritative decrees as mature, fully functioning adults with a well-developed ensemble of independent reasons and goals already in place.[73] This is of course the case in many contexts. What is more, Raz reminds us that someone subject to authority remains an individual, rightly enjoying and pursuing a range of activities as a free and independent agent. At the same time, however, the in-dividual is always, inextricably enmeshed in some community or other, which nurtured her in childhood and sustains her in maturity and decline. Not only does she rely on some community for the material means of life, including security as well as access to basic necessities; she also depends on the community for the full development and appropriate expression of her rational powers, including fundamental capacities for knowledge and ab-stract thought as well as the ability to form practical judgments. This process of formation presupposes some kind of participation in a system of ideas and structures which need not determine the full course of subsequent thought, but which does at least serve as a matrix for the agent's initial for-mation as a rational creature. And in particular, norms for action will neces-sarily be social norms, generalized standards for conduct, in contrast to or-ders or commands imposed by one individual on another, or the practical precepts generated through the autonomous functioning of practical reason. Distinctively human forms of social life are not just expressions of rational-ity, but are themselves preconditions for its emergence, at least in its fullest

72. Joseph Raz, *The Morality of Freedom* (Oxford: Clarendon Press, 1986), 53.

73. I do not believe that this is Raz's overall view. On the contrary, his defense of perfection-ism implies that social structures inevitably enable and limit individual choices, as he says; see *The Morality of Freedom*, 321-66. We will examine Raz's views on the incommensurability of ideals of human flourishing in more detail in the next chapter.

and most adequate forms. Prior to undergoing some such process of formation, the individual cannot be said to have reasons that authority can promote. He may have desires and interests, as infants do, but he cannot be said to grasp, or much less to act on, reasons properly so called.

At the end of the last section, I noted that the communal processes leading to the emergence of distinctive cultures and ways of life can be characterized in much the same terms as we describe authority itself. That is to say, they represent contingent and yet rationally defensible specifications of natural principles. It now appears that this is more than a superficial similarity. The relation between a community and its members is an authoritative relation, one of the few such relations which is in itself strictly necessary to human life. Without the authoritative specification of general natural principles represented by a communally specific way of life, men and women would not be able to function as rational creatures at all –which is to say, the fundamental natural form of human existence would be foreclosed. Thus, the authority of the community over its members is fundamental and foundational. As we will see further on, individuals do as such exercise a kind of authority over others, and over against the community itself. But even this kind of authority is necessarily conditioned, and exercised within the framework of the conventions of one's community, even though it does not depend for its legitimacy and force on the community. In its most paradigmatic forms, authority is intrinsically communal and therefore public.

For the sake of conceptual clarity, we should distinguish between the primal authority of a community over its members, and political authority properly so called, which is exercised by some designated individual or some impersonal agency on behalf of and for the sake of the community. At the same time, however, the primal authority of the community can be said to be a kind of political authority, in the scholastic sense of being consistent with the free status of its subjects. Not only does the political form of communal authority resemble political authority properly so called, but the distinctively political quality of communal authority is itself the ground and justification for political authority. What does this imply, practically, about the character of communal authority itself? As we saw in the last chapter, the scholastics first distinguished political authority from servile dominion by appealing to the purposes served by each; political authority is directed to the good of its subjects or to the community as a whole, in contrast to servile dominion, which directs the activities of the subject towards the good of the master. In itself, this does not seem to be a robust conception of freedom, but we need to keep in mind that the capacity for reasoned judgment and responsible freedom are themselves constitutive elements of human existence. This being so, the authority of a well-ordered community will necessarily provide its subjects with some scope for developing and flourishing as the free, self-determining agents that they are. What is more, since properly human freedom is intrinsically rational, the authority of the community will take the form of publicly accessible reasons for action, on the basis of which men and women can engage as free and rational agents in the shared activities which constitute the ongoing life of the community. Thus, any community in good order, sustaining the lives of its members in an appropriate way and exercising legitimate authority in that capacity, will be a political society, a polity.

The authority of the community over its members will of course be expressed through conventional forms, namely political practices which will be institutionalized in all but the smallest and simplest societies. The specific forms that these institutions take will be to some degree contingent. Inevitably, they will depend for their ongoing functioning and validity on (usually tacit) consensus and acceptance, through which the community generates what Hart would call rules of recognition for valid and binding authoritative decrees. In almost all cases, these rules will be more or less formalized at some point, in order to display their operative principles in a stable, easily accessible way. What is more, the resulting systems of formal norms will distinguish between the validity of authoritative judgments and decrees, and their wisdom, probity, or utility — a necessary distinction if authority is to retain its proper character as a normative power that can override or exclude otherwise relevant considerations. Thus, the relevant rules will operate more or less autonomously of the wider systems of ideals sustaining social life as a whole — more or less, because they are themselves ultimately justified in terms of these social ideals, and serve in their way to express and foster them.

In short, the authority of the community will normally be expressed, *inter alia*, through a formal, more or less autonomous legal system, at least in large-scale and complex societies. Legal authority thus represents one form of political authority and serves the same purposes as every other such kind of authority, albeit in a distinctive and delimited way. In the following two chapters, we will explore the ways in which political and legal authority serve natural purposes in more detail. At this point, however, it may be helpful to set out the broad outlines of a natural law justification of legal authority, seen as derivative from and closely interconnected with the authority that the community holds over its members.

Natural Inclinations and Social Structures

Once again, Aquinas offers a useful entree into the relevant considerations through his teleological account of natural human functioning, set out in terms of the natural inclinations from which our activities stem. As we recall, he gives a central place to the inclinations proper to us as a social animal, through which we spontaneously pursue associations with others and seek an active role in society. Men and women naturally desire each other's company, they care about the regard of their fellows, and they enjoy activities carried out in concert with others. Of course, the natural inclinations towards sexual union and procreation imply associations with at least a few others, and will almost certainly draw the individual in a wider mesh of familial ties. All these associations give rise to, are indeed constituted by shared practices and activities, which themselves can be analyzed and justified in terms of the natural purposes that they serve — the purposes of the individual, and also the purposes intrinsic to human nature in its properly communal forms of expression.

Correlatively, the virtues associated with these practices reflect complex, intertwined ideals for individual action and social practices, mutually informing, constraining, and challenging one another. The ideals informing a society's sense of itself as a decent, admirable, upright community sustaining a worthwhile set of values, and its correlative ideals of individual justice, responsibility, proper patriotism, and the like, offer the most obvious example of the ways in which communal ideals and individual virtues emerge together, reinforcing or sometimes challenging one another. But probably every sphere of human life incorporates some reference to communal as well as individual well-being. Consider, for example, the extended debates current in Western societies about the ways in which a temperate restraint with respect to eating — or the lack of it — can have an impact on communal ideals of sustainable production, familial structures of shared meals, and the proper relation to the wider environment.

The natural activities of individuals and communities thus yield — or better, spontaneously take the forms of — social virtues and legal categories of thought, providing the fundamental structures within which political authority can take concrete shape. Yet considered as the natural forms of human desire and reasoning, these categories are still too indeterminate to guide individual or collective activity in any meaningful way. Ideals of virtue and categories of obligation and harm are indeterminate and must be specified through processes of deliberation, involving, again, an irreducibly contingent element of preferential judgment. What is more, these ideals and norms for action will necessarily be social norms, generalized standards for conduct, in contrast to an individual's commands or her own practical maxims. By no means would I deny that the individual can and should arrive at his own independent judgments with respect to these matters, but even so, rational deliberation of this kind will inevitably presuppose that the individual has been formed in normative categories mediated by his society. He may well transform or even reject the ideals of his society, but without some ordering structure of social norms, he would not be able even to begin an effective process of practical reasoning.

Thus, we need an account of the social processes through which the natural inclinations and values intrinsic to human nature are translated into relatively concrete ideals and behavioral norms. To a very considerable extent, we already have a good idea of what the relevant processes are; they are nothing other than the processes through which distinctive cultures emerge and are sustained in human societies. It is important to keep in mind that this is a dynamic process, within which individuals play an active role. As Parish says,

> Looked at one way, culture is the flow of meaning in social life, but it is a meaning constructed and animated in a community of diverse selves, who voice culture in different ways, not meaning passively received in symbols. These voices, or selves — always social actors — take up culture (from others and experience) and constitute themselves in cultural ways, but as active agents of cultural lives, not simply as passive receivers of cultural tradition. Bound within a social and political structure, people form a community of cultural agents, at times working in concert, but at other moments set discordantly against each other, as they construct lives, and relationships, and aspects of what they know and experience as "reality," by activating and animating shared cultural models in different ways, for different purposes.[74]

Culture, understood in this way as a complex, dynamic, and open-ended set of standards of belief and action, cannot be reduced to practical norms and the ideals governing them, but these play a central role in the wider systems of beliefs and practices sustaining a society. This is clearly indicated by the fundamentally teleological form that culture takes. As Shweder construes it, culture is not just any sort of system of meanings, it is

74. *Moral Knowing in a Hindu Sacred City*, 279.

a system centered around what is "true, good, beautiful, and efficient."[75] What is more, culture thus understood both stems from and responds to the problem generated by the under-determination of human nature, and the need felt at both social and individual levels to give specificity to very general norms in self-reflective and self-directive — or as Shweder would say, self-monitoring — ways. It represents, therefore, a kind of social analogue to the Aristotelian and Thomistic idea of virtue as *habitus,* that is to say, a development of some human faculty in and through reflective choices, through which the agent is able to act in a coherent, directed way.

We come now to a key point. That is, culture as Shweder understands it is integrally connected to law, insofar as law is one of those distinctively human forms of activity (like speech) that manifests the "goals, values, and picture of the world" constituting a culture. By the same token, formal law could not emerge or function outside this context of shared, socially embodied meanings, commitments, and values. This observation might appear to call into question the autonomy of law — and as Rosen observes, it would accordingly be resisted by many Western jurists, who are committed to a view according to which the law "is quite separable from other elements of cultural life."[76] Yet on any showing, the autonomy of law is relative and provisional, as we have already noted. In most Western legal systems, we safeguard the relative independence of law from other spheres of social life, for good reasons having to do with the purposes of formal law itself and the exigencies of the kinds of societies that we inhabit. But these boundaries are themselves motivated by, and embedded within, a broader framework of shared commitments and purposes — and for that very reason, they cannot be drawn too sharply or maintained too rigidly. Fuller suggests as much by his remark that any formal system is sustained through a matrix of shared assumptions and purposes, which serves to head off absurd or self-defeating actions even when these would be formally sanctioned by the system itself.[77] These assumptions and purposes, in turn, are generated by the culture, as Rosen goes on to observe:

> context is crucial: When we hear a court speak of "the conscience of the community," "the reasonable man," or "the clear meaning of a statute," when we watch judges grapple with parenthood as a natural or functional

75. *Why Do Men Barbecue?* 11.

76. Lawrence Rosen, *Law as Culture: An Invitation* (Princeton: Princeton University Press, 2006), 6.

77. Lon L. Fuller, *The Morality of Law,* revised edition (New Haven: Yale University Press, 1969), 148-51, 232-37.

phenomenon, or listen to counsel debate whether surrogate motherhood or a frozen embryo should be thought of in terms of "ownership," we know that the meaning of these concepts will come not just from the experience of legal officials or some inner propulsion of the law but from those broader assumptions, reinforced across numerous domains, that characterize the culture of which law is a part.[78]

Thus, as Rosen indicates, the analysis of culture currently being worked out by cultural psychologists, among others, offers a fruitful way of rendering the purposes and functions of formal law intelligible in terms of a wider context of shared meanings and values. The culture of a society is analogous, on a communal level, to the individual's personal conception of happiness, or more generally, his overall conception of the way in which he would expect or hope his life to go. It provides the cohesive ideals and commitments necessary if the society is to sustain a life as a society, that is to say, a cohesive community of reasonable men and women, and at the same time it generates the practices and institutions which give actual expression and substantive meaning to those ideals. This analogy must be kept in mind if we are to understand the purposes of political and legal authority and their relation to individual virtue.

According to a long-standing tradition, adopted by Aquinas's teacher Albert and ably defended by some of our contemporaries, the law exists in order to render its subjects virtuous.[79] Aquinas himself appropriates this tradition in only a carefully qualified sense (ST I-II 92.1), and we ourselves have good reasons to worry about it. Yet there does seem to be one sense in which this claim is true. As we noted above, the virtues can only develop and function through a process of rational reflection on what it would mean to attain one's proper perfection as a rational agent — that is to say, one's happiness, fully and comprehensively considered. Again, this necessity emerges from the spontaneity of human rationality. The characteristic pursuits and satisfactions of human life must be brought together in some kind of coherent order if they are to be pursued in a consistent and satisfying way, and this order cannot simply be read off from the immanent structures of human functioning, taken by itself. They must be ordered by reference to something

78. *Law as Culture*, 6-7.

79. Albert affirms this view, which he takes from Cicero, at the beginning of his analysis of formal law *(lex)*, in *De bono* V, 2.1. For a good contemporary defense of the same claim, see Robert George, *Making Men Moral: Civil Liberties and Public Morality* (Oxford: Oxford University Press, 1993).

beyond themselves, some standards of reasonableness, meaning and value more comprehensive than the life of the individual — which is to say, by standards constituting a particular culture. Correlatively, insofar as the law serves to sustain and express these standards, it may be said to serve the purpose of promoting virtue — not so much by encouraging virtuous behavior on the part of individuals, or punishing vices, but by sustaining the fundamental structures of meaning without which the virtues could not emerge.

This brings us to a final point. The distinctively human way of life, characterized by reasoned deliberation and responsible judgment, presupposes a distinctively social way of living, informed by its own proper natural values and virtuous ideals. In one way at least, Aristotle has been vindicated: the human person is most fundamentally a political animal, naturally oriented towards the free yet orderly pursuit of common goals. For this reason, a full account of the properly human form of life will give a central place to the polity, that is to say, to a community structured through and sustaining the political activities of its members. This will be the focus of the next chapter.

CHAPTER 3

Political Authority

We began the last chapter with the problem of legal authority — a problem sharpened, although not generated, by the high degree of autonomy characteristic of Western legal systems, taken together with ideals of integrity and independence of the laws implied by that autonomy. What might serve as a basis for legal authority, in such a way as to secure the legitimacy and non-arbitrary character of the law without compromising its integrity? In other words, can we provide an analysis of law that is itself normative and yet leaves the law properly independent of some kinds of normative claims? Or to put the same question in another way, can we offer a plausible account of properly legal, yet rationally cogent, normative criteria? I propose that a natural law jurisprudence offers a promising way of addressing these questions by providing an analysis of the purposes of law, in terms of which we can both vindicate the authoritative status of the law, and begin to identify its proper normative structures.

According to one ancient and still widespread view, the law serves the purpose of restraining evil-doers through force, directly or by way of punitive sanctions. But alongside this view we find another, almost as ancient, according to which law exists to promote the exercise of the virtues. At the end of the last chapter, we saw that this latter view, while easily misunderstood, nonetheless makes a critical point. That is, the law serves to express and safeguard the specific complex of ideals, values, and commitments that bestows cohesion on a community through generating a shared culture and a way of life. On the proposed account, formal law is therefore not just ameliorative, in the sense of providing correctives for the effects of sinfulness. It plays a direct role in sustaining the life of human communities; as such, it expresses and safeguards positive values intrinsic to natural human functioning.

By the same token, legal authority is derivative, insofar as it rests on a more fundamental form of natural authority, namely, the authority of a community over its individual members. The authority of the community, in turn, rests on its necessary role in specifying natural principles of judgment and choice, in and through spontaneous social processes giving rise to a language, a structure of background beliefs and assumptions, shared ideals, commitments, and a rough consensus on the boundaries of behavior, all jointly constituting the conceptual framework necessary for any developed rational thought. This specific framework might have developed in a different way, and it is thus to some extent contingent. Yet it stems from, and can be defended in terms of, rational and natural principles. Considered as an expression of communal authority, it is therefore both reasonable and bounded in its proper exercise. Thus, the authority of the community over its members reflects the seemingly paradoxical quality of contingent reasonableness which is characteristic of authority as such, distinguishing it from advice or exhortation, on the one hand, and arbitrary power, on the other.

Seen in this context, legal authority represents one key way in which the authority of the community is expressed in a self-reflective way, through a system of formalized secondary rules which presupposes, yet goes beyond, the primary rules comprising a distinctive way of life. Thus understood, legal authority rests most fundamentally on the authority that the community bears as an association of reasonable creatures, whose individual functioning as rational agents depends on, and is integrally bound up with, the structured life of the community as a whole. A formal, publicly accessible legal system expresses the community's sense that certain of its practices and commitments are so centrally important, not just as ideals but as presuppositions for a shared way of life, that they call for formal, public expression. Very often, legal rules will be attached to some kind of sanctions, which serve both to safeguard the laws and the commitments that they express, and to underscore the importance of these for the community's sense of its collective ideals. In any case, from the standpoint of the individual, the law thus understood provides a publicly accessible way to participate in social practices of all kinds in a properly rational way, through some reflective sense of the purposes they serve. By the same token, the law offers a framework within which communal commitments and practices can themselves be identified as objects for reflective analysis and possibly reform or rejection.

Thus, legal authority serves the overarching purpose of expressing, promoting, and safeguarding the natural purposes served by the community, as expressed through its authority over its individual members. For this reason, legal authority itself, and the cogency of particular systems and enactments, can only be rationally defended by appeal to natural purposes that the subject more or less shares — purposes that she might freely choose and pursue, appropriate therefore to her status as a free person. In scholastic terms, this is tantamount to saying that the authority of the judge or lawgiver is a political authority. As such, it is tethered to the natural law through the mediation of the commitments and ideals structuring the political community, its shared objects of love, which are constitutive of any true community. This implies further that the ground and proper function of legal authority cannot be separated from its place within ongoing processes of communal deliberation and decision-making through which the community exercises authority at the most fundamental level. These processes, in turn, cannot be understood except through an analysis of what it means to deliberate, and what kinds of arguments and considerations count as legitimate in a properly political context. As MacCormick observes, politics and law, while properly distinct, nonetheless operate in tandem, in such a way that each presupposes and qualifies the other in some respects.[1]

In the first section of this chapter, I begin by tracing some of the ways in which the early scholastics develop these interrelated claims through an account of political authority and the common good. I then turn to a consideration of the ways in which rhetoric functions within this context to identify and formulate the natural purposes in terms of which laws and other kinds of social conventions can be assessed. It might seem that this topic does not merit extensive theoretical analysis, but as I hope to show, a closer consideration of the forms of rational persuasion is vital to understanding the way in which natural inclinations are brought to a level of self-aware appropriation and formulation — the distinctively human way in which we are both receptive to the intelligible structures of our own nature, and spontaneous with respect to these. In the last sections of this chapter, I will turn once again to the questions, and especially the practical challenges, raised by the inevitable plurality of cultural forms and ethical systems. To what extent does this plurality rule out the possibility of cross-cultural ethical assessments, or participation in shared aims and projects? To what extent does it

1. Neil MacCormick makes this point in *Institutions of Law: An Essay in Legal Theory* (Oxford: Oxford University Press, 2007), 182-85. I believe that I would give a more unqualified priority to the political than MacCormick would do, but that is because I understand "political authority" in a more comprehensive sense. I fully agree with him that the legal system in a modern Western-style democracy is, and properly should be, independent of what we might call the formalized political process, tethered to actual institutions of governance and democratic procedures.

undercut our whole-hearted commitments to our own ideals and practices, or shape the way in which we commend these to others? These questions are salient for us, in ways that they were not for our early scholastic forebears. Yet, as I hope to show, they offer unexpected and fruitful resources for addressing them.

1. Reason, Freedom, and Community: The Parameters of Legal Authority

Political Authority and the Common Good

Let us take stock of what we established in the last chapter. Relationships of authority, understood in natural law terms, are natural relations, grounded in and justified in terms of purposes intrinsic to human nature — in this instance, the exigencies of shared practices and cooperative behavior as these are carried out by rational agents. Within this context, authority is tantamount to a claim to determine the concrete meaning of natural and reasonable principles in some relatively definitive way. Political authority is a claim to do so in virtue of one's role as a representative or governor of a community of free men and women, and legal authority is a claim to exercise political authority in view of the more specific purposes of formal law. These kinds of authority may well be regarded as paradigmatic for understanding authority in all its forms, and yet they are not the only forms of authority; the individual likewise enjoys authority in her relations with the community, and with other private individuals, in virtue of her capacities to exercise her *jura*, her rights, stemming (as we will see further on) from her participation as an individual in the eternal law. Nonetheless, the public character of law implies that legal authority as such can only be a form of public authority, grounded in some way in the claims that the community can properly make on its individual members. This suggests that if we are to continue to learn from the scholastics, we might profitably ask how they justified the public authority of the lawgiver.

The short answer to this question is, they do so through an appeal to the common good, well-being, or utility, in order to draw a fundamental distinction between private interests and the communal aims properly pursued by the lawgiver.[2] We observed in the first chapter that Aquinas distinguishes

---

2. This is a familiar point. I develop it at greater length, with attention to a range of scholastic

between political authority and servile dominion on the grounds that the former is exercised on behalf of its subject, or on behalf of the common good, and for him the common good is almost always linked to public authority in some way. Of course, private individuals also should and do act in such a way as to promote the common good, but private action on behalf of the common good is typically understood by reference to the activities of public authority — either by way of contrast, as when Aquinas compares what private individuals can do on behalf of the common good with what public authorities can do (ST II-II 64.3 *ad* 3), or by way of dependence, insofar as legal justice and political prudence in individuals presuppose a right relation to public authorities and to the community as a whole (I-II 92.1; II-II 47. 10-12; II-II 58.7). His views are summed up by his claim that justice (together with prudence) is paradigmatically a kingly virtue, since justice "is ordained to the common good, which pertains to the office of the king" even though he goes on to say that his analysis of regnative prudence would apply to any kind of morally legitimate rule (II-II 50.1 *ad* 1, 2). In order to reclaim the scholastics' distinctive perspectives on political and legal authority, we therefore need to look more closely at their ideas about the common good, paying particular attention to what is distinctive about those ideas.

Today the idea of the common good functions as a unifying ideal and a point of reference for broad traditions of social ethics, especially but not only within Roman Catholic circles. In its most widely influential current form, the concept of the common good stems from modern Catholic social encyclicals and the social ethics tradition which has developed from them. The *Pastoral Constitution on the Church in the Modern World (Gaudium et Spes)*, promulgated by the Second Vatican Council in 1965, provides what has become a classic definition of the term: "Every day human interdependence grows more tightly drawn and spreads by degrees over the whole world. As a result, the common good, that is, the sum of those conditions of social life which allow social groups and their individual members relatively thorough and ready access to their own fulfillment, today takes on an increasingly universal complexion and consequently involves rights and duties with respect to the whole human race."[3]

This definition indicates why the motif of the common good is so dura-

texts, in "The Common Good in Thomas Aquinas," *In Search of the Common Good,* ed. Dennis P. McCann and Patrick D. Miller (New York: T&T Clark, 2005), 94-120.

3. *Gaudium et Spes,* 243-335 in *The Gospel of Peace and Justice: Catholic Social Teaching since Pope John,* ed. Joseph Gremillion (Maryknoll, NY: Orbis Books, 1976), 263.

ble, especially within Catholic circles, while also pointing to its limitations as understood within official Catholic social teachings. It suggests a distinctively theological approach to social issues, which nonetheless is open to other traditions and approaches — as indeed it must be on this interpretation, since it is unlimited and potentially universal in scope, implying "rights and duties with respect to the whole human race." Thus understood, an appeal to the common good underscores the importance of attending to communal and public, in contrast to private goods, and yet such an appeal does not encourage despotic disregard of individual claims and aspirations. On the contrary, because the ideal of the common good is equated with a set of conditions necessary for the fulfillment of all members of society, it gives a central place to equality and sufficiency as norms for social life. But by the same token, the idea of the common good, thus understood, cannot serve as a foundational norm for social reflection. In order to develop this idea into a full-fledged social ethic, we would need first to determine independently what fulfillment as a human being means, and then to resolve hard questions about the access and distribution of the social goods sustaining individual fulfillment.

More recently, David Hollenbach has developed a theory of the common good as a normative ideal, considered in the light of recent work on the social context for rationality and responsible agency. He insists that, given this context, the common good cannot be regarded as purely instrumental or (by implication) reduced to "the sum of those conditions of social life which allow social groups and their individual members relatively thorough and ready access to their own fulfillment." Rather,

the common good of public life is a realization of the human capacity for intrinsically valuable relationships, not only a fulfillment of the needs and deficiencies of individuals. It is true, of course, that social life is necessary to meet a person's needs for food, shelter, familial nurturance in childhood, basic education, the protection of public safety, etc. From one point of view, therefore, these dimensions of the common good are instrumental to the good of the individual. Human beings are vulnerable and needy. But it is also true that eating with others, sharing a home with others, and benefiting from education, intellectual exchange, and friendship are all aspects of a life of positive social interaction and communication with others. They are not merely extrinsic means to human flourishing but are aspects of flourishing itself. This shared life of communication and interaction with others, in all its aspects, is good in itself. This helps explain

why the common good of social life cannot be disaggregated without remainder into the private goods of the people who are members of the society.... The common good, therefore, is not simply a means for attaining
the private good of individuals; it is a value to be pursued for its own sake.
This suggests that a key aspect of the common good can be described as
the good of being a community at all — the good realized in the mutual relationships in and through which human beings achieve their well-
being.[4]

Hollenbach thus points towards a promising way to develop and extend
the scholastic conception of natural law and natural purposes in the light of
recent work on the properly social character of human rational functioning
— just what we need at this point, in order to continue with the analysis begun in the last chapter. At the same time, it is worth noting that when
Hollenbach refers to "the good of being a community," the kinds of communities that he mentions represent what early modern Catholic social
thought, following Leo XIII, described as orders of society and voluntary societies — marriage, institutions of education and intellectual inquiry, and
the like.[5] He has relatively little to say about the overall good of the community considered as a distinctive and cohesive entity, sustained by a shared
culture constituting a comprehensive and stable way of life. He does insist
that "social communication in a democratic polity is itself a constitutive dimension of the shared public life of free, self-governing citizens," giving rise
to non-instrumental values of a distinctive kind:

> These non-instrumental values include the relationships that come into
> existence in public speech, joint action, and shared self-governance. These

4. David Hollenbach, *The Common Good and Christian Ethics* (Cambridge: Cambridge University Press, 2002), 81-82, emphasis in the original.

5. For further details, see the illuminating analysis of Leo XIII's social thought, its background and ongoing influence, by Russell Hittinger, "Pope Leo XIII: Commentary," in *The Teachings of Modern Roman Catholicism on Law, Politics, and Human Nature*, ed. John Witte Jr. and
Frank S. Alexander (New York: Columbia University Press, 2007), 39-75. From the standpoint of
my own theory of the natural law, these orders and associations would more accurately be described as social conventions expressing fundamental human inclinations, in such a way as to give
determinate shape and direction to human activities. For this reason, it is misleading to regard
them as paradigmatically self-contained, self-governing units (although voluntary associations,
especially, often will be). As structured ways of expressing natural human purposes, these orders
place normative constraints on political and legal authority, but they do not typically stand over
against the political community as independent — as it were, quasi-political — entities.

are all dimensions of a kind of freedom that can exist only in a community linked together by bonds of reciprocal solidarity. They are goods that, by their very nature, cannot be enjoyed privately. They exist in the relationships between people talking and acting together, and they evanesce when people fall silent or disperse. The freedom they bring is the power that arises when men and women are free together.[6]

Hollenbach's observation that democratic political processes constitute what is itself an intrinsic good, enabling a distinctive kind of freedom, is timely and important. Yet on this view, the common goods shared comprehensively by all members of a political community is largely, if not completely, identified with participation in political processes, narrowly construed. Thus, it leaves little space to acknowledge and affirm the more comprehensive complex of ideals and commitments, the shared culture, that brings cohesion to any political community and enables its individual members to develop and function as rational agents, participants in a shared rational way of life. This account also suggests that the ideals and commitments structuring a political community, and by implication the cohesiveness of the community itself, are generated by the existence and the operations of the regime: the government creates the polity, in other words. Yet surely it is the other way around. If a particular regime is to bear the authority of the community, it must itself be constituted (perhaps tacitly) by the community, in such a way that the identity of the community can meaningfully be said to antedate, ground, and outlast any particular regime.

Political Virtues and Civic Happiness

At this point, the scholastics can helpfully be brought back into the conversation. Admittedly, they do not offer much in the way of a developed concept, much less a theory of the common good. Nonetheless, when we attend to the ways in which they use this motif, the contexts within which the common good is invoked, and the ways in which these appeals further their arguments, we see that an appeal to the common good functions to tie together certain kinds of considerations in an increasingly focused way. Most importantly for our purposes, the scholastics systematically link the com-

6. *The Common Good and Christian Ethics*, 82, 83.

mon good with certain kinds of virtue — namely, the civic or political, seen in contrast to the theological virtues.[7]

Aquinas, for his part, does not take up this distinction (although he acknowledges that it is legitimate; ST I-II 61.5), but he does offer a suggestive comparison between the common good and the happiness of the individual, the latter of which, as we know from earlier remarks, is comprised of the practice of the virtues, at least in its properly connatural form.[8] Significantly, he does so in order to make a point about the purposes of law. After noting that "law pertains to that which is a principle of human actions, since it is their rule and measure," he goes on to observe that in practical matters, the first principle pertaining to activities and operations is the final end, formally understood as happiness, and therefore "the law depends above all on the order which is in happiness." What is more, "since every part is ordained to the whole as imperfect to perfect, and one human being is a part of a perfect community, it is necessary that the law depends most properly on an ordering to the common felicity . . . for the political community [*civitas*] is a perfect community" (I-II 90.2).

Aquinas does not develop this comparison at greater length, but given the context of his thought it is highly suggestive, because it points to a kind of link between the common good and individual perfection that we might otherwise overlook. That is, it suggests that the connection between the common good and individual flourishing is not simply instrumental, and it implies that neither the claims of the individual nor the needs of the community take precedence over the other in any straightforward way. On this view the community, in and through the distinctive configuration of meaning and value that it instantiates, offers its individual members possibilities and capacities for flourishing as rational creatures which they could not develop or enjoy in other ways. At the same time, the distinctive values of the community can only be realized in and through their attainment by individuals, singly and in relation to one another.

In the last chapter, we saw that Aquinas equates happiness, understood as the ultimate aim of all human actions, with the form of perfection proper to a rational or intellectual creature. He thus moves directly from his analysis of the end of human life, generally considered, to a more focused analysis of

---

7. For further details, including extensive documentation, see Odon Lottin, *Psychologie et morale aux XIIe et XIIIe siècles* (Paris: Louvain, 1949), Vol. 3, parts 1 and 2.

8. I am very grateful to Benjamin Smith for pointing this out to me, and helping me to appreciate the significance of the comparison.

the concept of happiness (ST I-II 2-5). He sets out, first of all, to give objective content to the formal concept of happiness, considered as perfection, and after rejecting various alternatives, he concludes that the object of human happiness, understood in the most unqualified sense, can only be God, who is in a manner of speaking attained through contemplation in the beatific vision (I-II 2.8; cf. I 12.4; I-II 5.5). At this point, it begins to appear that the similarities between individual happiness and communal well-being are limited at best. It is difficult to say what it would mean for a community to contemplate God, to attain an end transcending its natural powers, or — what comes to the same thing — to attain salvation. The individuals comprising a community can do all these things, but unless we are prepared to make very strong claims indeed about the existence of a group mind or a collective consciousness, it would appear that communities as such cannot. What is more, even if we bracket these specific complications, Aquinas's general analysis of happiness as perfection, considered as the optimal development of an individual substance in accordance with the proper potentialities of its form, suggests that the comparison to communal happiness is limited at best. Not only is the community not the kind of entity that enjoys contemplation, or anything else, except metaphorically; a community is also not a substance, and therefore does not possess a substantial form in virtue of which it could attain perfection in the Aristotelian sense.

Yet we can perhaps extend the Aristotelian analysis of perfection to a community in the following way. We have just seen that Aquinas links the idea of communal felicity to the claim that the polis is a perfect community — meaning, in this context, not a flawless or morally impeccable community, but a self-sufficient association of persons, what Shweder would describe as a self-monitoring and self-perpetuating community.[9] Any such association will necessarily consist in something more than an aggregate of persons or even a voluntary or limited association; it will comprise individuals interacting together in stable, ordered ways, participating in a shared way of life. What is more, since we are speaking of an association of animals, these interactions will be largely (although not entirely) comprised of the activities and processes through which individuals pursue and attain the fundamental aims of any kind of life — security, growth and proper development, and reproduction. Because this is an association of social primates, the constitutive interactions of a community will furthermore be the kinds

---

9. Again, see Richard Shweder, *Why Do Men Barbecue? Recipes for Cultural Psychology* (Cambridge, MA: Harvard University Press, 2003), 9.

of interactions proper to social life, which implies that they will be structured in and through individuals' more or less knowing relationships to one another. The interactions structuring a community will, in other words, reflect and embody the form of life proper to the kind of social primate that we are. Even though the community as such is not a substance, it is nonetheless something more than an aggregate of substantial individuals. Considered as a set of dynamic processes and interactions, the community embodies and sustains the ongoing expression of the unified set of goal-ordered capacities that constitutes the soul of a living creature — a mode of expression which necessarily takes the form of interactions among individuals, in accordance with the kind of social animals that we are.

So it appears that we can, after all, make some sense of the idea that a community can attain perfection in an extended, yet plausibly Aristotelian sense of the term. Even though the community cannot attain perfection in the full sense, because it is not itself an individual substance, nonetheless it stems from and sustains the dynamic tendencies of entities that are substances, of such a kind that they cannot attain their individual perfection except in and through structured interactions with one another. By the same token, the happiness of a community will reflect the natural structures and inclinations of the dynamic human form that it represents. This is important, because it implies that the common good itself has a kind of form, a proper structure, grounded in the structured interactions proper to human life as such. Certainly, the common good cannot simply be equated with any kind of collective interest or aspiration, or narrowed down to real but partial aims such as security or material prosperity. Neither can the common good be equated with the sum of the conditions necessary for the full flourishing of its individual members, if only because a "sum" implies an aggregate of goods and enabling conditions, and leaves out the critical point that the common good comprises an ordered way of life, grounded in the dynamic processes natural to human existence.

Grounded in, yet not fully determined by these structures. Otherwise, we would have no way of accounting for the diversity of cultural forms, except perhaps to argue, implausibly, that a genuine common good can only be attained in one specific way. The common good reflects the receptivity of human associations to the natural structures from which they stem, but it must also remain open to rational spontaneity with respect to these. Yet these two considerations actually operate in tandem with one another. After all, the human person is by nature a rational social primate, and the forms of life proper to him will necessarily comprise ways of life in which rational capacities, together with the individual's orientation towards organic and social goods, can develop and find expression. How does this observation qualify our conception of the common good?

We can take a further cue here from Aquinas's analysis of what it means to attain happiness, considered as the perfection of a rational creature. I mentioned above that Aquinas holds (as we would expect) that happiness in the most proper sense can only consist in the direct contemplation of God in the beatific vision. Subjectively, this represents the highest possible kind of perfection proper to a rational or intellectual creature — so much so that it exceeds the natural capacities of any created intellect, and can only be attained through operative principles of grace and illumination directly bestowed by God. But in addition, as we have noted in the last chapter, Aquinas also acknowledges the existence of a kind of happiness that is connatural to the human person, considered as a rational creature. More specifically, the characteristic human form of happiness, of a sort that can be attained through the appropriate development of our natural powers, consists in the sustained practice of the acquired virtues (ST I-II 5.5; cf. I-II 62.1, 109.2). The virtues are not merely instrumental to the attainment of connatural happiness, therefore; rather, the practice of the virtues is constitutive of the life of happiness in its natural, properly human form. This is so, precisely because the virtues are perfections. That is to say, taken singly they represent the fullest possible development and exercise of the discrete faculties of the human agent, and operating in tandem they comprise the perfection of the rational agent, that is to say, its happiness. At the same time, however, Aquinas does not sever all connections between the practice of the virtues and the pursuit of the more fundamental components of a naturally good human life. Rather, the virtues are dispositions through which the relevant desires and capacities of the human agent, as these are naturally directed towards the pursuit and enjoyment of the many components of organic well-being, are oriented towards rational and appropriate operations. It is easy to focus on Aquinas's emphasis on the ways in which the virtues bring rationality to our diverse desires. It is important to remember, in addition, that in order to count as perfections of the relevant capacities, the virtues must also preserve and even strengthen the agent's orientation towards the natural goods, without which human life could not be sustained or developed.

What does any of this have to do with the common good? Our reflections on happiness, perfection and the practice of the virtues took their starting point from Aquinas's analogy between individual and communal happiness, considered as the architectonic final end of the individual and the lawgiver, respectively. The Aristotelian/Thomistic conception of happiness as perfection, that is to say, the fullest development of one's natural capacities as a specific kind of creature, suggests that this analogy may extend further than we might at first have assumed. Even though a community is not as such a substance, and therefore has no form of its own to develop and express, it does embody the structured operations and activities in and through which a certain specific kind of animal — our kind — develops and exercises its proper potentialities. Nor should this communal process of embodiment be understood as if it were simply the sum total of innumerable individual activities and interactions — rather, precisely because it comprises structured relationships and shared practices, the community provides the necessary framework within which the activities and interactions natural to social animals like ourselves can take place. In this way, a community functioning in good order manifests distinctively human forms of perfection in a more complete way than any individual could do, and for that very reason, participation in communal life is itself a fundamental natural aim of human life.

This comparison further suggests that just as we can speak of communal happiness in an extended, yet legitimate sense of the term, so we may be able to speak of a kind of communal virtue, or virtues, considered as being in some sense perfections of the form of life embodied by the community. The claim that the common good presupposes virtue on the part of its individual members is familiar, of course, as is the more general idea of civic or political virtues, which have the well-being of the community as their proper object. The claim that the community could itself be a proper subject of the virtues, and not only an object or condition for their exercise, seems initially harder to understand, because once again a community does not seem to be the kind of entity that could develop and exercise virtues. Yet the closely related idea of virtues proper to an institution is familiar from contemporary political philosophy and jurisprudence. Justice is the first virtue of social institutions, according to John Rawls, whereas Ronald Dworkin identifies equality of concern as the foundational ideal, the "sovereign virtue" of political communities and institutions.[10] Of course, neither Rawls nor Dworkin believes that communities and institutions acquire and express virtues through the medium of some kind of subjectivity. They equate the

---

10. See, respectively, John Rawls, *A Theory of Justice* (Cambridge, MA: Harvard University Press, 1971), 3, and Ronald Dworkin, *Sovereign Virtue: The Theory and Practice of Equality* (Cambridge, MA: Harvard University Press, 2000), 1-7.

virtues they identify with the proper ordering and functioning of the relevant institutions and social processes, in such a way as to express, sustain, and promote ideals of justice or equity. Yet this approach would seem to be quite consistent with a conception of the happiness of the community, considered as the ongoing embodiment and development of the kind of social life that is specifically characteristic of humankind.

In this sense, we can speak of the common good as the object of a virtue, namely, the virtue that the community possesses when it is functioning in good order, in such a way as to express and foster an appropriate expression of a distinctively human form of social life. Correlatively, the common good, understood as the communal expression of a distinctive set of ideals and shared purposes, provides an object for individual virtue, or more exactly, for a related set of virtues, through which the individual identifies herself with, participates in and promotes these ideals and purposes. Thus understood, the common good is more or less equivalent to what Dworkin describes as the political morality underlying legislation and adjudication — with the important proviso that Dworkin does not appear to entertain the possibility of deep substantive differences among the defensible political moralities of diverse communities.[11]

Common Good, Cultural Ideals, and Social Norms

This brings us back to what has so far been a recurring issue. I mentioned that the common good is attained when a community expresses and fosters an appropriate expression of our nature as social animals. But what counts in this context as appropriate? We have many times noted that the diverse communities of the world exhibit irreducibly distinct ideals and ways of life. Surely it is not plausible to say that any one of these should be regarded as *the* optimum, or much less the only legitimate shape that human social life can take. And if this is so, then how can the idea of the common good, considered as an object of communal and individual virtue, offer any kind of normative purchase on matters of social policy? At best, what we seem to have here is a highly abstract formal principle which must be filled in from elsewhere in order to be applied in any concrete way.

Certainly, the ideal of the common good cannot simply be equated with

---

11. Admittedly, this way of reading Dworkin would be controversial; we will look more closely at his conception of political morality in the next chapter.

any of the specific configurations of values comprising the cultures of diverse societies. Yet even so, this ideal is not simply an abstraction, offering no purchase on normative judgments in concrete cases. We can give it some content by reflecting further on the claim that communal life embodies the ongoing expression of distinctively human forms of social existence. This claim, by itself, does not go so far as to point to one communally specific expression of human social life, to which all other communities must aspire. But it does suggest that all such candidates for an authentic common good will exhibit certain features, determined by the exigencies of human existence and happiness. And these commonalities, while they can be expressed in a wide range of ways, are not consistent with any and every kind of human association or set of conditions. As such, they provide a limited yet genuine starting point for developing a substantive conception of the common good, one which can meaningfully be applied within a range of diverse cultures and which can also provide a plausible basis for critical assessments within and even across the boundaries of specific cultural traditions.

One such commonality is suggested by prior observations on the relation between virtue and the pursuit of the natural goods of human life. The ideals constitutive of the common good cannot simply be equated with the pursuit and enjoyment of human well-being, not even the collective well-being expressed by such standards as common utility or shared wealth. Rather, just as the virtues are expressed in and through the pursuit and enjoyment of basic human goods in a particular, rationally informed way, so the ideals constitutive of the common good in a well-ordered community must at least be plausible ways of configuring and sustaining the fundamental operations and activities proper to the human person, considered (first of all) as an animal of a certain kind. To put the same point in another way — in whatever way these ideals are constituted, they must at least sustain, and be plausibly embodied by, what are recognizably variants of the fundamental activities of human existence. They must be grounded in, and supportive of, such basic, ordinary pursuits as eating and drinking, pursuing and maintaining sexual partnerships, offspring, and kinship systems, and engaging in productive work to sustain these activities. What is more, a community in good order will provide its members with sufficient security and support to sustain these activities, at least for most parts of the community, functioning under normal circumstances.[12]

---

12. I am especially indebted here to Henry Shue, *Basic Rights: Subsistence, Affluence, and U.S. Foreign Policy,* 2nd edition (Princeton: Princeton University Press, 1996), 13-34.

It may appear that these criteria are so general, and at this level so obvious, as to be banal. And when a community is fortunate enough to be functioning in reasonably good order, men and women do enjoy the luxury of taking for granted that they will have some possibilities for participating in the fundamental operations of a properly human form of life — to live, to sustain one's life through productive activities, to form sexual partnerships and rear offspring, and the like. These may not be ideal possibilities, they may be too restricted or limited or even unfair, but so long as a community is sufficiently well-ordered to function as a self-sufficient association of human beings, some such possibilities will be open, at least for a significant segment of the population.[13] By the same token, when these possibilities are foreclosed or break down on a broad scale, it is apparent that something has gone wrong. Customary practices, formal laws, or institutional forms that once sustained viable forms of life can now no longer do so, or perhaps changed circumstances have magnified the bad effects of previously tolerable flaws. In many cases, the relevant judgments will imply no condemnation of earlier practices, beyond simply acknowledging that they are no longer workable. But in some instances, we may well find ourselves making stronger claims — that a given set of social norms is so clearly contrary to the ongoing natural well-being of the community that we can and should reject it out of hand, and that the failure to do so constitutes grounds for reproach.

Thus, this distinction offers us at least a rough and general, yet centrally important criterion for distinguishing among and evaluating a wide range

13. This raises the difficult question of whether a genuine common good can be attained in a society that relegates a significant portion of its population to what would be, in name or effect, a kind of servitude — a condition in which one's activities are coercively directed towards the aims of others, or of society as a whole. In my view, the ideal of the common good, understood in the light of a sound conception of human nature, is inconsistent with servitude of this kind, although it is not inconsistent with every kind of social inequality. For reasons to be spelled out in the last chapter, I believe that this ideal can be, and in fact increasingly is, persuasive among the peoples of the world. Yet it is undeniably the case that it would not have been persuasive in most times and places until relatively recently. Until the modern period, nearly all societies included institutions of slavery or servitude of some kind, and yet it is difficult to deny that they typically attained limited and flawed, yet genuine forms of a common good. Indeed, it is difficult to see how any society, however morally ambiguous it may be in some respects, could sustain itself over time unless it did attain the minimal common good of self-regulating existence, sustained by a shared culture. On theological grounds, we should perhaps not be surprised that even relatively successful human communities are flawed by sin — but on the same grounds, we must nonetheless affirm their fundamental goodness and value as expressions of human existence, while also working to bring about substantive social change where needed.

of practices and enactments, within and among diverse communities. A set of social arrangements within which individuals can live, pursue a secure livelihood, and form stable families, may well appear from a Western perspective to be inequitable or unjust in all kinds of ways, but so long as it offers a framework within which men and women can live in a recognizably human way, it cannot be ruled out as a legitimate and worthy expression of the natural goodness of humankind. But a way of life that undermines human life at this level is at the very least problematic. At any rate, it cannot be defended as an expression of the culturally specific values of a community. No community can sustain (supposed) values that undercut its very existence and orderly development indefinitely. Still more to the point, such "values" cannot meaningfully count as human values, expressions of the distinctive modality of goodness embodied by human existence.[14] By the same token, this distinction offers a criterion for a different, yet closely related set of judgments — between legitimate regimes, laws, and policies, which are at least defensibly directed towards the common good of the community, and those enactments and policies which are manifestly directed towards the good of the ruler, or of some distinct sect or class within the community. In other words, it enables us to distinguish in a persuasive way between legitimate political authority, appropriate to the rule of free persons, and diverse forms of tyranny, and to head off the argument that what are manifestly self-serving acts and policies should be accepted as legitimate expressions of cultural diversity.

So far, we have focused on the common good, seen in relation to those activities that sustain human life at its most basic animal level. It is vitally important to keep the exigencies of the common good at this level in mind, because unless these are secured, nothing else of any lasting or genuine value can be attained. At the same time, however, the scope of the common good goes beyond sustaining human life at the level of well-being — just as the dispositions and practices of virtue are integrally connected with, and yet cannot be reduced to, the pursuit of individual well-being at the organic level. In addition, the common good as it is embodied in a particular community will also comprise a set of ideals, expectations, and values, through which the community expresses its collective ideals of truth, goodness, beauty, and efficiency. These judgments and ideals cannot be detached from the more basic exigencies of organic human life. On the contrary, they will

---

14. This point is developed in a very illuminating way by Daniel Bell, *Beyond Liberal Democracy* (Princeton, NJ: Princeton University Press, 2006), 52-83.

be comprised, largely if not entirely, of ideals about the best, the most comely or satisfying, the most efficient, or at least the defensible ways in which men and women should live, support themselves, come together in sexual partnerships, and the like. At the same time, the relevant judgments will also be informed by some overarching sense of the proper structures of human life and cosmic order, together with judgments about the realities and values transcending these structures. In other words, they will incorporate what Shweder refers to as some sense of the divine — which may be very different from, or even opposed to familiar theological conceptions. To the extent that these transcending ideals are emphasized, the common good of a particular community will be seen, more or less explicitly, as an exemplification of or point of access to some overarching value, in terms of which the community itself, and its individual members, derive a sense of ultimate purpose and worth.

At this level, the common good of a particular community, objectively considered, is equivalent to its culture, understood in Shweder's sense as a socially embodied set of value judgments about what is good, worthwhile, or simply workable. Subjectively considered, that is to say, as an appropriate target for individual respect and pursuit, the common good in a given community will be understood in terms of the individual's best understanding of the values at stake, and it will give rise (in a well-disposed person) to love and admiration for the values for themselves, and for the community insofar as it embodies and expresses these. At the same time, however, the ideal of the common good cannot be altogether detached from the fundamental well-being of the human population comprising a particular community. We have just noted that in order to count as such, an ideal of the common good as instantiated in a particular community must be a plausible, livable ideal for structuring the organic activities proper to human life — a set of dispositions directed towards pursuing these activities in a specific way, therefore, rather than a set of ideals detached from, or worse, antithetical to the values of ordinary human existence. What is more, the common good considered at this level is grounded in the exigencies of natural human life in a further way. That is, the common good considered as the idealization of a culture reflects the way of life natural to us as social primates, whose functioning reflects both immersion in a complex social network and a high degree of spontaneity vis-à-vis both society and the broader natural context.

We need here to recall the conclusions of the last chapter. In order to function as social primates and especially in order to develop and exercise rational judgment, a human agent needs to be both formed and sustained in the norms and practices of a particular community. No adult can function without some sense of his place in the complex web of roles and expectations that structure his immediate social world — even if he chooses to opt out of it or to define himself over against it in some ways. What is more, the exigencies of practical judgment themselves require a framework of judgments regarding the relative worth and proper ordering of at least some broad categories of desiderata — some judgments, for example, regarding whether it is more worthwhile or important to maintain freedom of action or to preserve social bonds. Without some such structure, the individual could not even begin to make the kinds of comparative assessments that she must make on a daily basis, in order to make real choices among the diverse and incommensurable goods and values of life. Again, once an adult has the structuring framework of her society in possession, so to speak, she can then go on to modify it or even to jettison it. But without the starting points provided by some initial set of practical judgments, she would be unable even to begin the rational processes of ordered judgment and systematic, self-reflective scrutiny. In each instance, receptivity to the givens of one's culture provides the necessary tethering, in the form of starting points and structures of coherence, for rational spontaneity — even vis-à-vis these givens themselves.

This line of analysis confirms Cicero's claim that the common good of a particular community, subjectively understood in terms of its idealized sense of the values embodied in a particular way of life, constitutes it as a true republic, a polity within which free men and women can join together in shared deliberation, fruitful debate, and communal activities of all kinds. We might also regard them, in Augustine's terms, as the shared objects of love constituting a commonwealth, a city.[15] Once we appreciate this point, we can more readily appreciate the insight behind the distinction — admittedly, overly simple as it was typically formulated — between political and theological virtues. Here is an explanation of the distinction by the early-twelfth-century theologian Simon of Tournai:

> What are the kinds of virtue? There are two kinds of virtue, which are distinguished by their duties and ends. For if a quality constitutes the mind in such a way as to carry out political duty for a political end, it is said to be a political virtue. By this means, citizens, even unbelievers such as Jews

---

15. See, respectively, *De Republica* 1.25.42 and *De Civitate Dei* 14.28. This is not the place to enter into an exposition of Augustine's political theory, but I believe he is in fact closer to Cicero on this point than he realizes.

or pagans, are said to have virtues, if their minds are so constituted by a firm resolve directed toward the carrying out of incumbent duties in accordance with the institutes of their homeland, for the purpose of preserving and building up the republic. And political virtue is so called from a "polis," which is a multitude or a city, because it is approved by the judgment of the multitude or the city, granting however that it is insufficient for salvation. But Catholic virtue is that which establishes the mind in a firm resolve to carry out Catholic duty for a Catholic end. By this means, the faithful are said to have virtues, if their minds are so constituted as to carry out their duties in accordance with the institutes of the Catholic religion, ultimately on account of God, that they might enjoy him.[16]

We see here an echo of the two loves, which, as Augustine tells us, have built two cities, the earthly and the heavenly. But unlike Augustine, Simon identifies the love animating political virtue in positive terms: it is not self-love, but love for the commonwealth, out of which men and women are motivated to act in accordance with its laws, in order to promote its well-being. By the same token, the qualities stemming from this orientation are said to be genuine human virtues, even though they are admittedly not sufficient for salvation.

It is worth emphasizing once again that the common good, thus understood, is not merely an instrumental good. On the contrary, the dynamic structure of reasonable and equitable interactions, informed by the ideals that constitute the "shared objects of love," the culture or ethos of a given community, and embodied in its customs, practices and institutions, is good in itself. It reflects the inherent goodness of the dynamic form of human existence which it embodies and sustains. More specifically, it embodies the values characteristic of the specific culture in question. By the same token, participation in these structures, provided that it is informed by reflective understanding and approval of the values they instantiate, is itself a great good for the individual — indeed, one of the greatest of the purely human goods that we can attain. By taking part in the ongoing life of her culture in a knowing, whole-hearted way, the individual exercises and perfects her own natural capacities to act as the rational, social creature that she fundamentally is. She acts in accordance with her own proper principles of action, namely, reason and the capacity for self-determination; she participates in a network of communal relations, within which she enjoys a secure and re-

16. This is taken from the Latin text excerpted by Lottin in *Psychologie et morale*, 106-9, 107.

spected place; and she identifies with and contributes to communal values which will transcend and survive her as an individual. By doing so, she perfects her capacities for social existence by exercising the properly political virtues, which have the good estate of the community as their proper object. Moreover, since the common good comprises a set of ideals for the proper ordering of human life, the individual who participates wholeheartedly in the common life of her community will practice a wide range of properly human virtues as a matter of course — not perfectly, to be sure, but nonetheless in a genuinely good way.

Communal Well-being and Individual Freedom

These considerations bring us back to the fundamental questions we are exploring. What is the ground of political and legal authority, and how is this to be distinguished from other kinds of dominion and power? Recall that for Aquinas, a properly political form of authority (as opposed to the kind of dominion exercised over slaves) turns on the orientation of political authority towards the good of the subordinate, or the common good. That is why political authority does not compromise the freedom of those who are subject to it. On the contrary, to the extent that it promotes the common good, political authority serves and promotes the proper aims of its subjects, insofar as the latter are presumed to desire and to seek their proper good, their happiness. It now appears that the common good is itself a key part of individual happiness, because it is both the object of a virtue, and a condition for sustaining virtuous practices in every sphere of life. So much can be found in Aquinas's own political theory, or so I believe. We now turn to an earlier point, which Aquinas does not develop at length, but which is nonetheless critical to understanding how political authority stems from the life of a particular community.

That is — political authority is appropriately exercised over *free* men and women. What do we mean by freedom in this context? It cannot mean freedom from any kind of authoritative restraints, since that is just what political authority itself provides. More fundamentally, an ideal of freedom as independence from all constraints is ultimately incoherent. As we saw in the last chapter, human action presupposes some kinds of orderly structures, both of judgments and of purposes. These structures will inevitably constrain and limit individual choices in some way, even though they are fundamentally enabling and in that way freeing. Paradoxical though it may sound, we are free agents because we are constrained in various ways — constrained by the ways in which our mind and sensibilities have been shaped by the community in which we live, through education and formation in a language, a set of theories and values, a way of life. Certainly, mature men and women can detach themselves from these structures in such a way as to critique and revise them or perhaps to move into another such set. But without the coherence provided by a culture, with its limitations and possibilities, we could not even begin the reflective processes necessary to such a critique.

Aquinas suggests (without developing) a more persuasive ideal of political freedom when he links political authority to the aims of the individual who is subject to governance. The point I want to underscore here is that political authority is compatible with freedom, because even though it is directed towards the common good, it nonetheless stems from, and ultimately serves, the aims of the individuals who are its subjects. That is to say, those who are subject to political authority are enjoined to act for reasons that they can recognize and affirm as their own, or at the very least, as reasons that they could plausibly make their own. The exercise of political authority thus does not compromise the status of its subjects as rational agents, agents who are free precisely in virtue of, and through the exercise, of rationality. On the contrary, when it is functioning in good order, political authority both presupposes and promotes the rational freedom of its subjects.

Does this mean that political authority, in and through its promotion of the common good, promotes the freedom of its subjects by constraining them in ways that they should accept — whether they actually do, or not? To some extent, this is indeed the case. Otherwise, we would have no grounds for establishing the coercive and punitive functions of political authority, which is obviously exercised over individuals whose aims are at odds with the commonwealth. Nonetheless, taken as a general construal of political authority, this line of analysis would lead to the affirmation of an idealized general will or, worse, to a totalitarian state that enslaves and kills its own people in order to free them for ideals that they should want to embrace. We have seen more than enough of such polities over the past century, and a theory of authority that lends support to such regimes is surely not credible.

The account of political authority that I propose does not carry these implications. On the contrary, it implies a set of constraints on the kinds of ideals that political authority can promote, and the forms of coercion that it can employ. The key point here is that political authority promotes aims that its subjects can accept as their own precisely as rational human agents, acting in pursuit of the natural goods that are constitutive of the natural course of a human life. This is the critical respect in which political authority, and the rationality that it embodies, is receptive to and constrained by the natural structures inherent in human nature itself. A putative political authority that attempts to do away with these constraints undercuts its own legitimacy, and may well undermine the minimal consensus without which no society can function over any period of time.

What this means, practically, is that political authority, so long as it is functioning legitimately and in good order, will necessarily be informed by the *sensus communis* — not in every respect, but at least to a considerable degree. It will stem from the community's sense that certain ways of life and common objects of human desire are good, worthwhile, praiseworthy, or attractive in the light of natural considerations that individuals can regard as actually or potentially persuasive to them. For just that reason, the subjects of political authority will be able to grasp the point of its enactments and to interpret and follow these intelligently, in the way proper to rational agents — in contrast to the kinds of rote and mechanical observance exhibited by slaves or the subjects of totalitarian rule.

This brings us to a further sense in which the kind of authority that is compatible with freedom is properly political in form. That is, not only does the authority in question respect the natural aims of its subjects; it is also grounded in, and continually constrained by, communal processes of practice and deliberation through which these aims are formulated and appropriated by the community itself. Understood in this way, political rule is thus described not only on account of its orientation towards the good of those ruled, but also on account of its tethering to some kind of deliberative process — to politics in the everyday sense. Political processes are important precisely because they mediate, however imperfectly, between the practices, institutions, and laws of a given society, and the collective sentiments and judgments that inform the practices of the community and come to be formulated in public debate. In and through these processes, the free subjects of political authority participate actively in the formation of the norms through which they are governed — in the first instance, through generating and sustaining customary practices, and then through ongoing processes of communal discernment and decision-making. Correlatively, through participating in deliberative and decision-making processes, men and women actively appropriate the purposes to which enactments are directed, precisely because they have played some part in formulating these.

By no means are the relevant practices limited to the forms of Western democracy. Nor will they necessarily always be formalized, or even open to

the equal participation of all subjects. As John Rawls points out, there are societies that organize their common life around associational groupings,
which represent the interests and claims of their individual members
through what he calls a decent consultation hierarchy. In such a society, individuals may not enjoy formal equality or general access to public processes,
but they are protected, and given scope for influence, through their mem-
bership in the associations which are the central actors in public life.[17] So
long as these associational groupings provide their members with opportunities to participate in reasoned deliberation, and to exercise effective influence in the community through the mediation of the group, the society may
be said to be a genuinely political society of free men and women.

Once again, we see that the common good as instantiated in a particular
community is tethered to the distinctive ways in which that community embodies natural human goodness, with its own particular construals of what
it means to live a worthy human life in relation to some wider context of
meaning and purpose. No society can achieve any kind of genuine common
good apart from local processes of deliberation and decision-making in accordance with its own accepted practices and norms, which may be different
from Western norms and practices. Not only is there no other effective and
secure means towards social change; this process is also itself an intrinsic
component of a common good, and to short-cut it is precisely to undermine
the common good. By the same token, insofar as legal authority stems from
the lawgiver's orientation towards the common good, it can only be exercised in and through the contingencies of a particular society. This brings us
back to a consideration of customary practices and laws, seen as the mediating structures through which the natural law in its most basic sense is specified by social norms and by formal legal enactments.

17. See John Rawls, *The Laws of Peoples* (Cambridge, MA: Harvard University Press, 1999),
62-88 for the development of this idea. For an extended contemporary example of associational
societies, emphasizing the plurality of ways in which power is diversified and expressed through
various groupings, see Lawrence Rosen, *The Culture of Islam: Changing Aspects of Contemporary
Muslim Life* (Chicago: The University of Chicago Press, 2002), 3-74. Similarly, Bénézet Bujo shows
how the African process of the palaver can serve to represent the interests and views of the diversity of associational groupings in *Foundations of an African Ethic: Beyond the Universal Claims of
Western Morality,* trans. Brian McNeil (New York: Crossroad, 2001), 45-74. Hollenbach, in contrast, seems to believe that the common good is only attained, or at least only fully attained,
through processes of Western-style democracy; see *The Common Good and Christian Ethics,* 77.

2. Public Reasons and Persuasive Rhetoric

Political Authority and Justification

By now, it is apparent that political authority can only function appropriately and effectively through ongoing processes of justification, by which reasons for public actions are formulated and then defended through public deliberation. So much is implied by the claim that a properly political authority operates in such a way as to preserve the freedom of its subjects. Whatever else this may mean, it implies at least that the enactments of public authorities can be defended to their subjects in terms of reasons and purposes that they can recognize as plausibly their own. *Plausibly* their own, because in any complex society, not everyone will share in or endorse the reasons and purposes furthered by specific enactments; but at least these must be persuasive enough to secure general recognition that they reflect defensible ways of pursuing decent ends, even if these are not attractive or compelling to all. Plausibly *their own,* however, because even though the free subjects of political authority will not necessarily accept the justifying reasons for every specific enactment, they must at least be able to recognize these as imaginable reasons for themselves, seen in relation to their actual aims and circumstances. *Plausibly their own,* finally, because in a political society in good order, most people, most of the time, will have played some effective role part in shaping the practices and formal enactments by which they live, in such a way that these will express their actual commitments and values — reasons that are in fact, and not just potentially, their own.

This, I believe, is the key point being made when the scholastics (and others) claim that the community is itself a bearer of authority, and is as such the agency conferring authority on its public officials. Political authority properly so called is exercised by individuals or institutional agencies empowered to act on behalf of the community through the relevant rules of recognition. At the same time, however, the proper authority of the lawgiver or other public official is justified and constrained by its relation to the authority of the community, as expressed in its overall way of life. These practices and enactments, in turn, cannot simply be identified with the deliberative choices of the community's individual members, even taken in the aggregate. Yet they could not take shape or continue in operation without the ongoing active participation of these men and women, whose individual judgments and choices may be said to be mediated to the lawgiver through these structures.

At the most fundamental level, the practices of a society will emerge out of the spontaneous and largely unconscious processes giving rise to distinctive forms of activity, leading on to the formation of accepted customary practices and institutional forms, all comprising a culture, a more or less coherent way of life. But as Hart reminds us, almost all communities will find it necessary at some point to develop a formal system of rules, drawn from the primary rules of the community but expressed in such a way as to confer a distinctive force and stability. The processes in question may very well take the form of what we would recognize as a formal legislative process, whether carried out by an individual enacting laws in accordance with accepted form or by a legislature of some kind. But this is by no means always the case, and at any rate, legislative practices and institutions do not just come into existence, fully formed, out of nowhere; they take shape over time, through processes that we can very often trace, processes which leave no doubt about the contingency of the corresponding rules of recognition.

The close connection between authority and justification in political and legal contexts suggests that in this sphere of human life, at least, we cannot distinguish sharply between criteria for rational validity and the requirements for effective, persuasive discourse. An account of validity in the processes of political reasoning needs to include some inquiry into the kinds of reasons that actually persuade, together with an analysis of the force, the scope, and the limits of these persuasive considerations. This claim is likely to strike some as wrong-headed. It is difficult to deny that men and women are very often unmoved by what are objectively very weighty considerations indeed, being swayed instead by trivialities. These experiences suggest a sharp distinction between the valid and the persuasive: the former expressing the theoretical, necessary, and unconditionally cogent implications of rationality itself; the latter expressing considerations that are particular, concrete, hostage to some extent to contingent circumstances, and persuasive, or not, depending on the acuity and good will of one's interlocutors.

Certainly, any adequate account of reasoning, whether practical or otherwise, will need to distinguish between good and bad reasons, valid and invalid forms of argument, and the like. Yet granting this, we may still question whether, in political contexts, the distinction needs to be drawn quite so sharply, or spelled out in just this way. Once we grant that the laws appropriate to a community of free people must not only be reasonable but also broadly accepted as such, then it becomes apparent that we cannot separate questions of validity and persuasiveness so sharply. If a community is to preserve its actual political character as a deliberative and self-determining association, then the reasons that it judges to be valid will depend to some extent, and in some ways, on what its members regard as genuinely persuasive; in this qualified sense, validity depends on persuasiveness. For this reason, there has been a renewed interest in the formal characteristics of arguments that are defensible and persuasive, while nonetheless falling short of the dispositive and compelling force that was once thought to be intrinsic to reason as such. This renewed interest, in turn, has led a number of legal and political philosophers to turn once again to the ancient discipline of rhetoric, regarded as the science of determining and deploying persuasive — although not necessarily compelling — reasons.

Here, once again, we find a point of contact between scholastic and contemporary jurisprudence. As we observed in the last chapter, the scholastics did not take the convention and laws of their society as immediate and necessary expressions of natural principles. Rather, these were regarded as expressions and determinations of natural principles, as formulated through rational deliberation and rhetorical persuasion. This line of analysis was more or less forced on them by their conviction that natural law principles are in themselves too abstract and general to have practical force, apart from some intermediate processes of specification. In addition, they were very conscious that they were living through far-reaching processes of institutional development and reform, which left them in no doubt about the contingent status of actual social practices. On the contrary, they were themselves deeply involved in the deliberative processes generated by, and then furthering these developments. They turned to natural law principles as touchstones for analysis and critique in terms of fundamental principles, which were then elaborated and given practical specification and force in the process of making a case for legitimacy or reform with respect to some specific set of practices.

Rhetoric in Law and Political Processes: Contemporary Perspectives

When we turn to our contemporaries, we find that the renewed attention to rhetoric in law is motivated by very similar considerations. If anything, contemporary legal scholars and political philosophers give more emphasis than did the scholastics to the ways in which the proper functioning of the law itself gives salience to rhetorical analysis. As Neil MacCormick points out, it is generally acknowledged that the kinds of reasons that are adduced in the processes of legislation and adjudication are not dispositive. That is to say, almost everyone acknowledges that men and women of good will can reasonably disagree, even with respect to the force and practical consequences of the reasons that they generally accept. Practical rationality depends on considerations that are too general to admit of only one legitimate determination in specific contexts. What is more, the complexity of most practical judgments adds a further element of indeterminacy, since the diverse and incommensurate considerations that we must take into account can be brought together in more than one defensible way.[18]

And yet, MacCormick is also well aware that we cannot just equate validity and persuasiveness. Indeed, his sense of this problem sets the agenda for much of his groundbreaking work on rhetoric and legal reasoning. As he explains,

> The rhetorical turn in analysis of practical reasoning must not be understood as reducing the rational acceptability of an argument to its actual persuasiveness, if that means whether or not it persuaded (or failed to persuade) a particular concrete person on a particular occasion. "Rhetoric" has a bad name among many people because of the notorious possibility that a good speaker can win an audience around with a bad case. . . . One way to counter this is to relate persuasiveness to an ideal or a universal audience. If what you said had to be persuasive in the sense of "persuasive on the same terms to everybody" (not just to your particular audience of the moment) your tricks would find you out. Yet there is a difficulty about using as a test "the universal audience," or even some supposed consensus of reasonable contemporaries. To do so seems question-begging, since we possibly have to work out what would persuade the universal audience by reference to what is sound, rather than vice versa. Moreover, we have no guarantee that a contemporary consensus, where it exists, is correct.[19]

In other words, the appeal to a persuasive consensus, or even to the necessarily hypothetical ideal of a universal consensus, raises the specter of the arbitrariness of authority from another direction. If the proper force of political and legal reasons is tethered to their actual persuasiveness, doesn't it follow that these depend on considerations that are not only contingent, but to some extent irrational? Is there after all no basis for distinguishing be-

18. Neil MacCormick, *Rhetoric and the Rule of Law: A Theory of Legal Reasoning* (Oxford: Oxford University Press, 2005), 26-27.
19. *Rhetoric and the Rule of Law*, 20.

tween the reasons that actually persuade a community and those that should (or should not) do so? If this is so, then it seems that we have substituted the arbitrary whims of a particular community for the arbitrary decrees of a lawgiver, and we may well question whether that represents much progress. MacCormick's own strategy for addressing this problem focuses on an analysis of the logical and procedural constraints that legal discourse must respect, if it is to count as a kind of reasoning at all and to conform to the standards implied by the ideal of the rule of law.[20] Taken as a way of spelling out rational constraints on legal interpretation, his analysis is quite persuasive. Yet in his analysis, MacCormick focuses on processes of argumentation and justification within a formal legal system, which presupposes that fundamental political judgments have already been made. This is entirely legitimate, given that that is after all his purpose, but it still leaves open the question of whether, and in what ways, we can distinguish between valid and invalid, more or less appropriate, better or worse, in the prior sphere of rational deliberation, rhetorical persuasion, and political action.

In order to address this question, a number of political and legal philosophers have argued that public deliberation should ideally be carried out in terms of justification in light of universally shared standards, while granting that the practical necessities for, and limitations of, interpretative judgment and reflective inquiry mean that we will seldom or never attain this ideal. In this way, these philosophers try to do justice to the importance of interpretative judgment and rhetorical discourse, and to maintain a proper humility about what any of us can actually accomplish through these processes. Nonetheless, they would also insist that we can move progressively from indeterminate and partial to systematic, specific, and universal reasons, and that we should continually strive to do so. Ronald Dworkin's account of ideal political morality, which always yields one correct answer to every question of legal interpretation (whether we know it, or not), represents one version of this line of reasoning. Among political philosophers, the most influential such proposal is surely John Rawls's theory of justice, which he analyzes in terms of the norms that would be agreed upon through negotiation of agents whose identity is subsumed in their rationality.[21]

This line of analysis is itself informed by normative ideals — above all, an ideal of equality. As Bryan Garsten explains,

---

20. See *Rhetoric and the Rule of Law*, 32-77 for the central arguments.
21. See John Rawls, *Theory of Justice*, 118-94.

Justification treats different audiences similarly, in deference to the ideal of equality. When we justify a course of action, we argue that it is just, legitimate, or reasonable. We ask for our listeners' consent insofar as they take on the role of impartial or reasonable judges and adopt the shared public perspective that John Rawls and others have called the standpoint of "public reason," but we do not ask for more than that. We stop short of what persuasion might require. We show why any reasonable person would accept our view but not necessarily why these particular people listening here and now should do so. Instead, we ask our listeners to join us on a different plane, a place where "questions of political justice can be discussed on the same basis by all citizens, whatever their social position, or more particular aims and interests, or their religious, philosophical, or moral views." We treat every citizen as being equally capable of giving and receiving public reasons.[22]

There is no denying that this ideal of public reasoning is deeply attractive. It reflects ideals of equality and respect for individual liberty that are central to the political morality informing Western democracies. It calls for a stance of respect for one's fellow citizens as rational agents, capable of participating in shared deliberation within a shared framework of generally recognized rational considerations. The difficulty, however, is that men and women do not reason on the basis of universally valid rational considerations alone. We are generally reasonable, certainly, but we are also passionate, self-interested, and even prejudiced, inevitably limited in our perspectives and in the scope of our concerns. The danger with Rawls's ideal of public reason — and, I would add, with Dworkin's ideal public morality, or other similar universalizing ideals — is that it leads all too readily from respect for rational agents as they ideally are to a disregard for the views of men and women as they actually are. As Garsten says, "efforts to leave the politics of persuasion behind often ask citizens to alienate their judgment in a way that leaves them stranded from both the activity of public discourse and its outcomes."[23]

22. Bryan Garsten, *Saving Persuasion: A Defense of Rhetoric and Judgment* (Cambridge, MA: Harvard University Press, 2006), 6-7.

23. *Saving Persuasion*, 175. My critique of Rawls's ideal of public reasonableness owes a great deal to Garsten's text, in particular 174-202. For a similar critique and alternative proposal, see Hilliard Aronovitch, "Reflective Equilibrium or Evolving Tradition?," *Inquiry* 39, 399-419. Raz likewise argues against Rawls's presumptions of neutrality and universal persuasiveness in *The Morality of Freedom* (Oxford: Clarendon Press, 1986), 110-33. For a powerful defense of the centrality of

In contrast, he goes on to argue, a politics of rhetorical persuasion begins with an encounter with our interlocutors as they actually are — rational, but also passionate, self-interested, and prejudiced — and attempts to
engage them on the basis of their actual perceptions and desires, in such a
way as to move them to adopt a new perspective which is nonetheless in continuity with their own actual purposes. Garsten frankly admits that this process is inherently political, even when its explicit subject-matter is not: "In
trying to bring an audience from the conventional wisdom to thoughts or
intentions they might not otherwise have adopted, rhetoric intends to wield
influence over them. In this sense rhetoric is a form of rule."[24] Nonetheless,
Garsten insists on a contrast between persuasion and the many varieties of
manipulating or pandering discourses on offer: "To persuade people is to induce them to change their own beliefs and desires in light of what has been
said," in such a way as to preserve the "active independence" of one's interlocutors.[25] Thus understood, rhetorical persuasion is political in the proper
sense, that is, a form of ruling appropriate to a community of free men and
women (in our terms, not Garsten's). Its aim is to induce people to change
on the basis of, and in continuity with, aims and considerations that they
can recognize as their own, in such a way as genuinely to engage them, preserving their "active independence" in the process.

The process of rhetorical persuasion draws on and preserves the freedom of one's interlocutors in another, still more fundamental way. That is, it
draws on and respects the intrinsic character of practical judgment itself,
through which we respond to "particular situations in a way that draws
upon our sensations, beliefs, and emotions without being dictated by them
in any way reducible to a single rule."[26] Practical judgments require us to
bring together a range of diverse considerations in some defensible way, taking account of all relevant factors, but there will almost always be more than
one such defensible construal. The deliberative processes preceding practical
judgment thus preserve the combination of receptivity and spontaneity that
is characteristic of human rationality: "We only deliberate about how to respond in situations where there is no clear or definite answer, where we can
control our responses to some extent, and where certain responses seem to

---

particular and localized traditions to legal judgments, see James R. Stoner, Jr., *Common Law Liberty: Rethinking American Constitutionalism* (Lawrence: University Press of Kansas, 2003), 1-29,
65-77.

24. *Saving Persuasion,* 6.
25. *Saving Persuasion,* 7.
26. *Saving Persuasion,* 7

be better than others."[27] This characteristic interplay of receptivity and spontaneity, in turn, opens up the possibility for a genuine rhetoric of persuasion, which induces one's interlocutor to change her mind without manipulating or coercing her, because it is entirely possible to construe one's aims and perceptions in a new way without thereby renouncing them.

Seen from this perspective, the strategy of rhetorical persuasion, no less than the alternative strategy of justification within the sphere of public reasoning, reflects a political ideal. It honors the equality of one's interlocutors, not seen as the rational agents that they are in the abstract, but seen as the opinionated and limited individuals that each of us actually is. It fosters genuine democratic accountability by forcing office-holders (and even more, aspiring office-holders) to meet their fellow-citizens as they are, and to engage them on that basis. Most importantly, it honors and promotes the freedom of those it engages, by respecting the actual processes of practical deliberation that are at the core of all authentic human freedom:

> Because of the link between persuasive rhetoric and judgment, an argument for saving the possibility of persuasion in democratic politics is an argument for protecting the practice of judgment. It seems to me that this is a crucial project. Today we are more than ever governed by rules that eliminate space for even the smallest exercises of judgment. These rules are created by both private and public authorities, by legislators, bureaucrats, and corporate managers, all interested in minimizing the uncertainty associated with judgment. . . . Of course, persuasive rhetoric does not address these problems. The point is rather that the modern suspicion of rhetoric arises from the same impulse to minimize the risks of judgment that is on display in our culture more generally.[28]

Yet the processes of rhetorical persuasion and deliberative judgment do carry risks, as we have already intimated. They can degenerate into a kind of knowing manipulation, on the one hand, or a craven pandering to one's constituencies on the other. Garsten not only acknowledges these dangers, he also repeatedly insists that we take them seriously. Nonetheless, he remains convinced that the processes of public persuasion and judgment are worth saving, because they reflect the most authentic kind of respect for one's interlocutors, and because at the end of the day we have no good alternatives: "There exists no sovereign authority to settle our disputes, neither a

27. *Saving Persuasion*, 8.
28. *Saving Persuasion*, 9-10.

king nor an enlightened statesman nor a shared conception of public reason nor even a common public conscience deep within our hearts. Only once we have acknowledged that fact will we find it necessary to engage in the work of trying to persuade one another."[29]

Parameters of Freedom: Self-Love and Communal Happiness

I have engaged with Garsten at some length because he sets up the problem that must now be addressed. Legal authority is a kind of political authority, and in modern Western contexts its exercise and operations presuppose a framework of political judgments, in the form of systems of formal law. This framework does not do away with the need for interpretative judgments, which will always be to some extent contestable, but it does place generally acknowledged constraints on what counts as salient, cogent, and legitimate in legal deliberation. Actual political processes, in contrast, operate within a much looser and more contested framework of shared commitments and judgments. They do presuppose such a framework — namely, the shared customs, beliefs, and commitments that go to make up a common culture. Nonetheless, even the most harmonious and homogeneous society will be able to presuppose only so much in the way of generally agreed upon parameters for discourse, and today's societies, by and large, are neither homogeneous nor harmonious. (Nor should we wish them to be.) The contingencies inherent in any kind of deliberative judgment occur at a more basic level, so to speak, in political deliberation, and by the same token, the arbitrary quality of any authoritative judgment is more apparent at this level.

This brings us back to the question that MacCormick and Garsten both raise, in different terms. That is, how can we arrive at criteria for better or worse, more or less appropriate, more or less reasonable, in evaluating the processes of persuasion, deliberation, and judgment? If the processes of lawmaking and adjudication are to represent genuinely political forms of authority, which preserve the freedom of their subjects, then they must in some way stem from, and remain contextualized by, processes of rational deliberation and rhetorical persuasion, along the lines Garsten indicates. That is to say, they must be tethered, to some extent at least, in the convictions and purposes that those subject to the authorities can recognize as actually or imaginably their own — not in the terms of abstract public reasonableness

29. *Saving Persuasion*, 210.

but as an extension and reconfiguration of one's actual beliefs and desires. Yet if we are to avoid substituting the arbitrariness of despotic power with the arbitrariness of public sentiment, we still need to identify criteria for accounting for and, where necessary, critiquing these beliefs and desires — criteria which are, again, plausibly grounded in the actual exigencies of human life.

At this point, the theory of the natural law outlined in the previous chapter can be brought to bear, by indicating, at least in general terms, which kinds of reasons and forms of argument can be expected to be persuasive over a wide range of contexts, and furthermore, defending these as legitimate considerations, appropriate to the political discourse of free men and women. The starting point, as we would by now expect, lies in the identification of certain kinds of reasons as natural, insofar as they stem from the intelligible structures, and the corresponding purposes, characteristic of a distinctively human way of life. They are grounded, in other words, in the objective normative structure of human existence itself, and that is why they constitute legitimate, non-arbitrary, and non-coercive starting points for deliberation and persuasive rhetoric. Not only should men and women respond to these kinds of reasons; to some extent, they can also be expected to do so, insofar as these represent natural objects of the will, spontaneously desired even before the individual is capable of fully rational deliberation and choice.

So much is implied by the metaphysical theory of human existence, seen as one distinctive form of animate being. Before proceeding, we should pause to ask whether the appeal to natural law, construed along these lines, is not after all just another attempt to impose a theory — a rather esoteric theory, some might say — on the diverse and unpredictable dynamics of legal and political deliberation. Aren't we at risk of substituting an abstract ideal of naturalness for the abstract ideal of public reasonableness? Certainly, there is a risk here. But we can at least minimize it, by keeping the context of actual deliberations in view. If this theory is broadly correct, and if we can identify classes of reasons that should naturally be persuasive to all or most people, then we should be able to show that people are in fact persuaded by these kinds of reasons across a broad range of contexts or at any rate that these kinds of reasons are widely regarded as sound, even if not decisive in every instance.

This, it seems to me, can readily be done. After all, there is nothing esoteric about the natural objects of the will, which tether individual and communal deliberation to an objective set of values. These are very largely comprised of the kinds of objects or states of affairs that almost everyone spontaneously desires, at least apart from extraordinary circumstances — to live, to enjoy the pleasures naturally attendant on the basic activities of life, to be in good health, and to enjoy unimpeded activity in accordance with one's own spontaneous desires. They include, in addition, many other desiderata which are perhaps not so universally held but which are nonetheless broadly shared and readily appreciated as playing a central role in human life, for most people at any rate — to form a close sexual or affective bond, to bring forth and raise children, to participate in the life of one's community. Almost everyone has some curiosity about the world around her, some appreciation for beauty and exercises of skill, and some desire to fit one's life into a wider context of meaning and value. All of these are recognizably expressions of the natural and proper functioning of a human being, considered as a living, highly social animal capable of considerable spontaneity in her engagement with her environment.

As I hope to show in more detail in the next section, these natural desiderata inform the processes of persuasion and deliberation through forms of argumentation that are themselves defensibly natural and reasonable, even though not (generally) dispositive. Before turning to that analysis, however, there is a further question that we need to consider. That is, even if we grant that we can account for the reasonableness of persuasion and deliberation in natural law terms, can we similarly account for its authoritative status? This is critical, if the deliberative processes informing the generation of customs, formal legislation, and adjudication are to constitute rationally defensible grounds for the exercise of authority.

Seen from a natural law perspective, the authoritative force of natural reasons rests on what may appear at first to be a surprising, even paradoxical, foundation. Not only *are* these kinds of reasons broadly persuasive, they *should* also be recognized as (at the very least) valid and worthy of consideration, because they are tethered to the natural and proper self-love of the human creature. That is to say, reasons that appeal to the natural desiderata in the ways indicated will not be altogether foreign or external to the congeries of motives and desires informing any individual's practical judgments, because they will be at least imaginably similar to some components of those motives and desires. Again, these constitute natural objects of the will, and while that does not necessarily mean that every human agent desires all of them, we cannot imagine what it would mean to live a human life without desiring most of them, including at least those most fundamental to our animal existence. In responding to these reasons, therefore, the individual is either responsive to his own proper desire for his proper perfection or at least responsive to an empathetic identification with the proper self-love of others. And since the capacity for identification with others is itself an important component of one's existence and flourishing as a social being, even this latter response will be at least indirectly tethered to the agent's self-love.

This line of analysis is likely to sound paradoxical, because we are accustomed to think of self-love in terms of a selfish, or at best innocently narcissistic, desire for one's own immediate comfort and well-being. The important qualification, of course, is that the self-love in question be *proper* self-love — which is to say, an expression of the creature's natural desire to attain its proper form of perfection, in and through the full and appropriate development of its natural faculties. Aquinas insists that this kind of self-love is not only appropriate, it is also a metaphysical necessity (ST II-II 25.7, 26.4; cf I-II 1.7, 8). To exist is to function in accordance with some specific form, in such a way as to incline towards the fullest possible expression of that form; that is fundamentally what it means to desire the good. Of course, only a rational or intellectual agent experiences a desire for its own perfection consciously, and in explicit terms. That is why only rational and intellectual agents can adopt, and act on the basis of, distorted conceptions of what their overall perfection would mean. But when a human being acts in accordance with a (more or less) accurate sense of what it is to live a good human life, he will pursue what Aquinas, together with nearly all his forebears, would have characterized as a virtuous life, and we would be more likely to describe as a satisfying, worthwhile, meaningful, or admirable life.

So an appeal to self-love is not so problematic as we might have thought, and it does preserve the freedom of deliberative agents in the way indicated. But what makes it authoritative? At this point, a Thomistic theory of the natural and eternal law has real explanatory power. The appeal to proper self-love is authoritative because the agent's self-love represents the fundamental point at which the agent's existence and activity are tethered to the eternal law. This does not imply that every individual experiences a tacit desire for God, much less an explicit and conscious desire. Recall that every creature can be said to desire union with God, insofar as it desires its own proper perfection, which is neither more nor less than a created similitude of the divine goodness. That is why the intelligible order that God constitutes in creation, and sustains through providence, can be said to constitute a kind of law. As Aquinas explains, God's providence operates in all creatures in and through the natural inclinations that God has implanted in them, through which they pursue their proper ends:

It may happen, however, that some prince, who may be desirable in his own person, will nonetheless give onerous laws to his subjects, which he himself does not keep, and therefore his subjects are not effectively subjected to him. But since this is excluded from God, [Dionysius] adds that he sets *voluntary laws* over *all;* for the law of God is the proper natural inclination placed in every creature to do that which is appropriate to it, in accordance with nature. And therefore, since all things are held by divine desire, so all are held by his law. (*De Divinis Nominibus* X, 1.1, 857)

The inclinations of the human person similarly provide the intelligible principles in terms of which she attains her perfection, thus attaining union with God in the way connatural to her as a specific kind of creature. Yet precisely because she is the kind of creature that she is, not only the likeness but the very image of God, she pursues and attains this end in a distinctive way, through rationally grasping and acting upon the principles structuring her proper inclinations (cf. ST I 93.1, 2). Seen from this perspective, the political character of God's authority comes clearly into view. At the end of the first chapter, I claimed that the authority of law rests ultimately in God's eternal law, seen not in terms of the imposition of divine decrees but rather as the expression of divine wisdom and love. Now it appears that God's authority is itself binding, insofar as it is persuasive — as indeed God's perfection, mirrored in its proper way by one's own natural perfection, is supremely persuasive, and by the same token authoritative beyond cavil.

What, then, is the point of connection to political authority? At the end of the first chapter, I argued that it is a mistake to connect political authority to a specific act of divine authorization, as if God in some way confers legitimacy on lawmakers and rulers through a kind of targeted decree. We are now in a better position to offer a more satisfactory alternative, through which political authority is seen to be one component of the natural and proper flourishing of the human creature and, as such, a reflection of God's own goodness and perfection. In other words, we are in a position to defend political authority in terms of its status as a reflection of God's wisdom rather than seeing it as primarily a manifestation of God's will. We have already seen, at least in general terms, how the kinds of reasons appropriate to political rhetoric and deliberation are authoritative — within limits, and taken in conjunction with each other — because they are tethered to the properly authoritative self-love of the individual. How might we connect this analysis to a properly political form of authority?

The natural authority of the individual is tethered to political authority,

I would argue, through the common good of the community, seen in terms of the well-being of one's actual community and (even more) in terms of the ideals that the community (partially) embodies, and to which it aspires. When I say that individual and political authority are linked, I mean this to be understood in terms of a bi-directional relation between the two. The authority of the community is grounded in the natural authority that individuals possess as free and self-directing agents, although the precise character of this dependence needs to be spelled out with some care. We will return to this question in the last chapter. But correlatively, the ideals embodied by the common good as it is understood within a specific community are authoritative for its individual members, because these reflect the ideals in terms of which the men and women of the community collectively shape and direct their own lives — ideals which have given definition and order to their own efforts to pursue their natural perfection, and which they in turn, as free participants in a political community, have helped to shape.

None of this implies that political discourse will inevitably be couched in terms of explicit references to the common good or formulated in terms of appeals to what is natural, reasonable, or appropriate for creatures of our specific kind. Nonetheless, I do claim that familiar forms of political discourse can be analyzed in these terms, in such a way as to identify certain kinds of reasoning and forms of argumentation that should be, and generally are, persuasive. This analysis, in turn, lends support to the overall claim that political discourse tracks the natural inclinations of the human creature, and above all the natural orientation towards individual and communal perfection, as these are mediated through a community's commitments and ideals, comprising its conception of the common good. Seen from this perspective, a display of the forms of persuasive argumentation will be inseparably linked to their justification. That is, certain kinds of arguments will be broadly persuasive, precisely because they reflect the natural inclinations of the human agent in some intelligible way. This does not mean that these kinds of arguments will be, or even should be, dispositive or even persuasive in every context, or to every individual. It does, however, imply that we should expect to find that certain kinds of arguments are generally persuasive in a range of diverse contexts. This, I think, can readily be shown. In order to do so, however, it will be necessary to say something more about the scope and force of processes of political persuasion.

3. The Forms of Argument:
Natural Law, Common Good, and Justifying Considerations

Basic Goods, Capabilities, and the Structure of Practical Judgment

In the last chapter, I argued that human nature comprises an intelligible normative structure, out of which stem the ideals and practices comprising the natural morality of any given society. It does not follow that these normative structures exhaustively determine the mores of a particular community, since the specific ways in which natural ideals and claims are ordered and configured will always reflect some degree of contingency. That is why the natural law will always be mediated through the customs of particular communities, which embody a conception of the common good — or, as Cicero would say, the shared objects of love constituting a distinctive way of life. Nonetheless, seen from the perspective of the proposed account of natural law, the ideals and practices of diverse societies can be seen to track the intelligible structures of human nature in some recognizable way.

In this section, we will examine the implications of this account for political discourse, focusing on the ways in which certain kinds of considerations stem from the natural inclinations of the human agent as these are mediated through a particular shared conception of the common good. We thus begin by focusing on the perspective of individual interlocutors, in order to see how natural considerations inform deliberation, judgment, and choice. At the same time, it is important to realize that the processes of individual deliberation and public persuasion take place within a communal context, which initially frames individual deliberations and is in its turn shaped by these, leading to the formation of communally specific practices and norms. By tracing the kinds of arguments that are legitimately persuasive among free, rational agents, we will thus build up an account of the way in which the natural law, understood in terms of the most general principles of practical judgment, can generate specific practices and norms, and correlatively, in what way, and how far, an appeal to the natural law may serve to justify specific conventions, or alternatively, to provide criteria for reform and innovation.

The key point is that certain kinds of arguments are legitimate and persuasive because they reflect the kinds of objects that men and women naturally pursue. Anyone can appreciate that life, health, sexual pleasure and intimacy with another, children, and immersion in one's family and community life, are legitimate aims for action and salient concerns for assessing social policies — precisely because these are among the natural objects of the will, goods towards which each human being is naturally and properly oriented. Taken in broad terms, this observation would be accepted by moral and political theorists across a wide spectrum of theoretical commitments and political orientations. To take one widely influential example, the new theory of the natural law developed by Germain Grisez and John Finnis grounds moral reasoning in certain basic goods which are said to be self-evidently such to any rational agent, which are always in themselves reasonable objects of pursuit, and which are in no way to be forestalled or undermined.[30] Similarly, the widely influential political theories developed (with some variations) by Amartya Sen and Martha Nussbaum, which grounds rights claims in the agent's basic functions or capabilities, implies that all persons are oriented towards the pursuit and enjoyment of natural goods — those, namely, which are the targets of the capabilities in question.[31]

Nussbaum's theory offers an especially illuminating comparison to my interpretation of the natural law, because she too takes her starting point from Aristotle's teleological account of human functioning. As she explains:

> The intuitive idea behind the approach is twofold: first, that certain functions are particularly central in human life, in the sense that their presence or absence is typically understood to be a mark of the presence or absence of human life; and second — this is what Marx found in Aristotle — that there is something that it is to do these functions in a truly human way, not a merely animal way. . . . The core idea is that of the human being as a dignified free being who shapes his or her own life in cooperation and reciprocity with others, rather than being passively shaped or pushed around by the world in the manner of a "flock" or "herd" animal. A life that is really human is one that is shaped throughout by these human powers of practical reason and sociability.[32]

30. See Germain Grisez, *The Way of the Lord Jesus 1: Christian Moral Principles* (Chicago: Franciscan Herald Press, 1983), 173-274, and John Finnis, *Aquinas: Founders of Modern Political and Social Thought* (Oxford: Oxford University Press, 1998), 56-102 for basic statements of the theory.

31. Sen has developed his own version of the capabilities approach through a series of books and articles; for a good recent statement, see *Development as Freedom* (New York: Random House, 1999), especially 54-86. My comments on the subsequent reception of the theory are taken from Martha C. Nussbaum, *Women and Human Development: The Capabilities Approach* (Cambridge: Cambridge University Press, 2000), 70. She lays out the main lines of her own, slightly different version of the capabilities approach at 34-110.

32. *Women and Human Development*, 71-72.

Reading on, however, we find that Nussbaum departs from Aristotle (and from Aquinas as well) in one critical respect. That is, Aristotle offers what he regards as a morally significant analysis of the distinctively human activity comprising happiness, which he identifies with contemplation and the practice of the civic virtues.[33] Aristotle's account of human flourishing or happiness thus depends on a set of evaluative judgments about the relative worth of the activities and pursuits that might comprise a human life, and a proposal (in fact, two proposals) about the most appropriate and desirable ways of ordering and configuring these. Nussbaum, in contrast, resists making any such move. Rather, she holds that the basic functions and capabilities given by experience and observation, confirmed in a number of different societies; their moral significance depends on a "*freestanding moral idea,* not one that relies on a particular metaphysical or teleological view," and Nussbaum expects this view to be widely persuasive.[34]

Nussbaum's insistence that her moral conclusions are "freestanding" and need no metaphysical grounding is reminiscent of the claims of Grisez and Finnis to derive moral conclusions on the basis of self-evident intuitions of value, without any need to appeal to empirical or metaphysical claims. I suspect that she and Grisez and Finnis share at least one part of the motivation for this move; that is to say, they hope to develop moral theories that will be universally persuasive, in accordance with content-neutral criteria for public reasonableness. At any rate, the formal similarity between Nussbaum's capabilities approach and the new natural law is reflected in a further significant way. That is, Nussbaum resists any suggestion that the basic capabilities can in any way be ranked on the basis of some comparative evaluation. We apprehend their value and acknowledge the rights claims that they generate on the basis of moral intuitions that cannot be further analyzed or defended, and thus leave us with no ground — and no need — for ideals of what human life, taken as a whole, should be. Grisez and Finnis similarly resist any claim that the basic goods can only be justified, appropriated, or pursued in terms of some overall configuration. On the contrary, the point of identifying them as basic is precisely to deny that they can be ranked or ordered.[35] The upshot, in each case, is that normative claims rest on consid-

---

33. Annas's analysis of the distinction (not always explicitly recognized) between "nature" and "mere nature" in Aristotle is particularly helpful here; see Julia Annas, *The Morality of Happiness* (Oxford: Oxford University Press, 1993), 142-58.

34. *Women and Human Development,* 83, emphasis in the original.

35. For clear summaries of this fundamental point, see *The Way of the Lord Jesus,* 196-98, and *Aquinas,* 79-86.

erations that serve to set strict parameters around the kinds of actions that can be legitimately pursued — those which forestall or destroy a particular instantiation of a basic good, or those which violate someone's right freely to pursue one of her basic capabilities.

In contrast, seen from a more comprehensive natural law perspective, basic goods and human capabilities should be construed as expressions of the intelligible and normative structure proper to human existence, correlated with the discrete goods necessary to human life and well-being, or the operative faculties through which these are pursued and enjoyed. The new natural law and the capabilities approach thus converge on the same point that will be developed here, namely, that there are some kinds of considerations that anyone can recognize as proper and valid starting points for practical reasoning and justification. Yet both approaches fall short in one critical respect: neither takes full account of the way in which practical reasoning and deliberation actually function. Men and women do not choose instantiations of basic goods considered in abstraction, even though the choices that we make can subsequently be analyzed in terms of the basic goods comprising the natural objects of the will. Sometimes we do choose to exercise basic capabilities for the sheer joy of doing so, or else we choose to exhibit freedom and self-control through what may appear on the surface to be unmotivated actions. But more typically, we freely exercise our basic capabilities in pursuit of more complex satisfactions. In any case, the immediate object of human choice is always some kind of action (construed in such a way as to include instances of deliberately refraining from a contemplated act). For this reason, the deliberation informing choice reflects the normative contours of human action itself — and for that very reason, deliberation will almost always involve some element of contingency faced with an array of incommensurable aims.

The Contingency of Public Morality

What I am getting at is this. Human actions are always directed towards attaining, enjoying, or safeguarding something that the agent perceives as good or desirable, and this perception can always be analyzed in terms of the natural objects of the will, pursued through characteristically human kinds of activities. But by the same token, any particular action will also represent, at the very least, a choice to pursue one set of desirable objectives over against others, if only because any act forecloses the possibility of doing something else at a specified time. This choice is only possible because the natural objects of the will, while desirable in themselves, are not in themselves *necessary* objects of desire. Indeed, the natural objects of the will, taken in the abstract, will almost never comprise the objects of someone's actual choices. Typically, choice is informed by a rational judgment to the effect that some state of affairs is desirable on the whole — with the criterion of desirability being supplied by reference to the agent's overall happiness, as the individual conceives it, or (perhaps) by reference to another's good or the well-being of the community.

No one can pursue an ideal of the good life, or promote this ideal on behalf of others, through a seriatim pursuit of basic goods or a focused exercise of distinct capabilities. In order to pursue and develop almost any of the activities that we regard as worthwhile, we must choose among competing satisfactions and possible ways of developing our abilities, in such a way as to renounce some and to bring a rough ordering of priorities to the others. Probably most or all human actions will nonetheless be targeted on the natural objects of the will, but there is nothing irrational about choosing to forego natural goods — nor is there any apparent reason why it is irrational to act in ways that might broadly be described as "acting against" these natural goods. By the same token, there is nothing irrational about placing the possible objects of choice into some kind of ordering relative to one another, in such a way as to choose to instantiate one set of desiderata over against others. On the contrary, ordinary processes of deliberation and choice will almost always call for these kinds of comparative and preferential judgments, in order to make definite choices in the light of diverse kinds of considerations.

At the same time, as we saw in the preceding chapter, no one forms an ideal of happiness or carries out the complex deliberations necessary to pursue such an ideal in isolation. Without some process of formation in a preexisting set of ideals, disposing the individual to desire some kinds of alternatives and to reject others, one's capacities for desire and judgment would be too unformed to allow for much deliberation at all, much less for deliberation over the proper shape of one's life. Once again, we are reminded that the individual's practical reasoning, no less than his language or his knowledge of the world, depends in the first instance on formation in communally shared norms, even though these may later be subject to critical scrutiny. These shared norms, as they pertain to practical reasoning, comprise the ideals for individual and communal life that constitute the shared objects of love, the common good that constitutes an association of persons as a coherent, self-governing community. So much follows from our earlier analysis of the scholastic account of the common good.

This brings us to a further point. That is, the processes of communal discernment and custom-formation, through which ideals of the common good emerge, are themselves marked by the same dialectics of renunciation and affirmation that shape individual deliberation. No community can bring together the diverse natural goods proper to human life in such a way as to give equal weight to all of them, or even to leave individuals with a purely neutral set of alternatives. Any set of ideals for human flourishing, however wide the range on offer may be, will inevitably shape and direct individual deliberation in such a way as to give enhanced weight to one set of options, and to foreclose some others, perhaps to the extent that they do not even occur as possibilities for men and women in the community in question. Correlatively, public deliberation guided by some ideal of the common good (or contested versions of such an ideal) will necessarily require complex assessments of relative worth and priority across a range of incommensurable goods, just as do the ideals of happiness guiding individual deliberation.

In the last chapter, we observed that the political morality of our own society gives priority to individual freedom in the processes of developing and pursuing an ideal of life. Indeed, for many exponents of this ideal, individuals deserve respect precisely because they are, or potentially could be, autonomous in this way. Correlatively, respect for persons is spelled out in terms of respect for one's dignity as someone who does, or ideally would, adopt and pursue an ideal reflecting one's best sense of what it means to be human, what men and women should attempt to achieve and to be.[36] So far, there is nothing in this ideal that would be incompatible with the theological account of political and legal authority being proposed. On the contrary, it offers a clear point of contact with Aquinas's interpretation of the image of God motif in terms of human capacities for free judgment and rational action, and his further claim that we can only attain connatural happiness through our own free activities, directed towards an ideal for human existence that we have ourselves reflectively adopted.

But at this point, we come to a critical difference between much con-

36. Among contemporary legal philosophers, Dworkin is perhaps the strongest proponent of this view; see *Is Democracy Possible Here? Principles for a New Political Debate* (Princeton: Princeton University Press, 2006), 9-23 for a succinct statement. Christopher Insole offers a qualified but strong defense of contemporary liberal ideals in *The Politics of Human Frailty: A Defense of Political Liberalism* (Notre Dame: University of Notre Dame Press, 2004).

temporary liberal political theory and the account of the natural law under consideration. (Raz is a noteworthy exception to this generalization.) Among our own contemporaries, respect for human capacities for free self-determination implies that at the communal or political level, we must remain neutral with respect to ideals of human existence. The worry is that men and women cannot make their own self-determining judgments regarding the overall course of their lives if social expectations or legal strictures make these choices for them. This is true up to a point. Certainly, if the state of Indiana were to attempt to require me to marry, my (hypothetical) deliberative choice to pursue the life of a cloistered Carmelite would be severely compromised. But at a more fundamental level, our political morality cannot presuppose complete neutrality at the social level with respect to ideal or appropriate forms of human life. As Raz reminds us, "Supporting valuable forms of life is a social rather than an individual matter."[37] No society can remain neutral on these matters, for much the same reasons that no individual can function as a free and reasonable individual without some sense of the overall aims she is pursuing. In order to function as a cohesive society, a community needs settled conventions of some kind, through which the many activities of individuals can be directed and coordinated in some cohesive way. This implies the formation of institutions, with their attendant practices and expectations concerning at least the central purposes of human life. These processes, in turn, cannot take place apart from some kinds of discriminating judgments about the relative weights and the appropriate configurations of diverse and partially incommensurable aims and values. Apart from the structures generated through these processes, human activities could not take place at all, and rational deliberation would have neither starting points nor the needed context of intelligible choices. And yet, these structures, which human freedom presupposes, also constrain it — if only because our communal commitments to one set of institutional arrangements rules out certain possibilities for human activity which a different set of arrangements would have provided.

Autonomy itself, considered as a social ideal and a personal value, cannot be pursued outside a communal structure that forecloses some alternatives, even as it opens others. Again, Raz makes this point clearly: "An autonomy-supporting culture offers its members opportunities which cannot be had in a non-autonomous environment, and lacks most of the op-

---

37. *Morality of Freedom*, 162; he develops this point at greater length in his analysis of personal well-being and its dependence on communal forms at 288-320.

portunities available in the latter."[38] Speaking in reference to the growing emphasis on individual choice, rather than family control, in the formation of marriages, he remarks that "The move away from pre-arranged marriages affects in a profound way the nature of the marriage bond. . . . The change to marriage as a self-chosen partnership increased personal autonomy. But it did so not by superimposing an external ideal of free choice on an otherwise unchanged relationship. It did so by substituting a relationship which allows much greater room for individual choice in determining the character of the relationship for one which restricted its scope."[39] The point to underscore is that this social judgment in favor of autonomy foreclosed some options, even as it opened others. No participant in Western cultural forms today can choose to enter into the kinds of marriage that were available to their nineteenth-century forebears — forms which were more restrictive, but which also offered satisfactions, including a high degree of stability and solidarity within extended kinship and social networks that most contemporary Western forms of marriage cannot provide. We need not denigrate our own way of life and its distinctive values in order to recognize that these inevitably presuppose constraints, and come with some costs.

This is my point. Social neutrality has its limits, and that means that one of the most cherished myths of the liberal state must be surrendered; we do not, and cannot, live in a society governed by pure norms of a universal morality only. This does not mean that we cannot and should not pursue a political morality grounded in an ideal of respect for individual freedom and self-determination. We can, and we do — and as I will argue below, those of us who are Christians have a particular stake in promoting this ideal. But we must nonetheless recognize that it is more substantive in its normative content, and less transparently reasonable and universal, than we often assume. Even the liberal European polities of our own day are informed by a distinctive conception of the common good, within which commitments to equality and liberty play a key role. Our common objects of love include, centrally, a way of life characterized by a high degree of individual freedom and mobility and our devotion to these ideals takes the practical form of respect, even reverence, for the political and legal institutions, even the very texts, that express and safeguard them. This ideal of the common good represents a powerful, widely attractive construal of the diverse values and potentiali-

---

38. *Morality of Freedom,* 392; more generally, for an illuminating analysis of the social conditions necessary to sustain individual freedom and to express autonomy as a social ideal, see 369-99.

39. *Morality of Freedom,* 392.

ties of human existence. But it is not the only one on offer among the peoples of the world, nor is it necessarily the only legitimate or even the best such construal.[40]

We have already observed that the open-ended and partially contingent character of practical reasoning gives rise to relations of authority in both political and non-political contexts. At this point, I want to call attention to a different, but closely related point. That is, in practical deliberation, both individual and public, no one of the natural goods can offer a compelling reason for choice. Indeed, it is difficult to see what could count as a compelling reason for choice at the outset of a deliberative process, since the point of deliberation is precisely to arrive at some overall configuration of competing considerations that will serve as the basis for a compelling, or at least a satisfactory choice. Thus, we cannot expect to find goods, or claims, that would definitively resolve the open questions informing deliberation. That kind of resolution can only come about through the formation of practices and their associated precepts, near the end of a process of deliberation, not at its first beginnings.

It follows that it would be a mistake to hold practical deliberation to the same standards of certainty and definitiveness that we appropriately apply in some empirical and theoretical contexts. Rather, the appropriate criteria for reasonableness in the context of public deliberation are salience and a kind of conditional, all-things-considered persuasiveness. What we want to identify, as we trace the contours of a legitimate political rhetoric of persuasion, are the kinds of considerations that would be generally recognized as relevant and important, and which are broadly persuasive to most people across a wide range of contexts. We are not trying to identify considerations that are, in themselves, persuasive to every individual, or (much less) generate a universally valid, comprehensive political morality. We are simply trying to spell out the kinds of aims and considerations that reflect the normative structure of human nature, as these are revealed through the contours of genuinely persuasive rhetoric. There will always be room for good-faith, reasonable disagreement over the ways in which the desiderata of human life should be assessed and brought together — but what we are looking for, in the first instance, are those kinds of considerations that everyone would recognize as carrying some weight, and calling for some kind of (at least provisional or conditional) consideration.

---

40. Again, Raz offers a powerful defense of these claims; see *Morality of Freedom*, 110-33 and 369-99.

Persuasive Reasons and the Natural Objects of the Will

Even at this basic level, we can readily identify some kinds of considerations that are generally recognized to be relevant in deliberative contexts, and which are widely, albeit not universally persuasive. These will be familiar, at least in broad outline, by now. Almost everyone acknowledges that it's good to be alive, under most circumstances anyway, and therefore, basic considerations of security and a due concern for safety are almost always acknowledged as having appropriate public force. Practices and choices which threaten human life in some way are generally regarded as problematic, in need of some kind of special justification. Even more, choices which involve directly taking human life, through a declaration of war or capital punishment, are widely seen as calling for justification in terms of very serious considerations indeed; it is telling that if these considerations are not forthcoming, public officials generally attempt instead to minimize the expected levels of casualties. Almost everyone acknowledges that individuals legitimately pursue their own health and physical well-being, and that the community should support these efforts at some level — through maintaining standards of hygiene and providing some means of access to wholesome food and water, if in no other way. To take a third, very important example, almost everyone acknowledges that one's family ties, close personal relationships, and especially one's children matter. Of course, we also realize that these bonds can be overridden for sufficiently serious reasons, but here again, the reasons need to be very serious, especially when what is at stake is the bond between parent and child.

These kinds of reasons are grounded in the natural objects of the will, and that is why a persuasive rhetoric, which takes its starting-points from the "arguments, images, and emotions most likely to appeal to the particular audience in front of us," will almost always include some appeal to these, or to other similar desiderata proper to human life.[41] These considerations thus reflect the universal normative structures underlying diverse social norms and cultural ideals, underlying even the uncountable variety of individual aspirations and desires, rendering these intelligible as expressions of natural values which are thus generally shared, albeit in a variety of expressions. By the same token, an appeal to these kinds of considerations will always be appropriate to political discourse among free men and women. We can recognize these kinds of considerations as among those that we our-

41. *Saving Persuasion*, 5.

selves share, even though we interpret them differently or give them different weight.

In order to be effective, however, a persuasive appeal grounded in naturally shared considerations will usually need to go beyond invoking the individual's own desires for life, security, and the like. It will also need to engage her regard and (even better) her sympathy for other people or for the community as a whole. It will need, in other words, to engage human capacities for empathy, concern for the regard of others and respect for their claims, civic pride and responsibility — in short, to call upon those attitudes and desires that are directed away from the individual himself, towards a more or less altruistic concern for others. After all, we are focusing here on the exigencies of public deliberation, which by its nature involves some kind of engagement with the well-being of someone or something other than oneself. Even at this level, rhetorical persuasion will often effectively focus on the individual's own self-interest; debates over taxation policies typically proceed in this way, for example. But appeals to the self-interest of one's interlocutors will only go so far in most public contexts — or indeed, in most personal relationships. We cannot live together unless at some points, and in some ways, we are prepared to take the needs and concerns of others into account.

Does any of this imply that public deliberation will necessarily include an appeal to considerations that are alien to the individual's own natural and proper desires and aims? Altruism is all very well, but aren't we in danger here of introducing another kind of despotic manipulation, directed in this case to the interests of someone else under the cover of exhortations to self-lessness and self-sacrifice? Certainly, this danger does exist. To take one egregious example, consider the sentimental exaltation of the silent, selfless woman, whose every thought is directed towards serving others. Yet appeals on behalf of the needs and claims of others, or on behalf of the community itself, need not be manipulative or despotic, even when they attempt to tap into our deepest feelings of responsibility, sympathetic suffering on behalf of others, or even good, old-fashioned guilt. The reason that these kinds of considerations can be persuasive in an appropriately political way is precisely that these, too, are natural to the human person. Attachment, the regard of others and a secure, recognized place among one's immediate circle are themselves natural objects of the will, intelligible and proper expressions of our nature as social primates. We depend on others for our very survival, our sense of our own identity, and whatever structures of meaning and purpose inform our thinking and desire. Without some receptivity to the norms and practices of the community, we could not exercise the spontaneity of individual judgment and choice. And for that reason, appeals to our feeling and regard for others are in themselves tethered to considerations that each individual can naturally and properly recognize as in some way her own.[42]

At this point, a further objection may arise. That is, not everyone does care about the needs and claims of others. While most men and women do have at least some feeling for others, many of us are probably more selfish than we realize. And there do seem to be some who go through life in blithe disregard of anyone else's point of view, out of narcissism or — at the pathological and dangerous extreme — the sheer inability to grasp or be moved by the feelings of another human being.[43] In itself, this observation does not falsify the claim that human beings are naturally disposed towards empathy and attachment. Individual members of a specific kind may be limited, even to the point of incapacity, in their abilities to express the full range of activities proper to the natural life of the kind, as we have more than once observed. But if it is really the case that some individuals are incapable of perceiving or caring about the needs and claims of others, then this would seem to raise questions about the appropriateness of appeals in a comprehensive rhetoric of persuasion. So far as these individuals are concerned, an appeal to the needs and concerns of others, or to the community as a whole, would rest on reasons for action that the individual cannot recognize as in some way her own. In such a case, the individual's own interests would offer no

42. As we saw in the last chapter, there is a growing consensus among those working in the relevant fields that cognitive capacities depend for their development, both at the evolutionary and the individual levels, on capacities for shared intentions and reflection on oneself in relation to a social network that are characteristic of our lives as social primates. Again, see Michael Tomasello, *The Cultural Origins of Human Cognition* (Cambridge, MA: Harvard University Press, 1999), and Michael Tomasello et al., "Understanding and Sharing Intentions: The Origins of Cultural Cognition," *Behavioral and Brain Sciences* 28 (2005): 675-735. In addition to Tomasello, both Merlin Donald and Sarah Hrdy offer cogent reconstructions of the relevant evolutionary processes, which differ, of course, in many particulars but nonetheless converge on the central point; see Merlin Donald, *Origins of the Modern Mind: Three Stages in the Evolution of Culture and Cognition* (Cambridge, MA: Harvard University Press, 1991), and Sarah Blaffer Hrdy, *Mothers and Others: The Evolutionary Origins of Mutual Understanding* (Cambridge, MA: Harvard/Belknap Press, 2009). Drawing on this line of research, Katherine Nelson makes a cogent case that social contexts play a foundational role in the development of the cognitive capacities at an individual level, in *Young Minds in Social Worlds: Experience, Meaning, and Memory* (Cambridge, MA: Harvard University Press, 2007).

43. Admittedly, the proper classification and even the existence of genuine psychopaths — individuals who are very nearly, or entirely lacking in internal moral motivations — are controversial. For a good overview of recent research, see Robert D. Hare, *Without Conscience: The Disturbing World of the Psychopaths among Us* (New York: Guilford Press, 1993).

tethering for rational persuasion, and attempts to induce her to take account of the interests of others would constitute despotic forms of manipulation, rather than a genuinely persuasive political rhetoric.

Admittedly, an appeal to the interests of others is not likely to be effective when directed towards a confirmed narcissist or a psychopath, but that does not mean that such appeals are in themselves despotic. Two observations are in order. First, it may well be that there are some individuals, outright psychopaths, who really are incapable of caring about others, in the sense of experiencing genuine fellow-feeling, sympathy, or disinterested concern for them. But even with respect to such persons, we can expect to find some point of contact between the individual's own needs and concerns and an appeal to the perspectives of others — if only because he will have some concern for the way in which he appears to others. Independent, self-directed action requires some sense of one's place in one's immediate circle of associates, implying awareness of others' perceptions and therefore some insight into them. Without this minimal level of empathy, the agent cannot maintain the needed balance between receptivity to the constraints of one's community and spontaneity in negotiating these through independent action.

Secondly, and more fundamentally, we have good grounds for regarding a concern for others as a natural and proper component of human life, even if it is the case that not every human being exhibits such concern in anything like a fully adequate way. Admittedly, the level of empathy needed for minimally adequate capacities for action is not very high; it need not extend to any genuine feeling or regard for others' concerns. Nonetheless, these further capacities for concern and attachment are also natural to the human agent — a necessary precondition for the enjoyment of many of the central satisfactions of human life, including friendships and close ties with a sexual partner or with one's children; a life without these capabilities is stunted and pitiable. Precisely because these concerns are natural to humanity, we are justified in counting them as properly political kinds of considerations, appropriate grounds for persuasion among free men and women. That is why, as Garsten observes, "most people's partial attachments include certain loyalties and commitments to principle, perhaps a sense of honor or dignity or justice, or, most commonly, a sensitivity to injustice."[44] And in fact, appeals to other-regarding and community-regarding arguments are among the most common and effective forms of persuasive rhetoric, recurring in a wide range of contexts and generally acknowledged as legitimate appeals.

---

44. *Saving Persuasion*, 193.

In its simplest forms, these kinds of persuasive arguments will involve straightforward appeals to identify with another's perspectives, in such a way as to engage one's sympathies and one's sense of reasonableness or fair play. These are in effect Golden Rule arguments, which presuppose that one's interlocutors would be unwilling to accept policies or constraints that they themselves would regard as onerous or unfair. Fortunately, this is often the case. Garsten quotes a particularly telling example, of Lyndon Johnson's efforts during the 1960 presidential campaign to persuade Southern whites to accept the Democratic Party's commitment to civil rights. His strategy was simple; he went into one small Southern town after another, and at each stop he would ask his listeners how they would feel "if your child was sick, and you could not take him to the hospital in this town, but had to go twenty miles away? How would you feel if you were shopping and your child was thirsty, and you could not give him a cold soda at the counter in the drugstore? And again and again, he won the sullen audiences."[45] This is unsurprising, given that concern for the well-being of one's own children is one of the most fundamental forms of concern for another, a natural touchstone for identification and sympathy across a wide range of contexts.

Similarly, a straightforward appeal to what we might describe as the well-being of one's community, its security and prosperity, can be quite effective. These kinds of appeals are framed in terms of basic considerations stemming from our shared sense of what it is that we collectively need in order to live and flourish, as individuals and as a society. Anyone who follows city and state politics with any level of attention will quickly see that appeals to the economic prosperity of the community are a staple of American political life. Recently, political discourse at every level has been dominated by appeals to physical security from violent attacks. Of course, these kinds of appeals will typically and legitimately engage the self-interest of one's interlocutors, to a greater or lesser degree; every mature adult appreciates the importance of some access to a steady income, and we still typically expect the community, acting through its public agencies, to protect us from the violent attacks of others. At the same time, these kinds of appeals typically draw on altruistic as well as self-regarding considerations. When New Orleans, together with much of the surrounding region, was devastated by Hurricane Katrina in 2005, the near-total collapse of public provisions for the safety and well-being of the victims generated widespread outrage — even among

---

45. *Saving Persuasion*, 193, quoting Henry Fairlie, "The Decline of Oratory," *The New Republic*, May 28, 1984, 17.

those unlikely ever to suffer in this way themselves, either because they were not situated in an area prone to natural disasters or (more often) because they were sufficiently prosperous to insure themselves against the worst effects of such losses.[46] To take a still more striking example, many people respond to the force of arguments couched in terms of the future well-being of one's community, even when one's interlocutors cannot reasonably expect to experience that future. We do care about leaving a legacy of debt or a ruined environment to our children — even those of us who in fact have no children are sensitive to such appeals.

These kinds of considerations, and the forms of argumentation typically correlated with them, have a legitimate role to play in political rhetoric and deliberation, because they are grounded in natural objects of the will and meet the criteria for reasonableness proper to practical judgment. They presuppose that a given practice or policy reflects the normative structures of human nature, and by implication, reflects reasons for action that the men and women of the community can claim as their own. To that extent, these kinds of reasons and forms of argumentation lend support to the claim that the social arrangements in question represent conventional formulations of the natural law, not just in the sense that these are tethered to what is natural in some way, but more specifically that they reflect desirable or defensible expressions of human nature. In this way, these kinds of arguments serve as a bridge between the very general first principles of the natural law and the concrete precepts which give substantive content to those principles as they are applied in a specific context. By the same token, they serve to justify social conventions in natural law terms, provisionally and with qualifications, to be sure, but in such a way as nonetheless to have real force.

In the last chapter, we noted that for the scholastics, the natural law is first of all a principle of legitimation, and only secondarily a source of prohibitions. This point is, if anything, more important in our own circumstances than it was for the scholastics themselves. In our globalized society, we find ourselves increasingly drawn into contact — and conflict — with peoples whose practices and ideals are very different from those informing our own way of life. These differences cannot all be explained away or dismissed as non-essential modifications of shared commitments, if only because they include profoundly different ways of construing the fundamental relations

---

46. The devastating effects, and even more, the tragic aftermath of Hurricane Katrina have been extensively documented; for a good summary, see George Friedman, "The Ghost City," *The New York Review of Books* 52.15, Oct. 6, 2005.

between the sexes, within and among kinship associations and functional divisions, and most fundamentally between the individual and the community itself. From our perspective, these arrangements may appear to be problematic or even unjust, so much so that we may be tempted to conclude that we cannot relate to these peoples as potential interlocutors in shared deliberation — at least, not until we have persuaded them to be more like us.

Certainly, there is scope for critical appraisal and a persuasive rhetoric of reform between peoples as well as within any given community. But we cannot engage in a genuinely political discourse with others unless we begin from a standpoint of respect for their own perspectives, their sense of what is natural and appropriate, as they themselves apprehend it. In order to do so, it is essential that we begin with some appreciation of the ways in which their way of life — strange and even repugnant though it may be to us — reflects one defensible expression of the natural law, a natural morality which as such carries with it the authority of the sovereign founder of human life. Appeals to the well-being of a community, seen in relation to the well-being of its individual members, can play an important role in this context.[47] Does a given set of social arrangements promote the fundamental well-being of its members, or at least most of its members, most of the time? Does it provide most individuals with the opportunity to live out a normal lifespan in reasonable health and enjoyment? Does it offer wide access to the material conditions necessary for life and health? Can men and women come together to form sexual bonds, to bring forth and rear children, and pursue the activities intrinsic to family and kinship structures with relative autonomy and security? Does it offer them a secure place in a network of relations and a sense of participation in larger values, within which they can find a place that is satisfying and meaningful to them? In short, does a given set of social practices and institutions give expression to, and support and promote, the natural and proper operations of human existence? To the extent that it does, these arrangements deserve respect as expressions of natural norms. Evaluation at this level can at best be provisional, a starting point for shared deliberation rather than its conclusive end — but this is a critical starting point, if we are to arrive at even the minimal level of real respect for the other, as he or she is, which is necessary for genuinely political persuasion and deliberation.

---

47. Although they approach these issues from different perspectives, and none frames the relevant questions in natural law terms, Bell, Raz, and Rawls all develop similar criteria for evaluating the soundness of an overall way of life, whether one's own or that of another community. See *Beyond Liberal Democracy*, 52-83; *Morality of Freedom*, 369-99; and *Laws of Peoples*, 59-88.

Thus self-regarding and altruistic considerations typically come to-gether in rhetorical discourse and public deliberation, as these pertain to the well-being of the community. But so far, the connection appears to be loose and contingent. Deliberation over such matters as prosperity or security will normally appeal to one's self-interest and her concern for others, but we can readily imagine contexts in which only one or the other kind of appeal would be relevant, or effective. There is another kind of appeal to the well-being of the community that is still more significant, because it represents a point at which individual and communal concerns are intrinsically linked together. These are appeals couched in terms of the defining values, ideals, and commitments of a community, its shared sense of the common good. What is at stake in these kinds of arguments are not so much appeals to communal well-being in the broad sense, but some invocation of the ideals to which the community aspires and which it hopes to see maintained in its public life. Understood in this way, the common good functions in some-what the same way as Dworkin's ideal of public morality — that is to say, it represents the highest ideals embodied in a community's characteristic prac-tices and public institutions. His ideal of equal regard, as expressed in repre-sentative democracy and public openness to many kinds of individual aspi-rations, is a persuasive representation of the common good embodied in United States political institutions at their best — just as the ideals of mar-tial courage and political wisdom, exercised in service of universal peace un-der the rule of law, represented the common good of the Romans in late an-tiquity, and ideals of personal and familial solidarity, expressed in holy conformity to God's revealed law, represent the common good towards which many Muslims aspire today.[48]

Certainly, appeals to public morality or the common good, thus under-stood, can be powerfully moving and persuasive, if only because they invoke ideals that would have been formative for most of those to whom they are directed, and can therefore draw on images and sentiments familiar from childhood. Further, to the extent that individuals identify with their com-munity, such arguments can represent a powerful kind of flattery, an appeal to the individual's sense of self-respect and worth, as these are grounded in, and yet obscured by, his self-identification with a collective whole.[49] What is

48. Alasdair MacIntyre makes a similar point in his account of political liberalism as a tradi-tion; see *Whose Justice? Which Rationality?* (Notre Dame: University of Notre Dame Press, 1988), 326-48.

49. Reinhold Niebuhr makes this point forcefully in *Moral Man and Immoral Society* (New York: Charles Scribner's Sons, 1932), 92-93. The dangers he identifies are without doubt very real,

more, to the extent that we are social animals, with all that that implies, appeals to collective ideals are tethered to the natural inclinations of humankind, more specifically, to the natural necessity for shared conceptual and evaluative structures in order to make sense of one's world and to formulate and pursue one's own aims. Thus far, it is not apparent that appeals to the common good bring together individual and collective considerations in a more specific way. The point of contact between the natural objects of the will and collective concerns would seem to lie in the natural need for some kind of shared ideals and commitments or other — but this in itself would not go far towards justifying this or that particular ideal of the common good, or suggesting that it might reflect natural desires of individual men and women in any more specific way. This is particularly worrisome, because without some such tethering, appeals to shared ideals can readily take on manipulative and coercive forms — as is all too often the case. In the United States, for example, ideals of liberty and self-sufficiency are commonly invoked to justify market arrangements which leave most individuals with almost no scope for independence in their employment choices or secure access to an adequate standard of living.[50]

Nonetheless, in at least some formulations, appeals to the shared ideals that comprise the common good of a particular community do represent a particularly close point of contact between the individual's orientation towards his own proper perfection and communal concerns. In order to see that this is so, we need to remind ourselves of something obvious, yet easily overlooked — that is, while the ongoing activities constituting a community cannot be reduced to a summation of individual actions, there would be no community apart from individual men and women, who sustain the community even as they find meaning and purpose within its structures. This mutual interdependence between communal dynamisms and the trajectories of individual lives sets constraints on what the common good of the community can be. It implies that a genuine common good can only exist when its structures offer men and women real opportunities to pursue their own happiness through the exercise of the political virtues. Let me explain further what I mean.

---

but I do not accept his view that political society, or indeed self-love expressed through identification with one's polity, is always invidious.

50. This is by no means a new line of argument, but it is gaining in saliency as the problematic nature of current market arrangements becomes painfully clear; for a good recent example, see Tony Judt, "What Is Living and What Is Dead in Social Democracy?" *The New York Review of Books* 56.20, December 17, 2009, 86-97.

The Common Good and Political Virtues

On the one hand, the common good, understood as the congeries of values and aspirations informing public life, is an embodied ideal, reflected in the actual norms, practices, and institutions of a political community. In order to be genuinely persuasive as an ideal of the common good of a particular community, it must be spelled out in terms of the actual practices of that community in some plausible way, such that it can be expressed concretely in terms of the specific norms and institutions of the community in question. Correlatively, the ideal of the common good plays an indispensable role insofar as it confers legitimacy and coherence on communal norms, thus rendering them practically effective. This is apparent enough. Not so apparent, but equally important, the ideal of the common good also opens up possibilities for living meaningful individual lives, in and through its instantiation in communal norms. After all, the practices and norms embodying this ideal are somebody's practices, norms for someone's behavior, just as the institutional forms structured by these are embodied in interlocking social roles that are filled by individual men and women. What appears from the communal standpoint as a shared set of practices and norms will also appear to the individual as one integral component of an overall way of life, an ongoing dynamic of structured interactions with others through which the individual man or woman can grasp and pursue a properly human way of life. As Raz observes,

> it is of the essence of value that it contributes to the constitution of the agent's personal well-being just as much as it defines moral objectives. The source of value is one for the individual and the community. It is one and the same from the individual and from the moral point of view. Individuals define the contours of their own lives by drawing on the communal pool of values. These will, in well-ordered societies, contribute indiscriminately both to their self-interest and to other aspects of their well-being. They also define the field of moral value. There is but one source for morality and for personal well-being.[51]

In the last chapter, we noted that the natural law can only find expression in concrete norms through its tethering in the individual's natural ori-

---

51. *Morality of Freedom*, 318. Note, by the way, that when Raz refers to well-being, he means a state of comprehensive flourishing, similar to what I term beatitude or happiness; his notion of self-interest is similar to what I describe as well-being.

entation towards her own perfection or happiness, expressed through a life of practice of the virtues. We have also remarked, more than once, that a virtuous life can take more than one defensible form, and that the specific forms it takes will be determined, at least to some degree, by the possibilities for self-understanding and practice opened up by one's community. We are now in a position to draw out the full implications of these observations. That is to say, a community's ideals of the common good will reflect and embody conceptions of particular virtues, together with possibilities for practicing a comprehensive life of virtue, within which individuals can seek their own individual perfection as human agents. They offer individual men and women access to a way of life — typically, indeed, more than one — within which they can pursue and attain the fundamental goods of human life in decent and admirable ways, through which they can appropriately develop and express basic human capabilities, and in which they can enjoy the satisfactions intrinsic to human existence.

For example, Dworkin's account of equality as the sovereign political virtue implies a rich and attractive ensemble of individual virtues on the part of the men and women who embrace this ideal and attempt to put it into practice.[52] In order fully to respect the self-conceptions of others, one needs sufficient humility and at the same time a robust self-confidence to forego any demand that one's social or religious ideals be given a privileged status. One needs a sense of fair play, a capacity for empathetic identification with others' perspectives, or at least ready sympathy for their attachments to those perspectives. The point I want to underscore is that all of these are recognizably individual, as well as distinctively political, virtues — in this instance, dispositions developing and expressing in a coherent way the individual's capacities for cooperative behavior, altruism, and judgment that are central to our existence as social primates. Similarly, the Roman imperial ideal implied an individual ideal of courage, and the Muslim ideal implies an individual ideal of piety, both of which reflect comprehensible ways of developing and expressing fundamental human capacities to resist adversity and to align oneself with an originating source of meaning and value.

This brings us to a further point. We have already observed that the ideals constitutive of a particular conception of the common good will to some extent depend for their expression and practical force on the historical tra-

---

52. This is especially clear in Dworkin's defense of the ideal of equality targeted towards a general audience, *Is Democracy Possible Here?* See especially his comparison of religious and liberal views, as he construes the alternatives, at 52-88.

jectory and present circumstances of the community in question. In order to be effective in a genuinely political rhetoric, appeals to civic and individual virtue must be tethered to what are recognizably expressions and appropriate developments of fundamental human capacities and inclinations. But these capacities can be developed and brought together in more than one way, not all of them compatible with one another, and not all of them possible in every social arrangement. The same observations apply to the individual virtues correlative to these political ideals. The courage of the Roman nobleman and the courage of (let us say) a twentieth-century civil rights advocate facing down a snarling dog look very different. Yet these are recognizably two forms of one virtue, the virtue of courage, manifesting the reflective development of one's capacities to face down danger in fidelity to one's ideals and commitments. Even so, neither kind of courage would be possible apart from the historical trajectory and the social world sustaining it, and they may well not be compatible in an individual life or as components of a social ideal.

So long as we frame this point in terms of the Thomistic language of virtues, understood as perfections of the agent, it is likely to seem archaic and unpersuasive. After all, the language of civic virtue is reminiscent of old-fashioned fourth-of-July speeches by the mayor in the town square, the exhortations of ministers and earnest schoolteachers, or the reproaches of the respectable, scandalized by those who are not. In fact, we could do worse than to engage with small-town mayors, ministers, schoolteachers, and our respectable fellow-citizens; arguably, we have done much worse in recent memory. At any rate, under different rubrics, the general point that I am making here is widely recognized by political philosophers and jurists representing a wide spectrum of views. While there may be few defenders of civic virtue as such, there are very many defenders of communal values, the integrity of a way of life, and the possibilities for individual self-respect and excellence that these open up.

Through their detailed comparative analyses of moral discourse, Richard Shweder and his colleagues have identified three broad categories of human goods, namely, individual autonomy, communal solidarity, and divinity.[53] These are correlated with what they describe as three forms of discourse for understanding human experience. The discourse of autonomy, or personal agency, focuses on considerations of harm, individual rights, and claims of justice; the discourse of community emphasizes personal in-

53. For details, see *Why Do Men Barbecue?* 74-133.

terdependence, hierarchy, and duty; and the discourse of divinity frames its claims in terms of a sacred or natural order, the traditions of a society, and sanctity on the individual and communal levels. "All three goods enhance human dignity and self-esteem," as Shweder observes, but "The rub, of course, is that the three goods are often in conflict."[54] He goes on to argue that American society also embodies these three kinds of discourse — but it configures the three kinds of goods in question in different ways:

> In direct contrast to secular society in the United States, the discourse of autonomy and individualism is seemingly backgrounded in Hindu society, whereas the discourses of community and divinity are foregrounded, made salient and institutionalized. That does not mean that there is no personal experience of autonomy and individuality in India or no personal concern with these goods as essential to well-being. Instead, the themes of personal autonomy are often absorbed into the discourses of community and divinity. . . .
>
> Similarly, although ideas of community — and to an even greater extent, divinity — have been backgrounded and left out of much of the world-description produced and institutionalized by modernist Western social science, these communitarian concerns continue to live on, implicitly or explicitly, in the unofficial folk culture and its discourse.[55]

On the basis of an extensive survey of the literature, Shweder and his colleagues have concluded that these observations can be generalized; that is, cultures can generally be analyzed in terms of the ways in which they formulate and express these three broad categories of human concern. As he remarks, "different cultural traditions try to promote human dignity by specializing in (and perhaps exaggerating) different ratios of moral goods. Consequently, they moralize about the world in somewhat different ways and try to construct the social order as a moral order in somewhat different terms. Cultures differ in the degree to which one or other of the ethics and corresponding moral goods predominates in the development of social practices and institutions and in the elaboration of a moral ideology."[56] The resulting configurations will be to some extent contingent, because they take their starting points in the unreflective practices and customs that simply express "the way we do things"; what is more, they will reflect a community's

54. *Why Do Men Barbecue?* 101.
55. *Why Do Men Barbecue?* 101.
56. *Why Do Men Barbecue?* 102.

particular beliefs, ideals, and material and social constraints in innumerable ways. For these reasons, they will lead to incommensurably distinct prescriptions for life and action, even though each configuration may well offer an intelligible and defensible way of bringing together "goods that enhance human dignity and self-esteem," or as we might alternatively say, distinctive trajectories within which men and women can live satisfying, admirable lives in accordance with the proper inclinations of human nature. They represent, in short, distinct ideals of the common good, each recognizable as such, yet different from one another, in some respects deeply so.

It will be apparent by now that the conception of the common good offered here differs in one key respect from most contemporary Catholic interpretations. As the remarks of *Gaudium et Spes* illustrate, the common good is understood within the social encyclical tradition in terms of international society, as well as by reference to national or local political communities. Indeed, the common good of the human community, taken comprehensively without regard to political boundaries, arguably represents the paradigmatic ideal of the common good within this tradition. Hollenbach endorses a similar view, although he is considerably more conscious of the challenges presented by cultural pluralism in a globalized world order.[57] The common good thus understood looks a great deal like the political morality endorsed in broad terms by Dworkin and others, qualified in such a way as to give greater weight to economic and other positive rights.

According to the account just proposed, in contrast, the common good is fundamentally an ideal of communal perfection, closely bound up with complex ideals of human happiness, and the virtues and ways of life implied by them. Such a notion presupposes that any community in good order will sustain the life of its members through providing material sufficiency, security, and social stability, but properly understood, the common good of a community should be identified with its distinctive and value-laden way of pursuing and sustaining these desiderata. Thus, the ideal of the common good as appropriated within a particular community will necessarily be a thick ideal, laden with specific content. For that very reason, there are many, to some extent incommensurable ideals of the common good, just as there is a plurality of natural moralities. Correlatively, on this account the common good is intrinsically a political good, instantiated in the practices of particular communities and the processes of persuasion and shared deliberation through which these practices are developed and sustained. That is to say, no

57. See *The Common Good and Christian Ethics*, 212-44.

society can achieve any kind of genuine common good apart from local processes of deliberation and judgment. Not only is there no other effective and secure way to facilitate properly political processes of social development and reform; this process is also itself an intrinsic component of a common good, and to short-cut it is precisely to undermine the common good. Respect for the common good as understood in one's own community, or as embodied in another society, implies respect for political boundaries and the parameters for inclusion, deliberation, and accountability that they provide.

And yet, the universal ideal embodied in the encyclical tradition reflects the realities of our situation in ways that cannot be overlooked. The boundaries among peoples and ways of life are increasingly permeable, and as individuals make their way across these boundaries, physically or through the exchange of information, they bring their distinctive beliefs and ideals with them, and borrow from their new hosts in turn. The decisions of even the most isolated communities are open to the scrutiny of the world, and rightly so, since they may well have an impact on the rest of the world. And finally, the past century has been a century of atrocities, "crimes against humanity" perpetuated by political communities on their own citizens, let alone more traditional enemies. For all these reasons, we cannot avoid raising the question of whether we might be able to discern and justify a set of universal standards for human conduct, in terms of which to frame principled criticism and reform of local practices, one's own or those of another community. At least we should be able to arrive at the judgment that certain kinds of aggression and abusive behavior are so extreme that the world community can and should join in condemning them and enforcing these judgments in some effective way. That, at least, is the aspiration that the tragic twentieth century bequeathed to the twenty-first.

Does the natural law as I understand it offer any resources for responding to these challenges? It does. Not through the elaboration of a universally applicable conception of the common good, but through the more limited, yet more powerful aspiration towards what Roman and medieval jurists styled the law of nations. As they understood it, the law of nations is comprised of the customary practices and more or less explicit agreements among the peoples of the world, regulating the affairs of political entities and individuals as these act across or outside political boundaries. It is thus itself a product of a kind of deliberation, shaped by a rhetoric that is (ideally) political in the sense of being non-coercive and directed towards natural considerations. Our task, therefore, is to expand the account of persuasive rhetoric that we have been developing so far, in such a way as to identify persuasive arguments that might reasonably be expected to carry force across the boundaries of different conceptions of the common good.

4. At the Limits of the Natural:
Appeals to the Conscience of Humankind

Pluralism and Commonality in Communal Ideals

The ideal of a global common good reflects a broader modern and contemporary preoccupation with the idea of a universally valid morality, concrete enough to be practicable, and yet rationally defensible to men and women everywhere. Starting from this perspective, we readily assume that the natural law must similarly be understood, as Watson suggests, as a kind of secular Decalogue, perspicuously grounded in the natural order or the exigencies of practical reasonableness. The scholastics, in contrast, do not share our preoccupations with establishing a universally valid and rationally compelling moral system. This is not the most pressing issue for them. Their reflections on the natural law are situated in a context of dispute, diversity, and rapid development within one overarching culture, rather than in the contexts of encounters among representatives of quite different ways of life, and interactions of individuals and nations acting outside established political boundaries.[58]

However, we should not therefore conclude that there are no points of connection between the concerns of our scholastic forebears and our own. Admittedly, their contact with other societies, representing alternative ideals of political life, was limited, but their felt need for standards for internal critique, within the parameters of an established tradition, was if anything greater than ours. Above all, their reflections on natural law, political authority, and the common good were motivated by the need to establish some kind of critical perspective on the ideals and practices of their own rapidly expanding and developing communities. Whereas we are attempting to address conflicting ideals and claims in a pluralistic world society, they were confronted by competing alternatives for developing the political ideals of their own societies. Of course, these two sets of concerns overlap; the scho-

58. This section is taken from an article that will appear, in slightly different form, in *Listening: Journal of Religion and Culture*, Spring 2011, and is used here with permission of the editors.

lastics were not unaware of alternatives to their own political ideals and customary practices, and our ongoing engagement with alternative ideals and practices can and often does lead to internal self-scrutiny and reform. At any rate, the scholastics shared one of our concerns, at least — that is to say, they were well aware that any practically useful account of the natural law needs to offer criteria for critical assessment, as well as legitimation, of the actual ideals and practices of particular communities.

Yet so long as the natural law is identified with basic capacities for rational judgment, together with the natural inclinations informing these judgments, it is difficult to see how it can provide the needed criteria. Once again, we are faced with the problem that on this view the natural law appears to legitimize too much. If every practice, every custom, every conception of the common good, stems from and expresses natural inclinations, then a justification for some social arrangement in terms of its naturalness does not seem to be worth very much. What is worse, on this account it would appear that we can give a natural law justification for anything, including much that no well-disposed person would want to justify. How could there be any social arrangement, or any human action, which did not stem in some way from the natural principles informing human life and agency? Even the most flagrantly unfair and exploitative social arrangements reflect someone's natural inclinations, and serve and promote ongoing human life in some way or other. By the same token, even the most atrocious outrages against human dignity express someone's natural desires. Seen from any credible ethical perspective, nature would appear to be ambiguous at best. From the scholastics' perspective, the ambiguity of nature is not itself natural; it reflects the myriad ways in which the concrete expressions of what is natural are distorted by the human patrimony of sin. But this hardly helps — because once we admit that human nature as we know and express it is always to some degree distorted by sin, it is difficult to see how appeals to naturalness can carry any normative force at all.

But this conclusion would be too quick. We need to keep in mind, first of all, that naturalness as understood in an Aristotelian philosophy of nature is tethered to some account of the criteria for identity and flourishing proper to specific kinds of living creatures. Even at this level, naturalness properly so called is a normative concept, insofar as it reflects judgments about what it is for a given kind of creature to develop and flourish in accordance with the ordered dynamisms of activity informing its existence. Correlatively, even at this level, not every concrete manifestation of a natural principle, in the sense of an innate capacity or function, can be said to be natural in the fully normative sense. Malfunctions and diseases are manifestations of natural principles, in the sense of stemming in some way from something innate, and yet they cannot be said to be normatively natural because they undercut the overall, orderly functioning, full development, and sustained existence of the organism.

It might seem that any normative criteria that would emerge at this level would be too basic and under-determined to do useful evaluative work in political contexts. After all, we cannot equate full human flourishing, understood in terms of the practice of the virtues, with well-being understood as a healthy, unimpeded existence as a successful animal. Each can be obtained without the other. Nonetheless, there is a conceptual link between happiness and more basic forms of well-being. The virtues are dispositions informing the basic faculties through which we live and develop by pursuing and enjoying the natural goods of life, and if they are to count as genuine perfections of these faculties, they must consist in dispositions to pursue and enjoy specific goods in a reasonable and appropriate way. Illness is a misfortune, but a vicious tendency to pursue a life of fine dining (or snacking, anyway) even at the risk of one's health is appropriately a target for reproach.

In the same way, the concept of the common good proper to a given community cannot be equated with the ongoing activities and overall well-being of the population of human animals comprising it. But a sound ideal of the common good will consist, in key part at least, in a collective disposition to pursue and attain the basic conditions for human existence in a given way, appropriately and in harmony with whatever are taken to be higher purposes and ideals. By the same token, a putative conception of the common good that did not take due account of such considerations would be considered to be, at best, ill-advised and in need of revision, if not downright indefensible. Widespread poverty, social instability, vulnerability to natural disasters — these are appropriately targets for commiseration, and when possible, assistance, when they cannot be traced to human agencies within the community itself. But when these misfortunes reflect social arrangements and policies that could have been otherwise, and especially those which still could be altered through the political processes of the community itself, they become targets for reproach.[59]

---

59. By no means do I want to imply that we have no obligations towards those who have been victimized by their own rulers; they are not appropriate targets for our reproach, as I hope to make clear. My point, rather, is that a natural apprehension of what it means to sustain the common good (not necessarily understood in those terms) provides a widely persuasive basis for reproach, even among those who may not agree on much else.

Political Vices: Tyranny, Cruelty, and Callousness

Reproach against whom? At this point, the analytic and normative assessments implied by the natural law are again closely linked. When a human community is functioning in good order, sustaining and at the same time sustained by the prosperous, fruitful lives of its individual members, we can expect that its overall conception of the common good will reflect a plausible account of what it means for men and women to live together in appropriate, harmonious ways. This conception will reflect the ongoing practices and customs of the community itself, grounded in more or less tacit judgments rendered explicit through processes of political persuasion. And since this community is by hypothesis successful, its conception of the common good will be correspondingly sound and defensible, at least in most respects. But the same cannot be said of social arrangements that do not promote the overall well-being of the community and the flourishing of the men and women comprising it. It is at best unlikely that such arrangements would emerge from the ongoing activities of the community taken as a whole, since left to itself, a healthy, self-regulating community will find ways to correct practices that undermine and destabilize it. At any rate, pernicious practices could not be defended through an openly persuasive process of political deliberation. When we see such distorted arrangements, we can at least suspect that they have been set up and maintained by one limited segment or faction within the community, pursuing its own interests and directing the life of the community accordingly.

If this is indeed the case, we do have a target for reproach, namely, the faction responsible for arrangements that undercut the natural and proper dynamisms of the community in order to serve their own limited aims. What is more, we have terms of reproach. This kind of behavior is exploitative, insofar as it places communal life and the well-being of individuals at the service of the interests of others. Indeed, the idea of exploitation is foundational for any defensible conception of justice as a rational human virtue. Once men and women come to see themselves as placed at the mercy of others' aims in this way, they have a most persuasive focus for pre-rational sentiments of outrage, ill-treatment, and desires for revenge. As Judith Shklar observes, those who suffer the effects of culpable negligence, dishonesty, and corruption at the official level "would have seen injustice and cried out in anger and they would have been quite right to do so."[60] The virtue of justice

---

60. Judith Shklar, *The Faces of Injustice* (New Haven: Yale University Press, 1990), 3. She is speaking here specifically of victims of natural disasters whose sufferings are exacerbated by cul-

takes shape through an ongoing reflection on injustice, and the myriad ways in which it is experienced and felt.

So far, I have been speaking in terms of social dynamics, played out through the interactions of different factions within society. Of course, these same reproaches can also persuasively be directed towards individuals who act in exploitative and unjust ways in public contexts. They will be especially appropriate in the context of individual rulers whose practices and enactments are clearly aimed towards mainlining their own power, enriching themselves, and the like — those modern-day heirs of the ancient traditions of tyranny. Of course, lesser public officials and private citizens can and do behave in exploitative and unjust ways — ranging from some variety of outright fraud to the use of one's wealth or lobbying power to block inconvenient legislation. In either case, the exploitative character of the act in question will be especially apparent when it reflects a departure from the prevalent customs of the society itself. Lawrence Rosen has shown that the ideals of lawfulness look very different in many traditional Muslim societies, precisely because they do not draw sharp lines between legal and non-legal considerations. In such a context, it would make little sense to condemn what, in our very different legal and social situation, would constitute violations of due process.[61] In contrast, the legal system in Pakistan does follow Western models, and while this is no doubt a remote effect of colonial exploitation, it is by now a long-standing, deeply entrenched, and widely supported element of Pakistani society. This became apparent in March of 2007, when President Pervez Musharraf suspended the Chief Justice of the Supreme Court, Iftikhar Muhammad Chaudhry, leading to organized protests by lawyers across Pakistan. Subsequently, just before scheduled national elections in November of that year, Musharraf declared a state of emergency, suspended the constitution, and fired the chief justice of the Supreme Court. Again, these steps were widely and rightly condemned, both by his own fellow-citizens and by the world community — all the more so, since his actions were transparently aimed towards maintaining his own power.[62]

---

pable neglect and corruption on the part of state agencies, but we can readily generalize the point. My arguments in this section have been shaped throughout by her searching analysis of the sense of injustice and its centrality for a healthy discourse of deliberation and persuasion; see especially 83-126.

61. He spells this out in some detail in *The Anthropology of Justice: Law as Culture in Islamic Society* (Cambridge: Cambridge University Press, 1989); in addition, see his *Culture of Islam*, 21-38, 56-74.

62. For further details, see Trudy Rubin, "Musharraf War on Courts Hurts Terror Fight,"

These kinds of judgments are very basic, and yet they do important normative work in certain contexts. We are continually confronted by political leaders who exploit the natural resources of their countries for private or factional gain, threaten their own subjects with harm, and maintain their position through unilateral exercise of power, in despite of the norms and practices of their own communities. Sometimes they defend their actions by appealing to their cultural traditions, which, they say, are different from Western traditions.[63] But factionalism and tyranny are not defensible in terms of any tradition, and almost everyone, except for the partisans of the faction or tyrant in question, can recognize that these claims are spurious. The natural law analysis being developed offers an explanation for why men and women can so readily agree in condemning these forms of power, even across the boundaries set by diverse conceptions of the common good. That is, tyrannical forms of power represent perversions of the natural exigencies which any valid conception of the common good will necessarily respect, if the community is to sustain its ongoing life in such a way as to express the natural goodness of human existence itself. Men and women naturally recognize this (not, of course, in these terms) and formulate the corresponding judgments without necessarily drawing on any one particular conception of the common good.

We see another kind of activity that is similarly the target of almost universal condemnation, at least on the part of those not involved in the situation at hand — those kinds of actions, namely, that are so egregiously destructive that they "shock the conscience" of men and women throughout the world community. These are the atrocities, the crimes against humanity, with which we are all too familiar — acts of genocide and mass murder, mass rape as a means of warfare, recruitment of child soldiers, torture; the list could be extended almost indefinitely.[64] No one seriously claims that these kinds of actions can be justified in terms of the ideals and traditions of

Philadelphia Inquirer, December 26, 2007, and Somini Sengupta, "For Now, Musharraf Has Muzzled Legal Critics in Pakistan," *New York Times,* January 5, 2008.

63. Again, Bell offers a perceptive defense of this point; see *Beyond Liberal Democracy,* 52-83.

64. There is a very considerable literature on genocide, torture, and other kinds of "crimes against humanity." For an excellent introduction to this issue, framed with special attention to the relevant legal frameworks, see Geoffrey Robertson, *Crimes against Humanity: The Struggle for Global Justice,* second edition (New York: Penguin, 2002). Philippe Sands offers a thorough account of recent United States complicity, either directly, through the use of torture, or indirectly, through its refusal to participate in the International Criminal Court set up to try perpetrators of such crimes; see *Lawless World* (New York: Penguin, 2005), 143-73, 205-24, 257-81.

any political community. Those governments and peoples who perform them either do not attempt to justify them at all or they find ways to re-describe what they are doing, or plead extreme necessity or provocation — all of which can be seen, sometimes even by the actors themselves after the fact, to be spurious excuses. It seems almost improper to ask why it is that we can so readily agree in condemning atrocities of this kind, yet it is worth pursuing this question, if only because these kinds of condemnations reflect a more general set of considerations.

Since the middle of the last century, we have commonly condemned these kinds of atrocities as violations of the human rights of their victims. If the language of rights has any application at all, this claim is surely correct, but it also seems too weak fully to account for and to express our sense of the outrage that these kinds of actions represent. It is a very serious matter to deprive a priest of the right to say Mass, or to close down a newspaper owned by one's political opponents. But surely these kinds of affronts, blameworthy though they may be, are not equivalent to systematically butchering all the members of a hated ethnic group. "Crimes against humanity" are generally felt to be such because they go beyond most of the ways in which men and women violate the claims to forbearance and respect. They are not just harmful or unjust; they represent egregious violations of the common claims of humanity. In international law, this sense of outrage is expressed through the framework of peremptory or *jus cogens* norms, which are non-derogable and cannot be altered by the positive acts of nation-states or other agencies.

Sometimes, actions of this kind will be exploitative, and will therefore call forth a condemnation similar to that directed against factions and tyrants more generally. But again, our antipathy towards exploitation does not seem in itself to capture the full dimensions of the outrage that we feel, confronting an act of genocide or torture. What is more, these kinds of actions very often do not promote the long-term interests of those who carry them out, and may not be understood and pursued in those terms even by the perpetrators themselves. The most egregious forms of aggression tend to be driven by forces that go well beyond cool calculations of self-interest — above all, by hatred and the sheer joy of dominating and hurting the hated other. This, I suggest, is a key reason why these kinds of actions elicit unhesitating and universal condemnation; they are cruel, and the idea of cruelty, like that of exploitation, represents one of the evaluative touchstones for any communal appropriation of the natural law. Of course, no one of these kinds of actions is *merely* cruel. Each carries its own distinctive kind of malice against a way of life, the physical freedom, the mental and spiritual integrity of another, or the like. Nonetheless, I would claim that whatever else they are, these kinds of actions are cruel, and it is this quality which accounts for their immediate and universal condemnation.[65]

Why should this be the case? Not every infliction of pain or suffering on another is cruel, but when men and women are made to suffer gratuitously, without any credible justification that they might themselves accept, we should at least suspect cruelty on the part of the perpetrators. Add to this some delight in the infliction of pain and suffering on another, and we have pretty well captured what it means to be cruel. Cruelty thus represents something more specific than a disregard for the due claims of another (which may stem from almost any kind of motive), and it goes beyond exploitation, taking delight in the pain of another whether this promotes one's wider interests or not. These considerations account for the distinctive revulsion that we feel when confronted with crimes against humanity; these kinds of actions typically go well beyond ordinary, comprehensible forms of unfairness and self-serving greed, although they may well manifest these vices as well. And yet, even though almost anyone is repulsed by clear examples of cruelty, this seems to be very nearly a universal human tendency. Children are famously cruel, and we do not grow out of these tendencies so completely as we might wish. Who has not felt some guilty delight at the discomfort or distress of another, or taken pleasure in sarcasm or in humiliating another?

However we are to account for it, the tendency to cruelty appears to be deeply rooted in human nature as we now experience it, and if pervasiveness and innateness were in themselves the touchstones for naturalness, we would have to conclude that cruelty is enjoined by the natural law. But of course it is not, and the reason is that even though it is pervasive, cruelty nonetheless represents a perversion of what is natural in the proper, normative sense. It is a perversion, first of all, because it consists in the knowing infliction of pain and suffering, and thus, the orientation of the will towards what we can only describe as natural evils. But there is a still more fundamental reason why cruelty is perverse. Once again, we need to remind ourselves that the normative force of naturalness does not depend on considerations of innateness alone, but reflects the innate formal character of a given

---

65. Again, I am indebted to Judith Shklar; in this case, to her profound reflections on cruelty as a personal vice and social practice; see *Ordinary Vices* (Cambridge, MA: Harvard/Belknap Press, 1984), 7-44.

kind of creature, including an ideal state towards which its operations are naturally directed. Seen from this perspective, cruelty is a perversion because it undermines our natural inclinations as social animals to form complex bonds of intimacy and interconnection with one another. What is worse, it is itself an expression of these inclinations, in a form distorted by the agent's delight in pain and (usually also) her desire to dominate another. It is sometimes said that certain atrocities could only have occurred once the perpetrators dehumanized their victims. To some extent this may be so, particularly when a whole population has been mobilized to turn on its neighbors. But once we begin to examine the experiences of perpetrators and victims of cruelty, it becomes apparent that cruelty reflects and sustains deeply human sentiments towards, and relationships with, the victims of the cruel agent. The hatred that springs up in concentration camps, refugee camps, and secret prisons would simply not emerge in a slaughterhouse for animals, but in a population of despised fellow human beings, it is all too comprehensible.[66]

The peoples of the world can join in condemning crimes against humanity because these kinds of actions represent extreme examples of the deeply perverse, yet almost universal human tendency towards cruelty. In terms of the proposed account of the natural law, they reflect our innate sense that cruelty and its expressions represent a misdirection and corruption, at a very deep level, of the very inclinations and capacities for attachment that ground our humanity and offer the deepest satisfactions of our lives. What is more, the deep universal repugnance towards these atrocities also reflects a sense that almost any of us might be drawn into these or similar kinds of behavior. We condemn them so strongly precisely because on some level they attract us. The proposed account of the natural law cannot account for this, of course, nor can any other theory of morality. Only a theological explanation, couched in terms of the pervasive strain of sinfulness running through our historical experience, could do so.

In any case, the widespread tendency towards cruelty represents perhaps the most serious, but far from the only consideration that comes into play as we confront the crises that emerge in the world community. At the extreme, indifference to the suffering of another can be almost as bad as outright cruelty, particularly when it stems from a knowing disregard of the needs and pains of others, motivated by one's own self-interest. The deep, nearly uni-

---

66. This is not to say that the kinds of suffering inflicted in the slaughterhouse are morally justifiable, either. On the contrary, we always need very good reasons to justify the infliction of pain on another sentient creature, and indifference to another's pain is always to some extent vicious.

versal outrage following initial governmental responses to the aftermath of Hurricane Katrina reflected the sense that these responses reflected just this quality of callousness to the urgent needs and suffering of others, including especially the poorest and most vulnerable among us. We saw a still more striking example of public callousness more recently in Myanmar in 2007, following a devastating cyclone which left at least 100,000 people dead or injured, making this the worst natural disaster in its history.[67] Clearly, the ruling junta could not meet the needs of its people on its own (few regimes could have done so), and yet it first turned away, and then delayed, the entry of aid and assistance from the United Nations and other relief agencies. As a result, many of its own citizens died unnecessarily, and many more were forced to endure extreme suffering which could have been ameliorated or relieved by the timely assistance waiting, literally, at their shores. There was no reason to believe that the ruling authorities in Myanmar acted as they did out of any positive delight in the sufferings of their subjects — rather, they were apparently motivated by fear that the free entrance of foreigners would destabilize their society, thus undermining their own power. If this is so, they cannot be accused of cruelty, but they can be charged with an indifference to suffering, a callousness so severe as to approach cruelty in its gravity. Like cruelty, callousness represents a perversion of our natural inclinations to associate with others through bonds of empathy and attachment. Like cruelty, it is naturally seen as appropriately the target of reproach and condemnation. And like cruelty, it reflects an all too pervasive human tendency — all the better reason to condemn it so strongly, so as to contain an impulse that we can all see within ourselves.

We can thus account on natural law terms for the almost universal condemnation elicited by certain forms of exploitation, atrocious acts of cruelty, and egregious expressions of indifference to the suffering of others. In order to do so, we need not appeal to a universally valid, rationally compelling moral system. Rather, we can account for, and by the same token justify these judgments in terms of the proper structures and innate value of human existence itself, which are naturally perceived in such a way as to inform our spontaneous normative judgments, even though these may not be expressed in natural law terms. This in itself is significant, because it secures at least

67. Again, the Myanmar tragedy has been widely documented; for a good summary of events, placing these in the wider context of humanitarian interventions in a range of contexts, see Brian Urquhart, "The UN and the Race Against Death," *The New York Review of Books* 55.11, June 26, 2008.

these kinds of judgments from the corrosive effects of untethered moral relativism. Richard Rorty once famously remarked that if Socrates was wrong, and we have no intuitive grasp of the Truth, then "when the secret police come, when the torturers violate the innocent, there is nothing to be said to them of the form 'There is something within you which you are betraying. Though you embody the practices of a totalitarian society which will endure forever, there is something beyond those practices which condemns you.' This thought is hard to live with."[68] Indeed it is — but if the preceding analysis is correct, we do not need to live with it. On the proposed account of the natural law, it is difficult to see how a profoundly corrupt society could "endure forever." But even in the extreme circumstances Rorty envisions, it would still be possible to appeal to something "within," held in common by perpetrators and victims, namely, the normative structures proper to our existence as creatures of a specific kind. These structures do not come preformulated, as it were, into a fixed moral code, but they do provide persuasive reasons, in some cases cogent reasons, for joining together in condemnation of certain practices and actions.

Ambiguity, Imperfection, and Injustice in Political Institutions

What is more, we can extend this line of analysis in such a way as to identify legitimately persuasive criteria for assessing the quotidian structures of any given society, criteria which we may reasonably expect to carry weight both within and across the boundaries of particular traditions and ways of life. These are the kinds of considerations that come into play in the context of debates over contested ideals of life and conflicting practices within the world community, just as — and in much the same way as — they inform deliberative critique and reform within a given society. Arguments to the effect that a given set of policies, practices, or enactments is exploitative or inequitable, and therefore unjust, are among the staples of domestic politics and a recurring refrain in international fora. Examples could be multiplied indefinitely. In the United States, debates over the proper use of natural resources, especially water, are very often couched in terms of a charge that one state, or one segment of the population, is exploiting limited water supplies for its own particular interests, or taking more than its fair share. Inter-

68. Richard Rorty, *Consequences of Pragmatism* (Minneapolis: University of Minnesota Press, 1982), xlii.

national debates over farming and trade policies regularly bring up exploitative effects of protectionist policies within the United States and Europe, which are unfair towards farmers and producers in other nations. These examples have to do with policies and enactments, but similar critiques against practices, customs, and institutions are similarly familiar. Some thirty years ago, feminists within the United States developed a powerful argument that marriage as we practice it in Western societies is intrinsically exploitative towards women; similarly, the caste system in India is widely regarded, by outside observers as well as some within the society, to represent a kind of institutionalized exploitation along ethnic and class lines. These claims are controversial, of course, but my point is that all parties to the relevant debates understand what they mean; there is not much need for shared ideals and normative commitments in order to arrive at a level of shared understanding necessary to lodge, and to respond to, accusations of these kinds.

Similarly, accusations of cruelty and callousness play a central role in political deliberation in both domestic and international contexts. The practices of Islamic law have attracted a great deal of scrutiny because they seem to many — including some within the Islamic community as well as many outsiders — to be cruel. It is hard for many to comprehend, much less to sympathize with, legal arrangements that countenance mutilation and stoning as legitimate penalties. By the same token, it is difficult for most Western peoples outside the United States to sympathize with the seemingly cruel practice of the death penalty in that nation, and many domestic critics of this practice agree. To take a somewhat different set of examples, certain aspects of some arrangements for marriage and child-rearing are likely to seem callous from an outsider's perspective or indeed from the perspective of many within the relevant community itself. Arranged marriages and the strict prohibition of divorce may seem to presuppose considerable indifference to the deepest desires of the men and women involved, and the practice of isolating the different members of a family in sleeping arrangements may suggest a certain lack of sympathy towards universal needs for closeness and attachment, especially on the part of children. Again, even though these kinds of critiques are arguable, they are at least comprehensible even in contexts shaped by deep disagreements over normative specifics.[69]

69. For a good overview of debates over the limits of appropriate punishment at the international level, see *Crimes against Humanity*, 131-51. For an excellent recent study of differing perceptions of appropriateness, kindness, and boundaries in child rearing practices and family relations generally, see Barbara Rogoff, *The Cultural Nature of Human Development* (Oxford: Oxford Uni-

These comprehensible charges are arguable, however, in a way that the charges of exploitation, cruelty, and callousness directed against egregious tyranny and crimes against humanity are not. The very heinousness of these latter kinds of offenses would seem to foreclose any kind of serious debate over whether they are justifiable or not — although there is still a great deal of scope for debate over what we, as bystanders or as members of a responsible world community, can do or should attempt to do about them.[70] But when we turn to the examples just mentioned, it is apparent that in these and many similar cases, there is far greater scope for good-faith disagreement and debate. It is sometimes hard to appreciate this, in contexts that engage deeply different sets of ideals and normative commitments; it is so obvious to many in the West that the caste system is unfair, or judicial mutilation is cruel, that it can be hard to see how anyone could in good faith come to different conclusions. Yet these disagreements are not different in principle from debates in the United States over whether the death penalty is cruel. In each case, we are confronted with a set of social practices that involve real human costs — costs that are acknowledged by almost all parties to the debate. But this does not, in itself, resolve the debate, because defenders of the practices in question can also point to the values that the practice represents, the benefits that it confers, or the necessities to which it answers. These considerations outweigh those aspects of the practice that would otherwise be construed as unfair, cruel, or callous — the point being, that the practice in question should not be characterized in these terms because it reflects a justified sacrifice of some natural goods in order to secure others.

It would be easy to dismiss this line of argument as rationalization, and this may very often be the case. Yet we cannot dismiss it out of hand in this way. The fact is that the practices, customs, and institutions of human society are very often ambiguous in just the way that this argumentative strategy would suggest. We may readily see how these preserve and promote some aspects of human existence, or benefit the community in some other way,

---

versity Press, 2003). Sara Harkness, Charles Super, and Constance Keefer offer a good example of changing paradigms for appropriateness in this regard within one culture, namely that of the United States, in "Learning to be an American parent: How cultural models gain directive force," in *Human Motives and Cultural Models*, ed. Roy D'Andrade and Claudia Strauss (Cambridge: Cambridge University Press, 1992), 163-78. Examples of differing perspectives of marital practices abound; for a good example, see *Foundations of an African Ethic*, 34-39, and Don Browning, *Marriage and Modernization* (Grand Rapids: Eerdmans, 2003), 30-55.

70. Again, see Urquhart, "The UN and the Race against Death," for a good overview of recent crises and the practical and moral challenges that they present.

while at the same time recognizing that they do so at a real cost. As we noted above, any specific set of social arrangements will impose a set of alternatives while foreclosing others, thereby depriving men and women of possibilities for life and happiness that they might otherwise have enjoyed. By the same token, every stable way of life offers possibilities for the development of natural capacities, in such a way as to practice genuine virtue and to live in a satisfying, humanly happy way. When a society turns from one set of practices to another, for whatever compelling reasons, something of real value will inevitably be lost — very often, not without a prolonged struggle. These kinds of ambiguities are inevitable, given that no set of social arrangements can provide for every relevant value, or keep open every conceivable avenue for human happiness. In addition, a further level of ambiguity is introduced by the pervasive realities of sinfulness. Even the most admirable practices and institutions will inevitably reflect the distortions of collective egoism and self-seeking; what is more, the central institutional forms of human life, as we experience them, reflect harsh necessities of safeguarding the conditions of life against selfishness and violence. This does not imply that the institutional forms of human society are themselves fundamentally expressions of sinful impulses, or only or primarily safeguards against these, as generations of more pessimistic theologians have argued. With only a few exceptions, longstanding and pervasive practices and institutional forms express the positive purposes of human nature and reflect its goodness and its claims on us, and for this reason they are fundamentally targets for respect and gratitude, and only secondarily occasions for regretful submission.

Nonetheless, the ambiguities and the costs of almost any practice or institution have to be taken into account in the processes of political persuasion and deliberation. Indeed, this necessity gives rise to what may well be the most fundamental form of persuasive argument in political contexts, within as well as across the boundaries set by diverse cultural traditions. This argument takes the form of identifying the natural purposes served by a given practice or institution, acknowledging the ambiguities, limitations, and costs inherent in it, and making a case that it is, nonetheless, justified in light of its overall purposes, given the circumstances, history, and culture of the society in question. What it amounts to, in short, is an argument to the effect that, all things considered, a given set of social arrangements is justified, and its costs are worth it, in light of the values that it expresses or secures — where judgments of the form "it's worth it" are not to be construed in terms of a straightforward utilitarian calculus, but are themselves developed by reference to the specific considerations in play. These kinds of arguments will almost always call for resolution through some kind of considered judgment which configures the benefits and costs in a particular way. And since more than one such construal will always be possible, there will always be some scope for good-faith disagreement, even after an issue has been practically resolved. That is why the arguments in question call for persuasive rhetoric and political deliberation, processes which allow for defensible decisions while also leaving room for principled disagreement and incommensurable choices.

The processes of persuasion and deliberation presuppose at least some consensus of beliefs and commitments, without which genuine disagreement and debate are impossible. Ultimately, this consensus is rooted in the claims of a shared humanity, as expressed in the first principles of the natural law. But shared humanity and the natural law are only given concrete meaning and efficacious force in and through their active appropriation into a specific way of life, including the political processes of deliberation and persuasion. Thus, these general principles cannot be set over against the political community, as if they constituted an independent, efficacious, and authoritative set of criteria for common life. Once again, we are reminded, in Garsten's words, that "There exists no sovereign authority to settle our disputes," not in the domestic arena, much less at the international level.

Garsten goes on to say:

> Ultimately politics is not analogous to a courtroom; there is no judge to offer a final verdict; we are always, in that sense, in the state of nature. Instead of resolving our fundamental disputes all at once we are left to struggle over them as they arise repeatedly in different forms in particular cases over a long period of time. Seeing this path ahead and seeing how efforts to cover it up tend to produce more insidious forms of discord is what may convince us that the difficult project of persuasion is worth our efforts.[71]

It is true that legal authority serves the purpose, *inter alia,* of resolving disputes in a relatively definitive way. Correlatively, the distinctive forms of legal argumentation are somewhat different from the forms of deliberation and persuasion characteristic of political discourse, although as we will see, not radically so. At the same time, legal authority is itself a kind of political authority, and its characteristic purposes can only be understood as specifications or implications of the purposes of political authority more broadly con-

---

71. *Saving Persuasion,* 210.

strued. Ultimately, the law depends for its force on the authority of the community itself, and the distinctively legal values of independence and proper legality find their context and point in a larger framework of political virtues oriented towards the community's distinctive ideals of a common good. We turn in the next chapter to a closer examination of legal authority, as exercised in distinct and complementary ways by the judge and the lawgiver.

CHAPTER 4

Legal Authority

In the last chapter, I argued that among the natural relations of authority which structure our lives, political authority plays a distinctive and necessary role as an expression of the community's foundational authority over its own members. Building on the analysis of the natural law set out in chapter two, I tried to show that even though human nature is structured through normative principles of operation, accessible as such to rational inquiry, these principles under-determine the practical norms giving them expression. The community itself provides the necessary level of specification through generating and sustaining a culture, that is to say, a distinctive and more or less coherent ensemble of an overall worldview, beliefs, ideals, and practices expressed through the characteristic mores of the community. These norms inevitably take the form of contingent, and in that sense arbitrary, specifications of general principles. Nonetheless, these norms are rationally justifiable, insofar as they represent a defensible and persuasive expression of generally shared natural inclinations. Thus, the authority of the community, which is the basis for every kind of political or legal authority, is itself justified by the necessity for specifying the normative principles of human existence through concrete norms. Political authority, in turn, rests on its indispensable function as the institutional expression of the authority of the polity, as formulated through the community's authoritative judgments — comprehensively considered, we should now add, in contrast to legitimate but more restricted loci for communal authority, as, for example, a family or a professional association.

Is this sufficient to account for a properly legal form of authority? Much depends on the generosity of one's terms. Seen from one perspective, the customary practices of any community can be regarded as a kind of law.

Since every society is structured through customary practices of some kind, stemming from its distinctive culture, every human society will exhibit a kind of law, broadly understood. This seems to me to be a legitimate extension of the idea of law, but taken by itself it is too comprehensive to offer much in the way of conceptual clarification or analytic power. In addition, we find distinctively political kinds of authority, and corresponding to these, more or less formalized legal systems, in most communities of any size and complexity. As such, these institutional forms do seem to reflect pervasive, naturally grounded exigencies of human life, even though they only emerge in certain conditions and therefore cannot be regarded as universal features of human experience. The legal systems with which we are most familiar, exhibiting as they do a high degree of autonomy and formalism, are more distinctive still, and especially characteristic of a distinctively modern form of political arrangements; although formalized, independent legal systems are by no means only a modern phenomenon, as we have seen.

If formalized legal systems of this kind are taken to be paradigmatic instances of law, then we cannot say that legal systems are as such universal features of human life, although certainly such systems are very widespread. What is more, the highly formal, self-referential norms and procedures of modern legal systems might seem to be far removed from the forms of life, values, and ideals intrinsic to human functioning, so much so that it would be pointless to try to justify the former through any kind of appeal to the latter. Yet as I will argue in what follows, the law as we experience and understand it in modern Western societies does reflect one defensible, albeit socially specific, expression of broader natural purposes. As such, these legal systems can be both justified and critiqued in terms of natural values, in such a way as to bring them within the scope of rational inquiry, deliberation, and rhetorical persuasion. In this way, we can justify the authority of modern legal systems and particular laws, while at the same time, and in much the same terms, subjecting them to normative critique and revision. The conventional character of law is thus not inconsistent with its grounding in what is natural; on the contrary, the law, like every other well-grounded human institution, can only be understood as a conventional expression of natural forms of functioning, which as such only makes sense in terms of the natural purposes that it serves. At the same time, the natural purposes that justify legal authority also set boundaries to its proper exercise — normative constraints that are not extrinsic to a legal system, but stem from properly legal values and the operative principles expressing these values. Thus, the proposed account will address both the questions pertaining

to legal authority, as identified in the first chapter — concerning its legitimacy, and the normative constraints on its exercise — in terms of one theoretically unified natural law theory of legal authority.

In this chapter, I will develop and defend these broad claims through a
more extended analysis of legal authority as one legitimate and salutary expression of political authority, closely tied to those kinds of institutional arrangements that are today characteristic of nearly all sovereign states. In the
first section, we will look more closely at political authority and its relation
to law broadly construed, moving then to a closer analysis of the distinctive
characteristics of modern states and the kind of legal systems that they exhibit. This will lead on to a defense of legal systems in terms of the natural
purposes that they serve, which will bring us in turn to a fuller consideration
of the authority of the judge and the lawgiver, considered, in two distinct
senses, as "ministers of the law." (For stylistic reasons, I refer to the lawgiver
as an individual, but of course in most modern societies the lawgiver is in
fact a legislature, or some other kind of communal body.) We will next consider the normative constraints on the law, which will turn out to be inextricably bound up with the processes through which laws are formulated, promulgated, and received. This will bring us finally to a closer look at the ways
in which the values and characteristic forms of human existence constrain
political authority, and by implication, legal authority — a line of inquiry
that will lead us on, in the next chapter, to consider the boundaries set by the
nation-state itself, considered as a law state, by individual rights claims, and
by international law.

1. Political Institutions, Sovereignty, and the Authority of Law

Political Authority and the Practice of Judgment

Every community has the authority to determine the specific ideals and precepts informing its common life, if only because this determination medi-
ates between the values intrinsic to human existence, and the specific norms
enabling men and women to grasp and pursue them in a knowing, rational
way. Is this primal kind of authority sufficient to account for a properly legal
form of authority? Once again, we cannot address this question without attending to the scope and specificity of its terms. Seen from one perspective,
the customary practices of any community can be regarded as a kind of law.
Culture, which is sustained through these customary practices, is a human

universal, and so on this view law too would be a universal phenomenon, authorized by the primal requirements of rational functioning. Yet considered at this level, the law of a community will be more or less equivalent to what the scholastics called its mores or practices, and what Hart would identify as the first-order ideals and practices constituting its moral system. This overarching system may be more or less unified (and for that matter, more or less systematic), but at any rate, it need not include an independent system of practices, distinguished from the overall morality of the community by virtue of the distinctive purposes it serves — something like a legal system properly so called, in other words.

Law properly so called appears to be inextricably bound up with the emergence of institutionalized forms of political authority, through which designated individuals or agencies act in the name of, and on behalf of the community. We learn from the scholastics that political authority is characterized by its orientation towards the common good. Correlatively, the agencies through which political authority is exercised will necessarily operate in accordance with formal, relatively abstract, and publicly accessible rules. Otherwise, they would not function as impersonal representatives of the community, but as vehicles for private interests or idiosyncratic judgments.[1] For this reason, political agencies and institutions will be absent or rudimentary in small, intimate societies which function best through interpersonal interactions and relationships. Less benignly, political agencies will be absent, truncated, or perverted in communities such as those Bisson identifies in early medieval Europe, dominated by the tyrannical and self-interested exercise of power.[2] In contrast to both alternatives, political authority properly so called relies on established norms and procedures of judgment and action, through which common ends are articulated and pursued, and individuals exercise power and receive their proper due by refer-

1. That is why the emergence of effective forms of political authority goes hand in hand with the development of bureaucracies; for cogent accounts of these processes in the early scholastic context, see James A. Brundage, *The Medieval Origins of the Legal Profession: Canonists, Civilians, and Courts* (Chicago: University of Chicago Press, 2008), 126-63, 283-343, and R. W. Southern, *Scholastic Humanism and the Unification of Europe,* vol. 1: *Foundations* (Oxford: Blackwell, 1995), 134-62. In addition, for an illuminating account of the ways in which the transition to a market economy, structured through impersonal mechanisms of exchange, fostered the emergence of bureaucratic forms of government and correspondingly impersonal criteria for equity and fairness, see Lester K. Little, *Religious Poverty and the Profit Economy in Medieval Europe* (Ithaca: Cornell University Press, 1978), 1-58, 173-229.

2. Again, see Thomas N. Bisson, *The Crisis of the Twelfth Century: Power, Lordship, and the Origins of European Government* (Princeton: Princeton University Press, 2009), 1-83.

ence to impartial, generally recognized standards of justice, in accordance with the community's overall conception of the common good. These norms and procedures comprise what Hart identifies as secondary rules of obligation, amounting to a more or less well-developed system of formal law.

By now, it will be apparent that governmental and legal authorities will in practice emerge and operate together, in mutual interdependence. By no means do I want to imply that the legal system and judicial institutions of a polity must be, or should be, subordinated to political institutions and processes, as these are commonly understood. The judiciary should be, and normally is, largely independent of the legislature and the executive branch. Nonetheless, the legislature, the executive arm of government, and the judicial system all derive their authority from the fundamental authority that the community holds over its members, an authority which in a well-ordered society will itself be political in character, insofar as it serves, *inter alia,* to promote the proper ends of its individual members. Among the institutions that we typically associate with the political process, some bear legal authority, namely, legislatures, and others do not, namely, representatives of the executive and security functions of government. The judiciary is typically — and rightly — regarded as operating in relative independence of political processes, which in turn depend for their integrity and continued acceptance on this very distinction. What MacCormick says about the modern nation-state can be generalized to include any kind of formal, organized political authority: a properly political state of any kind is necessarily a law state, informed by and in its turn sustaining a rule of law through distinct and relatively independent lawmaking, judicial, and executive agencies.[3]

Approached through the natural law analysis set forth in the second chapter, political authority in all its forms, including legal authority, may be construed as a kind of natural authority, to be understood and justified in terms of the broad natural purpose that it serves. Generally speaking, these derive from the natural purposes of the foundational authority of the com-

---

3. Here and throughout this section, I draw extensively on the analysis of constitutionalism, legal systems, and political processes in Neil MacCormick, *Institutions of Law: An Essay in Legal Theory* (Oxford: Oxford University Press, 2007), 39-60 and 171-83. As MacCormick rightly notes, a full account of the institutional forms necessary to sustain a constitutional state would include some discussion of the executive and enforcement agencies of the state, especially since these do carry out some quasi-legal functions, both legitimately (for example, through determining specific regulations) and illegitimately (for example, through the use of so-called signing statements by the U.S. President, qualifying the legal force of the law he signs).

munity. More specifically, they serve the purpose of expressing and fostering the well-being of the polity in a distinctive way. What, more precisely, does this imply? In order to move forward, it will be illuminating at this point to compare the natural law account of the purposes of authority with another account, similarly grounded in a theological appraisal of the purpose of political authority, but more directly dependent on an appeal to divine decree.

In his *The Ways of Judgment*, Oliver O'Donovan offers perhaps the most fully developed and illuminating recent theological account of the rationale for political authority: "The authority of secular government resides in the practice of judgment," which O'Donovan goes on to define as "an act of moral discrimination that pronounces upon a preceding act or existing state of affairs to establish a new public context."[4] As he explains, the act of judgment is an act of moral discrimination, insofar as it sets out to "resolve moral ambiguity and to make the right and wrong in a given moral situation clear to our eyes." It is reactive, a determination elicited by some previous act or state of affairs, so much so that according to O'Donovan it can never be forward-looking, as for example the act of founding a city would be. And finally, it establishes a public context, within which subsequent actions, public or private, may be performed. I would add that it does so by determining the status of some general kind of action, or of some individual considered under an impersonal description of some kind, in such a way as to set up what Raz describes as protected reasons for action, which are regarded as salient for everyone in the political community. Thus understood, the distinctively political act of judgment is not in itself a legislative power, since legal enactments, as expressed through legislation, are forward-looking acts. This seems to me to reflect an unjustifiably narrow construal of the act of judgment, as I will go on to argue. Nonetheless, O'Donovan's analysis is valuable precisely because he points the way towards an understanding of legislation as the necessary correlate to, and thus justified in terms of, the defining purpose of political authority itself — namely, the formulation of normative determinations which are meant to have enduring public force.

If we are to follow O'Donovan's lead, we need to look more closely at the purposes served by the political act of judgment in order to see why these purposes lead on to distinctively legal acts of adjudication and legislation. I say "purposes" advisedly, because for O'Donovan himself the act of judgment serves only one paradigmatic purpose. It is "a response to wrong as in-

---

4. Oliver O'Donovan, *The Ways of Judgment* (Grand Rapids: Eerdmans, 2005), at 1 and 7, respectively.

jury to the public good," a line of analysis he describes as "the reactive principle."[5] Thus understood, political authority is grounded in the exigencies of our fallen condition — and that is why O'Donovan would probably not describe it as natural in an unrestricted sense. By the same token, political authority rests on a divine concession, as he says elsewhere, through which God mercifully leaves us the "rump of political authority which cannot be dispensed with yet, the exercise of judgment."[6]

Certainly, O'Donovan's assessment of political authority reflects our experience, up to a point. Given the ambiguities inherent in every actual ideal and practice, we can at most expect political authority to secure what Reinhold Niebuhr frequently described as a rough justice and a tolerable peace. What is more, O'Donovan's views fit well with a well-established tradition, taken up by Gratian among others, according to which laws are instituted in order to secure public peace and to protect the innocent by restraining malefactors.[7] There is no doubt that this is one of the central purposes of law, and what is more, it is fundamental in the sense that unless a legal system can accomplish this much, it cannot accomplish anything else. Yet as we also observed, at least some scholastics took a more positive view of political authority, and Aquinas, for one, insisted that a distinctively political form of authority would have existed even if we had never sinned (ST I 96.4). This is of course tantamount to saying that political authority is a fully natural and proper aspect of a specifically human form of existence (although it may emerge under only some conditions), and is as such intelligible and good in itself, prior to and apart from the functions imposed on it by our sinful condition. Of course, this claim is not true just because Aquinas says it, but his straightforward defense of the naturalness of political authority should at least prompt a further consideration of the issue.

Innocent Authority: A Thought Experiment

As we saw in the first chapter, that defense turns on the distinction between political authority, which is consistent with the free status of its subjects, and a kind of self-interested dominion which reduces its subjects to servility.

5. *Ways of Judgment*, 59.

6. Oliver O'Donovan, *The Desire of the Nations: Rediscovering the Roots of Political Theology* (Cambridge: Cambridge University Press, 1996), 151; this point is developed at some length in *Ways of Judgment*, 52-66.

7. For Gratian's view of the purpose of law, see the *Decretum* D.1, C.4.

Aquinas concurs with the universally held view that the latter would have been entirely absent from paradise. Nonetheless, he adds, political authority would have been necessary and salutary even in a community uncorrupted by sin, for two reasons: "the first, because the human person is naturally a social animal; hence, human beings in the state of innocence would have lived socially. But the social life of many is not possible, unless someone presides, who aims at the common good, for many in themselves aim at many things, whereas one aims at one. And secondly, because if one person were to have preeminence over another with respect to knowledge and justice, this would be inappropriate, unless the former pursues and sustains the utility of the other" (ST I 96.4). The second of these arguments depends on the claim, which Aquinas goes on to defend, that even apart from sin, there would almost certainly have been differences of ability, experience, and even rectitude among individuals, without however implying any kind of defect or malice on anyone's part. He draws here on a Aristotelian presupposition that recurring features of organic functioning generally do admit of some kind of teleological explanation. But at best, this line of argument can only provide supplemental support for Aquinas's primary argument, especially since any conjectures on the exact conditions of humanity in a prelapsarian state are necessarily highly speculative.

At any rate, Aquinas's distinction suggests a thought experiment. Can we envision a place for a properly legal form of authority in a community in which no one is a malefactor and no one needs protection, a society in which sanctions and coercive force have no place? I believe we can. It is worth emphasizing that my aim in what follows is to bring the properly natural principles underlying political and legal authority into sharper focus by reflecting on what it would mean to live a human life, absent the corrosive effects of sin. I am not engaging in biblical exegesis, much less historical speculation. If Rawls can go behind the veil of ignorance, surely a theologian can venture into the earthly paradise — with just as much commitment to its literal existence as Rawls had to the historicity of the original position. In that spirit, let us ask what kinds of practices and institutions we might find if we were to enter into a society of limited, finite, yet sinless men and women.

Aquinas's defense of the naturalness of political authority relies primarily on the claim that such authority serves a purpose intrinsic to social life itself, namely, the coordination of diverse agents in pursuit of a shared goal.[8] We

8. Of course, the significance of Aquinas's point has not been lost on modern Thomists; for a particularly illuminating example, see Yves Simon, *A General Theory of Authority* (Notre Dame:

have already noted that coordination represents only one aspect of the purposes served by political authority. Aquinas's claim is nonetheless significant in this context, because it implies that a diversity of viewpoints and desires is not in itself sinful or a reflection of sin, although it may well be construed as one of the necessary consequences of human finitude. Thus, he does not take the view that if it were not for the divisions introduced by sin, the individual members of a community would spontaneously agree together on shared aims and the proper ways of pursuing these. Not only would (expected) differences among them lead to greater or lesser degrees of insight into the common good and its appropriate pursuit, but each individual, considered as such, would necessarily desire and pursue his or her own happiness — in close conjunction with the pursuit of the common good, to be sure, but nonetheless sought as an irreducibly individual aim. Thus, the need for coordination by some agency directly responsible for social existence reflects the conditions of human social life itself, rather than stemming from sinful divisions and self-interested desires. Because this need reflects exigencies of human sociability as such, it would have been felt in paradise — just as men and women in that happy state would have expanded their community through sexual reproduction and provided themselves with the material necessities for life.

Aquinas does not distinguish between political authority and the primal authority of the community over its individual members, as we do, but there is nothing in his account to rule it out. Indeed, if our preceding analysis is valid, it seems that a community of sinless men and women would necessarily be authoritative, for just the same reasons that actually existing communities exercise this kind of authority. That is, this primal authority rests on the community's mediating function, through which general natural principles are specified through concrete practical norms. This mediating function is necessary because of the general conditions for rational functioning and not because of bad will or other expressions of malice, and thus we would expect it to be operative, in a supremely appropriate way, among sinless, rational animals. Thus, political authority within a sinless society would stem from the primal authority of the community and would serve the purposes of that primal authority in its distinctive way — just as we find in our own experience.

Yet even granting that political authority serves natural purposes, in vir-

University of Notre Dame Press, 1962, 1980), 23-80. Simon does not, however, consider the constitutive (as opposed to coordinating) function of political authority, nor does he devote much attention to legal authority as such.

tue of which it would have existed even in paradise, why should we assume that such authority would have expressed itself through judgments, in O'Donovan's terms, or through adjudication and the promulgation of laws? The short answer to this question is that there is no necessary reason why authoritative figures in paradise would necessarily have had to resort to either judgments or laws — but neither is there any reason to assume that these would not have existed even in a community freed from sin. The critical variable, I want to suggest, is not the presence or absence of sin, but the size and complexity of the community in question. In order to defend this suggestion, it will be necessary to continue with the thought experiment of life in paradise — asking now about the kinds of communities that might be sustained under such conditions, and the ways of life that we might expect to find there.

When we try to imagine what a sinless human community would actually look like, we might assume that it would be small, consisting perhaps of an extended family, within which all human relationships and shared activities take place within a context of face to face, interpersonally rich interactions. Within such a context, there would indeed be no space for a division between private and public spheres of human interaction, and therefore little or no scope for legal judgment, let alone the promulgation of laws. But why should we assume that a pre-lapsarian society would necessarily remain at this level of size and complexity? According to one scriptural narrative, our first parents are told "be fruitful and multiply, fill the earth and subdue it" — before there is any suggestion that sinfulness has begun to compromise the primal goodness of the created order (Gen. 1:28). This is not in itself probative, of course, and yet it does call our attention to what appear independently to be aspects of natural human functioning. That is, human populations do tend to be both expansive and relatively independent and directive in their interactions with the non-human environment. This being so, there is no reason to deny the possibility, perhaps even the likelihood, that a sinless human community might expand to the point at which coordinated activity and social interactions could no longer be managed through personal directives and responses, embedded in thick webs of personal relationships. Certainly, there would be no enemies in paradise, but the human population might well reach a point at which some men and women would encounter each other as strangers. In order to relate to one another in meaningful and productive ways, they would need to rely on some shared framework of differentiated duties, liberties, and expectations — a system of norms, in other words, in which all persons participate as a matter of course and on whose regular operations all can rely. In this way, the complexity of human life, even apart from sinfulness, would generate a public realm, distinct from the web of interrelationships through which individuals generate and sustain relationships with their intimate associates.

Once we envision this kind of distinction between public and private spheres of interaction, can we rule out the possibility that authoritative judgments might have some place in even a sinless society? At this point, O'Donovan might object that judgment as he understands it would still have no scope under such circumstances, because political judgment "is a response to wrong as injury to the public good," which he goes on to identify as the "reactive principle."[9] But this, I want to suggest, presupposes an unnecessarily limited construal of what might count as a moral, or more broadly, a normative judgment. Suppose, for example, that a man and a woman exercise their natural right to marry, or that two individuals enter into some arrangement for a mutual exchange of services. These are surely licit and positive actions, since they reflect natural human desires and needs and also serve, more or less directly, to promote the well-being of the community. An authoritative acknowledgment of actions of this kind would not involve any kind of negative judgment, and yet it would be a retroactive moral judgment in O'Donovan's sense — only, positive rather than negative, a confirmation rather than a sanction.[10] It may not seem that even these kinds of judgments would be necessary in paradise, but keep in mind that we are presupposing a society large and complex enough to generate a public realm, structured through roles which generate relatively abstract and impersonal claims and expectations, in contrast to a private sphere of interpersonal interactions.

By the same token, it is difficult to imagine that a pre-lapsarian society at this level of complexity could function without some overarching framework of normative precepts which serve to express and clarify the principles underlying political judgments, thus enabling men and women to arrange their private affairs in such a way as to reflect these principles, when relevant and appropriate. Again, we may be misled at this point by the commonly held view that the central purpose of law is to restrain malefactors and by the correlative view that law properly so called implies some kind of sanctions. Certainly, there would be no need for either restraint or punishment in paradise — yet that does not mean that there would be no need for a formal, publicly promulgated law under such circumstances. On the contrary, a

---

9. *Ways of Judgment*, 59.

10. H. L. A. Hart makes a similar point, albeit in different terms, in response to a "command/response" model of political authority; see *The Concept of Law* (Oxford: Clarendon, 1994), 27-38.

law code would be salutary and probably necessary even in a sinless society of any considerable size, for much the same reason that authoritative judgments would be necessary in such a society. That is to say, it would serve the purpose of expressing and sustaining the ideals and principles of the community, in such a way as to render these readily accessible to each of its members. As such, the law would exhibit the principles underlying discrete acts of judgment, and in addition, it would provide a framework of established roles, within which men and women could enter into states of life and relationships having public effect. Under these circumstances, the law would be enabling and permissive, but not restrictive or punitive. Yet as Hart observes, the claim that the law is only or primarily concerned with forbidding and ordering certain kinds of behavior is not plausible in any case. People need legal forms in order to marry, to acquire and to sell property, and to enter into contracts, yet none of the relevant legal forms can plausibly be described as prohibitions or commands. By the same token, there is no conceptual necessity that law, as such, be backed by punitive sanctions.[11]

This brings us to a further point. Even in a sinless society, the law would serve to express and safeguard the properly political character of public authority, in such a way as to preserve the free status of those subject to it — a critical function given the conditions of human life as we know it, in which the uses and abuses of public power seem to be inextricably intertwined. Yet given a situation in which the law operates without sanctions, because its subjects accept its rule willingly and gladly, it may be difficult to see a place for this aspect of legal functioning. We may well appreciate the values of explicitness and consistency as these are sustained by the rule of law in our own, very much post-lapsarian societies; at its best, the law holds public officials accountable and constrains them from the arbitrary or self-interested exercise of state power. Yet surely there would be no need to safeguard the political character of public authority in a sinless society?

Admittedly, under such conditions there would be no need to safeguard against anyone's self-interested or misguided exercise of public authority, since by hypothesis the rulers of the community would be both appropriately disinterested and wise enough to pursue the common good in a suitable way. Nonetheless, under even these circumstances, formal law would still play a necessary role in preserving the political character of public authority — not as a safeguard against abuse but as an expression of the common ideals and principles structuring the community and informing dis-

11. Again, see *Concept of Law,* 27-38.

crete acts of judgment. In this way, the law would render these principles accessible to each individual within the community, in such a way as to enable each mature person to grasp them, to appreciate their attractiveness considered as expressions of shared ideals, and to express that reasoned appreciation through appropriate actions. In other words, the law would offer the necessary framework enabling men and women to exercise genuine virtues of justice and political prudence (of a kind appropriate to subjects, rather than to those in authority), to act as free persons rather than simply following someone else's directives.

At this point, we should recall that in addition to the restraint of malefactors, the classical and Christian tradition of jurisprudence identifies another purpose of law, namely, to render its subjects virtuous. I argued above that, properly understood, this traditional dictum is correct. That is, the law exists to make men and women virtuous with respect to a limited, yet critically important set of virtues — those political virtues, namely, informed by the ideals and principles constituting the community's vision of its common good. It does so by rendering these principles explicit and manifest through general formulations grounded in a casuistry of paradigmatic lawful or unlawful acts. Since we presuppose good will on all sides, we should not assume that men and women in paradise would need these explicit principles to provide inducements for doing the right thing. But they would still need, in greater or lesser degree, assistance in coming to understand the practical implications of their shared ideals. Without some such insight, they might well function as docile subjects, but they could not act as rational, free, and appreciative participants in a common life. They would want to be fair in their dealings with everyone, but without some grasp of the norms of justice they could not knowingly render the community or its individual members their due. For similar reasons, they could not take an intelligent part in shared deliberation or joint activities, nor could they manage their private affairs in such a way as deliberately to bring these into some appropriate harmony with wider concerns. In short, without access to a legal framework, men and women within a sinless, but large-scale community would at best function at the level of good children: they would be conspicuously deficient with respect to the proper perfection of social life. They would lack the critical foundation of all genuinely virtuous activity, namely, a rational understanding of the relevant aims and the overall point of one's actions, and correspondingly an intelligent appreciation and enjoyment of these as genuinely good. This deficiency with respect to the distinctive hallmark of human nature, namely, the pursuit and attainment of virtue in accordance with rational principles, can hardly be consistent with a prelapsarian condition. Even in paradise, men and women living in an extended community would thus need the law to provide a developed, relatively final, and publicly accessible formulation of the practical implications of shared ideals, precisely to enable them to function as mature adults, as knowing, independent and appreciative participants in a common way of life.

At this point, someone might object that while the law might well serve the purpose of inculcating political virtues, it is not necessary to this purpose. A reflective articulation of the relevant principles, standing on its own merits without any kind of authoritative promulgation, would likewise offer a set of articulate principles by which men and women could inform their practical judgments. If the function of the law were simply pedagogical, this might be so — although even so, public laws might serve a useful function for those who are unable to pursue the needed inquiries themselves, or simply prefer to do other things with their time. (Recall Aquinas's remark that differentials of ability in paradise would be incongruous, if these were not put at the service of others.) But besides providing insight and guidance into the practical meaning of a shared political morality, the law provides in addition something that cannot be supplied in any other way. That is, it offers institutional forms and structures through which men and women can actually practice the political virtues, through publicly sanctioned individual activities and through participation in shared activities and practices. Without these institutional forms, individuals could of course still promote the common good through all kinds of private contributions to public utility. But they could not act specifically as citizens of a polity, because they would have no way in which to carry out publicly recognized and sanctioned legal actions, nor could they participate in activities which by their nature require the coordinated activities of many individuals.

The Purposes of Law, Natural and Ameliorative

We can now more fully appreciate the force of Rosen's claim that law exists in order to express and sustain the distinctive principles and ideals informing a particular culture.[12] We might put the same general point in this way: formal law at its best expresses the ideals and principles informing the com-

---

12. Again, see Lawrence Rosen, *Law as Culture: An Invitation* (Princeton: Princeton University Press, 2006), 6-7.

mon good as it is understood in a given community, in such a way as both to instantiate these ideals through explicit precepts and public institutions and to render these readily accessible to the rational grasp of those who are subject to them. Not only is this one legitimate purpose of law, the preceding analysis indicates that it is the fundamental and definitive purpose of law, stemming from the exigencies of human nature as such, apart from any further purposes that it may serve in the light of human sinfulness. It does not follow that a formal, more or less autonomous legal system is a cultural universal, exhibited in some recognizable form in every human community, as language (for example) would be. Nonetheless, as Wickham observes, we do seem to find some system of rules dedicated to "collectively sponsored redress" and organized as a distinctive sphere of activity in all but the simplest human societies.[13] In other words, legal systems presuppose that a community has reached a certain level of complexity, but once that threshold has been passed, they emerge out of the exigencies of the social way of life that is natural to humankind.

It therefore follows that the authority of a legal system rests on the purposes that it serves as a necessary feature of human social life under almost all conditions, and these purposes, correlatively, are reflected in the distinctive contours of legal systems. The law rests on the distinctive ideals and commitments of a specific community, and as such, it represents a contingent, yet rationally defensible specification of general normative principles, justified as such by the foundational authority of the community over its common life. In addition, the law adds a further level of specification, both by expressing previously implicit or ambiguous customary precepts explicitly and clearly, and by pronouncing upon what had been open questions, in such a way as to resolve controversies in a contingent, yet reasonable way. What is more, it adds a second order of precepts to the mores of the community, in the form of procedural rules, forms for legally recognized individual acts, and structures for shared activity. These too will be contingent and yet rationally justifiable (and therefore authoritative) expressions of more general principles, in this case predominantly principles of reasoned deliberation and choice. These latter conditions, and the last especially, give rise to the relative independence of legal systems, and serve to account for the dis-

13. "Conclusion," *The Moral World of the Law,* ed. Peter Coss (Cambridge: Cambridge University Press, 2000), 242. This clearly does presuppose a conception of law that identifies redress as the primary purpose of legal systems. I don't deny that in our fallen condition, this would indeed be a typical and paradigmatic purpose of the law; I simply want to claim that this is not a necessary or definitive purpose of the laws.

tinctive authority of the law, considered precisely as a relatively autonomous sphere of social activity.

Grounds and Limitations on the Authority of Law

One further comment is in order. So far, we have been analyzing the purposes of the law by means of a thought-experiment focused on identifying the exigencies of life in a large-scale, complex, and yet sinless human society. We approached the question in this way in order to focus on those purposes of law that are grounded in human nature itself, in their own way manifesting the goodness of God's creation. As we saw in chapter two, a theological natural law analysis will attempt in addition to distinguish between the properly natural purposes served by a pervasive practice or institution, and the purposes it will generally or necessarily serve in view of the distortions of the natural order introduced by sin. We described these functions as ameliorative, insofar as they serve to remedy the effects of our sinful and vitiated condition as far as may be possible, given the circumstances in which we find ourselves. In the first instance, these ameliorative functions will serve to safeguard and promote the primary natural purposes of the practice or institution under adverse conditions, but they may extend more broadly towards safeguarding natural aims and addressing natural needs in whatever ways are appropriate. In the case at hand, we can readily see that the purpose of the law which Gratian and many of our contemporaries take to be fundamental, namely, the restraint of the wicked, is best understood as the most characteristic ameliorative function of the law, one that attaches to it in almost any set of actual conditions that we can envision. By the same token, systems of law emerging in the world as it is will necessarily function in such a way as to promote common utility, preserve the conditions for cooperative behavior, and promote good order and peace, even among men and women who are very often self-absorbed, selfish, disorderly and fractious. As MacCormick remarks, most people, most of the time, are neither especially virtuous nor particularly well-informed about the substance and spirit of the laws, and the law as we have it must be of such a kind that it need presuppose only a minimal threshold of virtue and intelligent commitment among its subjects.[14]

---

14. *Institutions of Law*, 61-74. In a similar spirit, Aquinas observes that the common good depends on the citizens of the community being virtuous enough — sufficiently so, that is to say, to ensure that most of them are compliant with the laws (ST I-II 92.1 *ad* 3).

This cautionary reminder is in no way inconsistent with the claim just defended, that the primary natural purpose of law is to render its subjects good, by expressing ideals of political virtue and making these accessible through public forms of activity. Even in our sinful societies, the law at its best can and does serve these purposes for those who are willing and able to pursue them. By the same token, it preserves these ideals in such a way as to shape the practices and sensibilities of all members of the community to some degree. That is why it is especially important, precisely in view of the pervasive effects of sinfulness, to preserve an ideal morality of law, as best we can. Sinfulness does not render our best ideals meaningless, or hopelessly corrupt; on the contrary, precisely because we are sinners, it is urgently necessary that we preserve these ideals, in the best way that we can, until better ones emerge as real possibilities for us.

This second level of analysis is especially relevant with respect to the purposes served by the highly autonomous, formalized and abstract systems of law that characterize modern Western societies. For as we observed in the first chapter, these distinctive characteristics emerged (in key part) in reaction to the resurgence of seigneurial power and servile dominion in the late eleventh and twelfth centuries. In this context, it was particularly urgent that the law express and safeguard the properly political character of public authority and the freedom of those subject to it. Thus, the appropriate expressions and operations of a legal system in this context were inextricably bound up with an ameliorative function, namely, to provide safeguards against the resurgence of forms of servile dominion, which are antithetical to any kind of meaningful freedom. That is why early scholastic jurisprudence places such a heavy emphasis on the independence of the law and also its impersonal character, in virtue of which judges can be said to be "ministers of the law," whose individual judgments and responsibility are to some degree submerged in the law. This approach is not without its own ambiguities, but at its best it serves to safeguard the consistency of the laws and to protect those subject to the law from arbitrary impositions of power.

We now come to a critical point. The grounds for the authority of legal systems also set normative constraints on its legitimate expressions — constraints grounded in part in the fundamental requirements of publicity, efficacy, and consistency identified by Fuller as the intrinsic morality of law, but also stemming from the congeries of political ideals and commitments constitutive of the community — its political morality, in Dworkin's terms. These two sets of constraints are integrated through the operations of the law in accordance with its properly natural function of articulating ideals of the distinctive political virtues of the community and offering the paradigms for action necessary to the effective practice of these virtues. If the law is to serve this fundamental purpose, its prescriptions must meet at least minimal standards for clarity, consistency, and appropriate stability; otherwise, individuals could not grasp the norms being proposed, or pursue them through action, in such a way as effectively to participate in the ideals of their society in an informed and appreciative way. By the same token, the political morality itself must be genuine — which is to say, it must reflect a defensible construal of natural ideals and purposes that can be justified through an open process of rhetorical persuasion. Of course, we are well aware by now that natural human flourishing can take a wide range of legitimate forms, and by the same token, the political morality of a community will be a contingent specification of what human flourishing means. But if this morality is to sustain a legal system that really functions to promote political virtues, then it must leave at least some space for individual freedom of choice and action, and some room for individual participation in processes of communal deliberation; otherwise, the laws might generate docile compliance with ideals of conduct but could not form and enable a fully virtuous appropriation of those ideals.

So far I have spoken in terms of more or less autonomous and formalized systems of law, in order to take account of the fact that legal systems take a wide range of forms, some of them more closely integrated with the general mores of the community, or more deeply interconnected with wider systems of social interaction (such as family or tribal groupings) than we would consider consonant with "proper legality." But we have also observed that modern Western legal systems are autonomous to a marked degree, operating at a level of abstraction, formality, and self-referential justification that renders them practically inaccessible except through the mediation of highly trained legal professionals. Can we account for and justify the distinctively formal, abstract, and independent character of these legal systems in terms of the overall line of analysis just set forth? There is of course no denying that the abstract, formal, and self-referential qualities of legal functioning can be perverted, or simply carried too far. The law can become so complex and convoluted in its operations that it simply grinds to a halt, and the need for practitioners with specialized skills, inaccessible to most outsiders, constitutes an open invitation to abuse. Nonetheless, the formality and autonomy of law do preserve and exemplify real values, intrinsically and not merely as instrumental means towards external ends. Lawyers can take genuine pride in being officers of the court and agents of justice, and Western societies generally preserve ideals of due process, equitable and open adjudication, and judicial independence. Can we account in natural law terms for these as genuine values, grounded in the distinctive form that legal authority takes under commonly recurring circumstances?

In the first chapter, we traced something of the trajectory through which the transition from personal fealty and servile dominion to properly political forms of authority and obedience led Western societies towards impersonal, role-structured, and bureaucratic forms of social organization. We concluded that these features of social systems are not hallmarks of modernity as such, much less reflections of a widespread process of secularization. Rather, they reflect the exigencies of life in large-scale, complex societies, in which face to face interactions simply do not provide a feasible framework for anything other than the exercise of sheer power and servile submission. What is more, these forms of social organization are likely to be especially prominent in societies comprised of heterogeneous populations, communities of communities, as it were, each of which reflects its distinctive commitments and way of life — conditions that are especially characteristic of modernity, even though they were not unknown in the medieval world or antiquity. In this kind of pluralistic society, a relatively sharp distinction between public and private spheres serves the purpose of maintaining considerable freedom for communal as well as individual pursuit of distinctive ideals and ways of life, while still expressing the values unifying the society as a whole through maintaining a structured public realm, readily accessible to all citizens.[15]

These considerations point the way towards a natural law analysis and justification of Western legal systems that takes account of the high degree of independence characteristic of these systems, while also indicating the normative constraints operative on and within these systems. We have already observed that every legal system serves to express and promote the ideals and commitments informing a polity's distinctive conception of the common good. In Western contexts, this generally takes the form of the political morality of classical liberalism, a morality that gives priority to individual freedom and to the respect that is due to each man or woman as (at least potentially) an agent of freedom and self-determination.[16] Thus, Western legal

15. Raz makes a similar point with respect to the rights of identifiable, culturally cohesive minority groups vis-à-vis wider communities, in *The Morality of Freedom* (Oxford: Clarendon Press, 1986), 250-55.

16. I attempt here to capture, in broad outlines at least, the main lines of political liberalism as they would be understood by our contemporaries working in the philosophy of law and politi-

systems tend to give priority to individual choice and to private arrangements over the claims of collective agencies — for better or for worse — and correlatively, rely largely on individual rights as a safeguard for all kinds of personal interests. At the same time, the abstractness, complexity, and independence of these systems reflect the bureaucratic forms of social organization that are characteristic of most Western societies. As we might expect, the forms and the substantive commitments of Western societies are closely intertwined. The characteristic forms of our societies give special salience to the individual considered simply as an agent, not essentially constrained by personal characteristics or communal ties, and therefore, someone who can move in and out of a range of roles and relationships in a complex society. Correlatively, our commitments to individual freedom are expressed, in key part although not entirely, through procedural norms of due process and proper legality which, by their very abstractness and formality, embody our sense of what it means to respect persons as actual or potential agents.

Understood in these terms, formal law in its distinctively Western forms embodies a particular construal of justice, considered both as a characteristic of equitable social systems and a personal virtue disposing the agent towards right relations to others and the community as a whole. Of course, every human society gives a central place to ideals of justice, but without attempting comparative judgments, we can still take note of the fact that Western political ideals are framed, to a remarkable extent, in terms of an ideal of justice. It is telling that the most influential book in Anglophone political theory, Rawls's *A Theory of Justice,* proposes that all public institutional arrangements be evaluated in terms of their functions as safeguards and promoters of justice — justice, as is well known, interpreted in terms of the social norms that would be acceptable in a community of pure agents, negotiating behind a veil of ignorance of any particular features of human life.[17] Dworkin's construal of the ideal political morality gives more empha-

---

cal philosophy. For good summaries of the views of key figures, see Ronald Dworkin, *Sovereign Virtue: The Theory and Practice of Equality* (Cambridge, MA: Harvard University Press, 2000), 1-7, and *Is Democracy Possible Here? Principles for a New Political Debate* (Princeton: Princeton University Press, 2006), 9-23; John Rawls, *Political Liberalism* (New York: Columbia University Press, 1993), 1-46; and Joseph Raz, *The Morality of Freedom* (Oxford: Clarendon Press, 1986), 1-23. For a perceptive and, with qualifications, affirming theological appraisal of modern liberalism, see Christopher Insole, *The Politics of Human Frailty: A Theological Defense of Political Liberalism* (London: SCM Press, 2004), 1-40.

17. See in particular John Rawls, *A Theory of Justice* (Cambridge, MA: Harvard University Press, 1971), 118-94.

sis to equality, but he similarly places normative weight on individuals' capacities for free choice and self-determination. It goes without saying that seen from this perspective, legal systems are justified by reference to the key purposes of rendering justice and preserving the forms for just interactions among individuals — and in this way, expressing and sustaining the ideals that are central to our best sense of ourselves as a polity. Thus, the purposes characteristic of legal systems generally — to express and sustain a community's sense of itself as a polity, pursuing a common good through the promotion of political virtues — are not at odds with the more distinctive purposes of Western legal systems, including the key purpose of expressing a specific conception of justice. In these societies, the ideals of justice and fair treatment are constitutive of the common good, that is to say, the values and commitments that hold us together as a unified polity.

It is often said that the complex of social conditions and ideals of freedom characteristic of modern Western societies are themselves products of modernity, and more specifically, reflections of secular modernity — for better, or for worse. It is worth emphasizing once again, therefore, that in key respects, medieval European ideals, social forms, and legal systems are similar to our own. As we saw in the first chapter, the bureaucratic organization of European society, its emphasis on abstract procedural norms, and correlatively, the emergence of independent legal systems, are all well underway by the early twelfth century, and the ideals informing common life are correspondingly formulated, to a very considerable extent, in terms of impersonal standards of fairness and equitable treatment. This set of circumstances helps to explain what is otherwise puzzling to contemporary readers — namely, the emphasis that the scholastics place on legal arrangements as the proper locus for the virtue of justice. This emphasis is especially marked in Aquinas, who identifies the proper act of justice simply so called with the act of adjudication, in terms reminiscent of O'Donovan's analysis of political authority. (The act of justice properly so called, that is to say, in contrast to the proper acts of commutative and distributive justice; ST II-II 61.) In response to the question of whether judgment is an act of justice, he says that

> judgment properly names the act of a judge insofar as he is a judge. Now the judge is said to be, as it were, "justice speaking" *(jus dicens),* and the just is the object of justice, as was said above. And therefore judgment implies, in accordance with the primary sense of the word, a definition or determination of the just, or the right. Now if someone appropriately determines some matter in virtuous operations, this properly proceeds from

the *habitus* of the virtue; as, for example, one who is chaste rightly determines those matters pertaining to chastity. And therefore judgment,
which implies a right determination of that which is just, properly pertains to justice. (II-II 60.1)

But when he turns to the next article, which asks whether the act of
judgment is licit, he does not base his defense of judgment directly on God's
divine authorization; rather, he appeals in the first instance to the rational
purposes of law, along lines similar to those developed above: "as was said
above, three things are required in order for a judgment to be an act of justice: first, that it proceed from an inclination of justice; secondly, that it proceed from the authority of the one presiding; and thirdly, that it be produced
in accordance with the right reason of prudence" (ST II-II 60.2). The judge is
indeed constituted as a minister of God (*ibid. ad* 2), but that does not mean
that his judicial acts rest directly on divine authority, much less that they
cannot be challenged or deemed invalid. On the contrary, they are both justified and constrained by the implications of the virtue they express, considered (I would add) as a distinctively full and appropriate expression of natural purposes. Aquinas makes this clear in the body of the article, where he
observes that deficiency with respect to any of these three conditions renders
a judgment vicious and illicit. Presumably, a judgment would not be vitiated
by any kind of vicious motive, but an intention contrary to what he calls the
rectitude of justice does so, resulting in what is said to be a perverse or unjust judgment. Secondly, a judgment is invalid if it stems from some kind of
usurpation of authority; it is also invalid if it rests on inadequate or dubious
grounds, leading to what Aquinas calls, respectively, temerarious judgment
and judgment from suspicion.

According to Aquinas, the ideal that sets the mean of the virtue of justice is an equality of exchanges, specified as rendering to each his or her due
(ST II-II 58.10, 11). Thus, the paradigmatic act of justice, the kind of act
which best displays the proper rational character of the virtue, is an act of
impartial judgment, expressed through and safeguarded by standards of impartial treatment. In this way, an ideal of equality as respect for persons, considered as far as possible in abstraction from personal characteristics or affective relationships, governs Aquinas's analysis of what it means to respect
the fundamental equality of interpersonal interactions that for him is the
central ideal of justice properly so called.

This emphasis on equality construed as impartiality continues through
Aquinas's analysis of commutative justice, the ideal governing relations

among individuals. Here too Aquinas rests his analysis on the traditional dictum that justice requires rendering to each person his or her due, construed in terms of parity in exchanges of all kinds (ST II-II 61.4). The paradigmatic act of commutative justice is thus restitution, the restoration of some equitable balance of burdens and benefits among individuals (II-II 62.1). This need not be a legal action, of course, and yet it is plain that legal exchanges, governed by the ideal of equality before the law, have shaped the way in which Aquinas envisions just exchanges between private individuals. This impression is further reinforced when we read further that the ideal of commutative justice requires that we render to each individual the honor due to him *as a human individual,* that is to say, prior to whatever is due to the individual as the beneficiary of a specific arrangement or as the occupant of a social role or status (II-II 72.1). In this way, equality as a normative standard is expanded to include not only equality of exchanges, but all the central norms of non-maleficence and positive obligation, which Aquinas analyzes as stemming, directly or indirectly, from a general first principle of practical reason according to which we ought not to wrong another person. In this way, Aquinas draws on the language of personal fealty and differential status as a way of articulating a very different set of ideals, those appropriate to courts of law and the structured, bureaucratic societies that sustain them and render them necessary. "Modern" ideals of impartiality, procedural due process, and the integrity of law have made an earlier appearance than we might have thought, in service of ideals of freedom and self-direction that are deeply rooted in the experiences and theological commitments of Europe in this period.

This brings us to a further point. Formal law, understood along characteristically medieval and modern lines, is both justified and constrained by the natural purposes that it serves. So much is implied by the natural law analysis set forth above, and we are now well along the way to developing such an interpretation. But at this point, we should guard against a misunderstanding. We can make sense of law, and value it, as one central component of human flourishing under almost all actual conditions. At the same time, to flag a point to which we will return, a legal system is not merely an instrumental means towards external ends. Rather, a legal system in good order embodies distinctive and characteristic values, intelligible as such in relation to other human values but not simply a means to their attainment. Once again, it is helpful to compare social goods with individual virtues. The virtues represent the full development and exercise of capacities that are in themselves naturally oriented towards well-being at a basic, organic level.

But as we have seen, that does not mean that they should be regarded as means towards the attainment of these desiderata. Rather, they are good in themselves, as active perfections of the human agent and therefore components of human flourishing in the fullest sense. They represent integral components of human existence at its happiest and best.

In much the same way, a formal legal system in good order represents the full development of the community's capacities to form and sustain itself in accordance with shared ideals, but it is not simply a means towards attaining these ideals. Rather, the law comprises one intrinsically valuable component of this common life, with its own integrity and its own claims to respect. The integrity of the law is expressed in various ways — through ideals of proper legality and the rule of law, norms of legislative procedure and procedural due process, and the independence of the legislative and judicial functions in a constitutional state. The integrity of the law, thus understood, places claims on each of us, and on society as a whole. It also places claims on the law itself, as it were, generating norms governing proper legal functioning. Once again, any kind of authority, considered as a natural relation, is both justified and bounded by the natural purposes from which it stems. We turn now to a closer examination of what this general observation might mean in the case of formal law.

2. Custom and Constitution: The Parameters of Legal Authority

*The Law before the Law: Custom as the
Enabling Context for Legal Authority*

At this point, it will be helpful to take stock of the argument so far. The authority of law, considered as one distinctive kind of political authority, is grounded in the natural authority which a polity holds over its individual members. As such, it is both justified and constrained by the natural purposes and needs that it expresses, most fundamentally (in this case) the expression and practical embodiment of the values and mores which sustain the common life of the community. For this reason, it can be misleading to speak of the authority of the law in the abstract. The authority of law is always tantamount to the authority of a particular legal system, which is itself an expression of the authority of a specific political community, setting up a relation (in the first instance) between a polity and the individual men and women who comprise it. It would thus be a mistake to analyze or defend the authority of law on the basis of some abstract conception of law or to appeal directly to shared standards of reasonableness or cosmopolitanism, or to a supposed universal common good, or even, in the first instance, to international law. At the same time, however, the authority of law, and the communal authority on which it rests, is not an undifferentiated or unbounded claim to power, any more than is any other kind of authority. Legal authority is bounded and constrained by the same considerations in terms of which it is justified and by the exigencies that it must meet in order to serve the natural purposes towards which it is directed.

This implies that the laws and legal institutions of a particular society are genuinely authoritative because, and only to the extent that, they serve the general purposes of law in the concrete circumstances of a particular community. More specifically, the legitimacy of these enactments and institutions depends most fundamentally on their character as public expressions and embodiments of a society's key values, the common objects of love holding it together as a society. Secondarily their legitimacy rests on their effective functioning in serving the complex of natural and ameliorative purposes that can best or only be served by the rule of law, including especially the critical ameliorative purposes of securing public peace and protecting the members of the community from those who would otherwise do them harm. Of course, the laws must serve these functions, and must be seen to serve them, in order to preserve the minimal level of acceptance necessary for their effectiveness. But more fundamentally, on the account of authority being developed here, the laws derive their normative force, their status as norms that ought to be followed, from the fact that they are rationally defensible public expressions of the values and mores of a given society, which additionally serve the secondary but critically important functions just noted.

I emphasize this point because it helps to explain why certain prominent accounts of the ground of legal authority have run into the difficulties noted in the first chapter. That is, these accounts have located their analysis at the level at which laws are enacted, or rendered effective through interpretative application. They have settled, in other words, on the authority of the lawgiver or the judge as the proper focus for inquiry. In doing so, these theories reflect the critically important fact that, as MacCormick notes, modern law states are necessarily structured in terms of a rough constitutional division of powers, comprising at least distinct legislative and judicial functions working independently, yet in coordination with one another.[18] Important

---

18. Again, see *Institutions of Law*, 39-60; Anthony King makes a similar point in his analysis

as it is to acknowledge this point, the recent history of jurisprudence makes it clear that we cannot adequately account for the authority of either, much less explain their interrelationships in a satisfactory way, without explaining how both express the community's authority over the lives of its members.

If we are to analyze legal authority in terms of its relation to the basic authority of the community, it would seem that we could find a promising starting point among the many theories of representative democracy on offer today. But while these are undoubtedly relevant to the issues at hand, they cannot provide an account of the origins of legal authority, for the simple reason that the institutions and practices of representative democracy are themselves creations of law.[19] What is more, this approach implies that legitimate laws presuppose a democratic system of governance, and while this view is widely held, as we saw in the previous chapter, it does not take account of the many examples of stable, reasonable, and to all appearances genuine legal systems that have emerged and flourished in non-democratic regimes. Whatever we make of the latter, we should not begin our analysis by ruling them out as genuine examples of legitimate legal systems.

I propose that if we are to develop a persuasive and comprehensive account of legal authority as a natural relation, we need to focus initially at an earlier stage of quasi-legal functioning, at which we find the "law before the law" which provides the basis and legitimacy for formal legal systems. That is, we need to begin our analysis at the point at which communal life begins to yield norms for conduct which express the community's core values in some systematic and generally recognized way through its settled mores and customs. In doing so, we need not attempt to settle the old conundrum of whether we can properly speak in terms of a customary law, standing alongside formal legal enactments as an alternative body of coherent laws. We noted above that in some relatively small-scale communities, customary practices alone seem to suffice for governing common life, and in these cases, there seems to be no good reason to describe these as laws, except in the most general sense. However, in those communities which do display a distinction between public and private realms, expressed through a more or less formal and autonomous legal system, it does make sense to speak of the customs of a community as a kind of law — not a legal system in the full

---

of constitutionalism as a normative political order in *The British Constitution* (Oxford: Oxford University Press, 2007), 10-14.

19. Both Lon Fuller and MacCormick insist on this point; see *Morality of Law*, rev. ed. (New Haven: Yale University Press, 1969), 148, and *Institutions of Law*, 171-85.

sense of the term but a system of norms and practices standing in an integral and ongoing relation with formal legal systems. These represent, as it were, the threshold of the law, the immediate and enabling context of normative practices that mediate between the fundamental authority of the community over its members and the specifically legal authority expressed in formal laws. Thus customary law cannot be law in the full sense, precisely because it provides the immediate foundation for legal authority. Yet by the same token, it is juridically significant and may appropriately be described, in an extended and qualified sense, as a kind of law.

As Fuller observes, customary law did not fit well within the positivist theories that dominated jurisprudence up to his own day.[20] The difficulty here is generated by the early positivists' analysis of legal authority, according to which there is a vertical, one-way relation between legal authority and the specific enactments resting on that authority. Yet customs, if they are taken to have legal effect, would seem not to be imposed by anyone, unless it is the community itself, as it were legislating for itself. And this, Fuller observes, is a problem for the positivists, because for them, "Unlike morality, law cannot be a thing self-imposed; it must proceed from some higher authority."[21] At the same time, early modern theories of the natural law offered, if anything, even less space to construe customs as a kind of law. The natural law — and much more, the eternal law — has long been regarded as quintessentially universal and timeless. Customary law would seem to represent the very antithesis of natural law, so understood, being local, mutable, and fluid, and clearly on the conventional side of the classical division between nature and convention.

When we turn from contemporary to scholastic understandings of natural and customary law, however, a more complicated picture emerges. The idea of customary law plays a more central role in scholastic jurisprudence than in most modern legal thinking. In itself, this is hardly surprising, since at this point customary law was still very much a part of both ecclesiastical and civil legal systems — even as custom began to be supplanted by reliance on written laws. At the same time, precisely because it was so central to their experience and legal thought, the scholastics were well aware of the ambiguities of customary law, and devoted considerable attention to its legitimacy, force, and scope. In the process, they distinguished customary law from natural law. Yet this distinction was not framed in terms of a sharp dichotomy; rather,

20. *Morality of Law*, 232-36.
21. *Morality of Law*, 233.

customary law was seen as (ideally) one kind of specification of the natural law, standing towards it in a relation of dependency and exemplification, rather than outright opposition. Thus, customary law represents the point at which the particular and fluid norms by which a society functions emerge out of the natural needs and inclinations of humankind, and the norms of this law provide the basis and ongoing context for the further specification of natural law through legal enactments. Or so I will argue in what follows.

Gratian Revisited: Custom, Written Law, and Natural Right

In developing this argument, I will once again take my starting points from the foundational text of systematic Western jurisprudence, Gratian's *Decretum*.[22] As we noted in the first chapter, Gratian's work appears during the early stages of the transition from predominantly customary to predominantly statutory legal systems, and perhaps for that reason, he devotes considerable attention to spelling out the interrelationships among custom, written law, and natural law. On his view, the relation between customary and written law can only be rightly understood, and placed on a practically usable basis, in terms of the relation of both to natural law. Thus, he points the way towards an account of law as grounded in natural law, mediated through custom, and justified and assessed in terms of the natural purposes it serves, deriving their goodness and compelling force — their authority — from the goodness intrinsic to a well-ordered, created nature.

We have already examined Gratian's account of natural law and legal authority in earlier chapters. As we have seen, Gratian identifies natural law in its primary sense with the Golden Rule, thus establishing that natural law is vindicated by Scripture and is properly and supremely authoritative within a Christian community. At the same time, in good scholastic fashion he also recognizes that natural law can be understood in a number of ways, all more or less proper and legitimate, which he analyzes by relating them to what he identifies as the paradigmatic understanding of the term. Thus understood, natural law can be identified with almost any defensible, pre-conventional warrant for a concrete normative practice or demand. This ap-

---

22. Again, I draw on an interpretation of Gratian's treatment of custom first set out in my "Custom, Ordinance and Natural Right in Gratian's *Decretum*," in *The Nature of Customary Law: Legal, Historical and Philosophical Perspectives*, ed. Amanda Perreau-Saussine and James Bernard Murphy (Cambridge: Cambridge University Press, 2007), 79-100.

proach to natural law allows for a rich and flexible analysis of the claims of
the natural law, but by the same token, it implies that natural law as such has
no direct juridical effect. Natural law is always expressed in and through social conventions of some kind, and so it makes no sense to try to separate
those norms and practices which are natural, from those which are "merely"
conventional. The distinction between natural and conventional is not a distinction running between two sets of laws; rather, it is an analytic distinction
that applies to every law and legal system, focusing analysis on the way in
which a given convention expresses (whether well or badly) natural principles of reasoning and activity. Seen from this perspective, the mores of a particular society appear as more or less direct and adequate expressions of natural law, and for that very reason, they provide the starting points, and much
of the substance, for the processes of natural law analysis and rhetorical persuasion discussed in preceding chapters.

When Gratian turns his attention to the distinction between custom
and ordinance (that is to say, written law) he reminds us that this distinction
presupposes a basic parity between these kinds of law, considered as two
ways of expressing the principles of natural law. He does so by way of a citation from Isidore, who says that "Law is written ordinance," whereas

> Custom is a kind of right instituted by practices, which is taken for law
> when law falls short. Nor does it make a difference whether it relies on
> what is written, or on reason, since law is also approved by reason. Fur-
> thermore, if law relies on reason, law will be anything that may now rely
> on reason, or at least that which is consistent with religion, that which is
> congruent with discipline, that which leads to salvation. Moreover, it is
> called custom because it is in common use. (D.1, C.5)

These remarks suggest that the boundary between custom and written
law is not sharp. Both kinds of law rely on reason, and what is more, any customs confirmed by reason can take on the force of law. This implies that custom is not merely a supplement to written law but exercises independent legal force. At any rate, custom is a source for written law, as Gratian goes on
to say in the same passage: "When therefore it is said that it does not matter
whether custom relies on writing or reason, it is apparent that custom is in
part put into writing, and in part is preserved only by the practices of its followers. That which is put into writing is called ordinance or right. That
which is not rendered in writing is simply called by the general name of custom." In contrast to law *(lex),* which is by definition a written ordinance (D.1,

C.3), "Practice *(mos)* is longstanding custom handed down only through practices" (D.1, C.4).

Reading further, we find that custom is more or less equivalent to common practice — more or less, because long-standing practices apparently have a greater claim to be regarded as customary law (D.12, C.6, 7; cf. D.12, p.c. 11). As Bisson shows at some length, not every custom is of long standing, and not every custom is good.[23] That is why the author of the Ordinary Gloss on Gratian adds that not every commonly accepted practice constitutes customary law; some practices are merely tolerated, or else they go on in spite of a society's contrary commitments (gloss on D.1, C.5).[24] In order to count as customary law, a practice must not only be congruent with natural law; it must also reflect social approbation and a collective intent to establish or endorse norms for behavior. Just as written law must be promulgated in order to have legal force (D.4, p.c. 3), and legally authoritative judgments presuppose power or authority as well as rational discernment (D.20, pr), so the practices of a community must in some way reflect the will of the people in order to count as customary law. This line of interpretation gains credibility when we read further that no one should promulgate laws that are at odds with the customs of the people for whom the laws are intended (D.8, C.2) This need not imply that such a law would be invalid. The text cited goes on to say that even though long-established custom ought to be respected, it nonetheless yields to divine authority. Given the context, this would seem to be the point Gratian wants to underscore. Nonetheless, this text offers one more indication that Gratian (and his sources) place a high value on the normative force of custom, suggesting at the very least that legislators should maintain a conservative attitude vis-à-vis the long-standing customs of their community, respecting and preserving them as far as possible and departing from them only when necessary.

This is just the kind of attitude that we would expect, given the kind of society inhabited by Gratian's immediate forebears — that is to say, given the predominantly rural and decentralized character of European society

---

23. Again, see Thomas N. Bisson, *The Crisis of the Twelfth Century: Power, Lordship, and the Origins of European Government* (Princeton: Princeton University Press, 2009), *passim.*

24. This refers to the gloss, or line by line commentary, on the *Decretum* composed (probably) by Johannes Teutonicus around 1215 and subsequently accepted as the standard or "ordinary" gloss. As such, it was traditionally published together with the *Decretum.* For further details, see the introduction to *Gratian: The Treatise on Laws (Decretum DD. 1-20), with the Ordinary Gloss,* trans. Augustine Thompson and James Gordley (Washington, DC: Catholic University of America Press, 1993), xvii-xviii.

through the end of the eleventh century. In this kind of society, local custom was in fact central to legal practices, and it would generally not be necessary or wise to challenge these customs. But this conservative stance was harder to maintain in the expansive and increasingly centralized European society taking shape in Gratian's own day. More immediately, jurists in this period were faced with the urgent challenges posed by "new customs," which were in effect lawless impositions of sheer power. In this context, legislators and judges had to enjoy some flexibility and freedom to innovate if they were to respond to changing conditions. Most importantly, they needed a set of standards for developing a principled normative critique of customs, on the basis of which abuses could be curbed, while the long-standing customs of a society, stemming from long-standing reflective practices, could be given due recognition.

Given this context of social and political tensions, we should not be surprised to find that Gratian's positive remarks on custom are carefully qualified and delimited. Most fundamentally, custom apparently only has legal force with respect to matters not covered by written law: "Custom is a kind of right instituted by practices, which is taken for law when the law is deficient" (D.1, C.5.1). Further on, we read that custom yields to written law (D.11, a.c. 1). What is more, respect for custom should not be taken so far as to undermine the authority of the legitimate rulers of a community; when custom conflicts with the decrees of such an authority, it must give way (D.11, C.4). Nor can we appeal to custom to justify practices that are unreasonable, depraved, or even just pointless. Gratian quotes the patristic commonplace to the effect that Jesus did not say, "I am the custom," but "I am the truth" (D.8, C.5). At the very least, these comments would seem to reflect a different spirit from the distinctions cited above, one that prizes reasonableness, innovation, and change in contrast to tradition, conservation, and stability. What is more, at least some of these distinctions seem to come into direct conflict with those cited above, considered precisely as matters of law. How is it possible to say both that a decree must be confirmed by custom in order to be firmly established, and that written law overrides contrary custom — which by definition would not confirm the law in question?

The Ambiguity of Customary Law

Gratian is aware of these tensions and sets out to resolve them. Most fundamentally, his analysis of custom, developed at some length over the first twenty distinctions of the *Decretum*, reflects his desire to maintain a proper balance between the claims inherent in customary law and the claims of centralized authority typically expressed through written law. Gratian is commonly, and rightly, regarded as one of the most influential early supporters of a strongly centralized form of church governance, and more specifically in the newly emergent monarchial papacy.[25] Whatever we may think of this development today, we can see why Gratian and so many of his contemporaries would have welcomed it. Some kind of centralized government was necessary if the church was to function effectively in a rapidly expanding society. What is more, the papacy had been a force for reform since the time of Gregory VII. At the same time, however, a close examination of the treatise on laws suggests that Gratian was also sympathetic to the countervailing demands of the local churches. This sympathy is expressed through his generally positive treatment of customary law, which, we should recall, is typically the law of relatively small, internally cohesive and isolated communities. This comes through very clearly in D.12, in which Gratian approvingly cites a whole series of authorities defending the legitimacy of *local* customs over against those who would disregard or extirpate them without good reason (D.12, C.3-10) — significantly, placing these within the context of the general principle that no one is permitted to act without regard for justice (D.12, pr). In reading these texts, the emphasis should be placed on "local"; Gratian is here expressing a concern to protect the autonomy and integrity of local communities as far as possible, given the conditions of the time. To be sure, he also insists that written law can depart from custom, or even override it, but at the very least, these texts drive home the point that written law should not undercut local custom without good reasons for doing so. Uniformity as such is not a value, even in the centralized church that Gratian defends.

The tensions in Gratian's remarks on custom thus stem both from his sources and, more importantly, from the social conditions and legal practice in his own day. At the same time, however, he indicates how these tensions can be harmonized — not perfectly, perhaps, but adequately, given the practical aims of lawmaking and litigation. In order to see how he does so, we must keep in mind that throughout the *Decretum*, Gratian is attempting to

---

25. Gratian's strong support for papal authority has often been noted. For a clear and persuasive argument, grounded in a comprehensive review of relevant texts, see Jean Gaudemet, "La primauté pontificale dans le Décret de Gratien," in *Studia in Honorem Eminentissimi Cardinalis Alphonsi M. Stickler*, ed. R. J. Card. Castillo Lara (Rome: Libreria Ateneo Salesiano, 1992), 137-54.

reconcile diverse elements of a complex and sometimes inconsistent textual tradition, in the process eliciting a coherent conception of law from the manifold perspectives incorporated in his sources. The placement of diverse approaches relative to one another carries much of the interpretative weight here. Gratian indicates which elements of this tradition he takes to be central or paradigmatic by identifying them as the general categories; these, in turn, provide a framework for interpreting the specific claims and approaches found in what follows.

With respect to customary law, the immediately relevant general category is that of *mores,* practices, which are comprised of customs and ordinances, that is, written laws. As we noted above, practices are mutable and provisional, in contrast to the unchanging and universal natural law. Both custom and ordinance are valid only insofar as they are in congruity with the standards of natural law, and yet natural law cannot serve as a basis for actual legal practice unless it is specified in some way. Custom and written law represent two centrally important forms of specification, and correlatively, they are legitimate only insofar as they can be construed as expressions of natural law in some way. In order to identify the proper boundaries between them, we must begin by placing them as two kinds of expression of the rational standards that are alone normative in the proper sense — that is to say, standards that ought to be obeyed because they reflect demands of natural right, reason, and equity. Given this starting point, these criteria themselves go a long way towards determining the relative force and authority of customary and written law.

Seen from this perspective, the priority of written law to custom is not so prejudicial to custom as we might assume. Recall that both custom and ordinance are initially presented as expressions of reason (D.1, C.5). Seen from this perspective, it does not much matter whether a given practice is expressed through written law or handed down through custom, since whatever reason confirms will have the force of law (D.1, p.c. 5). Gratian is not denying the necessity for legally authoritative promulgation (in the case of written law), or confirmation that a custom reflects the approbation of the people, normally by way of long-standing usage; on the contrary, elsewhere he explicitly affirms both of these claims (D.4, C.3.1). His point, rather, is that custom and ordinance represent two distinct but interrelated ways of expressing the demands of natural law in a particular time and place. Certainly, written law will normally represent a more perspicuous and clearly authoritative expression of natural law than does custom — if only because written laws are intentionally and (we hope) clearly formulated to serve just that purpose. Yet there seems to be a presumption here that written laws will often be formulations of what has hitherto been customary practice, at least on the assumption that the custom in question is well-established and genuinely rational.

By the same token, Gratian introduces the negative appraisals of custom collected in D.8 with a dictum asserting that neither customs nor written laws should be received as law if they conflict with natural law (D.8, a.c. 2). In such a case, the practices in question would not deserve to be regarded as customary usages or rights, claims having force of law, but would count, rather, as depraved or (at best) as mere usages. In cases such as these, the (so-called) customs of a community can and should be set aside by written law. Yet written law also yields to natural law, and any ordinance of civil or canon law is to be rejected if it is contrary to natural law (D.9, passim; see especially C.11). Seen from this perspective, Gratian's claim that an ordinance is established when it is promulgated and confirmed by the practice of the people, and correlatively abrogated by non-observance, appears as counterweight to the claim that written law supersedes custom (D.4, p.c. 3).[26] That is, when an ordinance is irrational or unjust, or in some other way at odds with natural law, the non-reception by the people offers one way of rejecting and correcting the putative ordinance in question. Thus, there is no necessary inconsistency in saying that written law can abrogate (some specific) custom, while at the same time custom (broadly considered as an ensemble of practices) can abrogate (some specific) written law.

Precisely because they stem from rational principles, at least in some ways and up to a point, the customs of a people can be subject to self-reflective, rational scrutiny, developed, made explicit, and where necessary reformed or abandoned. This is the process that will normally lead to the articulation of written laws. Because written laws serve to formulate and correct custom, they will normally supersede and override customary law; and yet, these only make sense, and can only be interpreted and implied, within the context of practices comprising the customs of the people. What is more, written law will have no purchase on a community, unless it reflects the practices of that community in some way; even a law that sets out to correct custom will necessarily reflect other aspects of the customary

26. Although he focuses on a somewhat later period, Geoffrey King offers a helpful introduction to the complex of ideas and practices informing the early medieval references to reception and communal abrogation of the laws; see "The Acceptance of Law by the Community: A Study in the Writings of Canonists and Theologians, 1500-1750," *The Jurist* 37 (1977): 233-65.

practices of a community, or it will lack purchase in the community for which it is intended.

Custom thus stands in a mediating role between natural law in the most basic sense and written law. The customary practices of a community reflect a historically informed and socially located expression of natural principles of action. As such, they reflect the particularity and mutability proper to human, as opposed to divine and natural law. Yet the contingency of customary practices is not sheerly arbitrary or unbounded. To the extent that these practices stem from natural and rational principles, they reflect something of the universality and stability of these principles, and can be understood and applied accordingly. At the same time, custom is of course not written law, and in this respect too it resembles natural law properly so called. Considered relative to natural law, customs are particular formulations — albeit, not verbal formulations — which are under-determined by the rational principles from which they stem. Yet considered relative to written law, the customs of a community, to the extent that they reflect rational and equitable standards, function much as natural law itself does. That is to say, they provide the unarticulated starting points and the necessary contexts for interpretation and application that must be in place in order for a system of written laws to get off the ground in the first place. To put it another way, the customs of a people mediate between natural law and written law in such a way as to provide a framework for the formal processes of legal enactment and the implementation of law.

Hart Revisited: Customary Practice and Rules of Recognition

This is the context in which to return to Hart's claim that legal authority rests on a rule of recognition, which is as such both extra-legal and in some way contingent.[27] As we have already observed, Hart's claim has proven to be both compelling and problematic, precisely because he tries to ground a norm of legitimacy in what is necessarily a contingent judgment, namely, a communal consensus to the effect that legal authority should be vested in a given set of offices and procedures. By now, it is apparent that he is right on this point. Formalized legislative authority is a derived authority; it is a formal determination of the authority of the community, typically mediated through customary practices. This implies that the rule of recognition as

27. Again, see *Concept of Law*, 93-96, although, strictly speaking, the rule of recognition acknowledges the legitimacy bestowed on legal forms by the community.

instantiated in a particular community will indeed represent a contingent determination, out of an indefinite range of other possibilities. Yet — once again — this kind of contingency does not imply an irrational kind of arbitrariness. On the contrary, if a rule of recognition is to attain the necessary degree of acceptance, it will necessarily rest on rationally persuasive considerations, broadly seen to be such among the men and women who are subject to the laws. Under most circumstances, the customary practices of a community provide the starting points and, as it were, the initial rules of recognition, on the basis of which laws and legal authorities can be formulated, subject to critical scrutiny, and if necessary reformulated in more or less radical ways.

Within the context of contemporary Western legal systems, in which legal authority is commonly tethered to some kind of constitutional structure, it might seem that the customary character of a rule of recognition would be attenuated at best. Yet this is not the case, at least not within the Anglophone legal systems on which we are focusing here. The common law tradition informing the legal systems of England and its former colonies is itself a kind of customary law, extending well beyond those areas of law explicitly identified as falling within its scope. Thus, the diverse governing structures found among these polities — representative democracy and a strict separation of powers in the United States, parliamentary democracy in Great Britain and most of its former colonies — represent alternative ways of specifying the division and articulation of powers essential to a modern law-state.[28] This line of argument is perhaps more plausible in Great Britain, since the British constitution itself is apparently grounded in foundational customs of lawmaking and governing, never formally written and enacted as such, and yet widely discussed and generally acknowledged as providing the authoritative structure for British legislation — a very good example indeed of Fuller's observation that lawmaking authority is itself typically the product of law.[29]

Within the United States, the centrality of common, and therefore customary, law is not so apparent, precisely because legislative authority rests ultimately on a written, formally promulgated constitution. This set a context within which most American legal scholars before Fuller inclined to-

28. King offers a very helpful summary of classical British constitutional theory and practice, with attention to these distinctions, in *The British Constitution*, 1-14, 39-62. It should be added that he goes on to argue, in some detail, that the British constitution has recently undergone a profound and largely unnoted and probably irreversible transformation, not necessarily for the better.

29. See *Morality of Law*, 115.

wards positivist theories of law, and within which even the recognized forms of common law were denigrated and limited in scope. Oliver Wendell Holmes famously regarded the common law as "judge-made law" — by which he meant that even in those contexts in which the common law plays a generally accepted role, it ultimately rests on nothing more than judicial fiat on the part of judges who formulate what the law is under the guise of applying objective, yet unwritten principles.[30] Yet recently, Holmes's easy dismissal of common law within an American context has been challenged by James Stoner, who makes a persuasive case that the United States Constitution itself, together with the ongoing enterprise of constitutional interpretation, rest on foundations of common law — explicitly acknowledged in the eighteenth century — and cannot be adequately understood or practiced unless this context is given due recognition and respect.[31] In the process of arguing his thesis, he shows the common law to be a communally held, largely intelligible body of principles, which must be applied to be sure, but which nonetheless reflect commitments and practices going beyond the fiat of any one judge or interpreter. Nonetheless, Holmes's remark contains an element of truth, and for that reason it offers a starting point for a closer examination of the two distinctive yet interrelated functions characteristic of legal authority in modern constitutional orders, namely, those exercised by the lawgiver and the judge.

3. Judicial and Legislative Authority: A Necessary Complementarity of Functions

The Judge and the Lawgiver as Ministers of the Law

Whatever we may think of his overall conclusions, Holmes's reservations about the common law, like the widespread worries about legal activism expressed by his present-day heirs, do reflect a legitimate concern over the

---

30. See Olivier Wendell Holmes, *The Common Law* [1881] (Cambridge, MA: Harvard/Belknap Press, 1963).

31. See James R. Stoner, Jr., *Common Law Liberty: Rethinking American Constitutionalism* (Lawrence: University Press of Kansas, 2003), 1-29 for a summary of the overall argument. Compare King's observation that the constitution of a country, understood as the central rules and shared understandings regulating relations among a country's governing institutions with one another and with citizens, may or may not be codified, but "are never — repeat, *never* — written down in their entirety." *The British Constitution*, 5, emphasis in the original.

proper function of the judiciary — and therefore, within the terms of the analysis here offered, the basis for judicial authority. The function of the judge is, after all, to adjudicate — to apply the law as it currently exists to the case at hand. In the scholastics' lapidary phrase, he is a "minister of the law," not its sovereign. The lawmaker is the legitimate and proper source for new legal precepts, authorized by the community to innovate, to generate new law on its behalf. The judge should not attempt to legislate from the bench because, in most modern democracies, judges are not authorized to create new laws. What is more, as Fuller reminds us, this kind of activism would generate uncertainty about the law among those who are supposed to be governed by it, thus rendering it difficult for men and women to plan and act in accordance with settled legal expectations. Only the lawgiver is authorized to generate new laws, on behalf of the community as a whole. As MacCormick rightly reminds us, these two roles are necessarily distinct and their boundaries ought to be respected.[32]

Yet adjudication is not always a straightforward process. It presupposes that relevant legal precepts are in place (whether through enactments or generally recognized customs) and their application to the case at hand is more or less clear. Under ordinary circumstances, these presuppositions will indeed reflect reality, but this will not always be the case. The judge may well need to determine the law through an extended process of interpretative judgment, because the precept in question is unclear, or the case at hand is unusual or ambiguous, or perhaps because more than one precept would appear to be pertinent, and the relation among them is not settled. In these kinds of cases, adjudication will necessarily involve a more or less prominent element of contingency, which is to say that the judge will necessarily exercise judicial authority through determining what the law is, in and through the process of applying it. This is in no way illegitimate, as defenders of judicial discretion rightly insist; on the contrary, it is a necessary element of the adjudicative process itself.

What is more, the discretionary and innovative element inherent in adjudication corresponds to an interpretative and receptive element in the exercise of legislative authority. This is not to deny that the lawgiver exercises a necessary and legitimate innovative role, or that she is sovereign over the law, in the sense that she is not bound by existing enactments or precedents, in the same way the judge is. Yet she too is a "minister of the law" — not the formal legal system generated by authoritative enactments, but the "law be-

---

32. Again, see *Institutions of Law*, 39-60.

fore the law," the mores of the community itself, insofar as these reflect justifiable and salutary expressions of, or safeguards for, natural forms of functioning and communal ideals of the common good. As we have just seen, Gratian makes this point clearly by insisting that customs of long standing should be respected by the lawgiver, unless these are clearly out of date, or in some way harmful. This does not mean that the lawgiver cannot legitimately innovate through the creation of new laws; on the contrary, that is her distinctive and proper function. Yet new law can never be completely new. If the innovations of the lawgiver are to reflect the ethos and will of the community in any meaningful way — if they are to stand as rhetorically defensible expressions of the community's distinctive formulation of natural ideals and practices — they will necessarily reflect the political ideals of the community, as expressed through a defensible continuity with its extended tradition of customary practices, taken as a whole and considered in the light of its ongoing development.

This line of analysis reinforces MacCormick's claim, although not in terms of an argument he himself develops. The judge and the lawgiver do indeed exercise necessarily distinct and yet complementary roles within a modern constitutional system. The proper functioning of each presupposes that of the other: the judge cannot judge in accordance with a legal system unless someone has actually enacted laws, while at the same time, legal enactments have no force apart from some authoritative interpreter, whose task it is to apply these to specific disputes. But more fundamentally, the judge and the lawgiver have complementary roles in the context of a more comprehensive system of shared ideals and customary practices, within which they serve mutually subordinated purposes which ground their respective forms of authority. The contingent specification of this authority rests, again, on the historically specific processes through which judicial and legislative institutions emerge and develop, leading over time to settled rules of recognition; their authoritative force depends on the distinctive purpose each serves as an expression of the self-determining authority of the community itself.

This analysis helps us to understand something that would otherwise be inexplicable, and indeed, should be impossible on a strict positivist theory of law. That is, in the European societies of the early Middle Ages, judicial functions and offices emerged before effective and generally recognized legislators.[33] As the historian R. C. van Caenegem remarks, from the late

---

33. The legal situation in early medieval Europe was, to put it mildly, complex, but in all its variant forms, the rule of law through the eleventh century appears to have relied almost entirely

ninth century until the beginning of the twelfth century, "the European Continent lived without legislation," either civic or ecclesiastical, being governed in this period mostly by customary law.[34] Yet disputes did arise, and these were adjudicated through what were recognizably settled, formal legal procedures. Far from it being the case that the office of judge is created by legislative authority, it appears that the judicial office is logically the more fundamental of the two: a recognizable legal system can emerge without a lawgiver, but there can be no such system without a judge. Here, again, Holmes's skepticism about the common law contains an important element of truth. There is one sense in which common law is indeed a judge-made law. It is not the case that the common law is made up by the judge out of whole cloth, nor is it fashioned by the collective decisions of the courts operating independently of the societies in which they function. The customary law out of which common law emerges cannot be regarded as the product of any one individual, or even any one system within the polity; it represents the collective judgments and practices of the community taken as a whole. Yet in order for these customary practices to become usable as law, someone must articulate them in such a way as to give them both specificity and authoritative force. "Someone," in this case, refers in the first instance to a judge, who necessarily specifies and articulates tacitly accepted practices and customary law in the process of drawing on these as a justification for a particular judgment.

It is thus not surprising that when Europe began the process of transition to a recognized system of settled, impartial law, this process began in the courts, together with the circle of learned men who began to form around the courts as their advisors and guides. For many of the early civil jurists, not only is the judge responsible for trying cases in accordance with the laws, he

---

on systems of courts, arbitration, or royal vindication of customary rights and privileges. For further details, see James A. Brundage, *The Medieval Origins of the Legal Profession: Canonists, Civilians, and Courts* (Chicago: University of Chicago Press, 2008), 46-74; R. C. van Caenegem, "Government, Law and Society," in *The Cambridge History of Medieval Political Thought, c. 350–c. 1450*, ed. J. H. Burns (Cambridge: Cambridge University Press, 1988), 174-210, and *An Historical Introduction to Western Constitutional Law* (Cambridge: Cambridge University Press, 1995), 54-71. For a detailed account of the transition from reliance on customary law and the royal vindication of accepted claims to the acknowledgment of lawmaking authority and legislative innovation — a process that was, in the present instance, only partially successful — see Gerhard Dilcher, "Der mittelalterliche Kaisergedanke als Rechtslegitimation," in *Die Begründung des Rechts als historisches Problem*, ed. Dietmar Willoweit and Elisabeth Müller-Luckner (Münster: Oldenbourg, 2000), 153-70.

34. "Government, Law and Society," 181.

is also said to be responsible for judging the laws themselves and rejecting
those which are not in accordance with reason and equity. By implication,
the advisor to the judge, the scholar of law, can also claim authority, simply
in virtue of his expertise and judgment. We recall the anonymous author of
the *Petri exceptiones,* writing in the late eleventh century, who flatly says that
"If anything useless, broken, or contrary to equity is found in the laws, we
trample it underfoot."[35] From our standpoint, this suggests a program for
judicial activism on a scale that we could scarcely imagine. Of course, it
would be a mistake to read early medieval legal practices through the prism
of our disputes over legislative intent and of judicial interpretation. At this
stage, there were very few recognized lawgivers, nor a comprehensive system
of duly enacted legal precepts. Rather, the author of the *Petri exceptiones* reflects a situation in which the law is regarded as simply given, implying a legal system that functions through judicial application guided by learned
commentary — a scholars' and judges' law, not unlike rabbinic and Muslim
legal systems today.

Given the appropriate contexts, this kind of legal system functions well
and there is no doubt that it secures some values, such as communal cohesion and the preservation of personal relationships, better than modern
Western legal systems can do.[36] Nonetheless, in the European societies of the
twelfth and thirteenth centuries, it was quickly apparent that this approach
could no longer work — both because of the sheer size and complexity of
these societies and, more urgently, because of the resurgent abuses of power
discussed in the first chapter. In these circumstances, it was necessary to establish legal ordinances through an authoritative decree, so that they could
exhibit the needed clarity, stability, and above all, legitimacy. Once again, we
find the ideas of reason and authority held together in a concept of law, this
time for eminently practical reasons.

35. Cited in Weigand, no. 21. As Paul Vinogradoff points out, the *Exceptiones Petri* is interesting for more than one reason. It indicates that some systematic study of secular jurisprudence existed in southern France in the eleventh century independently of the great center for legal studies
that emerged in Bologna towards the end of that century. It also reflects the practical significance
of these studies, since it is dedicated to one Odilio, a magistrate of Valence in Dauphine, for the
express purpose of guiding him in the exercise of his office. See *Roman Law in Medieval Europe,*
2nd edition (Oxford: Clarendon Press, 1929), 44-48; the whole chapter, "Revival of Jurisprudence,"
43-70, is indispensable for understanding the emergence and the social impact of secular jurisprudence in the late eleventh century.

36. Rosen makes this point very effectively; see *The Culture of Islam: Changing Aspects of
Contemporary Muslim Life* (Chicago: The University of Chicago Press, 2002), 3-74.

The theologians also take up the topic of positive law. Albert is the first to offer a definition of positive law, or *lex*, which incorporates the traditional four kinds of law: that is, the natural law, the law of Moses, the law of grace, and the law of the members, which is the innate tendency to sin which Paul mentions in Romans 7:23 (*De bono* V 2.1).[37] In order to do so, he synthesizes definitions of positive law drawn from Cicero, Augustine, and Gratian, all of which are interpreted in light of Aristotle's claim that the purpose of law is to make the members of a community good. As is well known, Aquinas also proposes an analytic definition of law, a definition, it should be noted, which is meant to comprehend every kind of law, from the eternal law to human law (ST I-II 90). For him, however, the key to the definition of law is not provided by its purpose in making men and women good. Rather, he focuses on the character of the law as a norm of reason (I-II 90.1, 2). At the same time, not just any rational norm can count as a law; rather, a genuine law can only be established by the community as a whole, or by those individuals who have responsibility for a community (I-II 90.3). Furthermore, he follows Gratian in saying that a law must be promulgated in order to have force within its community (I-II 90.4). This brings him to his much-quoted definition of law: "Law is an ordinance of reason directed towards the common good, instituted by one who has responsibility for the community, and promulgated" (I-II 90.4).

An Ordinance of Reason: The Authority of the Lawgiver

Aquinas's definition of law offers a good point of departure for further clarifying the distinctive function of the lawgiver, and correlatively drawing out the ground and scope of a distinctively legislative form of authority. Consider the first phrase of the definition, "law is an ordinance of reason." Modern Thomists have tended to emphasize the reasonableness of laws, but I would suggest that we place comparable weight on Aquinas's claim that a law is an ordinance; we are concerned here with reason as specified in a concrete norm that can readily be applied to a range of choices — not with reason in the sense of a faculty for norm-governed judgment or even reasonableness in the broad sense. Reason as such does not yield ordinances of this

---

37. As Odon Lottin points out, in "La loi en général: La définition thomiste et ses antécédents," in *Psychologie et morale aux XIIe et XIIIe siècles*, Volume 2, *Problèmes de morale* (Louvain: Abbaye du Mont César, 1948), 22.

kind by itself. It has to be specified, given determinate shape through rational processes of deliberation and judgment. This specification will necessarily be to some extent contingent, and thus introduces something genuinely new into the ensemble of practices and enactments governing the life of the community. In this sense, at least, the proper function of the lawgiver is innovative; he opens up new pathways for action and closes others, previously open (ST I-II 95.1, 2).

What is more, the law is an ordinance of reason directed to the common good — not, therefore, just any prescription leading to good behavior, but a norm which can be seen to promote the overall well-being and integrity of the community in some principled, systematic way. Further on, Aquinas adds that in order to count as a reasonable ordinance, a law must not only be oriented towards the common good, it should also reflect an equitable distribution of burdens and benefits among the individual members of the community (ST I-II 96.4). Our analysis so far suggests a third way in which the reasonableness of law depends, at least in key part, on its orientation to the common good. That is to say, if we construe the common good to include the community's sense of its core values and ideals, a law within that community can only count as reasonable if it represents a defensible expression of those values and ideals. So far as practical reflection within the context of this community goes, these are foundational in the correlative senses of neither needing nor allowing for defense in terms of more general principles in the political order and as themselves constituting the first principles, in terms of which practices and laws must in some way be justified. In this context, practical reasonableness implies, *inter alia,* some kind of continuity with the community's constitutive political morality.

If this is so, then it would seem that the proper function of the lawgiver is perhaps not so innovative after all. If practical reasoning in a political context is always tethered to a community's core ethos, then it is difficult to see what the lawgiver can add to the existing practices of his community, beyond a new element of specification — just as the judge will sometimes need to determine the meaning of the law in the course of interpretation, even though she should not legislate from the bench. But this conclusion would be too quick. As our earlier natural law analysis of political authority indicates, the authority of the community over its members is itself grounded in purposes stemming from the exigencies and form of life proper to human existence as such. For this reason, the complex of communal values and ideals that is foundational within the political order rests on extra-political values, and ultimately on the good order of human existence itself. These extra-political considerations can only be grasped in and through their expression in the distinctive culture of a particular community. We can only arrive at some sense of the human good through a process of reflective abstraction from the good as reflected in a specific way of life. And of course, it is more than likely that these natural principles would not be described in these terms today — we are more likely to speak in terms of reasonableness as such, or to appeal to general notions of appropriateness or congruity. But reasonableness, appropriateness, and congruity only make sense with reference to some standard, and that standard is set by the forms of life proper to human nature — or so the natural lawyer would claim, without insisting too much on terminology.

At any rate, once these natural principles begin to be established, they offer a vantage point from which to evaluate that way of life from a fresh perspective. This, in turn, provides a basis for both reform of bad practices and the introduction of new norms. If these are to express a genuinely political exercise of authority, they will still stand in some kind of defensible continuity with an existing way of life. Yet that does not mean that they cannot also constitute real, in some ways even radical departures from previous practices. Add to this the possibility, very often an actual occurrence in our shrinking world, that a community's grasp of what is natural and expedient may be both expanded and challenged through its encounters with other ways of life, which express what can be seen to be shared values and ideals in new, perhaps challenging ways. These too, together with the practices retained in historical memory, and, in a more limited way, the practices and ideals of international law, all offer starting points for the innovative activities proper to the lawgiver.

Certainly, innovation at this level is only tolerable within a community of free men and women to the extent that the innovator acts on their behalf, and is generally seen to do so. It is not enough, in other words, that her innovations are defensible in terms of a political process of rhetorical persuasion; she must also be authorized to act as she does, through some rule of recognition giving her not only a voice, but the decisive voice in determining the practical meaning of such a comprehensive set of considerations. Only in this way can her ordinances generate protected reasons, considerations which can be overridden only in extreme circumstances, or in carefully delimited ways. By the same token, if these ordinances are to have decisive force, in such a way as to put an end to processes of practical deliberation, at least here and now, then those involved in the political community must be aware of them, at least to some extent and in a general way. Thus, they must be promulgated. Otherwise, they could not count as ordinances of reason, practical norms for those falling under the authority of the law.

We can now more readily appreciate why it is that within a developed constitutional order, in which the legislative function is given its own institutional means of expression, the proper activities of the judge are dependent on and subordinated to those of the lawgiver. Judges should not legislate from the bench because they are not authorized to innovate vis-à-vis existing laws and practices, but only to apply recognized legal precepts (including, where appropriate, customary law) to the case at hand. Yet the more properly conservative element of the legal function should not be exaggerated, even in the context of a developed constitutional order. Interpretation always implies some new, contingent determination, specifying what had previously been implicit or ambiguous. Hart is thus right that even well-developed legal systems will always have some gaps, which can only be filled through innovative judicial determinations.[38] For this very reason, the judge cannot exercise her own proper function without some overall grasp of the rationale and point of existing laws. If the laws were self-interpreting, there would be no need for adjudication as such, although we would presumably still need courts to determine matters of fact and to enforce the laws in an appropriate way. In order to go beyond these functions, actually to interpret the laws, the judge must place them within the context of a set of broader principles that are not themselves articulated in the laws. What is more, in a complex legal system she will sometimes need to take the additional steps of determining what the law actually is, or arranging competing laws in some kind of order of precedence — again, processes calling for innovative interpretation and specification.

Dworkin Revisited: The Authority of the Judge

In order to bring out the significance of judicial interpretation, it will be helpful to return to Dworkin's claim that the judge should ideally interpret and apply the laws in terms of the best concept he can attain of the ideal political morality governing his community. As it stands, this is a program for judicial innovation of a very high order indeed. In the terms developed so far, Dworkin's ideal leaves no space for the contingency which is necessarily implied in any kind of authoritative determination. That, I would suggest, is why he insists that the judge should aim at the uniquely correct normative

---

38. See *Concept of Law*, 141-54.

judgment, and not simply a defensible judgment, in determining the ideal political morality of his community.[39] The contingency of an authoritative judgment is of course directly opposed to a necessary determination of this kind — and by the same token, Dworkin's insistence that judicial interpretation should aim at the uniquely correct determination of political morality implies that the processes of judicial interpretation should not be constrained in any fundamental way by the contingent enactments of legislative authorities. What Dworkin advocates is, in effect, a law of judges and learned commentators: "if anything in the laws is found contrary to ideal political morality, we trample it underfoot."

The difficulty with this approach, as I argued in chapter one, is that it gives insufficient weight to the properly and distinctively authoritative status of the legislative act. We are now in a better position to appreciate why this should matter. The rationale for interpreting laws in accordance with the will of the lawmaker — as opposed to interpreting them in accordance with general considerations of rationality or political morality — is grounded in the rationale for legislative authority itself, including above all its innovative role and function as a safeguard for the equality and freedom of the individual members of the community. The innovative character of legislation presupposes that the lawgiver is free to determine the general requirements of collective ideals in a contingent yet relatively final way, and its role in safeguarding the political freedom of individuals demands that its decrees be respected as expressions of legislative will. The lawgiver and the judge are both bound to respect the political morality of their community, but the lawgiver does so in a relatively unconstrained way, whereas the judge is bound by the specific determinations of the lawgiver.

At the same time, the lawgiver can provide a safeguard for the equality and freedom of the individual members of the community, only because and to the extent that the lawgiver, considered as such, does not act as an individual, pursuing private ends. That, once again, is the critical difference between political rule and servile dominion: political authority is exercised on behalf of the community as a whole, pursuing its common good rather than the good of any one person (or faction of persons), in contrast to servile dominion, which compels the slave to serve the private good of the master. Thus, as the scholastics frequently remark, the lawgiver as such intends to promote and safeguard the common good. That is precisely what consti-

39. Again, see Ronald Dworkin, *Law's Empire* (Cambridge, MA: Harvard University Press, 1986), 266-75.

tutes the occupant of this role as a lawgiver, a political authority, in contrast to a master exercising dominion over slaves.

Of course, in reality lawmakers will be individual men and women, acting as individuals or (more commonly) collectively. But my point is that the properly political character of authority implies that the lawgiver, considered as such, whether an individual or a legislature of some kind, should be regarded as the occupant of an impersonal role, and that the intrinsic character of the role, together with its location in a particular community with distinctive customs and history, jointly inform and constrain the legally significant intentions that are, so to speak, open to those occupying this role. To put the same point in another way, the intention of the lawgiver is not something that is formulated in someone's subjectivity and then expressed through legislation. Rather, the overall intention of the lawmaker as such is determined and shaped by those elements that are constitutive of the role that he occupies. The individual appropriates it and specifies it, certainly, but in order to do so, the individual (or group of individuals) must internalize and specify something that is objectively given, namely, the intent of the lawgiver to promote the common good. In this respect, too, the lawgiver and the judge stand in a mutually complementary and subordinate relationship to the law. If the latter is a "minister of the law," one whose individual judgment is to be subordinated to the objective demands of the law as it exists, the former is in another way a "minister of the law" whose private judgments and purposes are properly subsumed in the purposes intrinsic to the common good of the community.

This is the point at which the basis for lawmaking authority and the norms for interpretation of the laws come together. Those who defend "original intent" as an indispensable guide and constraint on judicial interpretation appeal — whether deliberately or not — to ideals of political authority and personal freedom and equality that institutionalized, impersonal legislative authority is meant to serve. To put it more plainly, the judge should respect the intention of the lawmaker rather than imposing his personal convictions about what the law should be, because only in this way can the judge maintain his own character as a "minister of the law" — itself an impersonal role, which for that very reason can adjudicate from a position of authority in the disputes of free men and women. But by the same token, the "intent of the lawmaker" cannot be identified with or limited to the diverse purposes and motives of the private individuals functioning in this capacity. Essentially, "the lawmaker" is a term of art for what is necessarily an impersonal, institutionalized agency within a complex society. It does act, and therefore it can be said to have intentions, but these intentions can only be formulated and accessed in terms of what the lawmaker objectively does, taken together with the context — linguistic, cultural, and legal — within which it acts. Unless we keep this in mind, our attempts to identify what it means to speak of the "will of the lawmaker," much less to determine actual legislative intent, will become hopelessly mired in confusions.

This brings us to a centrally important element of truth in Dworkin's theory of legal interpretation. That is, he is right to insist that the judge must interpret the intent of the lawgiver in terms of some overall construal of the principles undergirding the law, precisely in order to interpret the relevant decrees *as* laws, as expressions of the will of the lawgiver. Once again — the lawgiver, considered as such, intends the common good. That is the point or function of the role of the lawgiver, and it is only in the light of this purpose that the lawgiver's acts can intelligibly be regarded as laws at all. Correlatively, the courts, and society as a whole, can only take judicial cognizance of legislative acts which are in some way oriented towards the common good. Understood in this way, the ideal of the common good functions in much the same way as Dworkin's ideal of the integrity of the law. That is to say, it provides an overarching framework of values and ideals, in terms of which legal enactments can be construed as expressing the overall sense of the community, and interpreted and applied accordingly.[40]

Nonetheless, it still seems to me that Dworkin does not sufficiently acknowledge the contingency of the lawgiver's determination and the corresponding constraints on judicial interpretation. It is true that Dworkin acknowledges that legal interpretation is constrained by the legal system as it actually exists, not the ideal legal system that might be envisioned if we could create a legal system from the ground up. The judge's role is to interpret the laws in such a way as to render them consistent with the overall legal system, construed in the best possible way as reflecting a political morality: "The adjudicative principle of integrity instructs judges to identify legal rights and duties, so far as possible, on the assumption that they were all created by a single author — the community personified — expressing a coherent conception of justice and fairness."[41] It is telling, however, that the author of the legal system is the community personified — not an actual lawgiver, who can act on behalf of the community, precisely because she is

---

40. Dworkin develops his ideal of integrity most fully in *Law's Empire*, 176-224 and especially 225-75.

41. *Law's Empire*, 225.

distinct from the community.[42] Correlatively, as we saw in the first chapter, Dworkin regards the judge as the latest in a diverse range of authors, all jointly contributing to the law as if it were an ongoing chain novel; thus, the judge enters into a creative partnership with the lawgiver.[43] There is much to be said for a creative partnership, but it is not a relation of authority.

I would argue, in contrast, that the lawgiver stands in a relation of authority with respect to the judge, in such a way as to constrain the latter's activities of adjudication and interpretation in accordance with her contingent judgments and legislative will. We should recall once again that legislative authority always operates by way of determination. The lawmaker does not just intend to promote the common good; she intends to promote the common good with respect to a particular domain of action, and in a specified way, within the parameters set by a particular community's history, circumstances, and needs. This intent is expressed through an act of legislation, formulated and promulgated in such a way as to reflect the lawgiver's authoritative enactment. I would argue that respect for the properly political character of legislation can only be preserved if the judge takes the intent of the lawgiver, thus construed, to be the primary target for judicial interpretation. It may be that in the judge's own (private) opinion, a given law is directed towards the common good in a wrong-headed or perverse way, but so long as it can be plausibly construed as such, in accordance with the norms and procedures of rhetorical persuasion discussed in the previous chapter, then the lawgiver's judgments about the proper pursuit of the common good should prevail. In any case, the judge should aim to recover the actual intent of the lawgiver, construed as one intelligible expression of the political morality of the community, rather than construing the law in such a way as to accord with the best possible expression of that political morality.

For similar reasons, judicial interpretation should rely on recovering the intent of the lawgiver, rather than the objective meaning of an enactment regarded as a proposition, interpreted in light of the original context for its utterance. The latter view, forcefully defended in the United States by Antonin

---

42. On my view, the community does exercise authority, of course, but it does so through processes of self-formation and self-maintenance leading to the formation of a distinctive culture, tacitly accepted practices, and eventually customary law — all of which are themselves to some degree contingent, considered as specifications of natural principles.

43. See *Law's Empire*, 313-15, where Dworkin makes it plain that his ideal judge, Hercules, is not bound by what the lawgiver may actually have intended; he is only bound by the requirement that he interpret the law at hand in such a way as to "fit and explain" (315) the political acts and statutes comprising the body of the law in the best possible way.

Scalia, once again does not acknowledge that we have a stake in affirming the authority (and not just the reasonableness, or the integrity) of the act of will expressed in the legislative act.[44] Certainly, what the lawmaker specifically intends is most immediately expressed through the meaning of the enactment considered as a linguistic construct, and interpretation will necessarily take "the letter of the law" as its starting point. Yet just as the intent of the lawmaker is to be construed in an objective and external way, so the meaning of the law is contextually determined by a range of pragmatic factors. These will include both general features pertaining to any utterance in the language at hand, and the wide range of circumstantial conditions which set the immediate context for the lawgiver's specific legislative act. These factors set the necessary context for the intelligibility of the law itself, considered as a linguistic construct, and by the same token they provide indispensable starting points for any subsequent act of judicial interpretation.[45]

The range of meanings and circumstances which set the original context for the lawmaker's utterance provide the starting point for judicial interpretation, and yet the judge cannot, and should not, stop with these — not if she is to do full justice to the lawmaker's intent, and to the meaning of his enactment, regarded as a way of promoting the common good. Let me explain.

Precisely because he aims at promoting the common good through a specific enactment, the lawgiver necessarily wills that his law be effective, implying that it is received by the community and incorporated into its ongoing practices. That is why Aquinas includes promulgation among the formal requirements for the validity of a law, and why Gratian had earlier added community reception to promulgation as conditions for legal validity. When a law is promulgated, it enters into the complex of rules, customs, and practices structuring the life of the community, and establishes its own trajectory within that complex matrix. At the same time, the matrix of practices and assumptions within which the law in question takes its meaning and point are themselves likewise developing, in part, although not entirely, in response to the law in question. These processes of ongoing reciprocal devel-

<hr />

44. See Antonin Scalia, "Originalism: The Lesser Evil," *University of Cincinnati Law Review* 849 (1989): 57, and "Common Law Courts in a Civil-Law System," in Scalia et al., *A Matter of Interpretation: Federal Courts and the Law* (Princeton: Princeton University Press, 1997), 3-48.

45. MacCormick offers what I believe to be the best and most sophisticated analysis of the ways in which, and the extent to which, legal interpretation is constrained by the verbal formulae of legislation in *Rhetoric and the Rule of Law: A Theory of Legal Reasoning* (Oxford: Oxford University Press, 2005); see especially 32-100.

opment, between the formal law and the practices and beliefs that form its immediate context, cannot be predicted at the outset and will always elude exact identification, and yet they are not so complex and open-ended as to be empty of all content. We may not know for certain what impact the laws have had, but we can at least offer good reasons for construing the trajectories of their development in one way rather than another.

This process, I want to suggest, plays an integral role in justifying the interpretation of a law as being in accordance with the will of the lawmaker. In other words, these are the trajectories that count, when we are attempting to establish the scope of legitimate interpretation, reflecting respect for the authoritative will of the lawgiver. To some extent, and with all due caution, the judge must function as a kind of historian, in order to show that the interpretation she offers reflects — at least — a plausible construal of the trajectory set by the reception of the original law, or the development of the considerations that set the immediate context determining the meaning of the law, or both together. In this way, judicial interpretation does remain tethered to the will of the lawmaker as expressed by the meaning of its act — comprising not only the range of applications that could have been envisioned at the time of enactment (although these are of course partially constitutive of its meaning), but the fuller meaning that it takes on through the processes of reception and development that are integral to the life of the law. Only in this way can judicial interpretation respect the true will of the lawmaker — to promote the common good with respect to a particular domain of action, in a specified way.

The authority of the lawmaker and the judge both rest, therefore, on the distinctive purposes served by each in the ongoing process of generating and sustaining a system of formal law. As such, each exercises that authority through functions which are both justified and constrained by the exigencies of their distinctive roles, their proper interrelationships to one another, and their mutual dependence on the community which is the immediate ground for their authoritative functions. Once again, we find that authority is structured by the very considerations which justify it; the genuinely free and contingent element in authority remains a structured freedom, oriented towards purposes which set normative constraints on its proper exercise.

This offers us a good vantage point from which to approach the fundamental question of the normative constraints inherent in law itself. After all, on almost any showing, formal law is an enactment of a lawgiver, meant to be applied to specific cases through the interpretative judgments of a judge. It would seem to follow that the normative constraints inherent in the legislative and judicial functions would also apply to the law itself, at least in some way. At the very least, almost everyone would agree that an enactment cannot be an authoritative law unless it can be legitimately promulgated by a lawgiver, and many would add that the validity of a law depends on its vindication by a court, at least in some cases.

Are there further normative constraints on the authority of the law? Or to approach the same issue from a different perspective, does the natural law analysis offered here imply that enactments must meet some normative standards, beyond those set by the conditions for the authoritative promulgation and judicial interpretation of formal law, in order to count as genuine laws? Among the scholastics, these questions would have been answered in terms of the broadly accepted maxim that an unjust enactment is not a law. That was not the only or the final word that they had to say on this subject, and it cannot represent the final judgment of a contemporary natural law perspective on the authority of law. Nonetheless, we have already seen indications that there is, again, an important element of truth in this maxim, and we can best draw it out by contrast with the competing maxim, that the validity of an enactment depends solely on the legitimate authority of the lawgiver, acting in accordance with accepted procedural norms.

4. Legal Validity and Normative Constraints on Law

Fuller Revisited: When Enactments Fail to Be Laws

No one would deny that laws are properly subject to all kinds of normative evaluations — a given law may be unjust, immoral, ill-advised, inefficient, impractical, or confused. Like any other kind of normative evaluation, these suggest appropriate courses of action — the law in question should be amended, abrogated, perhaps disregarded, perhaps deliberately broken in pursuit of a larger strategy of reform. But do these judgments imply that the enactment in question is not really a law at all — that it fails with respect to the fundamental legal norm of validity, given that it was duly enacted by a legitimate lawmaking authority and duly promulgated? There are good arguments on either side of this question. On the one hand, if an enactment meets the formal criteria for inclusion in a legal system, then it would seem that we have compelling reasons to regard it as a genuine law. It will generate legal consequences, including enforcement through the police power of the state and through the processes of adjudication. This being so, it is difficult to see how this putative law is really different from "real" law. What is more, we have good normative reasons to acknowledge the validity of even bad laws. It is important that the expectations set up by the laws should be honored, as far as possible. Even more fundamentally, we have a stake in upholding a genuinely political kind of authority, precisely in order to safeguard the central ideal of civic freedom. This would seem to imply at a minimum that we should acknowledge the validity and authority of the enactments of such a lawmaker — even when those enactments are themselves problematic in some way.

Yet on the other hand, some kinds of normative failures do seem to undermine the validity of an enactment. If a law fails to meet the minimum threshold of what Fuller calls the inner morality of law — if it is too unclear, or complicated, or inconsistent to be put into practice through a consistent course of action — it hardly makes sense to insist that it is a fully valid law nonetheless.[46] As we saw in the first chapter, there is a growing consensus among lawyers and legal philosophers that an enactment can similarly fail as valid law because it fails to meet a minimum threshold of morality, justice, or equity. As MacCormick puts it,

> Disputable as most deep moral questions are, it is not disputable that some orientation to justice and the common good is . . . essential to legitimate participation in legislative and judicial law-making and law application. Moreover, the fact, if it be one, that reasonable people can reasonably differ about many questions concerning justice by no means entails that there are no outer limits of what can be reasonably represented as justice. . . . It is therefore perfectly possible and reasonable to set outward limits to what can be accepted as moral law. Provisions which are unjustifiable by reference to any reasonable moral argument should not be considered valid as laws.[47]

Clearly, what is at stake here are conflicting views over the meaning of legal validity. Should we construe legal validity in terms of purely formal requirements, spelled out perhaps in terms of legitimate authority and procedural norms, or should we also consider some kinds of substantive constraints, in terms of minimal standards of justice and morality, or even standards of the political morality of the community in question? At this

---

46. Again, see *The Morality of Law*, 33-94; Fuller expresses some reservations about this view, however, at 200-24.

47. *Institutions of Law*, 241-42

point, we need to resist the temptation to try to derive an answer from some abstract general conception of law. Rather, we are trying to identify the appropriate and proper, perhaps even necessary, conditions for legal functioning, given the natural purposes expressed by the kind of legal system that we actually have. Once we frame the issue in these terms, we can readily understand why the paradoxical tension between procedural and substantive criteria should be so acute. That is, the high degree of autonomy exhibited by Western legal systems implies that these are, by and large, self-contained systems, generated and sustained through internal processes which are deliberately isolated from other social systems. Yet as we have seen, even the most formalized legal system cannot operate in complete independence from other social systems and the framework of ideals and commitments sustaining the overall life of the community; indeed, the central function of legal authority is to express and sustain these ideals and commitments in a stable and public way.

We might accordingly proceed by identifying those kinds of failures that are so deeply contrary to the purposes of the law that they invalidate an attempted enactment. In such cases, either we cannot describe the enactment as a law, or else we have compelling reasons to deny the validity of a formally correct statute. Transgressions of what Fuller calls the inner morality of the law offer good examples of the first kind of failure. Legal enactments are after all norms for action, and more specifically, action in accordance with institutionalized practices, having generally recognized public consequences. A putative enactment that is simply too unclear to be put into practice, or one which lacks (and cannot by itself generate) the appropriate public, institutional context, simply fails as law at the most basic level. It cannot be put into practice through actions, or perhaps, actions with the appropriate kind of public force.

We should probably say something similar about an enactment that is not recognized, let alone obeyed, in the community for which it is promulgated. I noted above that for Gratian, a law is properly promulgated by a lawgiver and confirmed by its reception in the community. This seemed to many early commentators, and to some canon lawyers even today, to imply that the validity of an enactment (and not just its effectiveness or soundness) depends on communal reception as well as authorized promulgation — just as an enactment is abrogated once it is no longer generally obeyed. Given our analysis of the point of the law, this seems to me to be correct, for the reasons noted above. That is to say, if an enactment is to serve its key function of guiding action and structuring the public life of the community, then the community has to act on it, and to do so in such a way as to integrate the norm in question into a wider system of formal and customary norms and practices. Through its reception (or otherwise), the community exercises its primal authority over its own affairs, on which the authority of the lawgiver himself rests. It is worth noting that even in this form, the exercise of authority involves an element of contingency — which is to say that we should not presume that there is anything defective about an enactment, some underlying infelicity or moral flaw, just because the community fails to receive it.

I argued above that judicial interpretation should presuppose that the lawgiver intends communal reception, but I do not mean to imply that communal reception is a condition for the validity of a law because the lawgiver intends it. Rather, we should assume that the lawgiver intends such (as one of the implications of the role that she assumes) because communal reception is, independently, one of the conditions for the validity of a law. It is nonetheless worth flagging the lawgiver's formal intention that his law be received by the community, in order to indicate that in recognizing this constraint on legal validity, we do not deny the derivative yet legitimate authority of the lawgiver or the inescapably contingent character of legal enactments. What is more, this construal of the lawmaker's intention is practically important because it helps to set the framework for judicial interpretation — and this brings us to a more general point of considerable importance for our attempt to spell out an account of legal validity.

Let me try to get at the point in this way. So far, I have spoken in terms of enactments that fail to meet the criteria for legal validity, because they are incoherent or fail for some other reason to serve as efficacious norms for action. Yet it does not seem quite right to regard even these as having no legal force whatever. Barring some immediate action on the part of the lawgiver, they will presumably be promulgated and incorporated into the body of formal law. As such, they may generate attempts at enforcement, and they will also stand as presumptive constraints on adjudication, or as themselves standards by which a case should be judged. In short, they represent the lawgiver's minimal claims to recognition on the part of public officials and judges, and in that way they do have a kind of legal force. This is the element of truth in some older versions of legal positivism, according to which the validity of an enactment depends solely on the duly executed authoritative act of the lawgiver. We cannot construe validity in these terms alone, but it is true that the lawgiver's authoritative act is sufficient to give an enactment a place, at least provisionally, in the wider system of norms and practices constituting the formal law.

In particular, it serves to place the enactment within the restricted set of those explicit norms which ought to be taken into account, when relevant, in the adjudication of specific cases — even though it is itself subject to judicial review and abrogation for just the same reason. This brings us to the point at hand. That is to say, even though we may conclude that an enactment fails to attain legal validity, that determination still needs to be made in a publicly acknowledged and authoritative way — which, given the constitutional structure of Western legal systems, implies that invalid enactments are normally determined to be such in and through processes of adjudication and judicial review. Once again, the judge serves a necessary mediating function, in this instance, between specific enactments, and the wider set of norms and considerations informing the legal system itself. In this way, the judge serves as a gatekeeper, keeping unworkable or inappropriate enactments out of the body of the law, where they would otherwise generate confusion or undermine respect for the rule of law.

Iniquitous Statutes and the Limits of Legality

It is important to keep this in mind when we turn to the more difficult question of whether, and in what ways, an enactment can fail to be valid law because it is, in MacCormick's terms, "unjustifiable with respect to any reasonable moral argument." I want to argue that here, too, the judge serves as a gatekeeper, both by interpreting enactments, as far as possible, in such a way as to render them consistent with a broad political morality and minimal standards of equity and justice, and abrogating them when they are too problematic to be saved through even the most generous interpretation. Thus, even a morally problematic enactment should be regarded as valid law, in the sense that it can properly serve as a basis for a legal claim, and ought to be taken into consideration, when relevant, by the court. But of course, this does not imply that the court should automatically uphold or enforce it. On the contrary, if an enactment is morally flawed in some relevant way, the court should, if possible, interpret it in such a way as to render it consistent with the political morality of the community. If that simply cannot be done, then it can and should be set aside (at which point, it loses its validity as a legal enactment). Generally speaking, it should not be enforced in such a way as to affirm and perpetuate those aspects which render it problematic. Acts of civil disobedience and conscientious dissent directed against such a law should not be punished, and manifestly wicked actions should not be excused solely on the grounds that the law allowed or required them.

Seen from this perspective, the claim that an unjust (or otherwise morally problematic) enactment is not valid begins to be plausible, even within the context of highly formalized, self-contained legal systems characteristic of Western societies. After all, the judicial response to flawed enactments sketched above reflects what judges actually do in most Western legal systems. Laws are regularly suspended or struck down because they are inconsistent with an overall system of normative principles, as embodied in the overall legal framework of the society. Western legal norms and customs of adjudication allow judges wide scope for suspending the effects of an enactment, when strict enforcement would be unjust or otherwise problematic. Most of these systems allow, in addition, at least some scope for higher courts to, in effect, abrogate an enactment on the grounds that it is contrary to the overall constitutional structure of the polity. Of course, there is a difference between declaring a law to be morally problematic and declaring it to be unconstitutional. At the same time, the constitutional structure of a polity (whether formally enacted or not) reflects its central ideals and commitments, as these are expressed and sustained in the institutions structuring its public life. Seen from this perspective, a judgment that an enactment is unconstitutional may well express a sense that it is inconsistent with central elements of a political morality, as these are reflected in constitutional norms and practices. This need not be the case, of course — every constitution includes purely procedural norms — but very often it is, as when a law is struck down because it violates constitutional norms of equal treatment, or respect for core individual freedoms, or privacy, or the like.

The claim that adjudication can and should take account of value judgments, at least insofar as these are inscribed in the legal and constitutional structures of the polity, is not new; as we have seen, Fuller offers a restricted, and Dworkin an expansive defense of this claim. Yet until recently, most legal scholars would have been reluctant to say that in some cases, at least, legal judgments are also and inextricably moral judgments, admittedly limited in scope, but moral judgments all the same. To some extent, of course, this reluctance reflects widespread unease with the whole project of "legislating morality" — imposing moral standards for individual conduct on the unpersuaded or unwilling. But when we examine influential discussions of these matters more closely, a second and more fundamental reason for this reluctance appears. That is, most legal philosophers simply assume the existence of a robust, action-guiding and yet pre-conventional morality — in contrast to the constitutional order, customs, and laws of a polity, which are clearly conventional.[48] Given this assumption, any attempt to incorporate elements of the pre-conventional moral system into enactments of a conventional legal system will, at the least, call for special justification. Seen from this perspective, the project of "legislating morality" is bound to risk undermining the proper independence of law — perhaps a justified risk, but a risk nonetheless.

At this point, the early scholastic approach to the natural law offers a promising, and perhaps surprising, way forward.[49] As we saw in the first chapter, the scholastics in this period consistently identify the natural law in its primary sense with the capacities for rational judgment, or the formal principles through which these capacities operate. Understood in these terms, the natural law is universal, innately natural, and therefore pre-conventional, but it cannot be equated with normative standards specific enough to guide conduct. Unlike many contemporary natural law theorists, the scholastics also recognize that rational judgment is properly informed by the intelligible structures, purposes, and natural values intrinsic to human nature broadly considered, which are again innately natural and therefore pre-conventional. What is more, as we have seen, these do yield some specific normative content — but even at this level, the normative structures generated by the natural law fall considerably short of a comprehensive system of practical norms, specific enough to guide conduct. Natural norms and values, while real and universal, under-determine the conventional norms which give them direct practical force, and for this reason, they must be specified through the comparative judgments, practices, and customs of a specific morality. At this level, we cannot say that there is only one, or even one clearly preferable natural moral law. What we find, rather, are a plurality of natural moralities, expressing the diverse ways of pursuing and sustaining the human good that have emerged over the course of human affairs. That, in my view, is why the scholastics in this period do not speak in terms of a moral law, existing as a normative structure distinct both from the natural law and divine (that is to say, revealed) law. What we would describe as moral law comes closer to what they describe as the mores of a particular community, that is to say, its customs.

---

48. See, for example, *Institutions of Law*, 243-61. Hart is the most important recent exception to this generalization, at least among philosophers of law; see *The Concept of Law*, 79-99.

49. I defend the following interpretation in more detail in "Christian Ethics and the Concept of Morality: A Historical Inquiry," *Journal of the Society of Christian Ethics* 26.2 (2006): 3-21.

The implications of this approach for contemporary legal theory are clear. The antinomy between moral and legal norms presupposes a fundamental divide between a pre-conventional moral law and legal conventions. But if there is no good reason to construe the moral law in these terms, then the antinomy dissolves. Moral norms and what we might describe, broadly, as legal norms (not necessarily formal enactments) stand on the same side of the divide between the natural and the conventional as two ways of expressing pre-conventional norms of rationality and the values intrinsic to our natural existence and activities. There are still important differences between legal norms and the more general and comprehensive morality of a given society, but these are differences of scope and purpose, well expressed by Hart's distinction between primary and secondary rules. This is particularly true in the Western legal systems we are considering. We attempt to draw sharp lines between legal and broadly moral considerations because we have good, indeed exigent reasons for doing so, given our core commitments and social conditions — not because there is any deep difference between something we might style as the moral realm of judgment and legal norms and practices. The latter are formulated in such a way as to place them within a relatively self-contained normative system, bearing distinctive public significance. The boundaries that we place around that system more or less track the distinctions between law and morality, as these would be construed in most Western societies. These distinctions, in turn, partially reflect the limitations of a broad public order, and also express specific normative judgments implied by a particular political morality. Let me say something about each of these boundaries in turn.

In the Western legal tradition, it has long been acknowledged that some aspects of human behavior simply cannot be subject to legislative and judicial regulation, at least not directly. Human acts are construed and judged, in key part if not entirely, by reference to the intentions and motivations that they reflect. For example, almost every legal system draws some distinction between inflicting an injury on another by accident and deliberately harming another. Yet even so, an individual's inner desires and motivations are not always directly accessible, and to the extent that they are not, they cannot be subject to adjudication. Nor does there seem to be any point in judging desires and even intentions which are not expressed in some way in action.

There are other aspects of human behavior which do find expression in overt acts, but which nonetheless appear to be inappropriate or inopportune targets for judicial regulation. We may well question whether the legal system should concern itself with regulating actions that affect no one but the agent herself, or other willing participants in a shared activity. Admittedly, this is not apparent, since the expression and sustenance of a shared set of values and ideals is one of the key purposes of a legal system. Even so, a legal system can only accomplish so much, and even if there is a general social consensus that the regulation of some kinds of private behavior would be appropriate, it may simply be impractical, if only because no legal system can command unlimited resources. The attempt to correct even widely recognized social evils through legal regulation can do more harm than good.

What is more, we may well find ourselves in the position of tolerating deeply flawed institutions and practices because we have no practical alternatives, or at least we cannot imagine what they might be. This is a hard saying. Anglophone societies, especially the United States, have long been dominated by what Michael Walzer calls messianic politics — a style of public discourse and activity that combines great clarity about social evils with the conviction that they can and should be eliminated, immediately and comprehensively, through the agency of some secular messiah or messianic movement.[50] But the central practices and institutions structuring the common life of a polity cannot readily be changed, and can almost never be eliminated outright, without doing intolerable damage to the complex social structures with which they are bound up. For that reason, lawgivers and courts may sometimes find themselves in the unhappy position of giving legal recognition and force to problematic practices, if the society is to continue to function, or at least to do so in such a way as to sustain its character as a polity, sustained by the rule of law. Needless to say, we would not want to generalize this point too far. As we saw in the last chapter, there are some kinds of public acts so heinous that they cannot be justified even by claims of necessity. They simply should not be enjoined by law or official directives. Nor, if attempted, should such (supposed) laws or directives be carried out or sanctioned by the courts. That being said, however, we will still need to deal with social conventions that are seriously unjust or otherwise problematic, even though they are not on the same level of iniquity as recognized crimes against humanity, and which furthermore are so deeply ingrained in a given society that we cannot avoid giving them some cognizance at law. So long as these evils are thereby tolerated rather than endorsed or promoted,

50. The image is, of course, biblical; Walzer contrasts it with Exodus politics, which operates through the paradigms of provisional liberation, extended periods of consolidation, and persistent ambiguities, after the pattern of the Exodus narratives of liberation and wandering in the wilderness. This is his own preferred approach, and mine as well. The main lines of the argument are summarized in Michael Walzer, *Exodus and Revolution* (New York: Basic Books, 1985), 131-52.

and so long as the legal system taken as a whole remains oriented towards the common good, understood as the community's best ideals of itself as a polity, it does not thereby surrender its claims to legitimacy and authority.

As Reinhold Niebuhr so forcefully reminds us, no human society can be altogether free of the ambiguities and injustices that stem from the pervasive effects of sin.[51] Yet we can acknowledge this unhappy truth without thereby withdrawing from political life altogether, or else taking up a stance of regretful tolerance towards even the most egregious social evils. Societies do change, generally slowly, sometimes with remarkable speed, and in periods of rapid social change and institutional flux, we may well find ourselves presented with unanticipated opportunities for far-reaching social change. The late eleventh and twelfth centuries were characterized by just such processes of social upheaval and systemic change, and the institutional and legal reforms of the period demonstrate that far-reaching innovation and change can take place, offering real alternatives to seemingly intractable social evils.[52] In such a situation, practices and institutional arrangements which were once tolerable, and legitimately subject to legal regulation, may become unjust, in such a way as to bear legal consequences. At this point, we can cogently claim that our best standards of justice, as given concrete form through attainable reforms and transformed practices, do place normative constraints on the law. To take one obvious example, the iniquity of slavery was apparent to many even in antiquity, and yet it probably would have been impossible to eliminate this institution through any imaginable political or legal action until the early modern period. But by this point, both circumstances and the range of imaginable possibilities had changed, in such a way that it would have been entirely possible to refrain from introducing slavery into the fabric of Western societies, and possible, albeit more difficult, to eliminate it once introduced — as events eventually proved. At that point, the laws regulating and institutionalizing

51. This point is central to Niebuhr's work throughout his long career; one of the best and most comprehensive developments may be found in *Nature and Destiny of Man, Volume 2: Human Destiny* (New York: Scribners, 1943, 1964), 244-86.

52. I do not mean to imply that the reforms of the eleventh and twelfth centuries were altogether effective, or positive, or free of their own ambiguities. Nonetheless, as we saw earlier, in this period the rule of law was articulated and extended throughout western Europe, personal dominion was replaced by stable entities sustaining a genuinely political form of rule, marriage was reformed in such a way as to guarantee everyone the freedom to marry and to place men and women in a relation of rough parity, and claims to subjective, juridically salient nature rights began to be articulated and given legal effect. These seem to me to be genuinely innovative and salutary reforms.

slavery could only be regarded as profoundly unjust: they should not have been enacted, but being enacted, they should not have been obeyed, enforced, or affirmed as legitimate by the courts.[53]

This brings us to a more general point. So far, we have focused on the ways in which legal systems necessarily exclude some kinds of normative considerations, distinguishing between moral and properly legal considerations. Without drawing these distinctions in some ways, it would be impossible to maintain a body of law as a self-contained, self-regulating normative system, and given the distinctive ideals and circumstances of Western societies, we find ourselves compelled to draw the relevant distinctions fairly sharply. In this way, the purposes of law imply exclusionary constraints on the kinds of first-order considerations that should be given legal cognizance. At the same time, however, the characteristic purposes of law can also require us to take account of more general moral or broadly normative considerations, incorporating these into our legal systems in such a way as to give them properly legal force. Certain kinds of normative considerations can and should be taken into account, in distinctive and appropriate ways, by the lawgiver and the judge.

Above all, a legal system is both properly constrained and normatively structured by the demands of justice, understood formally in correlation to the act of rendering to each his or her due. The scholastics were disposed by the very terms of their analysis to presuppose an integral connection, at the very least, between the law and the *jus,* understood as an intrinsically just state of affairs, or between law and the legitimate claims or rights, the *jura,* that should be recognized at law. It is sometimes said that the central purpose of law itself is precisely to render justice. In my view, this is misleading. Justice is better construed in terms of a normative ideal internal to the law, rather than one of the natural purposes served by law. In much the same way, chastity is the regulative ideal for sexual behavior and marriage, but it would be odd, at least, to say that the natural purposes of sex and marriage include being chaste, or in the contemporary idiom, doing chastity. Chastity and justice are, rather, dispositions to pursue and enjoy the natural purposes of sexual behavior and political and legal activities in appropriate, rationally defensible ways.

53. I rely here on David Brion Davis, *Inhuman Bondage: The Rise and Fall of Slavery in the New World* (Oxford: Oxford University Press, 2006); see 1-11 for a summary of the overall argument. Also see Orlando Patterson, *Slavery and Social Death: A Comparative Study* (Cambridge, MA: Harvard University Press, 1982), 17-34 and *Freedom in the Making of Western Culture* (New York: Harper Collins, 1991), 9-46.

Nonetheless, the natural purposes served by law, and justice considered as an internal ideal governing the legal system, are closely interconnected. To return once again to a familiar point, human beings are highly social animals. As such, we exhibit a way of life that is structured in accordance with some sense of equity, appropriate respect and constraint, and defensible distributions, which we express through norms of justice, informed to some extent by pre-rational sentiments of entitlement, anger, deference, and assertion. No human society can sustain itself over any length of time unless the perceived claims of its individual members are acknowledged, at least in most cases and most of the time, and in most societies this is done chiefly through the rule of just laws. More fundamentally, the goodness intrinsic to the form of life proper to creatures of our kind can only be expressed through patterns of just and equitable interactions. To return to the point flagged above, a just rule of law is not merely instrumental for, but also partially constitutive of a distinctively good and happy human existence. At the same time, the substantive criteria for justice cannot be formulated or put into practice apart from a community's actual commitments and practices, its culture, as expressed in its distinctive ideal of the common good. To a very considerable extent, the law can only serve its distinctive purpose of expressing and promoting this ideal by rendering justice in accordance with the community's best standards of equity and fairness, seen in correlation with its ideal of the common good.

Practically, what does all this imply? The boundary norms discussed at the end of the last chapter constitute a most important set of demands that any legal system or society must respect, if it is to preserve any claims to legitimacy and allegiance. For the scholastics and for our own contemporaries, human or natural rights offer another, indeed perhaps the central example of normative constraints operating on a legal system. We will defer the consideration of the complex topic of natural rights to the next chapter. Meanwhile, I will conclude this chapter with a brief consideration of two other kinds of normative claims implied by an ideal of justice. Both of these, I will suggest, stem from general exigencies of forms of activity necessary to human existence as such, and both must therefore be recognized and upheld if a community's conception of itself, its common good, and its laws, are to be fully defensible. To add the now-familiar qualification, these exigencies will be perceived and addressed in irreducibly diverse and incompatible ways. They must be acknowledged in some way, nonetheless, if men and women are to live, and to live well, as the kind of creatures that we are.

Structures of Human Life, Ideals of Due Process, and the Limits of Law

The first set of normative constraints that we will briefly consider here stem from the exigencies of natural functioning, considered from the standpoint of communal, rather than individual activities. Human activity, as we have repeatedly seen, stems from a specifically distinctive way of functioning, which unfolds in a structured and broadly predictable way, embodying (if all goes well) the natural values constitutive of a good human life. Like every other kind of living creature, what we are is inextricably bound up with what we ideally can and should be, and this — so far as it goes — is not simply a matter of individual choice. We must immediately add that unlike other living creatures, the natural telos of the human agent can be attained in an indefinite number of ways, and, what is more, it can only be attained through her free and informed activities. It would be a very grave mistake to identify the properly human way of flourishing with a particular set of social conventions, embodying (for example) culturally specific norms of sexual behavior and forms of marriage, and to insist that the laws can or should enforce these conventions on this basis.

Nonetheless, the innate structures and purposeful activities that are characteristic of human existence as such — our characteristic ways of coming into being, maturing and sustaining life, participating in processes of physical and cultural reproduction — all these will properly inform the ideals governing any human society, and correlatively, they will set parameters on the shape of a society and especially on its legal system. By now, this claim should come as no surprise. In the last chapter, I argued that some values are intrinsic to the structured form of human existence, in such a way as to constitute salient considerations for rational deliberation and a legitimate, non-manipulative form of rhetorical persuasion. No genuinely political society, informed by the deliberative activities of free men and women reflecting on their deepest and most urgent needs and desires, would tolerate a social or legal system within which basic human needs were not addressed, and basic human desires could not be meaningfully pursued.

These include the necessary conditions for any kind of action, including centrally food and water, clothing, and shelter, access to transportation and information, and critically, the means to procure all these necessities. But they also include what we identified in chapter two as key natural institutions and relationships, grounded in purposes which are proper to human existence as such, serving to express and sustain these in a broadly accessible way. Once again, these are necessarily expressed in conventional forms, which are always in a process of development, and properly subject to ongoing reform through processes of rhetorical persuasion. It would be a grave mistake for political authorities to attempt to short-circuit these processes through narrowly restrictive legal regulations. And yet, the constitutive relationships and institutions of human life do reflect natural purposes, and correlatively, structured forms of interaction which give rise to more or less self-contained systems of activity. At the same time, these aims and activities can only be pursued in and through social conventions of all kinds, which, as Raz reminds us, will inevitably open up some kinds of options while foreclosing others. For that very reason, and given their central place in individual lives and in the sustenance of an overall way of life, the natural institutions and relationships yield claims which a just society is bound to respect, supporting these in whatever ways are possible and appropriate within the given polity. With qualifications, the same can be said of small-scale communities and associations which inevitably emerge in any sizeable political community, which very often offer alternative ways of life, embodying natural principles and values in a distinctive way.

To some extent, these kinds of claims can be formulated and addressed within the framework of a doctrine and practice of human rights, which on almost any interpretation include rights to pursue what are here described as natural purposes and satisfactions of human life, and to associate with other like-minded individuals in pursuit of common ideals. But as we will see in the next chapter, the idea of natural or human rights emerged out of, and continues to reflect, a commitment to safeguard individual freedom, and for that very reason the discourse of rights cannot well express claims of value on behalf of institutions, practices, and ways of life which cannot be understood without remainder in terms of the free associations of purely autonomous individuals. As Mary Ann Glendon puts it, speaking of a recent dispute in Detroit involving government seizure of land in pursuit of urban renewal:

> Thus, when Detroit's Poletown residents mounted their campaign to prevent the taking and destruction of their neighborhood, they found that the most readily available vocabulary — that of individual property rights — enabled them to speak about only part of the problem. They could not find a way to communicate effectively with legislators, judges, or the press about other kinds of losses: a rich neighborhood life; shared memories and hopes; roots; a sense of place. When, as a last resort, they brought a

lawsuit, they were, in effect, laughed out of court when they resorted to the only legal terms that even came close to enabling them to voice their deepest concerns — the analogy to environmental protection.[54]

I would not share Glendon's negative assessment of the liberal construal of rights, particularly as we find it in the United States — while I agree with her that this construal emphasizes individual freedom, I regard that as one of its strengths, not a weakness. But I do agree that when the language of individual rights offers the only effective language for political and juridical discourse, something of importance is distorted or lost — namely, those elements of human life which by their very character transcend individual lives, and are valuable in themselves in a way that cannot be reduced to the satisfactions of the individuals sustaining them.[55] What is more, these transcend individual lives precisely because they provide necessary structures or contexts for human activities and enjoyments of all kinds. If these are undermined, men and women will find their choices curtailed, their lives impoverished and rendered unnecessarily hard, their freedom diminished. And so, we have a stake in recognizing and promoting the good estate of these institutions, practices, and communities — not as a value to be secured over against the free choices of individuals but as a way of safeguarding and expanding possibilities for human freedom by providing a range of genuine, attractive alternatives. Given our own characteristic political morality, we will most probably do so in such a way as to promote what Raz calls an autonomy-promoting society. But as he immediately goes on to say, the resultant institutional forms and laws, including those pertinent to marriage, will still provide structured options for choice, in which some possibilities are foreclosed precisely so that others can be safeguarded or promoted.[56]

Let me illustrate this point through a necessarily sketchy example. We observed in chapter two that marriage offers the paradigm case of a natural institution, tethered to the fundamental natural purpose of reproducing the species. Yet marriage is always expressed through some set of conventional practices which will inevitably serve a range of other purposes proper to the kinship structures and personal interactions of the complex social primates

---

54. Mary Ann Glendon, *Rights Talk: The Impoverishment of Political Discourse* (New York: Free Press, 1991), 111.

55. We have already noted that David Hollenbach makes a very similar point; see *The Common Good and Christian Ethics* (Cambridge: Cambridge University Press, 2002), 81-82.

56. *The Morality of Freedom,* 192; he goes on to spell out what an autonomy-promoting society would look like at 369-99.

that we are. This being the case, I think we should be very hesitant to rule out unconventional forms of marriage too quickly on the grounds that these are contrary to the natural purposes of the institution. What seems from one perspective to be contrary to natural purposes might appear on longer experience as a legitimate expansion of those purposes, which does not undermine, and may well strengthen, the central purposes which the institution must serve if society is to continue at all. For this reason, I would support the legal recognition of same-sex unions as marriages, and I would grant legal recognition to some forms of plural marriages as well.

At the same time, the institution of marriage does express natural purposes which cannot be reduced to the rights of individuals to enter into (or for that matter, to leave) marriages. Whatever other purposes it may legitimately serve, the institution of marriage exists in order to facilitate the generation and upbringing of children in an appropriately human way, which fosters education and integration into a society as well as physical nurture, and which more broadly sustains the ties of kinship and generations in such a way as to give meaning to the natural development of a human life. These purposes cannot be reduced to, or much less safeguarded through, individuals' marriage rights. They presuppose a wider set of social arrangements, especially economic arrangements, which enable men and women to enter into marital relations freely and to build and enjoy a family life without having to undergo extreme financial hardships or drastically to curtail the freedom, the civic life, and the intellectual and spiritual development of one partner or the other.

Not to put too fine a point on it: it should be possible for a man and a woman to marry, start a family, and meet their responsibilities to their parents and extended family without driving themselves into penury or exhaustion, and without forcing one partner, usually the wife, into a set of impossible choices between family and financial security, family and personal vocation, husband and dependents, children and elderly parents. Fathers and mothers should be able to rely on decent social arrangements which enable them to care for and educate their children in the dense, complex, and mobile society in which we actually live, not the close-knit, cohesive rural communities that we think we would prefer. They should have ready access to the minimal material requirements for a decent, enjoyable home, including some access to housing itself and provisions for food, water, and hygiene — to say nothing of some protections for the physical and emotional privacy of the home. The fact that these conditions do not obtain in United States society, seem in fact almost utopian or dangerously socialist, reflect the deepest threats to "family values" in this country today. If we want to safeguard and promote the family, we can best do so by way of addressing these conditions. What is more, these reflect exigent claims on our society, stemming as it were from the natural goodness of human existence itself, and so long as we do not meet them we wrong our fellow-citizens, and ourselves.

This brings me to the second set of normative considerations that I want to mention at this point — considerations that return us once again to Fuller's inner morality of the law. We are by now familiar with his point that the law operates in accordance with normative standards, comprised of the practices and constraints intrinsic to legal functioning itself, and correlatively, the ideals of due process and legality corresponding to these. I want to focus at this point on these latter ideals, considered as another aspect of human activity that certainly generates rights claims, but cannot be reduced to individual rights and activities without remainder.

I argued above that the rule of law should not be regarded as an instrumental good. Rather, it is itself a constitutive element of the common good, an integral component of the flourishing of any community and, correlatively, one of the greatest social goods that men and women can share. We are now in a better position to appreciate why that should be the case. That is, the norms of proper legality reflect exigencies of rational action at the individual and communal levels — they are specifications of general principles of practical reason, partially contingent to be sure, but nonetheless necessary if men and women are to act in a public realm in accordance with rational principles. As such, they reflect a distinctive and centrally important constitutive structure of human life, which places direct normative constraints on the structures of law. Fuller's inner morality of the law thus turns out to be more important, and more closely tied to central human values, than we might initially have thought.

Let me conclude by saying something further about what seems to me to be the central components of Fuller's inner morality, considered precisely as correlative ideals of the rule of law and proper legality — namely, those principles and formal norms that comprise basic, procedural due process. These norms serve the critical function of enabling rational human activity at a critical juncture, at which the individual is rendered vulnerable to the overwhelming power of the state. They do so first by enabling him to pursue the most fundamental natural inclinations towards self-protection and self-defense, placing limits on his vulnerability and providing him opportunities to defend himself through reasoned arguments. Secondly, they do so by constraining the activities of public authorities in such a way as to safeguard basic standards of fairness and equity. It can be tempting to regard these as, once again, instrumental means towards maintaining a good balance between individual claims and public security, to be disregarded when overwhelming public interest or even the manifest demands of a larger justice require it. Yet this temptation should be resisted, because the norms of due process are themselves an intrinsic component of legal authority, seen as one kind of political authority. In a properly political society, not even the accused, nor indeed convicted criminals, can be subject to servile dominion; they too retain some status as political agents, who rightly expect to be treated in such a way as to take account of their intrinsic value and their claims to equity and (at least) minimal decency.

I noted in the first chapter that the scholastics liked to make the point that even God accused Adam in accordance with norms of due procedure, giving him an opportunity to respond to a formal accusation, even though God was of course not in doubt about the facts of the matter. Let me conclude this chapter with a more recent and very powerful defense of the same ideal, which also provides us with a fine example of persuasive rhetoric. The author is Leonard Pitts, a journalist and columnist for the Miami *Herald*. He is commenting on the bitter controversies over Attorney General Eric Holder's decision to try some of those accused of conspiring to carry out the attacks on the World Trade Center in New York City in 2001. Pitts begins by admitting that he understands and sympathizes with those who feel that Khalid Sheik Mohammed and the other conspirators should be subject to summary execution, or worse. Nonetheless, he says,

> It's worth remembering that even the architects of the greatest barbarism in history had their day in court. After burning away 11 million lives, the leaders of the Nazi regime found themselves facing not summary execution, but a trial before a military tribunal in Nuremberg, Germany.

It is certainly the case that the norms of due process formulate natural rights to equity, decent treatment, and the freedom to act on one's own behalf in an adversarial situation. But Pitts's point is that these norms serve in addition to safeguard the character of the community as a polity, structured in accordance with ideals of freedom and equity. We, as members of the polity in question, all have a stake in safeguarding these ideals, precisely because when they are compromised, we are all to some extent compromised. In order to bring this out, he goes on to quote a *New York Times* editorial written shortly after the conclusion of the Nuremberg trials which claimed that the

MINISTERS OF THE LAW

verdicts, while inadequate as a recompense for the crimes committed, nonetheless "help to assuage the conscience of mankind and to restore to honor
the concept of the dignity of man which cannot be violated with impunity."
He adds,

> Compare that with the Bush administration's original, Supreme Court re-
> buked justice — minimal rights for the accused, torture allowed, the gov-
> ernment's thumb on justice's scale — and maybe you'll agree. We need
> this trial more than [Khalid Sheik] Mohammed does. For all its risks —
> and they are real — it offers a prize worth risking for: the promise of feel-
> ing like Americans again.
>
> That feeling is arguably the most significant casualty of Sept. 11. On
> that day, we elevated a mob of stateless criminals, a mafia in clerics' cloth-
> ing, to the exalted level of rogue nation. But they were never that, never a
> threat to our national existence; they lacked the forces to take even one
> square inch of American soil. What they could threaten — and take —
> was our sense of ourselves as a brave, reasonable, and civilized people, in-
> habiting a nation of laws. They beckoned us into the mud with them, and
> we leapt.[57]

So we did — may we recollect ourselves sufficiently to reclaim our best
ideals, at least partially and provisionally, in the hard years that lie ahead.

---

57. Leonard Pitts, columnist for the *Miami Herald*, in an editorial reprinted in the *South Bend Tribune*, Nov. 22, 2009.

CHAPTER 5

Authority Within and Beyond the State

In the preceding chapter, I argued that legal authority derives from the more fundamental authority that a community properly exercises over its individual members, in and through the necessary processes of articulating background beliefs, normative boundaries, values, and commitments — all the ingredients of a specific culture, without which neither the community itself nor its individual members can develop and function in characteristically human ways. Legal authority is thus a kind of political authority, deriving from the foundational authority of the community — implying first, that it is directed towards the common good of the community and the flourishing of its individual members, and second, that it is in some way tethered to processes of rhetorical deliberation and persuasion, through which specific decrees and judgments can be justified by reference to broadly acceptable rational and natural principles.

All this suggests that legal authority is closely tied to the formal institutions expressing the political authority of the community in stable, publicly accessible ways — which is to say, up until now at any rate, through the institutional structures of the modern nation-state.[1] The analysis of the forms of

---

1. For a comprehensive historical account of the emergence of the modern nation-state system, see R. C. van Caenegem, *An Historical Introduction to Western Constitutional Law* (Cambridge: Cambridge University Press, 1995), 72-90, 194-243, and Hendrik Spruyt, *The Sovereign State and Its Competitors* (Princeton: Princeton University Press, 1994), 59-180. Neil MacCormick offers an illuminating analysis of what it means to characterize a modern nation-state as a "law state," that is to say, a political system supporting and sustained by the rule of law, in *Institutions of Law: An Essay in Legal Theory* (Oxford: Oxford University Press, 2007), 39-60. Finally, for an informative account of the theoretical principles undergirding the modern nation-state system, see Christopher W. Morris, *An Essay on the Modern State* (Cambridge: Cambridge University Press, 1998), especially 1-55, 172-227.

legal authority developed in the last chapter bear this out. As we saw, legal authority is characteristically expressed through processes of adjudication and legislation, carried out through the distinct yet mutually interrelated institutions of the court and the lawgiver. Today, these institutions are almost always constituted by a national government or by the joint act of governments setting up international tribunals, and for this reason courts and legislative agencies may seem to derive their authority from the regime (or treaty) that created them. What is more, the creation and functioning of courts and lawgivers in almost all modern societies is tethered to the system of sovereign nation-states emerging out of the Peace of Westphalia in the mid-seventeenth century. Within this system, the overarching governmental authority of the polity is tied to control over a defined territory, within which the national government exercises final and plenary power. Thus, courts and legislators operating within a modern nation-state properly concern themselves with every aspect of human existence — family life, property and financial institutions, education, religious practices, and the like — and they operate in independence of any authority external to the nation itself. Courts and legislators answer to each other in complex ways, and both are further engaged with the executive branch of government, but in their joint operations they cannot be held to account by any kind of world government or international court or, for that matter, by the Holy See or another religious authority. Or so the theory goes, and until very recently, so the practices of national governments went, as well.

These institutional practices seem to imply that the sovereignty of the modern nation-state within its own boundaries and over its own citizens is both fundamental and absolute.[2] For some of its defenders, and even more for its critics, the unconditional character of national sovereignty is indeed entailed by the modern nation-state system, in such a way that if we accept it, we will necessarily respect the unconditional authority of national governments over their own citizens and within their own boundaries. By implication, anyone who objects to the unconditional quality of sovereignty in the modern nation-state will necessarily be committed to rejecting the nation-state system itself and working to establish some alternative forms of governmental institutions, assuming that doing without governments is not a real option anymore. These are not happy alternatives.

2. However, van Caenegem points out that the principles and practices of absolute sovereignty were called into question almost as quickly as they emerged, and were very soon qualified both domestically and internationally; see *Historical Introduction*, 108-93.

But neither are they necessary alternatives, because even considered on its own terms, as a way of articulating the implications of the modern nation-state system, this way of construing the authority of the nation-state is unrealistic. Certainly, the legal and governmental institutions of the modern nation-state are not constrained by any external sovereign or court in the exercise of their powers, except insofar as the state itself freely concedes authority to some external agency, in delimited and revocable ways — as the nations of Europe have done vis-à-vis the agencies of the European Union. But that does not mean that legal authority within a nation is dependent upon, and without remainder subordinate to, the authority of the sovereign national government. By implication, the authority of the latter is not absolute and unqualified in its proper exercise. It may not be limited by external agencies but it is limited by the authority of the law itself and qualified by the constraints on proper legality set forth in the preceding chapter.

It may seem paradoxical to say that a nation-state is limited in some way through a body of laws enacted and interpreted through institutions that it has itself created and maintained. The appearance of paradox begins to dissolve, however, when we recall an observation from chapter one, that historically the legal systems, and to some extent the judicial and legislative institutions, of most Western nations pre-date the regimes currently governing them, in some instances by quite a long time. The institutions of government within these nations emerged in tandem with the generation of formal law codes through learned interpretation, institutional reform, and the creation of new institutional forms, through processes characterized by mutual interaction and dependence rather than strict relations of priority and derivation. Throughout the medieval and early modern period, these processes were spurred by the exigencies of a rapidly expanding, complex, and contentious society. In addition, and still more fundamentally, they emerged in response to the re-assertion of despotic forms of power in the eleventh and early twelfth centuries, which were widely perceived at the time to be a reversion from the ideals of a lawful, political society. Certainly, throughout the medieval and early modern period, political rulers laid claim to unlimited power, similar in form, if not in rationale, to the unlimited sovereignty of the nation-state as some would construe it. Usually, these claims were justified in theological terms. But throughout this period these claims were resisted, in terms which offered an alternative construal of the same theological commitments. These are the processes out of which modern institutions of national governments and legal codes emerged together, jointly laying the foundations for the modern nation-state system as we know it today.

Seen from a natural law perspective, these processes reflect a fundamental, yet easily overlooked point. That is to say, the distinctive form of sovereignty associated with the modern nation-state is itself a kind of political authority, dependent on the foundational authority that the community exercises over its individual members. Thus, the authority of the nation-state rests on the same basis as legal authority, in such a way that neither can be given absolute priority to the other. Each derives its ultimate normative authority from the same fundamental ground, in such a way as to reflect the properly political character of communal authority, that is, its suitability for a community of free, reasonable men and women. This does not mean that governmental authority derives from the law in any simple way, any more than that the legal system is wholly dependent on processes of governmental enactment, interpretation, and enforcement. It does imply that governmental authority is limited and constrained by the same broad considerations that emerged in our analysis of legal authority. That is to say, it must be tethered in some way to processes of rhetorical persuasion, in such a way that it reflects rational and natural considerations that can be appreciated, and to some extent shared, by all the members of the community. There is really no such thing as a properly unconditional authority; the pretension to absolute power is a mark of tyranny, and as such it exercises no proper normative force over its putative subjects.

Understood in this way, the authority of the modern nation-state rests ultimately on the fact that at its best, it operates in such a way as to safeguard and promote the well-being, the way of life, and the processes of deliberation and persuasion sustaining the community within its borders. These are of course very similar to the purposes served by the law, and once this becomes apparent, we can more readily appreciate the force of Neil MacCormick's claim that the modern nation-state is a law-state, which owes its legitimacy to its genuine and manifest respect for the laws and for some defensible ideals of justice and equity.[3] Thus, there is no real inconsistency between defending a robust modern conception of national sovereignty and insisting on the proper limitations of governmental authority, both within and outside the boundaries of the nation-state.

This still leaves us with the question of whether, and in what ways, the authority of nation-states is properly limited in their *ad extra* relations to

---

3. Again, see *Institutions of Law*, 170-85.

one another, and increasingly to non-state actors of all kinds. For all that has been said so far, it might be the case that the world of international relations remains in a state of nature — in Hobbes's sense rather than that implied by Genesis. Indeed, on the account of political authority developed so far, it is difficult to see how international relations could be informed by a genuine rule of law. The difficulty is that on this account, political authority is tethered to processes of rhetorical deliberation and persuasion, which presuppose a relatively cohesive community held together by a framework of shared beliefs, commitments, and ideals. And clearly, there is no such thing as a world community of this kind, constituting a polity held together by a comprehensive culture and way of life. Certainly, we can and do think in terms of an idealized world community and, to a limited extent, this ideal answers to reality; the nations of the world, intermediate agencies, and individual men and women continually engage in relations with one another, and at least sometimes they reflect together on what they are doing. Nonetheless, the diversity of cultures among the peoples of the world sharply limits the scope of rhetorical deliberation and persuasion — to say nothing of the obstacles raised by deep divisions of interest and the sheer practical difficulties involved in joint reflection on the necessary scale. Given this state of affairs, it is hard to see how we might argue for the existence of a genuinely political authority that can legitimately constrain the *ad extra* actions of nations — or indeed, of any other agency or individual acting outside the boundaries of one's own political community.

The prospects for establishing a comprehensive system of governing institutions at the international level are very dim indeed, even if such an arrangement were desirable. But as we have seen more than once, systems of law do not necessarily depend on the prior existence of a political regime, either practically or normatively. And we do seem to affirm and act in accordance with an international law that is genuinely, and not simply figuratively, an authoritative law — or at least most of us do, much of the time. As Mary Ellen O'Connell observes,

> International law has deficits, yet it persists as the single, generally accepted means to solve the world's problems. It is not religion or ideology that the world has in common, but international law. Through international law, diverse cultures can reach consensus about the moral norms that we will commonly live by. As a result, international law is uniquely suited to mitigate the problems of armed conflict, terrorism, human rights abuse, poverty, disease, and the destruction of the national environ-

MINISTERS OF THE LAW

ment. It is the closest thing we have to a neutral vehicle for taking on the world's most complex issues and pressing problems.[4]

As these remarks suggest, even though the peoples of the world do not constitute one unified polity, we can nonetheless speak of a world community in a more limited, yet realistic way. The peoples of the world do share enough by way of commitments and ideals as well as common concerns and ongoing mutual activities, to provide a context for a kind of political authority, even at this level. This context serves to legitimate international law, which, as O'Connell's remarks suggest, in turn provides a vehicle for further deliberation and persuasion.

At the same time, as O'Connell goes on to observe, "we accept the binding power of international law for the same reason we accept all law as binding. Our acceptance of law is part of a tradition of beliefs in higher things."[5] For O'Connell herself, these higher things include a moral law, generating *jus cogens* precepts that bind all nations and cannot be abrogated — much like the natural law as traditionally understood. I will argue below that even though the natural law does not yield a comprehensive, universally binding moral code, we can defend more limited, yet significant normative judgments at the international level through processes of rhetorical persuasion, drawing on natural principles in the way indicated in chapter three. These include both claims to basic natural rights, and some specific *jus cogens* norms — not enough, even jointly considered, to comprise a comprehensive, concrete moral code, but sufficient to set boundaries and criteria for legitimacy among peoples who share a common humanity but not a common culture.

Oliver O'Donovan has observed that in contrast to an ideal of world order sustained by imperial rule, the medieval legal (and I would add, theological) tradition "opened up an alternative, a world order defined not as a universal government, but as a unified law."[6] The authority of international law, on this view, does not presuppose the authority of a lawgiver, even on a theoretical or notional level. It reflects the authority of humanity as articulated and expressed through an ongoing history, reaching into (what we hope) is an open-ended future. Seen from the theological account of the natural law

4. Mary Ellen O'Connell, *The Power and Purpose of International Law* (New York: Oxford University Press, 2008), 14.

5. *Power and Purpose of International Law*, 16.

6. Oliver O'Donovan, *The Desire of the Nations: Rediscovering the Roots of Political Theology* (Cambridge: Cambridge University Press, 1996), 267.

that I have proposed, it ultimately reflects the authority of the supreme law-giver, whose eternal law is expressed in and through the free self-disposal of his creatures. This eternal law is the highest law, on which every other law depends — not through some special divine decree but through the media-tion of the rational creature's participation in the eternal law, through which men and women are themselves active agents of providence for themselves and others. As we will see in what follows, the diverse loci of legal authority — the nation-state, the individual, and humanity as a whole — all reflect some likeness to the eternal law, in virtue of which each elicits some measure of respect and reverence — and properly so. Natural piety is not necessarily faith, much less hope or charity, but it is a reasonable and praiseworthy re-sponse to what is good and admirable in human life.

1. The Nation-State and the Rule of Law

Purposes of National Authority

In the modern world, the ideals and practices associated with the rule of law are bound up, for better or for worse, with the modern nation-state. MacCormick goes so far as to say that "Law of the kind we are mainly con-sidering" — that is to say, everyday formal law, epitomized by the statutes regulating our day to day lives — "is a feature of a certain kind of state, and of transnational organizations established by such states to institutionalize a basis of supranational collaboration."[7] The institutional forms presupposed by any operative legal system are typically incorporated into the operative structures of the national government, and practically depend upon it for their continuing existence. This might seem to imply that within the mod-ern nation-state, the institutions of law are ultimately subservient to the po-litical interests of the nation, or whatever faction happens to be controlling the government at a given time. MacCormick, however, resists this conclu-sion, on practical as well as normative grounds:

> Mutual respect for the differences of roles in a constitutional regime of separated but mutually interactive powers is not only (in a trivial sense) essential to the security of such a regime; it is essential to a well-secured rule of law. The conceptual difference must be fully acknowledged be-

7. *Institutions of Law*, 170.

tween law as a normative order of right and wrong versus politics as a domain of statecraft guided by considerations of prudence. . . . Politics, however, depends upon the constitutional-cum-legal order, and politicians have to utilize the roles of executive and legislature within a constitutional separation of powers to achieve their ends legitimately. Their doing so is, in turn, essential to the ongoing viability of the state as a law-state operating under a functional constitution that remains fully in sympathy with the text of the formal constitution (wherever such a constitution exists) on some reasonable interpretation of it. Law and politics are conceptually distinct but reciprocally interactive in the dynamic processes of government and of law-application and interpretation.[8]

These remarks suggest that the modern nation-state, functioning in and through its governing institutions, represents yet another kind of political authority, which as such can only be justified in terms of the broad purposes served by political authority generally speaking, as these are expressed in specific kinds of circumstances. Of course, we have at this point moved to a further level of contingency and specificity — the modern nation-state represents only one out of many possible alternative political arrangements, ranging from small-scale, relatively cohesive communities, through various arrangements of tribal alliances, city-states, regional confederations, all the way to imperial systems with pretensions to world dominance. All these, except perhaps those that operate on a very small scale, sustain a rule of law, more or less formalized and independent of other systems within the wider society. The modern nation-state thus represents one contingent expression of the political authority of the community. But to return to a familiar point, contingency is one of the hallmarks of authority, and so the fact that we once might have chosen other kinds of regimes does not in itself call the legitimacy of the nation-state into question. Just as the particular forms and agencies bearing legal authority in a given community rest ultimately on the community's authoritative rules of recognition, so too do the forms of governance operative in the community. The question that we need to address at this point is not whether the modern nation-state is the necessary, or even the best possible governing system, but whether it is justifiable in the light of the natural purposes that it serves.

Most fundamentally, the modern nation-state, considered as a kind of political authority, serves to express and preserve the integrity of the com-

---

8. *Institutions of Law,* 184-85.

munity as a properly political community, given cohesion by a shared culture and way of life, within which men and women can pursue their affairs in peace and security and participate jointly in ongoing processes of mutual deliberation and rhetorical persuasion. This implies, among other things, that the nation-state serves to promote collective interests in such a way as to express and foster the ideals of justice and equity informing the community's ideals of the common good. What is more, since the political morality of the community and the regime's own legitimacy depend on respect for ideals of rule of law and proper legality, the nation-state will properly respect and foster these ideals, in this way also safeguarding the properly political character of the community.

In addition, the nation-state will play some role in preserving and fostering all the diverse activities that jointly comprise human life — family life, work and economic activities, artistic and intellectual pursuits, religious worship, and other fundamental aspects of human existence. By no means does the state itself generate or establish these practices and institutional forms; rather, they emerge out of the natural dynamisms of the community itself, as informed by the development of a culturally specific way of life. As such, these practices play an integral part in expressing the integrity and goodness of our natural existence as creatures of a certain kind, and in doing so, they set further constraints on the authority of the nation-state, or indeed of any kind of governing regime. Any attempt to do away with, for example, ongoing intellectual inquiry, or to place it completely under the control of the government, would represent a clearly unjust and normatively invalid exercise of governmental power. That being said, however, the fact remains that in any complex society, there will be a need, and a legitimate place, for some measure of regulation and coordination of these diverse practices, in such a way as to safeguard their integrity and to secure their harmonious functioning as elements of a comprehensive way of life. These regulatory activities will fall inevitably to the governing regime, and in carrying them out, the nation-state again may be said to serve natural purposes in a reasonable and praiseworthy way.

So far, we have identified the broad purposes that any system of governance must fulfill in order to be regarded as a legitimate conventional expression of natural purposes. It is no coincidence that these mirror the constraints on legal authority identified at the end of the last chapter, because the governmental institutions of any legitimate national authority will be structured and constrained in accordance with the rule of law, implying among other things respect for the normative boundaries on legal authority. In addition, the modern nation-state fulfills these broad purposes through a system of governance tethered to a defined territory, within which it exercises plenary and relatively final power — plenary, in the sense that it legitimately regulates every aspect of human life, and final, in that its governing agencies are not formally accountable to outside authorities except insofar as the national government voluntarily consents to such an arrangement. These, the hallmarks of modern national sovereignty, presuppose that national authority is tethered to control over a territory, for both positive and negative reasons. Control over an expanse of land guarantees stable access to the material means of life and also provides a defined space within which to defend one's community, and from which to mount (let us hope, only) defensive military operations. At the same time, because the modern state tethers its identity to a specific territory, it can maintain relative independence in a clearly defined way; it can claim freedom from interference within this specified territory, while by the same token it should forego interference in the internal affairs of other nations.

Most importantly, the nation-state provides the structures necessary to preserve the character of a community as a political community, within which men and women can deliberate together on matters of public concern as free individuals legitimately pursuing their own interests as well as the common good. In the words of Tony Judt, "the impetus to state-building as we have known it derived quite explicitly from the understanding that no collection of individuals can survive long without shared purposes and common institutions," and correlatively, at its best, the institutions and practices of the nation-state serve to "illustrate and promote our collective identity and common purposes."[9] This may seem like an unrealistic ideal. On the contrary, as he reminds us, it was attained, albeit imperfectly, in the social service state as it existed until recently in the United States and Great Britain, and as it continues to exist in much of the European continent today. If this ideal seems far removed from attainable reality in Anglophone societies today, that is at least partially due to a half century of efforts to undermine the legitimacy of political institutions and to substitute an ideal of individuals interacting with one another through the impartial mechanisms of post-industrial capitalism — mechanisms which have only the most ten-

9. Tony Judt, "What Is Living and What Is Dead in Social Democracy?" *The New York Review of Books* 61.20, December 17, 2009, 86-96; the first remark quoted occurs at page 92, the second at 96, and the third, again, at 92. He discusses privatization at some length, but the interpretation of this process in terms of relations of dominion and servitude is my own.

uous relation to actual processes of productive activity and consumption and, in themselves, no place for genuine rational deliberation. The inevitable result, as Judt shows, is the breakdown of any political community and the delegation of communal structures and provisions to private interests who direct human needs and activities to their own private aims — the late-twentieth-century version of dominion and servitude. If we are to regain our status as free citizens of a polity, we must, in Judt's terms, learn to "think the state" — and that will require us, first of all, to reclaim a sense of the nation-state as a legitimate kind of political authority, fully deserving of our support in view of the natural purposes that it promotes.

The Origins and Trajectory of National Authority

I noted above that the distinctive character of the modern nation-state rests ultimately on a contingent affirmation on the part of a cohesive community that this form of governance, and indeed this particular regime, legitimately expresses its sense of itself as a polity. We can in fact trace the modern nation-state system back to communal affirmations of this kind. Throughout the early medieval period, the peoples of Europe thought of themselves as comprising distinctive polities, sharing in a common way of life and aspiring to distinctive, praiseworthy ideals.[10] These aspirations were tethered to the monarchies of Europe, which continued in existence, albeit with little effective power, throughout this period. In the late eleventh century, these monarchies began once again to exercise real power, and that meant, practically, securing control of defined territories. Thus, as Hendrik Spruyt observes, the first sovereign, territorial state developed in the twelfth century under the Capetian monarchs.[11] Given the ideals and sensibilities of the time, this development offered much more than a practical arrangement for governing one's common life; it represented an effective self-assertion of the community's sense of itself as a people, unified under one ruler and enjoying

10. As Barbara Reynolds argues in some detail, national governments continued to exist and to function as forces for social cohesion throughout the medieval period; see *Fiefs and Vassals: The Medieval Evidence Reinterpreted* (Oxford: Oxford University Press, 1994), 34-46. As Bisson observes, this continuing sense of a political identity was one of the factors that made the reassertion of lordship and servile dominion in the eleventh and twelfth centuries so painful; see Thomas Bisson, *The Crisis of the Twelfth Century: Power, Lordship, and the Origins of European Government* (Princeton: Princeton University Press, 2009), 1-83.

11. *Sovereign State and Its Competitors*, 77-108.

the stable way of life tethered to a specific place. Above all, it offered an effective response to the forces which threatened a reversion to an older system of personal dominion and servitude. As Spruyt goes on to observe, the move to territorial monarchies involved a "qualitative shift" from "personal rule to public authority."[12]

Early in the modern period, experience and ideology combined to eliminate monarchial rule in many European nations, and drastically to curtail it in most others.[13] However, the principle of territoriality has persisted, so much so that it may be considered to be one of the hallmarks of the nation-state system itself. And with good reason. The territorial character of the modern nation-state goes a long way towards explaining why this kind of governance has proven to be so resilient, and why the nation-state system is likely to persist as the basic structuring framework for the human population for the foreseeable future. To a considerable extent, these considerations have to do with issues of scale. The nation-state began to emerge in the medieval period because only a large-scale political entity — large-scale, that is to say, relative to the scattered rural societies of the earlier medieval period — could sustain the institutional structures needed for dynamic, rapidly expanding urban societies. It persists in our own period because only a relatively small-scale entity — small-scale, relative to present-day forces of global interdependence — is compact enough to sustain political communities within which genuine deliberation can take place and the shared understandings presupposed by law can be sustained. It is difficult indeed to sustain a genuine political community on a large scale, and especially across national borders. Europe is just managing to do so, and Europe has centuries of shared history, overlapping cultural traditions, and a very long-standing ideal of a unified continent on which to draw.

At the same time, the territorial nation-state can only promote and safeguard the political character of a cohesive community so long as the peoples inhabiting its defined territory do constitute one, more or less unified community — or perhaps, a plurality of such communities, sharing enough in common to sustain an overarching framework for rhetorical deliberation and persuasion. Very often, this is not the case. Cohesive communities have been incorporated into nation-states against their will, or forced to cede control of their established territories through conquest and occupation, or found themselves living within national boundaries imposed from without, bound-

12. *Sovereign State and Its Competitors*, 81.

13. Again, see *Historical Introduction to Western Constitutional Law*, 108-93 for details.

aries that fit badly with the actual contours of communal life in a given region. These kinds of situations constitute an ongoing invitation to social unrest, insurgency, and violence, and it is telling that the worst examples of
state-sponsored tyranny tend to be associated with national governments
that have been imposed from without. Nonetheless, it is not so clear that
these injustices and incongruities can or should be addressed through a
whole-sale abandonment of the nation-state. It is telling that those who regard themselves as displaced or oppressed typically demand full incorpora-
tion into the nation-state system, not its repudiation. As Stanley Hoffman observes, the claim to national self-determination is a demand of justice, "for
there is no more certain injustice than alien rule imposed against the will of a
people. Self-determination is a precondition for peaceful co-existence. And if
one ever wants to go beyond the nation-state, recognizing the right of people
to their own nation is the first step; you cannot go beyond by avoiding it."[14]
Hoffman's observation suggests that for most of the peoples of the world, for
the foreseeable future, political processes and the rule of law — hence, the attainment of a genuine common good — will require a sustaining framework
of national authority, exercised within secure territorial boundaries.

What is more, the structures of international law presuppose a world of
nation-states, interacting with one another in accordance with well-
established mechanisms of negotiation, diplomacy, treaties, and mercantile
exchange — just as the enabling and constraining norms set up through
municipal law presuppose a context of free individuals, freely interacting
with one another.[15] Take away the nation-state system and almost the whole
fabric of international law — the laws of war, to take a most important example, the regulation of borders, allocation of shared resources, the maintenance of trade and monetary systems, and much more — would collapse.
Again, my point is not that this system is the best possible, or that it will last
forever. But until we can be confident that we have workable alternatives to
the nation-state system, we would be very foolish indeed to act as if it did
not exist, or to attempt to undercut it.

Of course, this system of interactions itself implies, and at many points
directly institutionalizes, all kinds of constraints and limitations on the sov-

14. Stanley Hoffmann, *Duties Beyond Borders: On the Limits and Possibilities of Ethical International Politics* (Syracuse: Syracuse University Press, 1981), 34.

15. O'Connell makes this clear; see *Power and Purpose of International Law*, 1-16. For an illuminating account of the ways in which processes of globalization and international interdepen-
dency work in and through the structures of national governments, see Anne-Marie Slaughter, *A
New World Order* (Princeton: Princeton University Press, 2004), 1-35.

ereign freedom of nations. It might even be said that this is one of the main purposes of international law, to transform the anarchic freedom of sovereign nations into an orderly system of agreed-upon constraints, within which cooperative actions of all kinds can take place. By no means are these constraints problematic in themselves or contrary to a proper political authority expressed through the governing institutions of sovereign nations. Just as some legal constraints on my freedom as an individual are both justified in themselves and advantageous to me, so some constraints on the freedoms of individual nations are both justified and advantageous to the nations themselves. I think there is a case to be made that the much-denigrated laws of war, and the conventions governing the treatment of civilians and prisoners of war, have placed checks on war and served to limit violence in wartime, although admittedly we can probably never be sure about this.[16] Similarly, international legal tribunals have so far had only limited success, and yet I think we have every reason to cooperate in genuinely international efforts to form and support such tribunals. These are controversial examples, but there are many others that would not be controversial — agreements pertaining to trade and the flow of money, laws of the seas, systems for facilitating the free movement of persons and information, and much else. All these constrain the sovereignty of nation-states without undermining the principle of national sovereignty itself.

It may be the case that we are witnessing the break-down of the nation-state system under the pressures of globalization — even though there is good reason to be skeptical about this sweeping claim. Nonetheless, even if this were so, it would be important to negotiate this transition in a lawful way — which means, practically, that so far as possible we must respect principles of national sovereignty and self-determination, even in the process of creating alternative institutional forms. Even when circumstances force us to violate these principles, it seems critical that we do so in law-like ways — which is to say, in cooperation with the wider international community, in pursuit of openly stated intentions, and with an aim to restoring conditions under which peoples can pursue ideals of justice within the context of a secure and self-determining polity. These constraints imply, among other things, that we should almost never attempt to intervene in crisis situations with military force, absent a clear *causus belli* on the part of the antagonists

16. For a good overview of the relevant issues, see Michael Howard, "Constraints on Warfare," *The Laws of War: Constraints on Warfare in the Western World*, ed. Michael Howard, George M. Andreopoulos, and Mark R. Shulman (New Haven: Yale University Press, 1994), 1-11.

themselves — in other words, humanitarian interventions or attempts to engage in a kind of international policing operation. Experience has shown that such efforts, even when they are seemingly well-justified and well-intentioned, almost always do more harm than good. What is more, military conflict presses the rule of law to its limit, even when conducted in accordance with accepted norms; extra-legal military actions are likely to strain the rule of law to the breaking point, thereby undermining whatever reasonable concord may exist among the nations.[17]

In chapter three, we observed that there is a strong tendency in Catholic social thought to emphasize the global character of the common good — a tendency that reflects the realities of our increased interdependence on a world scale and the imperative need to deal with the resultant challenges in a principled and humane way. Understood in this extended sense, the ideal of a global common good has a critical role to play, precisely as a regulative ideal. Yet the common good in its most proper sense is a political good, and that means that it will always be tethered to processes of rhetorical deliberation and persuasion which are by their nature grounded in the commitments and practices of some cohesive community. That is why the ideal of a universal common good would be problematic if we were to try to translate it directly into a set of institutional structures.

There is a pervasive temptation, appearing in characteristic forms on both the left and the right, to pursue the common good through means that set aside political processes, whether our own or those of other societies or the world community — as if we could implement a uniform ideal of freedom and human rights through just the right system of sanctions and tribunals, or establish democracy and free markets through a few surgical air strikes. Such programs strike me as not only futile and dangerous but fatally at odds with what the common good most fundamentally is. That is to say, no society can achieve any kind of genuine common good apart from local processes of deliberation and the implementation of just laws — in accordance with the practices and norms of the society in question, which may not always be our own. Not only is there no other effective and secure means

---

17. This is obviously a controversial point; however, I am persuaded by Mary Ellen O'Connell's arguments that so-called humanitarian interventions, conducted outside the strict guidelines set by existing international law, are neither appropriate nor effective. See "Responsibility to Peace: A Critique of R2P," forthcoming in *Critical Perspectives on the Responsibility to Protect: Interrogating Theory and Practice,* ed. Philip Cunliffe (New York: Routledge, 2010). For a powerful defense of the contrary view, see Geoffrey Robertson, *Crimes Against Humanity: The Struggle for Global Justice,* 2nd edition (New York: Penguin, 2002), 427-72.

towards social change; this process is also itself an intrinsic component of a common good, and by the same token, to short-cut it is precisely to undermine the common good. Even at the international level, we cannot set aside the legal forms and deliberative processes through which the common good properly so called can be pursued, or forget that even at this level, the common good will necessarily be a political good.

The Nation-State as an Agent of Violence

The modern nation-state exhibits a further, centrally important characteristic. It claims a monopoly on the use of violent force within its own territory. Significantly, this does not imply that the nation-state can legitimately use violence within its own boundaries for any purpose whatever. Rather, as MacCormick explains, "the use of physically coercive force is reserved under law to the state's own civil and (under tight restraint domestically) military agencies concerned with crime and its prevention, with the frontier security of the state, with public order, and with the safeguarding of public revenues."[18] As he goes on to note, this general norm is qualified to some extent; some polities allow limited use of coercive force in order to discipline the young, and all polities allow some right to the use of force in self-defense. Nonetheless, these are carefully delineated qualifications of a general norm, articulated by Aquinas as well as modern political theorists: violent force can legitimately be used only by political authorities, and only in lawful and equitable ways in defense of the common good.[19]

This norm is so well established in modern Western societies that we might assume that it is obvious. But that is not so. In many societies, collective as well as individual defense, social control, and family cohesion are maintained through violent coercion, in ways that are regarded as normal and proper. Some use of lethal force on the part of individuals outside the context of self-defense was allowed in the United States and some European nations well into the modern period — for example, dueling to settle questions of honor. The processes through which the nation-state gradually claimed an effective monopoly on the use of violent force reflected characteristic aims of the nation-state itself, both pragmatic and principled. On the

---

18. *Institutions of Law,* 209.

19. With respect to Aquinas, this is most clearly stated at II-II 64.3; for a summary of modern views on the state monopoly of force, see Morris, *An Essay on the Modern State,* 199-213.

pragmatic side, political authorities initially had to claim a monopoly on the use of force, in order to defend the population from those overlords who were attempting to reimpose servile dominion on their hapless subjects. In addition, and more generally, state control of the use of force was a strategy for minimizing violence and securing public peace — and there is in fact some reason to believe that the incidence of violence throughout Europe decreased as the effective power of national governments increased.[20]

Understood in this way, the state monopoly on violence serves the same ameliorative purpose as does the rule of law, namely, to secure general peace and restrain wrong-doers through the use of force. This is of course no coincidence, because in the world as we know it, the ameliorative purpose of the law cannot be secured through legal norms alone, even presuming that these are generally recognized and accepted. The laws must also be enforced against malefactors, and within the nation-state system, this implies that they are backed by the effective power of the state. Thus, those charged with enforcing the law — the executive branch of government and its agencies — are "ministers of the law," just as the judge and legislator are. And this brings us to the principle underlying the state monopoly on the use of violent force — namely, the principle that violent force can only legitimately be used under the direction of, and in accordance with, the rule of law. This is one of the constitutive principles expressing and safeguarding the political character of the modern nation-state, which commands an overwhelming preponderance of force in almost any conflict with non-state actors. In order to be reasonable and tolerable, any use of this force must be transparently gov-

20. With respect to the pragmatic necessity for state power in order to counteract the violence of overlords and castelians, see *Crisis of the Twelfth Century,* 471-572. As for the more general claim: almost a century ago, the sociologist Norbert Elias argued that the emergence of centralized authority in the later Middle Ages was one part of a far-reaching transformation in attitudes and mores, which had the overall effect of reducing private violence even as it led to the formation of warlike regimes. More recently, historians have begun to apply statistical analysis to court records and other similar documents from the medieval and modern periods, and the results of these theories seem generally to confirm Elias's thesis. More specifically, it appears that murder was much more common in Europe in the medieval period than now, and that murder rates dropped sharply beginning in the seventeenth century — about the same time as the modern nation-state system was becoming entrenched. Of course, this work is still controversial. Nonetheless, it suggests that empirical assessments of the effects of the nation-state system are difficult, and their results should be treated with caution. See Norbert Elias, *The Civilizing Process* [1939], revised edition, trans. Edmund Jephcott (Oxford: Blackwell, 1994), 365-447; the subsequent research and reassessments mentioned are described in "Did Knives and Forks Cut Murders?" *New York Times,* May 3, 2003, A21, 23.

erned by justifiable legal norms. By the same token, there is no more fundamental and tangible expression of disregard for another, no more immediately effective way to assert one's dominion over another, than to subject him
to violence at the aggressor's mere will, without some compelling justification. The harsh necessities of life render some use of violent force necessary
in every human community. But if these necessities are not to undermine
the political character of the community, the essential freedom of its individual members, and the respect due to them as members of the commonwealth, the use of violent force must be defensible through processes of rhetorical persuasion, tethered to basic natural purposes which can be very
generally shared. The norms generated through these processes must then
be scrupulously maintained. Within large-scale, complex modern societies
this further implies that they must be incorporated into formal law. As
O'Connell points out, this principle is also widely accepted in international
contexts, so much so that the general acceptance of coercive sanctions at this
level indicates that the rules thus enforced are regarded as genuinely legal
rules: "To allow coercive enforcement of anything short of a legal rule would
be to allow the use of force outside the confines of law. It is to prevent just
such unconstrained uses of force that law came to be instituted in human
communities."[21]

Yet as we noted in chapter two, even this delimited exercise of violent
force strikes many theological critics of the nation-state as deeply problematic, enough perhaps to call the legitimacy of the nation-state itself into
question. The past half century has seen a resurgence of Christian pacifism,
at least in Anglophone circles, leading to far-reaching pacifist critiques of
public authority and defenses of an alternative model of ecclesial solidarity
and witness.[22] At their best, these critiques reflect deep and serious elements
of the Christian tradition, including an abhorrence of violence and domin-

---

21. *Power and Purpose of International Law,* 10.

22. Noteworthy examples include Stanley Hauerwas, *A Community of Character: Toward a
Constructive Christian Social Ethic* (Notre Dame: University of Notre Dame Press, 1981); *The
Peaceable Kingdom: A Primer in Christian Ethics* (Notre Dame: University of Notre Dame Press,
1991); *Against the Nations: War and Survival in a Liberal Society* (Minneapolis: Seabury/Winston
Press, 1985); and *After Christendom? How the Church Is to Behave if Freedom, Justice, and a Chris-
tian Nation Are Bad Ideas* (Nashville: Abingdon, 1991); Richard Hays, *The Moral Vision of the New
Testament: A Contemporary Introduction to New Testament Ethics* (New York: HarperCollins,
1996), especially 239-65; John Milbank, *Theology and Social Theory: Beyond Secular Reason* (Oxford: Blackwell, 1990); and John Howard Yoder, *The Politics of Jesus,* 2nd edition (Grand Rapids:
Eerdmans, 1994).

ion in all its forms and a salutary suspicion of the moral pretensions of those in power. At the same time, a commitment to pacifism, especially when this extends to a rejection of any active participation in political life, once again raises questions about whether, and in what ways, the Christian is permitted or bound to acknowledge the fundamental goodness of political authority. Certainly, political authority as we experience it is inextricably bound up with the pervasive realities of human sinfulness. Yet ambiguity and even sinfulness are not tantamount to sheer evil; rather, they presuppose a more fundamental goodness, which we can identify, celebrate, and promote. Even if this conclusion were not analytically compelling — as I think it is — we would be led to it by the doctrine of creation, which rules out any kind of Gnostic dualism between Christian ideals and the irredeemably corrupt realities of the world as we experience it. A stance involving thoroughgoing rejection of political authority and governmental structures as fundamentally corrupt, even if these are tolerated as necessary evils, implies that some constitutive elements of human life are not just corrupted by sin, but beyond the scope of redemption. And we as Christians cannot allow ourselves to say that.

An Ambiguous Defense: Christian Realism and National Power

This brings us to Reinhold Niebuhr, who offers what is still perhaps the most influential defense of the nation-state from a theological perspective.[23] Niebuhr was arguably the greatest, and among the last of those theologians who played an important role in United States public life in the early decades of the twentieth century. His theological reflection was tethered to the defining struggles of that unsettled time, including the end of the Great Depression, World War II and its aftermath, and the beginnings of the Cold War. Throughout his career, Niebuhr was engaged with the ambiguity and sinfulness that are inextricably tied up with the world as it now is, harsh realities that he was already disposed to take seriously on theological grounds. Yet he refused to withdraw from political engagement and social activism, and remained active in the processes of deliberation and rhetorical persua-

23. For a valuable overview of Niebuhr's political theology, see the introduction by D. B. Robertson, in Reinhold Niebuhr, *Love and Justice: Selections from the Shorter Writings of Reinhold Niebuhr,* ed. D. B. Robertson (Louisville: Westminster/John Knox Press, 1957), 9-21. In what follows, I rely especially on Reinhold Niebuhr, *Nature and Destiny of Man, Volume 2: Human Destiny* (New York: Scribners, 1943, 1964), 244-86.

sion, within and across the boundaries of the churches. Out of this engagement, he developed what may well be the most powerful, nuanced, and theologically well-grounded defense of the modern nation-state that we have. It
is by no means an enthusiastic defense, since on Niebuhr's view the nation-
state represents a standing temptation to collective pride and the arrogant
transformation of one's own interests and ideals into universal norms.
Nonetheless, given our circumstances, and especially in the light of our collective responsibilities to defend the weak and to secure as much justice as
we can, we are obliged to participate in political life, implicating ourselves in
its ambiguities while bearing witness to the dangers of its pretensions.

Yet from the standpoint of a natural law analysis, Niebuhr's defense of
the nation-state is in one key respect more troubling than the pacifist critiques that he sets out to address. Niebuhr goes well beyond the claim that the
nation-state properly makes use of coercive violence as an ameliorative response to the effects of sinfulness. For him, the nation-state is itself fundamentally a manifestation of human sinfulness, an expression of a collective
egoism and the will to power. What is more, the scope of this critique is not
limited to the modern nation-state. For Niebuhr, any community will similarly reflect the collective egoism of its members, acting ruthlessly in pursuit
of its own interests. Individuals can sometimes rise to the level of pure altruism and self-sacrificing love, but it is impossible for a collective body to attain
this level of self-awareness and purity of aim. Nor is the collective selfishness
of the community balanced by any kind of positive values or ideals, since
even the highest standards of justice fall radically short of the evangelical
ideal of self-sacrificing love, exemplified by Jesus' sacrifice on the cross. There
is no space here for the acknowledgment of genuine political virtues, much
less any hope that these virtues, and the civic friendship they sustain, might
be transformed through charity into positive elements of a Christian life.

On the contrary, Niebuhr insists that the seeming altruism and self-
sacrifice associated with the civic virtues serves, paradoxically, to reinforce
the unqualified self-seeking of the nation:

> There is an ethical paradox in patriotism which defies every but the most
> astute and sophisticated analysis. The paradox is that patriotism trans-
> mutes individual unselfishness into national egoism. Loyalty to the nation
> is a high form of altruism when compared with lesser loyalties and more
> parochial interests. It therefore becomes the vehicle of all the altruistic
> impulses and expresses itself, on occasion, with such fervor that the criti-
> cal attitude of the individual towards the nation and its enterprises is al-

most completely destroyed. The unqualified character of this devotion is the very basis of the nation's power and of the freedom to use the power without moral restraint. Thus the unselfishness of individuals makes for the selfishness of nations.[24]

Very often, the seeming altruism of the patriot is nothing more than individual egoism and self-seeking, projected onto the community and thus disguised, even from the agent herself: "Unquestionably there is an alloy of projected self-interest in patriotic altruism. The man in the street, with his lust for power and prestige thwarted by his own limitations and the necessities of social life, projects his *ego* upon his nation and indulges his anarchic lusts vicariously. So the nation is at one and the same time a check upon, and a final vent for, the expression of individual egoism."[25]

Niebuhr has undoubtedly identified a serious and perennial danger in devotion to one's nation. Nonetheless, we may still ask whether these dangers represent potential corruptions of positive elements of human life or reflections of an arrangement that is, from the outset, radically corrupt. Niebuhr would apparently take the latter view. Certainly, the faithful Christian can and should make use of the contrivances of political society, including even the use of force, in order to secure some rough approximation of justice and to better the lives of his fellows. Christian charity demands no less. But this represents, at best, a strategy of accommodation to harsh necessities, inspired by a Christian realism about the constraints imposed by the effects of sinfulness.

Niebuhr's Christian realism and the conception of the natural law worked out by the early scholastics and further developed in this project resemble each other, to an extent that would probably have surprised Niebuhr himself. Both approaches take sin and its social effects to be deep and pervasive realities of human life, and correlatively, both give a central place to the ambiguities and limitations of human social life as we now experience it.[26] Both draw on paradigmatic ideals of a pre-lapsarian or redeemed existence in order to relativize the pretensions of those in power.

Nonetheless, these points of contact, important though they are, should not obscure the central differences between the two approaches. Niebuhr's radical critique of any kind of collectivity, his insistence that every human

24. Reinhold Niebuhr, *Moral Man and Immoral Society* (New York: Scribner's, 1932), 91.
25. *Moral Man and Immoral Society*, 93.
26. With respect to the scholastics, I develop the interpretation that follows in *Natural and Divine Law: Reclaiming the Tradition for Christian Ethics* (Grand Rapids: Eerdmans, 1999), 247-93.

inclination falls infinitely short of the radical ideal of Gospel love, leaves very little space to affirm the goodness of God's primal creation. God's creative activities and self-disclosure through revelation are read through the lens of the Gospel, and a narrow and restrictive construal of the Gospel, at that. More fundamentally, by denying that collective life and its political expressions can have any positive value, Niebuhr is in effect denying that the natural and proper forms of human existence are good in themselves. In all fairness, he did not consider, and may well have objected to, arguments to the effect that collective life in accordance with rational norms is one integral component of natural human life. But to the extent that we ourselves are persuaded by this line of argument, it would seem to follow that Niebuhr's radical pessimism could only lead to a rejection of the natural goodness of human existence itself. In this way, his Christian realism raises the same theological worries provoked by Christian pacifism.

There is a still more important difference between Christian realism and the conception of the natural law developed here, stemming from a fundamental disagreement over the character of self-love. We noted above that for Niebuhr, genuine Christian love is wholly self-sacrificing, following the paradigm of Jesus' self-sacrifice on the cross, and every form of self-love is therefore a deviation from a Christian ideal. There is no space here for a distinction between sinful and proper forms of self-love. Rather, for Niebuhr there can be only one real distinction in this regard, between true, self-sacrificial love and its similitudes.

Self-Love, Political Virtues, and the Love of One's Homeland

In contrast, the account of the natural law developed here presupposes that self-love can be legitimate, perhaps even praiseworthy, thus locating the relevant line between legitimate and illegitimate, well-ordered and perverse forms of self-love. Indeed, as we saw in chapter two, a natural and proper self-love plays an integral role in the development of the natural law at every level. Experienced through the rational creature's first inchoate inclinations towards the natural objects of the will, it sets in motion the dynamic of activity and reflection through which the maturing child comes to reflect on the overall course and aim of her life, and to shape her activities accordingly. Experienced through a mature sense of one's own interests, it provides a point of contact between the agent's own freely chosen aims and the considerations that are brought to bear in the political processes of rhetorical deliberation and persuasion. Extended through a natural empathetic identification with others, it enables the individual to discern, feel, and be genuinely motivated by the needs and interests of others. Further expanded by a rational grasp of comprehensive goods, it opens out beyond itself to a rationally informed love of the commonwealth and of the divine reality beyond the commonwealth.

Most importantly, the agent's self-love represents the point at which the fundamental orientation of the will, and God's creative and providential will with respect to this creature, come together in such a way as to tether the rational creature to the rule of God's eternal law. Aquinas brings this out very clearly through his analysis of self-love as the desire for one's perfection, experienced by rational creatures as a desire for happiness. The critical point here is that for Aquinas, happiness *is* precisely the attainment of perfection, in accordance with the ideal existence willed by God in creating an entity of this kind. Through desiring its own perfection, the creature desires what God wills for it — at this level, there can be no opposition, or indeed any distinction between human and divine will. In this way, the human creature is brought under the rule of God's providential eternal law — as is every other creature. Of course, self-love can become corrupted, oriented towards partial or false construals of one's final end — and to the extent that this is the case, the creature's desire for happiness is perverted and incongruous with God's creative will for her. But even in such cases, the primal desire for happiness, considered formally as the necessary tendency to pursue full and complete existence through one's natural activities, represents the point of contact between human and divine will, even in the sinner. By the same token, the self-love of the rational creature tethers the considerations informing the individual's practical deliberations to the rationality informing God's providence in such a way as to set the needed context within which God can enter into a rhetoric of persuasion, grounded in reasons that are in the deepest sense the creature's own. In virtue of this connection, every individual may be said to participate, more or less adequately, in the political rule established by God's creative and providential eternal law.

At the same time, the dynamics of self-love in the maturing individual naturally lead him outwards, towards other people and towards the political community that sustains their common way of life. Or so we hope, because this is of course one critical point at which self-love can become perverted, self-seeking, callous, or cruel. Yet we can only recognize these perversions for what they are because we have some grasp of the proper forms of the relevant relationships. We do know, more or less, what it would mean to relate to others on a basis of mutual care and respect, and we know what it would mean to devote ourselves to a wider community and to work for the distinctive values that it embodies. We can grasp these possibilities, and sometimes even act on them, because these too are natural to our existence as rational, social animals — creatures whose distinctively rational mode of operation is inextricably bound up at every stage with others, interacting together in a shared culture and political community. Through natural processes of mutual identification with others, and grateful acknowledgment of the particular way of life that has formed us, we expand our proper self-love into a love of our fellows and our community. Once again, we recall that reason in its proper operations is receptive to the intelligible principles and values of the world with which it engages — in this instance, the social world which quite literally makes us into the men and women we are.

By the same token, the receptivity of reason vis-à-vis one's relationships, and the community that sustains them, is properly balanced by a spontaneity, through which the individual arrives at a relatively independent and general grasp of the values and ideals that are constitutive of his formative culture. I have emphasized the point that a legitimate self-love will properly affirm the value of the local and particular because this is just the point that tends to be overlooked, whether through a high-minded universalism or a devotion to the cosmopolitan ideal of a citizen of the world. We cannot meaningfully comprehend universals, except in and through some grasp of particulars seen as instantiating formal principles; this is a general principle of intellectual inquiry of any kind. And yet, we can and do move from particular to more general expressions of universal principles, and to the extent that we do so, we can spontaneously envision new expressions, new formulations, even genuine alternatives to whatever our starting points may have been. In the realm of practical deliberation, the spontaneity of reason enables us to identify with those others who do not share in our community and way of life. It enables us to grasp and value the ideals that are constitutive of our shared culture in general terms that are relatively detached from the specific embodiments that we know — to love and pursue them as such, even over against or outside the boundaries of the actual polity we may inhabit. We can even move beyond the constitutive ideals of our community through a spontaneous reconstrual of what it means to pursue a properly human good with consistency and integrity.

We are potentially citizens of the world, but only insofar as we are actually citizens of this or that particular polity. Our community of origin shapes us in ways that remain inescapably a part of our identity, even if we are led to repudiate or transcend our origins — as, in one way or another, all of us are. This is the context within which to assess Niebuhr's charge that patriotism is a disguised form of self-love. There is a sense in which he is right; at least he is right that love of one's country represents a kind of expanded love of self. But this need not be disguised or perverted. On the contrary, a rightly ordered love of self will take the individual beyond the confines of her individual existence, towards a knowing and free embrace of a good that is greater than herself, naturally considered, in which she recognizes and affirms the formative ideals that are integral to her individual identity. As Aquinas remarks, "the good of the republic is the chief among human goods," adding that this, like all other human goods, can itself become divine by being referred to God (ST II-II 125.3 *ad* 3).

As we have already observed, on this view there can be no conflict between the good of the individual, comprehensively considered, and the common good rightly understood. This represents a foundational interpretative principle in terms of which both individual and common good are to be construed. There are of course real and important conflicts between individual and social interests, and it is by no means the case that these should always be resolved on the side of the community. On the contrary, as Aquinas reminds us, the attainment of the common good presupposes that conflicts between individual and community must not be resolved in such a way as to violate the just claims of the individual (ST I-II 96.4; II-II 64.6, 68.3). This way of formulating the ideal of the common good presupposes that individuals do have private interests and legitimate claims that are distinct from, and potentially at odds with, collective interests. Although Aquinas does not say so, this further implies that the individual enjoys subjective rights which carry normative force even over against exigent communal needs and claims. The subjective rights of the individual do not stand over against the common good, but that is partially because respect for these rights is a constitutive element of the common good, properly understood. We will return to these points in the following section.

At any rate, I want here to make a different point. That is, precisely because the individual's self-love is properly oriented outwards, towards a reflective embrace of a community and a way of life, he has a stake in promoting ideals of equity and the rule of law in order to safeguard the ideals and commitments that his community, at its best, embodies. Seen from this perspective, the observance of just laws, even at the cost of one's own individual advantage or security, is itself a great good for the individual. Through participating in the just laws of his community, the individual enjoys the greatest connatural goods possible to him as a rational creature. He acts in accordance with his own proper principles of action, namely, reason and the capacity for self-determination, in this way existing and acting as the image of God that he most fundamentally is. What is more, he acts as the social animal that he is by participating in a network of communal relations, within which he enjoys a secure and respected place. Finally, he identifies with and contributes to communal values which will transcend and survive him as an individual, thus respecting his nature as a reflective rational creature who wants to live and knows he must die.

Once again, we are reminded that the rule of law as enacted through just positive laws is not merely an instrumental good. On the contrary, a dynamic structure of reasonable and equitable interactions, embodied in the particular institutions and practices of a given society, is itself intrinsically good, as I argued in the last chapter. Seen from this perspective, the rule of law can itself credibly be described as a common good, insofar as it can only be attained in and through participation in the life of a well-ordered community. I emphasize this point in part because we are today faced with so many powerful temptations to disregard the rule of law or norms of justice in pursuit of other social aims, security and wealth in particular. And certainly, these are important social goods, but it is a mistake to think that they could be weighed over against the fundamental principles governing a society. It is not the case that we can trade a little justice here for a bit more security there, and then go on with our lives as if nothing had changed. The principles on which we act in pursuit of discrete social goods will themselves set the conditions under which those goods are enjoyed — and by the same token, by embracing unjust means to attain good social ends, we constitute ourselves into an unjust society, one in which, for example, we ourselves might be detained without trial or tortured in the name of security or some other social interest. This kind of liability constitutes a kind of insecurity in itself, and what is more, it transforms our identities as members of our society from free subjects to the servile objects of others' aims and plans. Even worse, to the extent that a society is unjust, it forecloses the possibility of enjoying those individual goods that can only be attained in and through participation in communal structures of justice, including the opportunity to act as a free and rational agent in concert with others and shared participation in communal ideals and values. Probably no community could ever be so thoroughly corrupted as to foreclose all such possibilities for its members;

but to the extent that the enactments of a given society are unjust, it inflicts a grave wrong on all its members, and not only those who are victimized by the injustice in question.

The Nation-State as a Minister of the Law

This brings us back to the point with which we began this section. The modern nation-state is a law-state, which as such derives its legitimate authority from the broader natural purposes of political authority to which it gives institutional expression. Correlatively, the sovereignty of the modern nation-state, like every other form of genuine authority, is bounded and constrained by the same rational considerations that justify it — among other things, fidelity to the rule of law and to ideals of proper legality, both in relation to its own citizens and in its foreign affairs. This implies, at the very least, observance of its own laws domestically and respect for the formal structures and settled norms of international law — implies, in other words, respect for the inner morality of the law, at home and abroad.

Are these the only boundaries that the modern nation-state is obliged to respect in order to preserve its legitimacy as an authoritative minister of the law? It seems not — as MacCormick observes,

> Fidelity to the rule of law is one condition for the protection of liberty against unwarranted incursions by agencies of government. Insistence on the character of a *Rechtsstaat* or law-state is one way of stipulating that the force of the state must always and only be deployed under general rules that can be interpreted quite strictly and in universalistic ways that preclude unjust discriminations. But this does not itself seem enough. General rules can confer extremely wide discretion on particular officials — a case in point is the law under which Hitler was granted the power to rule by decree in Germany after 1934.[27]

He goes on to say that there have subsequently been many other examples of "abusive grants of broad discretionary powers" on governmental authorities in Europe and beyond, although few have been so "egregious as that of the Nazi terror." What is more, even when formal limits are in place, they can be ignored or circumvented, as we have all too frequently seen over the past several years.

27. *Institutions of Law,* 190.

This leads him to the topic of fundamental rights:

Taken by itself, the rule of law, albeit essential, seems likely to be in some contexts insufficient to protect against evil doing by agencies of the state. It is a real virtue but, taken on its own, a formal one. Perhaps we need also some substantive limits as well as purely formal limits to state power. Recognition of fundamental rights is one candidate for providing such limits. It is one which has gained great contemporary prestige as a result of the various international instruments and national constitutional safeguards adopted in the aftermath of the World War of 1939 to 1945, and devised in response to the horrors revealed by that period of human history.[28]

MacCormick is certainly correct that appeals to fundamental, or natural, or human rights provide some of the most important ways in which men and women attempt to limit the power of the nation-state and other agents, both in domestic and international contexts. At the same time, his remarks bring us back to considerations of natural law, in a way that he himself probably would not have anticipated. Not only does the very language of rights imply some tethering in what is fundamental, natural, properly human. As we saw in chapter one, the development of a political theology of natural law was initially motivated by competing rights claims — to one's *jura* — which were evaluated in terms of some reconstruction of natural right, *jus naturale*. What is more, this line of thought was very often developed in such a way as to constrain the supposed rights of owners and overlords and to defend the rights of the relatively powerless individual in delimited, yet critically important ways. This point of contact opens up a fruitful way of thinking about the complex, critically important subject of rights — or so I will attempt to show in the next section.

2. Natural Rights and the Authority of the Individual

Rights as Constraints on National Power

MacCormick is scarcely the only legal or political philosopher to draw a connection between fundamental rights and the authority and power of the modern nation-state. According to Dworkin, human rights give rise to

28. *Institutions of Law*, 190-91.

claims which override any other kind of consideration, even the most strongly felt social sentiments or the most exigent common necessities. As he famously says, rights are trumps, and as such can only be overridden by competing rights claims.[29] Respect for human rights, thus understood, is central to political morality, and as such it serves as a regulative principle for legal interpretation, the implication for Dworkin being that any course of action that involved a violation of a basic right would be *ipso facto* both unlawful and illegitimate. Very few political theorists are prepared to go quite that far, but they would nonetheless generally agree that national legitimacy and respect for human rights are properly linked. Thus, for example, Rawls identifies respect for rights as one of the boundary conditions for any acceptable conception of justice as a social virtue. What is more, in his later work he identifies respect for human rights as one of the essential conditions for recognizing any community as a "decent society," entitled to full respect as a member of the community of nations.[30] At the same time, in order to be effective, rights claims require appropriate institutional forms, within which they can be asserted, judged, and where necessary enforced. As MacCormick observes with respect to the rule of law generally, this implies that rights claims generally rely on nation-states for their effectiveness — a line of thought which leads Jack Donnelly to argue that the conception of human rights enshrined in international law presupposes that nation-states are the proper respondents to rights claims.[31]

Thus understood, rights claims constitute a remarkable constraint on the proper authority of the nation-state, or indeed on any kind of political authority. Even those of us who are not utilitarians may hesitate to sacrifice the interests of many to the rights of the individual, particularly when the sacrifices in question include such vital goods as security or life itself. When the conflict at stake involves the survival of the commonwealth as a political community, it becomes very hard indeed to claim that even in this context, individual rights claims should be overriding — or at least, that is the argument advanced by those who claim that individual rights must give way in instances of "supreme emergency," when the very survival of the nation as a cohesive political community is at stake. There is also some danger that

29. For an important early development of this claim, see Ronald Dworkin, *Taking Rights Seriously* (Cambridge, MA: Harvard, 1977, 1978), 85-203.

30. For a helpful summary of this trajectory, see John Rawls, "The Law of Peoples," in *On Human Rights*, ed. Stephen Shute and Susan Hurley (New York: Basic Books, 1993), 41-82.

31. See Jack Donnelly, *Universal Human Rights in Theory and Practice*, 2nd edition (Ithaca: Cornell, 2003), 22-37.

those who defend a strong doctrine of rights might inadvertently subvert the give and take, the needed balancing of competing claims, that play essential parts in any political processes. Or worse still, they might subvert their own claims by rendering them unworkable. This worry leads Michael Ignatieff, among others, to insist that rights claims can only be lodged and defended through political processes of negotiation, characterized by pragmatic compromises on all sides.[32]

This line of approach does take rights claims seriously, but only as one kind of politically salient consideration among others, and this is hardly the kind of claim that could serve generally as a constraint on national power, as MacCormick and others propose. What is more, it would seem that the very point of rights claims is to safeguard the freedom or the vital interests of the individual over against what would otherwise be overriding considerations. We may still want to acknowledge that rights claims are properly qualified and limited by other considerations, but unless we are prepared to call for real and serious sacrifices on the part of the many in order to respect the rights of the individual, it is difficult to say that we are really committed to human rights in any meaningful way.

Fundamental Rights as Divine Decrees

If we are to defend the view that rights claims carry the overriding authority that MacCormick and others give them, it would seem that we must draw on exceptionally strong normative considerations to ground or justify these claims. Philosophers have notoriously found it difficult to come up with persuasive arguments along these lines, leading to the suggestion that the recognition of rights is a free-standing moral intuition, or perhaps an expression of a communal commitment to a way of life which is the product, as much as the justification, for the practice of rights claims.[33] Yet there is something plainly unsatisfactory about placing so much weight on individual intuitions or even — in this context — a communal rule of recognition. It is hardly surprising, therefore, that a growing number of theologically minded jurists and philosophers have argued that rights claims can

32. He develops this claim at some length in Michael Ignatieff, *Human Rights* (Princeton: Princeton University Press, 2001), 3-52.

33. For an example of the former approach, see Martha Nussbaum, *Women and Human Development: The Capabilities Approach* (Cambridge: Cambridge University Press, 2000), 83; for the latter, see *Universal Human Rights in Theory and Practice*, 7-21.

only carry the weight they do if they are in some way grounded in a divine decree, bestowing supreme dignity or value on the individual and, so to speak, throwing the weight of divine authority behind individual rights claims.

Nicholas Wolterstorff offers an especially clear and forceful account of the logic of this argument in his *Justice: Rights and Wrongs,* in which he lays out the case that human rights are grounded in respect for human worth.[34] In doing so, he begins with Dworkin's claim that rights are trumps, that is to say, overriding normative claims, and goes on to ask what is presupposed by this feature of rights claims. He argues that we can only account for this feature by introducing the concept of wronging another, thereby altering his or her moral status as a victim of a wrong. "To our failure to render people certain life-goods comes attached the all-important significance of thereby wronging them; to other examples of such failure, that significance does not come attached. That significance, wronging, is the source of rights."[35] This looks very much as if the language of rights serves as an alternative way of expressing Kant's claim that we should always treat human beings as ends in themselves, and indeed that is what Wolterstorff goes on to say: "Kant's famous principle . . . comes to the same as the principle I have been defending: always act in such a way as to allow respect for the worth of human beings to trump balance of life-good considerations."[36]

Yet as Wolterstorff goes on to argue, neither Kant himself nor any other secular philosopher has offered a compelling argument in defense of the principle he articulates. Only a theistic grounding of a specific kind will suffice: "What we need, for a theistic grounding of natural human rights, is some worth-imparting relation of human beings to God that does not in any way involve a reference to human capacities. I will argue that being loved by God is such a relation; being loved by God gives a human being great worth."[37] He goes on to say that this is an example of bestowed worth, generated by God's love of attachment for each individual human being. This love does not of course presuppose that an individual is in some way an instrument of God's purposes, nor is it conferred in response to anything in the creature that would render it antecedently attractive to God. Rather, God bestows worth on the individual man or woman through the free decision that

---

34. The central argument is laid out in Nicholas Wolterstorff, *Justice: Rights and Wrongs* (Princeton: Princeton University Press, 2008), 342-61.

35. *Justice: Rights and Wrongs,* 293.

36. *Justice: Rights and Wrongs,* 310.

37. *Justice: Rights and Wrongs,* 352.

this person is an object of divine attachment, a decree that thus places the individual in the supremely desirable relation of being God's beloved. And since God loves every human being in just this way, every individual is worthy of respect as an end in him or herself — or to put it another way, each individual enjoys basic human rights, correlative to an immunity from being wronged.

It would seem that we have now said all that is necessary to defend the claim that fundamental rights properly constrain the authority of the nation-state. After all, what considerations could possibly outweigh a divine decree, bestowing worth or value or a claim to respect? Nonetheless, human or natural rights as Wolterstorff understands them cannot account for the authoritative character of these claims vis-à-vis communal interests or national power. It is easy to be misled at this point by the metaphor of relative weight, as if the relative force of political and individual authority could somehow be determined by having God, as it were, place his thumb on the scale. But on closer examination, it becomes apparent that the issue at stake has to do with the specific substantive force of rights claims. In order to serve as a proper constraint on political authority, rights claims must themselves be authoritative claims of such a kind as to exercise juridical force. Otherwise, as Dworkin for one recognizes, they would not constitute a proper constraint on the lawful exercise of state power.[38] Wolterstorff's theistic defense of rights claims cannot account for their distinctively authoritative and juridical character, and it is at this point that the scholastics, the jurists in particular, can make a distinctive contribution.

In order to appreciate the significance of the jurists' approach, we need to begin with a distinction between objective and subjective rights which Tierney identifies as the decisive innovation in early medieval thinking about natural rights.[39] According to the more comprehensive construal of rights claims, sometimes described as objective rights, the language of natural or human rights offers one way of expressing normative claims that we could just as well express in other terms. This is sometimes described as a doctrine of objective natural rights. On this view, natural rights should be seen as expressions of the claims and duties which pertain to each of us as participants in an objective moral order. Someone may be said to enjoy a

---

38. See *Taking Rights Seriously* (Cambridge, MA: Harvard University Press, 1978), 184-205.

39. Brian Tierney, *The Idea of Natural Rights: Studies on Natural Rights, Natural Law and Church Law, 1150-1652* (Atlanta: Scholars Press, 1997). This distinction is explained at 20-22 and Tierney argues that it emerges in the scholastic period at 69-77.

right, therefore, because another person has a duty which affects her (although it may not be a duty towards her specifically); thus, for example, my right to life would be grounded in the duty which everyone else has not to kill people, including me. On this view, rights talk offers a particularly emphatic way of expressing our sense of our obligations to others, but it does not add anything in the way of justifying those obligations or modifying their content.

However, when present-day legal theorists refer to natural or human rights, they often mean something more than this.[40] On such a view, a human right properly so called attaches to a person as, so to speak, one of the individual's moral properties. In the terms of contemporary legal theory, it is a subjective, rather than an objective right. Furthermore, the duties correlative to such a right arise *in virtue of* the right, although these may well exist alongside other, more general or objective claims and duties. Thus, someone's subjective right to life, let us say, is grounded in her authoritative claim (perhaps, only tacitly expressed, and suitably qualified) for immunity from violence, and the correlative duty not to kill her is grounded specifically in that claim — thus raising the possibility that she could cede it, perhaps in a request for euthanasia, in a way that she could not release someone from a more general duty not to kill another person. Finally, while natural rights so understood do not depend for their justification or force on prior agreements or particular social arrangements, their effective exercise may require the existence of specific institutions, such as law courts. Thus, rights claims, once formulated and generally accepted, may well provide a compelling justification for the creation of legal forms within which they can be vindicated. In this sense, these claims may be said to generate law, or at least to provide a warrant, perhaps even an exigent demand, for the creation of legal and institutional forms within which they can be recognized and enforced. The concept of subjective natural rights is thus a jurisprudential, as well as a moral concept.

40. The idea of human or natural rights has been very widely discussed among lawyers and philosophers of law over the past several decades, and at this point any summary of prevalent views will necessarily be highly selective. Nonetheless, I hope that I have captured at least the main lines of a widely shared account of what it is that we are talking about when we talk about human rights. Neil MacCormick offers a good summary and analysis of recent work on the concept of rights in jurisprudence in *Institutions of Law* (Oxford: Oxford University Press, 2007), 187-207; in addition, see Kieran Cronin, *Rights and Christian Ethics* (Cambridge: Cambridge University Press, 1992), 1-56 for a thorough and illuminating review and analysis of recent theoretical work on the subject.

Wolterstorff endorses the view that the language of rights offers one powerful way of expressing normative claims that could also be formulated without loss of meaning in other terms. This approach is very common, especially but not only among those who offer theistic defenses of natural or human rights. Thus, Michael Perry remarks that "properly understood, rights talk is a derivative and even dispensable feature of modern moral discourse. . . . What really matters — what we should take seriously — is not human rights talk but the claims such talk is meant to express: the claims about what ought not to be done to or about what ought to be done for human beings. We can take rights seriously (so to speak) without taking rights talk too seriously."[41] As for Wolterstorff, we have already seen that he explicitly identifies his own normative analysis of rights with Kant's principle that human beings are to be treated as ends in themselves, never as means.

Thus understood, the concept of rights itself adds nothing of substance to the normative demands that we place on ourselves and others. Again, Wolterstorff makes this point clearly:

> Determining whether or not one person has treated another with disrespect (under-respect) usually requires taking a number of factors into consideration. A passage in Allen Wood's discussion of Kant's ethics makes the point well. "Proper expression of respect," he says, "is a contextual matter; it is not evident that it could be reduced to any set of rules or generalizations that could serve as premises in a deductive argument. It might instead be something that has to be apprehended in each set of particular circumstances, perhaps by a sort of educated moral perception."[42]

We are by now familiar with this general picture of normative judgment, which implies some assessment of diverse considerations in the light of one's overarching aims. Wood and Wolterstorff are surely right that in order to be adequate, any such judgment will necessarily be guided through a discerning sense of the ways in which these diverse considerations come together in the context of a specific situation. These are just the kinds of judgment calls that each of us makes in a wide range of practical contexts, each day of our mature, functioning lives, and they are also the kinds of judgments that are taken every day in our communities through processes of

---

41. Michael Perry, *The Idea of Human Rights: Four Inquiries* (Oxford: Oxford University Press, 1998, 2000), 56.

42. *Justice: Rights and Wrongs,* 300.

political deliberation. Understood in this way, a rights claim would express a deliberative conclusion to the effect that a given course of action would amount to wronging another, given a set of salient considerations. The diverse considerations that support this claim carry the actual weight of the argument, which is then expressed through the language of rights, to the effect that a given course of activity would wrong someone, and so this individual has a right to the contrary act or forbearance. There is no place here for rights claims considered as one distinctive kind of consideration, that should be factored in prior to an overall assessment of what would be objectively right or wrong in a given case.

This is a widely attractive way of construing rights claims, and we can readily appreciate why this should be so. After all, if rights talk represents a particularly effective way of signaling the force and urgency of any kind of moral claim, which need not be too closely examined on its own terms, this makes it all the easier to arrive at a practical agreement on at least some rights claims, even in a context of deep disagreements over fundamental moral beliefs. Apparently, this is just the way in which agreement on a range of fundamental rights has been secured within the international community, and this is without doubt a most important achievement in itself. Nor do we have any stake on logical or conceptual grounds for ruling this construal of rights language out of court. At this point in its long and complicated history, the language of rights offers a capacious and flexible moral vocabulary. For that very reason, it can conceal deep disagreements, but that can be an advantage in itself, particularly in situations of long-standing conflict.

But is this all that we can or should say by way of accounting for the conception of fundamental rights? The difficulty with interpreting rights solely as objective claims is that it renders the language of rights, as such, nugatory. As the historian Richard Tuck points out,

> If any right can be completely expressed as a more or less complete set of duties on other people towards the possessor of the right, and those duties can in turn be explained in terms of some higher-order moral principle, then the point of a separate language of rights seems to have been lost, and with it the explanatory or justificatory force possessed by references to rights. This result has been acceptable to many political philosophers, but others have been worried by it, feeling . . . that the point of attributing rights to people is to attribute to them some kind of "sovereignty" over the moral world. According to this view, to have a right to something is

more than to be in a position where one's expressed or understood want is the occasion for the operation of a duty imposed upon someone else; it is actually in some way to impose that duty upon them, and to determine how they ought to act towards the possessor of the right.[43]

This brings us back to the problem with which we began this section. It is difficult to see how we could develop an account of rights sufficiently robust to serve as an authoritative counter-weight to the political authority of the community, particularly when this authority comes backed by the power of the nation-state. If my rights can be exhaustively expressed in terms of others' duties towards me, then they can only be determined at the end of deliberative processes in which my individual needs and claims count as one set of considerations among many others. Rights claims would thus be lodged within processes of political negotiation — just as Ignatieff argues. It might just be possible to defend an account of objective right that would take rights claims out of the arena of political negotiation by construing them as positive expressions of absolute prohibitions, targeting certain kinds of actions which are intrinsically evil — so that, for example, I have a right to life because killing me would be murder, which is an intrinsically evil act. But this line of argument has proven notoriously difficult to cash out, and even if we could successfully do so, it would still leave us with a conception of rights that is inadequate in one key respect. That is to say, even this strong construal of rights as correlative to absolute obligations cannot account for the legal force of rights; it cannot explain why rights set up a claim to adjudication, even prior to or apart from the formal enactments of a given polity. And unless rights claims can be shown to have legal, as well as broadly moral force, they cannot serve as a principled constraint on the properly legal authority of the polity.

Near the end of his analysis of human rights, Perry raises this issue through a discussion concerning whether human rights are absolute. He poses the issue through consideration of a case considered by the Supreme Court of Israel "involving the use of physical force in the interrogation of a Palestinian detainee believed to have 'extremely vital information whose immediate extraction would help save lives and prevent severe terror attacks in Israel.'"[44] He goes on to quote the attorney for the government to the effect that "No enlightened nation would agree that hundreds of people should

---

43. Richard Tuck, *Natural Rights Theories* (Cambridge: Cambridge University Press, 1979), 6.
44. *Idea of Human Rights*, 94.

lose their lives because of a rule saying torture is forbidden under all circumstances."[45] So far as I can tell, Perry never does state his own view on this issue. He does describe the claim that torture is absolutely forbidden as "counterintuitive," but he acknowledges that it might nonetheless be true.[46] However, he turns immediately from a consideration of torture to the right to life, on the ground that the latter is widely regarded as "the most fundamental of all human rights — or certainly one of them."[47] After an extended consideration of Finnis's defense of an absolute right to life, he concludes that the right to life is not absolute. This at least suggests that he would not consider the right not to be tortured as an absolute.[48]

And given the terms of his analysis, why should he? If rights claims represent our final judgments regarding what is due to others and to the community on a case by case basis, judgments which emerge out of a contextual consideration of the diverse considerations that inform practical reasoning, then it would seem that we cannot rule out any substantive kind of action antecedently of some such situational judgment. This is particularly so when competing claims of the same kind are at stake. That is why Perry's defense of rights as an expression of sacredness of life may not rule out even very extreme assaults on the individual, as we might initially expect it to do. Indeed, the ideal of the sacredness of life, taken by itself, can actually provide a sanction for violence against others who are seen as threatening that ideal. If human life is taken to be sacred, and if other moral commitments are considered to be secondary at best, then the protection of life readily becomes an overriding value.[49] This might imply that no one at all should be subject to violent attack, and of course many do draw just this conclusion. But it can also be taken to imply that those who appear to be attacking human life are so profoundly depraved that they have forfeited any claims to consideration. Seen from this perspective, the humanity of the (alleged!) terrorist recedes from view, while the loss of life for which he may be responsible takes on overwhelming moral signifi-

---

45. *Idea of Human Rights*, 94.

46. *Idea of Human Rights*, 95.

47. *Idea of Human Rights*, 95.

48. *Idea of Human Rights*, 95-106; note that he does claim that the right not to be tortured is legally nonderogable — that is to say, its violation can never be juridically sanctioned, even though it may be justified in certain extreme and exceptional cases.

49. This line of argument is exemplified by the development of the relatively recent ideal of the sacredness of human life, widely invoked as an absolute to put an end to political deliberation; see Jill Lepore, "The Politics of Death: From Karen Ann Quinlan to Death Panels," in *The New Yorker*, November 30, 2009, 60-67.

cance. Jean Elshtain, for one, comes very close to defending earlier United States policies of torture on precisely these grounds.[50]

I do not want to ascribe a similar view to Perry, who does say that the right not to be tortured should be regarded as legally non-derogable, although he also thinks that torture might be morally justifiable in extreme circumstances.[51] Although I cannot find anyplace where he discusses the subject in print, I think it is exceptionally unlikely that Wolterstorff would allow for torture under any circumstances whatever. My point, nonetheless, is that neither he nor Perry can defend the view that an individual can properly claim an unconditional immunity from this, or any other kind of treatment, within the terms of the analyses of rights that they offer. By the same token, it is difficult to see how rights claims, understood as expressions of contextual practical judgments, could serve as a real counter-weight to the authority of the nation-state. My point is not simply that rights claims provide one important check on the abuse of state power, although that is certainly one of the main functions of rights talk in all its forms. More fundamentally, a robust doctrine of subjective rights sets boundaries on what counts as the legitimate exercise of state power. After all, governmental authorities are properly concerned with the well-being of the many, in addition to their responsibility for sustaining a communal way of life. Absent some strong normative claim to the contrary, we might conclude that governmental authorities properly should be prepared to sacrifice individual claims to the good of the whole. This is just the line of analysis that MacCormick rightly wants to forestall.

Towards a Doctrine of Subjective Rights

At this point, we can appreciate the significance of the jurists' distinctive contributions to the theory and practice of individual rights. Through a series of path-breaking articles and monographs, Tierney has decisively shown that substantive, explicit claims to natural rights, which are pre-conventional in origin and yet have moral and juridical force, emerge earlier than was previously thought, by at least the mid-thirteenth century.[52] These claims emerged

50. See Jean Bethke Elshtain, "Reflection on the Problem of 'Dirty Hands,'" in *Torture: A Consideration*, ed. Sanford Levinson (Oxford: Oxford University Press, 2004), 77-92.

51. Again, see *Idea of Human Rights*, 95-106.

52. The central lines of his argument are laid out in *Idea of Natural Rights*; in addition, Charles Reid offers a detailed account of the emergence of the language and practice of rights

out of a context of intense interest in human laws and the claims stemming from these on the one hand, and the pre-conventional origins of human law in a natural right or law on the other. Yet as they were understood by at least some canon lawyers — and as acknowledged to some extent by the practices of ecclesiastical courts — these rights implied unprecedented claims on the part of those who demanded them. On this view, someone who claims his or her right to some benefit or forbearance exercises a discretionary claim, perhaps grounded in more general obligations, but going beyond these by demanding that they be put into practice, here and now, on behalf of this particular individual. Thus, the recognition of natural rights added two things to the accepted framework of mutual obligations: first, the recognition that individuals enjoy a discretionary power to enjoin or forbid certain kinds of actions in their regard, and (by implication) second, that individuals have the power to specify general obligations in such a way as to render them concrete and exigent.

Correlatively, the language of natural rights — or as Tierney further specifies, subjective natural rights — captures two distinctive normative concerns, which are likely to be obscured so long as rights are simply identified with moral obligations *tout court*. The first, widely associated with rights talk by both its defenders and critics, is a concern with the autonomy or freedom of the individual, expressed and safeguarded by his or her power to assert a claim to some specific benefit or forbearance. The second brings us more immediately to the issues at stake in this section. That is, the language of subjective natural rights serves to define and protect the authority of the individual, vis-à-vis other individuals and the community taken as a whole.

In order to see why this is so, we need to return once again to the distinctive scholastic approach to the natural law or, as most of them preferred to say, to natural right — that is to say, to the natural claim, the *jus*, undergirding every legitimate claim, every *jus* to a specific liberty or power. As we noted in the first chapter, the scholastics generally identify natural right with the "inner law" referred to at Romans 2:14, where Paul asserts that the Gentiles discern what the Law requires through a natural law. Correlatively, they identify this natural law or right, in its primary sense, with either rational capacities for practical judgment or the foundational principles through which practical judgment operates.

This identification, in turn, tethers the idea of natural right to a deeply

---

claims in ecclesiastical marriage law in *Power over the Body, Equality in the Family: Rights and Domestic Relations in Medieval Canon Law* (Grand Rapids: Eerdmans, 2004).

rooted and centrally important strand of scriptural and theological reflection. Still following their patristic sources, the scholastics further identified the natural law, understood as a capacity for rational discernment, with the image of God, in which the human person is created and which therefore cannot be extirpated even, as we are frequently reminded, in Cain himself. It is found in every human person, man, woman, and child, including sinners as well as the righteous, and even the damned.[53] What is more, the image is not just identified with reason generically understood; it is interpreted more specifically in terms of the human capacity for autonomous self-direction, mastery over one's own choices and acts. This capacity is thus not just one human power among others, but the definitively human way in which a creature of this kind reflects God's active power, wisdom and goodness; by the same token, it is a distinctive reflection of that wisdom and goodness because it mirrors the distinctive notes of divine activity itself. As such, this capacity deserves not only appreciation as a likeness of God, but reverence as the very image of God.

So far, the scholastics' interpretation of the natural law tradition in terms of the key idea of natural right does not necessarily imply a doctrine of subjective natural rights, understood in terms of a normative power either to forbid or to enjoin certain kinds of actions at the individual's discretion. By and large, the theologians did not make this move, but by the thirteenth century, at least some canon lawyers had begun to do so. The decisive shift came about in response to the urgent practical necessities of the time. It is hardly surprising that this way of construing rights began to be formulated in the context of the re-assertion of properly political forms of authority, over against the eleventh-century resurgence of feudal forms of violent exploitation and dominion. In this context, the assertion and defense of the natural rights, the *jura,* of the individual offered a scripturally sanctioned response to the supposed *jura* of those who would subject others to their rule. Rights claims thus reflected the same fundamental distinction between servile and political subordination, offering one practical way to guarantee the genuinely free character of the latter. By the same token, the properly political character of rights meant that they could readily be construed as correla-

---

53. As Tierney argues, the scholastics' interpretation of natural law and natural rights is decisively shaped by the connection that they draw between natural law or right and the capacities for self-determination implied by the doctrine of the image of God; see *Idea of Natural Rights,* 43-77. I also argue for the centrality of this motif for the scholastics' interpretation of natural law in *Natural and Divine Law,* 259-77. For a contemporary theological defense of a similar view, see *Rights and Christian Ethics,* 233-66.

tives to, and where necessary constraints on, the political authority of the community itself — as they subsequently came to be understood.

For at least some canon lawyers, the assertion of natural rights claims, if not the development of a fully formed theory of natural rights, represented a logical extension of practices already in place, in both civil and ecclesiastical contexts, for safeguarding individual freedom. Tierney cites the example of the thirteenth-century canon lawyer Laurentius, who reformulates the obligation of the rich to supply the necessities of the poor in terms of a *jus*, a claim possessed by the poor individual himself: according to Laurentius, when the poor person takes from another under press of necessity, it is "as if he used his own right and his own thing."[54] Even more significantly, as Tierney goes on to show, this right came to be regarded as a claim having juridical effect, insofar as it could be asserted and secured through a public process of adjudication. Of course, such a process would require some kind of legal structure, but for that very reason, it is incumbent on society to put the necessary procedures in place. And indeed, as Tierney goes on to observe, scholastic canon lawyers did set up legal fora through which the right to surplus wealth could be publicly defended and enforced:

> Alongside the formal judicial procedures inherited from Roman law the canonists had developed an alternative, more simple, equitable process known as "evangelical denunciation." By virtue of the authority inhering in his office as judge, a bishop could hear any complaint involving an alleged sin and could provide a remedy without the plaintiff bringing a formal action. From about 1200 onward several canonists argued that this procedure was available to the poor person in extreme need. He could assert a rightful claim by an "appeal to the office of the judge." The bishop could then compel an intransigent rich man to give alms from his superfluities, by excommunication if necessary.[55]

Understood in this way, a right is itself a kind of authoritative claim, grounded in a relation of natural authority. Like any other relation of natural authority, this relation can only be understood and justified in terms of the purpose that it serves. More specifically, it safeguards the freedom of the individual to sustain activity in accordance with what she most properly and specifically is — that is to say, a rational creature capable of discernment, choice, and free action through which she pursues her aims and ultimately

---

54. Quoted by Tierney, *Idea of Natural Rights*, 73; for the more extended argument, see 69-77.
55. *Idea of Natural Rights*, 74.

shapes and perfects her own existence as an agent. Once again, we should underscore the point that these claims go beyond the general obligations of forbearance and equitable treatment which are recognized in some form in every sustainable community. My fellow citizens, and the community taken as a whole, are obliged to respect and support me, to the extent that I am appropriately an object of general obligations of forbearance and aid. Yet at least to some extent, I have the power to impose specific demands on these others for forbearance and aid in this specific way, here and now. Thus understood, when I claim at least certain kinds of rights, my demands are intelligibly grounded in a general framework of obligations, and yet add a contingent level of specification to these.

Natural Rights and the Image of God Motif

By now, the main lines of a natural law doctrine of natural rights have begun to emerge. In certain ways, within defined zones of personal liberty, the members of a community can rule their rulers — and this constitutes a powerful safeguard against any tendency to absolutize political authority and to bestow on it a uniquely divine status. At the same time, because they are grounded in a natural relation of authority having immediate public consequences, natural rights have juridical force. This implies that they can be appropriately expressed through enacted law, and it also implies that they can and sometimes should be recognized through processes of adjudication, even prior to their articulation in formal law. Again, this insight is confirmed by the historical trajectory of rights claims as Tierney traces it. These were first asserted and vindicated in canonical courts, and then in courts and tribunals more generally, before they became the targets of systematic theories and formal legislation. At this point, too, the judges served as gatekeepers, in this case through the process of recognizing what had been extra-juridical claims, in the process formulating them and translating them into legal claims properly so called.

What is the basis for this extraordinary authority? This is the point at which we need to appeal to a theistic justification of a specific kind, in such a way as to account for the distinctive authority, as well as the worth, value, or dignity of the individual. As we have just seen the scholastics do so by grounding natural rights in the *jus naturale*, the natural right, understood as the capacity for free, reasonable judgment and action, which represents the image of God in which each human being is constituted. This latter point should be underscored: the human person is said to be created, constituted, or set up in the image of God, in virtue of his or her creation as an individual substance of a given kind of nature. The constitutive structural capacities of the creature remain as long as the creature exists at all, even though at any given point she may be too immature, or too sick, or otherwise impeded from expressing her full potential as a rational agent. For this reason, the scholastics would not have shared our worries that the normative claims, including rights claims, proper to us as rational animals might apply only to those who are actually capable of exercising the relevant capabilities at any given time (or indeed, at all). By the same token, they would not have known what to make of the objection that any attempt to ground rights claims in this way implies that the human person enjoys some value antecedently to God's valuation of the individual.[56] Apart from God's creative act, there would be nothing to provide a target for anyone's esteem or desire, and by the same token, God confers value on the creature by virtue of creating it as an entity of an intelligible and good kind.

Even granting these qualifications, the scholastic construal of the image of God will strike many as a problematic starting point for normative reflection. After all — it may be said — why should we give so much weight to capacities for reason and independent action that not everyone shares, and which seem in any case to reflect strains of individualism and self-assertion? Shouldn't we keep in mind that we are, in MacIntyre's phrase, "dependent rational animals" who must always cultivate the virtues appropriate to those who have been, and may well again become, irrational, insensible, needy, and dependent?[57] These are legitimate worries, and I would agree that we can and should understand the image of God motif in a range of ways, including some which would de-center rationality by privileging relatedness and receptivity. Nonetheless, it seems to me that the patristic and medieval interpretation of the Image motif brings together two key components of Christian doctrine and theological reflection which we have a stake in preserving — it tells us something about who we are, and by the same token, it provides a key for understanding, so far as we can, who and what God is.[58]

---

56. Wolterstorff raises both of these points; see *Justice: Rights and Wrongs*, 342-61.

57. I take the phrase, and the summary of the main argument, from Alasdair MacIntyre, *Dependent Rational Animals: Why Human Beings Need the Virtues* (Peru, IL: Carus/Open Court, 1999).

58. At this point and in the following sketch of natural rights, I draw on an argument developed at more length in "Natural Right, Authority, and Power: The Theological Trajectory of Human Rights," forthcoming in *The Journal of Law, Philosophy and Culture*, Spring 2011.

First, and most evidently, this construal of the image of God motif expresses our sense of the incommensurate worth and the dignity of the human person, regarded simply as such, prior to any distinctive features of ability, merit, or grace. And yet, paradoxically, it gives salience to those aspects of human dignity which are most inward and personal — the individual's capacities for judgment and self-determination, her free self-disposal through the exercise of these capacities, and the inwardness out of which she perceives and acts. What is more — and prior to any claims about rights per se — this way of construing the image reminds us that this other person is not just an appropriate recipient of our beneficence, but someone who places an authoritative claim on us for certain kinds of consideration and forbearance. In somewhat the same way as God demands love, as well as inviting it, the human person elicits and also claims our justice and charity.

Reverse that last claim, and we come to the other key component of the medieval interpretation of the image of God. That is, just as the human individual places authoritative claims upon us, so too does God. Of course, Christian doctrine has long insisted on God's supreme authority. But my point is that the medieval interpretation of God's authority, at least as it is keyed to this motif, emphasizes certain aspects of that authority while downplaying others. It de-emphasizes God's sheer power, while underscoring the sapiential character of God's authority, its roots in God's freely bestowed love for creatures and the incomprehensible inwardness that that love reflects. At the same time, it invites a correlative response out of those capacities and deep choices within ourselves that mirror and reflect God's inmost life. At the very least, it predisposes us to regard God's authority over us as political, rather than despotic — a kind of authority, therefore, which safeguards human freedom, to which we respond out of capacities for freedom that are not unlike God's inward reality. I believe that this is the trajectory that leads at least some jurists to the claim that the individual right to self-disposal properly carries juridical force. By justifying natural rights in the way that they do, scholastic jurists imply that rights claims and political authority work in tandem, as two distinct yet ultimately congruous expressions of divine authority expressed through God's creative decree.

At the same time, rights claims can only exercise juridical force in and through some process of formulation and specification, incorporating contingent as well as natural elements. This is tantamount to saying that rights claims — like all other expressions of natural authority — will always be expressed through conventions of some kind, even though these may only be constituted through processes of individual assertion and communal response. The conventional forms through which rights are asserted must thus be evaluated in terms of the natural purposes that they serve, if we are to defend the claim that these do in fact express natural, human, or fundamental rights — the purposes in question being to express and safeguard properly human capabilities for rational reflection, free judgment, and self-disposal. I emphasize this point, first because a doctrine of natural or human rights loses credibility if its claims are too expansive, and secondly, because it is critically important to keep in mind that rights are not the only kinds of normative claims, even in political contexts. It would be a mistake, therefore, to presuppose that any and every supposed rights claim — including many that represent valid normative claims of some kind — can credibly be understood as a natural right. If we are to defend a rights claim through processes of rhetorical persuasion, we need to tether it specifically to fundamental human inclinations towards rational reflection and free self-disposal, in such a way as to relate what is claimed to the direct expression of these fundamental inclinations or to the forms of forbearance or assistance necessary for such expression.

A Sketch of Natural Rights

This is not the point at which to attempt a fully developed theory of natural rights. Nonetheless, it may be helpful to attempt to sketch the outlines of such a theory, if only to clarify what has been said so far. And first, we should establish some basic parameters. On the natural law account that I propose, a natural right is fundamentally an individual claim, stemming from the individual's power to constrain the behavior of others vis-à-vis himself, or to compel some performance from the other, again relevant to the agent himself. (Rights can be claimed vicariously, on behalf of another, but because rights claims stem immediately and directly from the individual's status as a self-governing agent, they are fundamentally self-regarding.) They include what are sometimes called positive rights, claims to particular forms of aid or subsistence, although these are by necessity always circumscribed. Rights claims can be lodged against both individuals and collective agents of all kinds, and they can be acknowledged and honored without any kind of formal public procedures. However, these kinds of claims are intrinsically juridical in force; thus, they can be claimed in court and the courts have a *prima facie* obligation to consider them, even in the absence of relevant prescriptions of formal law. If appropriate judicial mechanisms for doing so are lacking, it is incumbent on the government or the community generally to provide them. Very often, claims to positive subsistence will be of such a kind that they can only be lodged against the community as a whole.

Given what has been said so far, it will be apparent that whatever else they comprise, natural rights include claims to the free exercise of one's capacities for rational inquiry and reflection, the ability to develop and express one's own reflective judgments about the overall direction one's life should take, and at least some opportunities to put those judgments into place. Given our nature as animals that are properly dependent as well as rational, these presuppose rights on the part of the young to care and protection, basic education, and formation in the ideals and commitments of their care-takers. Given our proper nature as social animals and political individuals, these also include at least core elements of what we think of as civil rights, including rights to free expression, participation in political processes, freedom of assembly and the like. Negatively, individuals can claim immunity from any kind of violent coercion in pursuit of aims that they themselves could not reasonably be expected to acknowledge — from any kind of servile dominion, in other words. These claims rule out slavery and related forms of servitude, as well as all kinds of extra-judicial processes of detention and denials of due legal processes. To return to the example discussed above, individuals properly enjoy an absolute immunity from any kind of outrage directed towards destroying their capacities to function as free, appropriately responsive, and discriminating agents; there is thus an absolute right not to be tortured.

In addition, each mature individual member of a community properly demands acknowledgment and respect as a free man or woman, properly subject to but also actively engaged in political processes of deliberation and persuasion. (Children and those who are unable to exercise this right directly nonetheless continue to enjoy it, to the extent and in the ways possible and appropriate to them.) Within the context of bureaucratized nation-states, which structure public life through networks of impersonal roles, this fundamental right is properly expressed through a congeries of claims to equal treatment, non-discrimination, and full access to public goods, services, and opportunities. In societies structured in other ways, a fundamental right to respect as a political agent may be recognized, and yet construed in such a way as to be consistent with forms of differential treatment that would properly be regarded as unjust in the context of a modern national society. In order to be meaningful at all, this right to respect must at least provide for some kind of participation in what Rawls describes as processes of consultation. And in every case, the claim to equality of respect includes basic claims over against society as a whole to an adequate and equitable share in the material means of life and the protections and amenities of the community.

This brings us to a further point. That is, characteristically human capacities for rational inquiry and reflective, self-governing freedom are not simply exercised in the abstract; they are exercised in and through the body, and specified in the first instance as claims over the use and disposal of one's body.[59] It is critically important to bear this in mind when considering claims to equality, because with respect to the fundamental needs and capabilities proper to us as organisms of a certain kind, we are all equal — and for this reason, as Aquinas suggests, these set the boundaries beyond which no one can legitimately claim authority over another person (ST II-II 104.5). What is more, human freedom and self-disposal will necessarily always take the form of some exercise of one's agency in and through one's bodily capacities, and will include disposal of the body in fundamental ways. For this reason, those claims which reflect the agent's dominion over his own body, and safeguard or express activities proper to him as a natural creature of a certain kind, offer paradigmatic examples of natural rights. These would include rights to bodily integrity and at least minimal levels of sustenance, some kind of property rights construed as dominion over physical things, the right to engage in physical activities, to move freely, and to enter into sexual relations, and finally, the right to exercise one's procreative capacities in an appropriate institutional context.

It will be apparent by now that this account of natural rights has a great deal in common with leading secular liberal theories, including those developed or implied by Dworkin, MacCormick, Rawls, Nussbaum, and others. A fuller statement of this account would indicate important differences as well. To mention only one, because natural rights are tethered to the integrity and the capacities of the body, they are both more specific and in key respects more limited than some of our contemporaries would allow.[60] Even so, there is enough convergence to raise the suspicion that my account of rights is essentially a baptized version of secular liberalism. And of course, there is sure to be some truth to this charge; after all, I am a twenty-first-century woman with strong liberal sensibilities, and it would be very

---

59. As Reid documents, this aspect of rights claims emerged with particular clarity in the context of marriage law; see *Power over the Body*, 1-68.

60. I am grateful to Matthew Hamilton for calling this to my attention.

strange indeed if my theology were not shaped by this context to some degree. Nonetheless, I would argue that on the larger scale, the lines of influence go in the opposite direction. Western liberal ideals of equality and the commitment to fundamental rights reflect the pervasive influence of what were originally Christian ideals and practices — an influence so pervasive as to be almost invisible.[61] It is telling that so many of those who defend this value on secular terms do not even try to justify it, identifying it as a foundational moral principle or pragmatic choice of some kind, as we observed above.

Seen from a natural law standpoint, the endurance and the widespread attractiveness of these ideals and commitments lend credence to the claim that the worth and freedom of the individual are natural values which can effectively be introduced into processes of rhetorical deliberation and persuasion in a range of contexts.[62] At the same time, nothing would necessarily compel a rational, well-disposed individual to give these values the overriding importance that they have in Western democracies. Historically, we arrived at this comparative judgment under the influence of distinctively theological doctrines and sensibilities, and there is a good case to be made that, even now, the overriding value of the individual and his claims to freedom can only be justified in these terms.

None of this need trouble those of us who believe that this value reflects what are ultimately God's comparative judgments about the many components of human goodness. We can happily cooperate with those who apprehend the human good as we do, while acknowledging the good faith and fundamental reasonableness of those who do not. We can even say, with all due caution, that the observance of human rights in society at large represents one of the ways in which men and women of all faiths and none may participate in a kind of natural homage to God, whether knowingly or not. Those of us who live as Christians in Western democracies have the strongest possible reasons for promoting and safeguarding rights claims through appropriate processes of rhetorical persuasion, and protesting their violations, above all when the victims are dangerous or unattractive. Beliefs are empty without practices, and respect for natural rights represents one key

61. Paul Hyams makes this point in connection with Tierney's work in "Due Process versus the Maintenance of Order in European Law: The Contribution of the *jus commune*," in *The Moral World of the Law*, ed. Peter Coss (Cambridge: Cambridge University Press, 2000), 62-90.

62. I take this to be essentially similar to Maritain's view, albeit developed in terms of a somewhat different conception of the natural law; see Jacques Maritain, *Man and the State* (Chicago: University of Chicago Press, 1951), 76-107.

aspect of the practices through which we Christians give concrete meaning and effective expression to fundamental beliefs about who God is, and who we and our neighbors are in relation to God and one another. Through respecting the fundamental rights of another, even — especially! — when these are exercised to our detriment, or in pursuit of aims we regard as unworthy or sinful, we express our reverence for this individual, considered in herself, and as the icon of the divinity that she is.

3. Natural Law, Natural Rights, and *Jus cogens* Norms: The Parameters of International Law

The Claims of Humanity and the Authority of International Law

The authority of the nation-state is properly bounded by the authoritative rights claims of individuals. If we are persuaded by this, then we will more readily accept the claim that the authoritative claims of nation-states are also bounded by international law. Yet international law, like customary law, has long been regarded as problematic, especially for those who hold that legal force depends on the formal enactment on the part of a legitimate, authoritative lawmaker. The difficulty from this perspective is of course simply that there is no agency that can credibly claim comprehensive law-making authority over all the peoples of the world. In many instances, international law seems to emerge from what are, in effect, the customary practices of nations and peoples. Even those norms which look most like formal enactments — treaties, trade agreements, the decrees and conventions of international bodies, and the like — are grounded in the free agreements of formally equal political authorities rather than the enactments of some formally acknowledged legal authority. For the early legal positivists, who claimed that the lawgiver must rely on some authority above that of the community, these were insurmountable obstacles.

This particular construal of legal authority was decisively undermined by Hart, who argues, as we have seen, that the authority of the lawgiver is on the contrary dependent on the community, operating through a contingent rule of recognition. Seen from a natural law perspective, these rules of recognition are expressions of the political authority of the community itself, which has a reasonable claim to regulate its own affairs in such a way as to sustain a common way of life. Thus, there is nothing necessarily problematic about the claim that international law can be genuinely law, even though it is not formally enacted. As we have seen, the same may be said, in an extended but legitimate sense, of customary law.[63]

However, international law is problematic in another way, seen from a natural law perspective — and not only from that perspective. On a natural law account, political and legal authority stem from the authority of the community, insofar as the institutions of governance and the legal system serve the purposes of safeguarding and expressing the values and commitments that sustain the common life of the polity. International law does not, and by its intrinsic character cannot, represent the authority of a cohesive community in this way. Whatever else it may be, international law is first and foremost a set of norms or practices pertaining to the activities of collective entities, and secondarily, to individuals as they move across and outside the boundaries of organized political communities. And cosmopolitan fantasies to the contrary notwithstanding, the peoples and individuals of the world cannot form a polity in the relevant sense. The sheer fact of human diversity, and the irreducible plurality of cultures and ways of life stemming from that diversity, rule out the possibility of developing a deep, substantive conception of human happiness and the common good in which all the peoples of the world can share.

And yet, it is manifestly the case that the nations of the world do acknowledge and comply with the norms of international law, at least in most instances, even when compliance works against a nation's immediate interests. Nor should this state of affairs surprise us. Even though the peoples of the world do not form a polity, unified by shared ideals and commitments, nonetheless we do share enough to engage in processes of rhetorical deliberation and persuasion. We share a common humanity, and while this does not by itself yield a comprehensive, concrete moral system, much less sufficient basis for a comprehensive formal law, it does provide a basis for shared agreement on at least the outer limits of tolerable behavior and the scope and force of the most exigent demands for mutual aid. What is more, ongoing processes of rhetorical persuasion have given rise to a considerable body of shared agreements with respect to a very wide range of matters, including

63. Hart himself does not believe that international law can be understood in terms of primary and secondary rules, the latter confirmed through a settled rule of recognition. He goes on to say, however, that this does not mean that international law is not law, since this analysis reflects the typical structure of municipal law but does not represent necessary conditions for the existence of law as such. In fact, he goes on to defend the legitimacy of international law, considered as a form of law, on other grounds. See *The Concept of Law*, 2nd edition (Oxford: Oxford University Press, 1997), 213-14, and more generally 213-37.

everything from mundane agreements on the proper use of shared resources to the intricacies of shared economic structures. These are themselves conventional and contingent — they may well have been decided differently — but to a considerable extent they are so deeply entrenched as to seem natural, and to provide an uncontroversial framework within which more specific rules and agreements can be worked out as needed. As contingent expressions of judgment, which nonetheless stem from natural considerations, they reflect genuine expressions of authority, the authority of humanity itself arranging its own affairs in those contexts in which shared activity calls for some such arrangements. Thus, even though the peoples of the world do not constitute a polity, they do nonetheless constitute a kind of extended community by virtue of their ongoing mutual interactions and the limited yet vitally important shared interests that can only be pursued in common. We can therefore speak, in an extended but legitimate way, of a world community bearing its own proper self-governing authority.

This authority is in turn expressed *(inter alia)* by norms of international law, which are constituted as such through common consent. To a very considerable extent, the specific norms in question emerge through the customary practices of the nations. As Theodor Meron points out, "General practice of states which is accepted and observed as law, i.e., from a sense of legal obligation, builds norms of customary international law."[64] Acknowledged customary law, in turn, is typically codified through treaties and other instruments of international law, but as Meron goes on to observe, "It is, of course, not the treaty norm, but the customary norm with identical content, that binds such states."[65] This, as he goes on to say, helps to explain why the norms of customary international law can be regarded as binding on nation-states generally, even those who do not accept the treaty or instrument in question. Thus understood, treaties and other instruments are thus not enactments that create new laws, but attempts to formulate what is regarded as already existing law — identified, debated, and eventually given formal expression through the familiar processes of rhetorical persuasion, carried out in the court of world opinion. What is more, actual courts once again serve as the gatekeepers for the law, adjudicating the claims of collective entities and individuals on the basis of their best sense of what, substantively, the practices comprising international law are, and what they imply. To a very

64. Theodor Meron, *Human Rights and Humanitarian Norms as Customary Law* (Oxford: Clarendon Press, 1989), 3.

65. *Human Rights and Humanitarian Norms,* 3.

considerable extent, even more perhaps than with judges operating within the legal system of some polity, judges at this level must rely on normative construals of the law. As Meron explains,

> Elementary considerations of humanity reflect basic community values whether already crystallized as binding norms of international law or not. Professor Brownlie has observed that "considerations of humanity may depend on the subjective appreciation of the judge, but more objectively, they may be related to human values already protected by positive legal principles which, taken together, reveal certain criteria of public policy. . . ." The fact that the content of a norm reflects important considerations of humanity should promote its acceptance as customary law. Thus, in explaining why the Geneva Conventions can be regarded as approaching "international legislation," Hersch Lauterpacht stated that, among other reasons, "many of the provisions of these Conventions, following as they do from compelling considerations of humanity, are declaratory of universally binding international custom."[66]

The authority of international law thus does not presuppose the authority of a lawgiver, even on a theoretical or notional level. It reflects the authority of humanity as articulated through an ongoing history, reaching into an open-ended future. What is more, like every other authoritative decree, this communal consent expresses a shared judgment that these norms express rational and natural principles of action in a defensible way. And just as customary law and natural rights claims can be vindicated through judicial processes, even apart from formal enactments, so the authoritative judgments of humanity can be vindicated through courts of all kinds, whose authority is recognized — again — through contingent yet rational rules of recognition. This situation is not so anomalous as it may seem. Recall that throughout the early medieval period, European legal systems functioned without formal legislators, sustaining the rule of law through the judgments of courts. Even though there is no such thing as a generally acknowledged, comprehensive legislative authority governing the peoples of the world, legal authority is properly exercised at this level nonetheless, through customary practices as (partially) expressed through treaties and other instruments and adjudicated by generally acknowledged courts.

This brings us back once again to the problem of authority and constraint. If the affairs of nations are not regulated by some supreme lawgiver

---

66. *Human Rights and Humanitarian Norms,* 35.

or comprehensive world government, then who or what does regulate them? In fact, as O'Connell shows in some detail, international law is backed, and by and large effectively enforced through sanctions, which themselves provide further evidence that international law is regarded as genuine law by most of its subjects. But there is a deeper issue at stake. That is to say, if the authority of international law rests ultimately on the authoritative decrees of humanity itself, then what is the basis for defending proper and legitimate constraints on that authority? Most informed persons do believe that there are some such constraints — that even the common consent of humanity could not do away with fundamental rights, or sanitize certain kinds of atrocious conduct. As O'Connell observes,

> International law's claim to be law is based ultimately on belief. It contains peremptory norms, *jus cogens* principles, that cannot be altered by positive acts, including the norms against genocide, apartheid, extrajudicial killing, slavery, and torture. The third primary source of international law rules after customary international law and treaties is the general principles of law — which have counterpoints in principles articulated by the great jurists of classical Roman law. They understood them as requirements or implications of reason, inspired by the natural order of things. General principles from this category, such as necessity, proportionality, and good faith, play an important role in regulating enforcement measures. While most of international law is based on positive acts of consent, ultimately the ontology and legitimacy of international law is based on more than consent, just as it is more than sanctions.[67]

O'Connell herself refers to a higher law, which provides the ultimate grounding for formal enactments at every level, and which she herself is inclined to identify with a kind of natural law. The theological account of natural law developed here confirms this view, while also locating the natural law in the context of a yet higher, eternal law. This highest law rests ultimately on God's free, authoritative decree, but not in such a way as to imply that God confers authority on polities or governing agencies or serves as a kind of ultimate lawgiver, governing the peoples of the world through formal enactments. Rather, to return to a familiar point, God's eternal law is enacted and promulgated (for us) through the free divine decree to confer existence on creatures of a certain kind, rational animals who participate in a distinctive way in the eternal law, in and through their free self-disposal.

---

67. O'Connell, *Power and Purpose of International Law,* 9.

There is no unchanging formal law in the heavens, not even hidden in the mind of God. Rather, to the extent that the eternal law can be said to govern human affairs, it does so through the natural law, which is in turn specified through individual and communal processes of practical deliberation and free choice. At the same time, these processes are themselves constrained — by norms of reasonableness, by the contingent yet practically irreversible determinations shaping an ongoing common life, and by considerations of natural right and equity which can be justified as such through processes of rhetorical persuasion, even in the absence of any extensive framework of shared beliefs and practices.

The Inner Morality and Irreversible Trajectory of International Law

As O'Connell's remarks suggest, these constraints take a variety of forms, including general norms of reasonableness, norms expressing natural rights, and *jus cogens* norms, which cannot be abrogated even by the express agreements of nation-states.[68] At this point, we once again confront a familiar problem. That is, given the indeterminacy of natural norms and values, and the irreducible diversity of natural moralities giving concrete expression to these, how can we account for this level of agreement on substantive norms at the international level? More precisely, how can we justify practical norms concrete enough to govern actual conduct through processes of deliberation and persuasion at the international level? These are the questions that will occupy us for the remainder of this section.

The first point to bear in mind is that international law is not actually or by intent a complete legal system, regulating every aspect of human affairs — much less a formulation of a comprehensive moral system. A comprehensive normative code, rationally compelling to all and yet substantive enough to be put into practice, would indeed be out of the question, but fortunately the bar is not set so high. What we need, rather, is some account of the way in which we might arrive at a properly political consensus on delimited sets of norms of a specific kind, through processes of rational deliberation and rhetorical persuasion operating at the international level.

---

68. I believe O'Connell considers norms expressing fundamental rights to be *jus cogens*, and I would generally agree, but I think it is nonetheless important to distinguish analytically between rights norms and prohibitions against certain kinds of atrocities, for reasons that will become apparent below.

We can most easily see how to account for what O'Connell describes as "general principles of law," comprising "requirements or implications of reason, inspired by the natural order of things." To some extent, these will be equivalent to fundamental exigencies of rational deliberation and activity as carried out in communal and public contexts — norms of openness, consistency, and the like, comprising Fuller's inner morality of law. In addition, these include very general norms of non-maleficence and equity, for example, *pacta sunt servanda*, which following Aquinas we take to be formulations or immediate expressions of the intrinsic structure of practical reason itself. The general idea that the "law of nations" stems from the exigencies of reasonable action is, as O'Connell notes, very old. It dates back at least to the great Roman jurists, and in the scholastic period it is developed most extensively by those scholastics who focused on secular law.[69] These jurists, in contrast to both canon lawyers and theologians of the time, tended to distinguish between natural law in its primary sense, which they identified with a kind of pre-rational, spontaneous instinct, and the distinctively human law of nations, which stems immediately from reason. Yet many of them also allow that in an extended sense, the law of nations can itself be considered to be a form of natural law. Certainly, the law of nations is a product of human reflection, and thus not, strictly speaking, pre-conventional, as the natural law properly so called is. The law of nations is nonetheless a reflection of human reason operating at the most general level of human affairs, dealing with matters which arise perennially in the interaction of nations and of individuals acting across or outside recognized national boundaries. It is thus both universal, in the sense of enjoying widespread recognition, and relatively general seen in relation to systems of municipal law.

Although this is not their point, the civilian jurists indicate why it is that we so readily identify at least some norms of international law with natural law properly so called, and by implication they remind us why this would be a mistaken conclusion. That is, these relatively general principles of reasonableness are necessarily specified to some degree through the generally accepted customary practices of the nations, if not through explicit agreements. Even at this level, there is a significant degree of contingency, sometimes recognized as such, sometimes not. At the same time, even though the specifications of rational norms may be contingent — they might have been defensibly specified in some other way — they may become so generally accepted, and so deeply entrenched in the overall structures of

---

69. For further details, see *Natural and Divine Law,* 46-48, 76-78.

international law, as to be generally binding and practically irreversible at this point. Again, these norms look a great deal like natural law as classically understood — they are binding everywhere, here and now — and yet they are not timeless, since they emerged through extended processes of practice and deliberation, and might conceivably be changed through similar processes in the future.

I emphasize this point because the contextual, time-bound, and partially contingent character of the norms of international law must be taken into account if we are to understand one important category of what O'Connell refers to as peremptory or *jus cogens* norms, namely, norms expressing natural rights claims and prohibitions against certain kinds of atrocious conduct. In each case, we need to account for norms that only emerge over time through extended processes of deliberation and persuasion — but the routes to justifying these two sets of norms differ, in ways that reflect substantive differences between them.

Norms expressing natural rights reflect a distinctive set of value judgments concerning the distinctive worth of the individual, the centrality of freedom and self-disposal for a fully developed human existence, and the equality that all men and women enjoy as actual or potential agents of this kind. As such, they offer a persuasive and powerfully attractive way of structuring communal life. We can, of course, also envision other such persuasive, attractive ways of life, grounded in a different set of judgments about the central values of human existence and the proper relation between individual and community. Yet for whatever reasons, the rhetoric of natural or human rights, together with corresponding practices of claim and adjudication, are by now deeply entrenched in international law — so much so that humanity might be said to have made a practically irreversible commitment to this specific set of commitments and practices, as enshrined in international law. No doubt, this general consensus can conceal deep disagreements at the level of substantive commitments, and to some extent it reflects dynamics of power at the international level. Nonetheless, we have good reason to believe that international law and practice also reflect a genuine, rationally informed commitment to safeguarding individual interests and liberties. The ideals and practices of international courts may not always reflect a fully developed doctrine of subjective rights, but they certainly presuppose something more specific than a commitment to objective right.

Of course, the widespread success of the general idea of natural or human rights owes a great deal to the ambiguity built into the language of rights, as we noted above. Nonetheless, substantive commitments to safeguarding human rights are by now central to international law, and what is more, these commitments are at the least very similar to the core commitments embodied in the idea of subjective natural rights. They are explicitly and centrally focused on the claims of individuals, vis-à-vis national governments and every other kind of agency, as Meron observes:

> Although international human rights also implicate obligations running from one state to another, or even from one state to all states (obligations *erga omnes*), they primarily seek to protect individuals, the beneficiaries of human rights, from governments and sometimes from other individuals or non-state actors. Unlike most other fields of international law, the observance of human rights is not based on reciprocal interests of states, but on the broader goal of states to establish orderly and enlightened international and national legal orders. In human rights instruments, the contractual (interstate) elements are far less important than those which are objective and normative.[70]

International law is thus committed to the value of the individual, apart from and over against interests of state. What is more, international courts increasingly recognize that individuals can legitimately claim their rights at law, even prior to, and outside of, previously existing boundaries of political affiliation and jurisdiction.[71] This latter practice is still controversial, but to the extent that it is recognized at all, it unmistakably confirms that for at least some courts, at least some rights claims brought by, or on behalf of, individuals carry juridical weight — and that is tantamount to saying that these courts recognize the juridically significant natural authority of the individual, expressed through her claim to natural rights.

We can trace the history of natural or human rights doctrines to a specific set of theological beliefs and values, developed in response to acute social needs and practically expressed through the available forms of speech and practice. Yet these doctrines have proven to be powerfully persuasive and adaptable, especially but not only at the international level. To a very considerable extent, the widespread diffusion of rights doctrines at this level continues the historical trajectory that began in the scholastic period, as traced by Tierney, Tuck, and others. Briefly, we can trace the development of modern ideas of natural or human rights through a period of eclipse during the Enlightenment, followed by retrieval and systematic de-

70. *Human Rights and Humanitarian Norms,* 99-100.
71. For further details, see *Crimes against Humanity,* 253-59.

velopment by the so-called fathers of natural law in the early modern period. Here too, a doctrine was developed in response to exigent social needs — social unrest, violent revolution and the breaking and creation of nations, in Europe and beyond, the emergence of the modern system of sovereign nation-states, and correspondingly, the growing importance of norms governing conduct between and outside the boundaries of these entities. In these circumstances, there is no agreed-upon legislative authority and no generally accepted body of comprehensive laws. In such a situation, if peoples and individuals are to relate to one another in rationally defensible, publicly acknowledged ways at all, they urgently need to find some basis outside formal law for rhetorically persuasive claims that can then be vindicated in judicial processes.

The language of human or natural rights does not offer the only such basis, but the experiences of over half a century have made it amply clear that it does offer one powerful and widely persuasive option, which has commended itself to men and women representing a wide variety of cultures and ways of life. Rights claims are justified through appeals to very fundamental values of freedom, responsible judgment, and more broadly, claims to respect, which any man or woman can recognize as values that he or she shares in some way or other. This does not render rights claims logically compelling on pain of rational inconsistency, as some have argued, because these values must always be configured in a specific way, and held together with other, sometimes inconsistent, commitments and ideals. Nonetheless, the wide and general appeal of the values at stake does practically guarantee that rights claims will be rhetorically persuasive much of the time, in very many disparate contexts. At any rate, no matter how we account for it, the fact remains that the language and practice of rights is by now one of the central organizing principles of international law and informal trans-national practices of all kinds. Human society might collectively have taken a different direction, but we did not, and it is difficult at this point to see how the practical consensus on rights could be effectively reversed. Now, and for the foreseeable future, norms protecting human or natural rights have attained the status of the scholastics' law of nations: they are universally recognized (among, if not always within the peoples of the world), they constitute an enduring structure of laws, and they may be regarded as binding on all, at least in the contexts of international public life.

At the same time, rights claims do reflect only one defensible construal of human values, broadly persuasive and structurally fundamental at the international level, but not as such compelling to all well-disposed men and women. In this respect, they differ from norms prohibiting certain kinds of atrocious conduct — for example genocide, or torture — which, as we have seen, represent forms of cruelty or callousness that can never be justified. Considered as explicit norms, these too emerged through situated processes of persuasion and practice which shaped them in specific ways, and they are in that sense contingent. But now that these norms are, so to speak, in the possession of the human race, we can no longer consider them to be justifiable or reversible through any sound, normatively defensible procedures. Considered as relatively concrete and articulate norms for behavior, these norms reflect the contingencies inherent in specific historical trajectories of reflection. But they are not contingent with respect to the intrinsic integrity and value of human life. That is to say, these kinds of behaviors simply are not consistent with any kind of meaningful acknowledgment of human worth or dignity. They offer paradigmatic examples of what theologians traditionally described as intrinsically evil kinds of actions, and we should surely regard them as paradigms of *jus cogens* norms as well.

Although I cannot here develop the argument in detail, it seems to me that the same line of reasoning can be extended to address a key question for international law and relations between nations generally. We might pose the question at hand in this way. What kinds of normative criteria — if any! — must a governing regime meet, in order to be regarded as a fully legitimate participant in the community of nations? In chapter two, I addressed this question in a preliminary way, arguing that despotism represents a perversion of the proper orientation of governing authorities towards the common good. But this argument is incomplete. It might be said that for some societies, the common good is compatible with what is in effect servitude for some of those within the community — meaning, not only some measure of mutual constraint and inequality in a hierarchical system, but systematic practices whereby the energies of some are directed entirely towards the interests of others, or to the attainment of some overarching ideal or set of public goods. These would be forms of servitude, tantamount to what Kant would call treating some as means to the aims of others.

In the previous chapter, I suggested that we have arrived at a point at which the condemnation of slavery, once seen as reflecting an unattainable ideal, now appears as one of the exigent demands of justice. Although I cannot argue the point here, this condemnation would seem to represent one of those *jus cogens* norms that can be acknowledged by all the peoples of the world to be universally binding. The example of slavery, which after all is a kind of denial of political relations at the individual level, further suggests that we have good grounds for condemning those forms of communal associations in which the lives of some are placed without remainder at the disposal of others. At the least, we have good reason to expect that most men and women can come to agree that despotism, understood in terms of the self-regarding dominion of a whole community or some segment of the community by an individual or another segment of the community, is always wrong. Again, this does not necessarily imply that we can or should secure agreement with respect to the specific ideals and practices of Western liberal democracies. Our own construal of a properly political freedom, while legitimate and indeed powerfully attractive, is not the only one possible. Once we realize that natural inclinations towards freedom of action, social integration, and communal cohesion can be expressed in more than one way, it becomes easier to recognize that the peoples of the world do generally share in their desire for political freedom and their hatred of despotism, and this provides a common starting point for reflection on law and the practical task of law-making, both domestically and among the nations.

In diverse and mutually interconnected ways, the polities of the world, the men and women comprising them, and humanity itself all act as ministers of the law, deriving their authority from the supreme authority of God's eternal law through the self-constituting principles and practices of natural law. For Christians, and for those who share the Christian vision of an active, benevolent Providence, this authority extends beyond the boundaries of human history and its future, promising the eventual return of all peoples to one polity, one homeland, under the rule of a perfect law of freedom: "A law will go out from me, my justice as a light for the peoples. . . . Raise your eyes to the sky, look at the earth beneath! — for the sky will be dispersed like smoke, the earth will wear out like a garment, its inhabitants will die like gnats, but my salvation will endure forever, my triumph will not be eclipsed" (Isa. 51:4-6).[72] This promise, with the hope it contains, offers great comfort to those who share the faith it expresses. But it also offers one more reminder of an authority that is hidden from the clear view of humanity, even as it is exercised and expressed through the ongoing processes of human life and history. Those of us who do hold onto this faith and hope are called on to recognize, affirm, and whole-heartedly support all that is good in these processes, including the precious, fragmentary intimations of God's providential law in political life

---

72. Taken from Joseph Blenkinsopp, *Isaiah 40-55*, part of the Anchor Bible Commentary Series (New York: Doubleday, 2002).

and formal laws. These are at best limited and provisional, but they are not evil nor are they simply the reflections of human sinfulness. They reflect the human goodness that we receive with gratitude, and offer tokens of hope forbidding us the easy evasions of cynicism and despair.

Bibliography

1. Ancient and Medieval Sources

Albert the Great. *De Bono.* Vol. 28 in *Alberti Magni Opera Omnia ad fidem codicum manuscriptorum.* Münster: Aschendorff, 1951.

Augustine. *De Civitate Dei,* book 14. Translated by W. C. Greene. In *City of God,* vol. 6. Cambridge, MA: Loeb Classical Library, 1969.

Cicero. *De Republica, De Legibus.* Translated by Clinton Walker Keyes. Cambridge, MA: Loeb Classical Library, 1928.

Hugh of St. Victor. *De sacramentis.* Vol. 176 in *Patrologiae Latina,* edited by J.-P. Migne. Paris: Garneri Fratres.

Glossa Ordinaria. *Biblia Latina cum Glossa Ordinaria.* Vol. 4. Brepols: Turnhout, 1992.

———. *Patrologiae Cursus Completus.* Vol. 114. 1852.

Gratian of Bologna. *Decretum Gratiani Emendum et Notationibus Illustratum una cum Glossis.* Rome: in aedibus Populi Romani, 1582.

———. *Gratian: The Treatise on Laws (Decretum DD. 1-20), with the Ordinary Gloss.* Gloss translated by Augustine Thompson and James Gordley. Washington, DC: Catholic University of America Press, 1993.

Justinian. *The Digest of Justinian.* Philadelphia: University of Philadelphia Press, 1985.

———. *The Institutes of Justinian.* London: Longmans, Green and Company, 1888.

Thomas Aquinas. *Summa theologica.* Vols. 4-12 in *Opera Omnia iussa edita Leonis XIII P.M.* Rome: Ex Typographia Polyglotta S.C. de Propaganda Fide, 1888-1906. Abbreviated ST in the text and notes.

———. *Super Librum Dionysii De divinis Nominibus.* Vol. 29 in *Opera Omnia.* Parisiis apud Ludovicum Vives, 1871-80.

2. Modern and Contemporary Sources

Adams, Robert. "A Modified Divine Command Theory of Ethical Wrongness." In *The*

Virtue of Faith and Other Essays in Philosophical Theology. Oxford: Oxford University Press, 1987.

Annas, Julia. *The Morality of Happiness.* Oxford: Oxford University Press, 1993.

Anscombe, Elizabeth. *Intention.* Ithaca: Cornell University Press, 1957.

Ariew, André. "Teleology." In *The Cambridge Companion to the Philosophy of Biology,* edited by David L. Hull and Michael Ruse. Cambridge: Cambridge University Press, 2007.

Aronovitch, Hilliard. "Reflective Equilibrium or Evolving Tradition?" *Inquiry* 39: 399-419.

Bastit, Michel. *Naissance de la Loi Moderne: La Pensée de la Loi de Saint Thomas B Suarez.* Paris: Presses Universitaires de France, 1990.

Bell, Daniel. *Beyond Liberal Democracy.* Princeton: Princeton University Press, 2006.

Bisson, Thomas N. *The Crisis of the Twelfth Century: Power, Lordship, and the Origins of European Government.* Princeton: Princeton University Press, 2009.

Blenkinsopp, Joseph. *Isaiah 40–45,* Anchor Bible Commentary, with translation. New York: Doubleday, 2002.

Browning, Don. *Marriage and Modernization.* Grand Rapids: Eerdmans, 2003.

Brundage, James A. *The Medieval Origins of the Legal Profession: Canonists, Civilians, and Courts.* Chicago: University of Chicago Press, 2008.

Bujo, Bénézet. *Foundations of an African Ethic: Beyond the Universal Claims of Western Morality.* Translated by Brian McNeil. New York: Crossroad, 2000/2001.

Charles, David. *Aristotle on Meaning and Essence.* Oxford: Oxford University Press, 2000.

Cole, David. "The Same-Sex Future." *New York Review of Books* 56.11 (July 2, 2009): 12-16.

Coleman, Janet. "MacIntyre and Aquinas." In *After MacIntyre: Critical Perspectives on the Work of Alasdair MacIntyre,* edited by John Horton and Susan Mendes. Notre Dame: University of Notre Dame Press, 1994.

Constable, Giles. *The Reformation of the Twelfth Century.* Cambridge: Cambridge University Press, 1996.

Coss, Peter. "Conclusion." In *The Moral World of the Law.* Cambridge: Cambridge University Press, 2000.

———. "Introduction." In *The Moral World of the Law.* Cambridge: Cambridge University Press, 2000.

Cronin, Kieran. *Rights and Christian Ethics.* Cambridge: Cambridge University Press, 1992.

D'Andrade, Roy. "Cognitive Anthropology." In *New Directions in Psychological Anthropology,* edited by Theodore Schwartz, Geoffrey M. White, and Catherine A. Lutz. Cambridge: Cambridge University Press, 1992.

Davis, David Brion. *Inhuman Bondage: The Rise and Fall of Slavery in the New World.* Oxford: Oxford University Press, 2006.

"Did Knives and Forks Cut Murders?" *New York Times,* May 3, 2003, A21, 23.

Dilcher, Gerhard. "Der mittelalterliche Kaisergedanke als Rechtslegitimation." In *Die Begründung des Rechts als historisches Problem,* edited by Dietmar Willoweit and Elisabeth Müller-Luckner. Münster: Oldenbourg, 2000.

Bibliography

Donald, Merlin. *Origins of the Modern Mind: Three Stages in the Evolution of Culture and Cognition.* Cambridge, MA: Harvard University Press, 1991.

Donnelly, Jack. *Universal Human Rights in Theory and Practice.* Second edition. Ithaca: Cornell University Press, 2003.

Dworkin, Ronald. *Is Democracy Possible Here? Principles for a New Political Debate.* Princeton: Princeton University Press, 2006.

———. *Justice in Robes.* Cambridge, MA: Belknap Press/Harvard University Press, 2006.

———. "Law, Philosophy and Interpretation." *ARSP* 80 (1994): 463-75.

———. *Law's Empire.* Cambridge, MA: Belknap Press/Harvard University Press, 1986.

———. *Sovereign Virtue: The Theory and Practice of Equality.* Cambridge, MA: Harvard University Press, 2000.

———. *Taking Rights Seriously.* Cambridge: Harvard University Press, 1978.

Elias, Norbert. *The Civilizing Process.* Revised edition. Translated by Edmund Jephcott. Oxford: Blackwell, 1994; originally published in two parts in 1939.

Elliott, Dyan. *Spiritual Marriage: Sexual Abstinence in Medieval Wedlock.* Princeton: Princeton University Press, 1993.

Elshtain, Jean Bethke. "Reflection on the Problem of 'Dirty Hands.'" In *Torture: A Consideration,* edited by Sanford Levinson. Oxford: Oxford University Press, 2004.

Fairlie, Henry. "The Decline of Oratory." *The New Republic,* May 28, 1984, 17.

Finnis, John. *Aquinas: Founders of Modern Political and Social Thought.* Oxford: Oxford University Press, 1998.

———. *Aquinas: Moral, Political, and Legal Theory.* Oxford: Oxford University Press, 1998.

———. *Natural Law and Natural Rights.* Oxford: Clarendon, 1980.

Foot, Philippa. *Natural Goodness.* Oxford: Oxford University Press, 2001.

Friedman, George. "The Ghost City." *The New York Review of Books* 52.15 (October 6, 2005).

Fuller, Lon L. *The Morality of Law.* Revised edition. New Haven: Yale University Press, 1969.

Garsten, Bryan. *Saving Persuasion: A Defense of Rhetoric and Judgment.* Cambridge, MA: Harvard University Press, 2006.

Gaudemet, Jean. "La primauté pontificale dans le Décret de Gratien." In *Studia in Honorem Eminentissimi Cardinalis Alphonsi M. Stickler,* edited by R. J. Card. Castillo Lara. Rome: Libreria Ateneo Salesiano, 1992.

Gaudium et Spes. In *The Gospel of Peace and Justice: Catholic Social Teaching since Pope John,* edited by Joseph Gremillion. Maryknoll, NY: Orbis Books, 1976.

George, Robert. *In Defense of Natural Law.* Oxford: Oxford University Press, 1999.

———. *Making Men Moral: Civil Liberties and Public Morality.* Oxford: Oxford University Press, 1993.

Glendon, Mary Ann. *Rights Talk: The Impoverishment of Political Discourse.* New York: Free Press, 1991.

Grene, Marjorie. "Hierarchies in Biology." *American Scientist* 75 (1987): 504-9.

Grene, Marjorie, with David Depew. *The Philosophy of Modern Biology: An Episodic History.* Cambridge: Cambridge University Press, 2004.

Grisez, Germain. "The First Principle of Practical Reason: A Commentary on the *Summa theologiae*, 1-2, Question 94, Article 2." In *Natural Law Forum* 10 (1965).

―――. *The Way of the Lord Jesus, 1: Christian Moral Principles.* Chicago: Franciscan Herald Press, 1983.

―――. *The Way of the Lord Jesus, 2: Living a Christian Life.* Chicago: Franciscan Herald Press, 1993.

Grisez, Germain, Joseph Boyle, and John Finnis. "Practical Principles, Moral Truth, and Ultimate Ends." *American Journal of Jurisprudence* 32 (1987): 99-151.

Gustafson, James. *Ethics from a Theocentric Perspective,* volume 1: *Theology and Ethics.* Chicago: University of Chicago Press, 1981.

Hare, Robert D. *Without Conscience: The Disturbing World of the Psychopaths among Us.* New York: Guilford Press, 1993.

Harkness, Sara, Charles Super, and Constance Keefer. "Learning to Be an American Parent: How Cultural Models Gain Directive Force." In *Human Motives and Cultural Models,* edited by Roy D'Andrade and Claudia Strauss. Cambridge: Cambridge University Press, 1992.

Hart, H. L. A. *The Concept of Law.* Second edition. Oxford: Clarendon Press, 1994; first edition, 1961.

Hauerwas, Stanley. *After Christendom? How the Church Is to Behave If Freedom, Justice, and a Christian Nation Are Bad Ideas.* Nashville: Abingdon, 1991.

―――. *Against the Nations: War and Survival in a Liberal Society.* Minneapolis: Seabury/Winston Press, 1985.

―――. *A Community of Character: Toward a Constructive Christian Social Ethic.* Notre Dame: University of Notre Dame Press, 1981.

―――. *The Peaceable Kingdom: A Primer in Christian Ethics.* Notre Dame: University of Notre Dame Press, 1983.

Hays, Richard. *The Moral Vision of the New Testament: A Contemporary Introduction to New Testament Ethics.* New York: HarperCollins, 1996.

Hittinger, Russell. *The First Grace: Rediscovering the Natural Law in a Post-Christian World.* Wilmington: ISI Books, 2003.

―――. "Pope Leo XIII: Commentary." In *The Teachings of Modern Roman Catholicism on Law, Politics, and Human Nature,* edited by John Witte, Jr., and Frank S. Alexander. New York: Columbia University Press, 2007.

Hoffman, Stanley. *Duties Beyond Borders: On the Limits and Possibilities of Ethical International Politics.* Syracuse: Syracuse University Press, 1981.

Hollenbach, David. *The Common Good and Christian Ethics.* Cambridge: Cambridge University Press, 2002.

Holmes, Oliver Wendell. *The Common Law.* Cambridge, MA: Harvard/Belknap Press, 1963; originally published 1881.

Howard, Michael. "Constraints on Warfare." In *The Laws of War: Constraints on Warfare in the Western World,* edited by Michael Howard, George M. Andreopoulos, and Mark R. Shulman. New Haven: Yale University Press, 1994.

Hrdy, Sarah Blaffer. *Mothers and Others: The Evolutionary Origins of Mutual Understanding.* Cambridge, MA: Harvard/Belknap Press, 2009.

Hursthouse, Rosalind. *On Virtue Ethics.* Oxford: Oxford University Press, 1999.

Bibliography

Hyams, Paul. "Due Process versus the Maintenance of Order in European Law: The Contribution of the *jus commune*." In *The Moral World of the Law*, edited by Peter Coss. Cambridge: Cambridge University Press, 2000.

Ignatieff, Michael. *Human Rights*. Princeton: Princeton University Press, 2001.

Insole, Christopher. *The Politics of Human Frailty: A Theological Defense of Political Liberalism*. London: SCM Press, 2004.

Judt, Tony. "What Is Living and What Is Dead in Social Democracy?" *The New York Review of Books* 61.20 (December 17, 2009): 86-97.

Kant, Immanuel. *Critique of Practical Reason*. Translated by Lewis White Beck. Indianapolis: Bobbs-Merrill, 1956, reprinted 1981; originally published 1788.

King, Anthony. *The British Constitution*. Oxford: Oxford University Press, 2007.

King, Geoffrey. "The Acceptance of Law by the Community: A Study in the Writings of Canonists and Theologians, 1500-1750." *The Jurist* 37 (1977): 233-65.

Landau, Peter. "Der biblische Südenfall und die Legitimität des Rechts." In *Die Begründung des Rechts als historisches Problem*, edited by Dietmar Willoweit and Elisabeth Müller-Luckner. Münster: R. Oldenbourg, 2000.

―――. "Wandel und Kontinuität im kanonischen Recht bei Gratian." In *Sozialer Wandel im Mittelalter: Wahrnehmungsformen, Erklärungsmuster, Regelungsmechanismem*, edited by Jürgen Miethke and Klaus Schreiner. Stuttgart: Jan Thorbecke, 1994.

Lennox, James. *Aristotle's Philosophy of Biology*. Cambridge: Cambridge University Press, 2001.

Lepore, Jill. "The Politics of Death: From Karen Ann Quinlan to Death Panels." *The New Yorker*, November 30, 2009, 60-67.

Little, Lester K. *Religious Poverty and the Profit Economy in Medieval Europe*. Ithaca: Cornell University Press, 1978.

Lloyd, G. E. R. *Cognitive Variations: Reflections on the Unity and Diversity of the Human Mind*. Oxford: Clarendon Press, 2007.

Lottin, Odon. "La Loi eternelle chez saint Thomas d'Aquin et ses predecesserus." In *Psychologie et Morale aux XII et XIII siècles*. Vol. 2 of 6 vols. Louvain: Abbae du Mont César, 1942-60.

―――. "La Loi en general: La definition thomiste et ses antecedents." In *Psychologie et Morale aux XIIe et XIIIe siècles*. Volume 2, *Problèmes de morale*. Louvain: Abbae du Mont César, 1948.

―――. *Psychologie et morale aux XII et XIII siècles*. Volume 3, parts 1 and 2. Paris: Louvain, 1949.

Lowe, E. J. *The Possibility of Metaphysics: Substance, Identity, and Time*. Oxford: Clarendon Press, 1980.

Luhmann, Niklas. *Law as a Social System*. Translated by Klaus A. Ziegert. Oxford: Oxford University Press, 2004.

MacCormick, Neil. *Institutions of Law: An Essay in Legal Theory*. Oxford: Oxford University Press, 2007.

―――. *Rhetoric and the Rule of Law: A Theory of Legal Reasoning*. Oxford: Oxford University Press, 2005.

MacIntyre, Alasdair. *After Virtue.* Second edition. Notre Dame: University of Notre Dame Press, 1984.

———. *Dependent Rational Animals: Why Human Beings Need the Virtues.* Peru, IL: Carus/Open Court, 1999.

———. *First Principles, Final Ends and Contemporary Philosophical Issues.* Milwaukee: Marquette University Press, 1990.

———. *Three Rival Versions of Moral Enquiry: Encyclopaedia, Genealogy, and Tradition.* Notre Dame: University of Notre Dame Press, 1990.

———. *Whose Justice? Which Rationality?* Notre Dame: University of Notre Dame Press, 1988.

Maritain, Jacques. *Man and the State.* Chicago: University of Chicago Press, 1951.

Marmor, Andrei. *Social Conventions: From Language to Law.* Princeton: Princeton University Press, 2009.

McDowell, John. *Mind and World.* Cambridge, MA: Harvard University Press, 1994.

Meron, Theodor. *Human Rights and Humanitarian Norms as Customary Law.* Oxford: Clarendon Press, 1989.

Milbank, John. *Theology and Social Theory: Beyond Secular Reason.* Oxford: Blackwell, 1990.

Milsom, S. F. C. *A Natural History of the Common Law.* New York: Columbia University Press, 2003.

Morris, Christopher W. *An Essay on the Modern State.* Cambridge: Cambridge University Press, 1998.

Moss, Lenny. "Representational Preformationism to the Epigenesis of Openness to the World? Reflections on a New Vision of the Organism." In *From Epigenesis to Epigenetics.* Volume 981 of the *Annals of the New York Academy of Sciences,* December 2002, 21-230.

———. *What Genes Can't Do.* Cambridge, MA: MIT Press, 2003.

Murray, John Courtney. *We Hold These Truths: Catholic Reflections on the American Proposition.* New York: Doubleday, 1964.

Nederman, Cary. "Aristotelianism and the Origins of 'Political Science' in the Twelfth Century." *Journal of the History of Ideas* 52 (1991): 179-94.

———. "Nature, Sin and the Origins of Society: The Ciceronian Tradition in Medieval Political Thought." *The Journal of the History of Ideas* 49 (1988): 3-26.

Nelson, Katherine. *Young Minds in Social Worlds: Experience, Meaning, and Memory.* Cambridge, MA: Harvard University Press, 2007.

Niebuhr, Reinhold. *Moral Man and Immoral Society.* New York: Charles Scribner's Sons, 1932.

———. *Nature and Destiny of Man.* Volume 2: *Human Destiny.* New York: Scribner's, 1943/1964.

Nobles, Richard, and David Schiff. "Introduction." In *Law as a Social System* by Niklas Luhmann. Translated by Klaus A. Ziegert. Oxford: Oxford University Press, 2004.

Nussbaum, Martha C. *Women and Human Development: The Capabilities Approach.* Cambridge: Cambridge University Press, 2000.

O'Connell, Mary Ellen. *The Power and Purpose of International Law.* New York: Oxford University Press, 2008.

Bibliography

————. "Responsibility to Peace: A Critique of R2P." Forthcoming in *Critical Perspectives on the Responsibility to Protect: Interrogating Theory and Practice,* edited by Philip Cunliffe. New York: Routledge, 2010.

O'Donovan, Oliver. *Church in Crisis: The Gay Controversy and the Anglican Communion.* Eugene: Cascade Books, 2008.

————. *The Desire of the Nations: Rediscovering the Roots of Political Theology.* Cambridge: Cambridge University Press, 1996.

————. *Resurrection and Moral Order: An Outline for Evangelical Ethics.* Grand Rapids: Eerdmans, 1986.

————. *The Ways of Judgment.* Grand Rapids: Eerdmans, 2005.

Padgen, Anthony. *The Fall of Natural Man: The American Indian and the Origins of Comparative Ethnology.* Cambridge: Cambridge University Press, 1982.

Parish, Steven A. *Moral Knowing in a Hindu Sacred City: An Exploration of Mind, Emotion, and Self.* New York: Columbia University Press, 1994.

Pasnau, Robert. *Thomas Aquinas on Human Nature: A Philosophical Study of Summa theologiae Ia 75-89.* Cambridge: Cambridge University Press, 2002.

Patterson, Orlando. *Freedom in the Making of Western Culture.* New York: Basic Books, 1991.

————. *Slavery and Social Death: A Comparative Study.* Cambridge, MA: Harvard University Press, 1982.

Peirce, Charles S. "Questions Concerning Certain Faculties Claimed for Man." Originally published 1868, printed as pp. 64-118 in *Charles S. Peirce: The Essential Writings,* edited by Edward Moore. New York: Harper and Row, 1972.

Pennington, Kenneth. *The Prince and the Law, 1200-1600: Sovereignty and Rights in the Western Legal Tradition.* Berkeley: University of California Press, 1993.

Perry, Michael. *The Idea of Human Rights: Four Inquiries.* Oxford: Oxford University Press, 1998, 2000.

Pitts, Leonard, columnist for *Miami Herald.* Editorial run by the *South Bend Tribune,* November 22, 2009.

Porter, Jean. "Christian Ethics and the Concept of Morality: A Historical Inquiry." *Journal of the Society of Christian Ethics* 26.2 (2006): 3-21.

————. "The Common Good in Thomas Aquinas." In *In Search of the Common Good,* edited by Dennis P. McCann and Patrick D. Miller. New York: T&T Clark, 2005.

————. "Custom, Ordinance and Natural Right in Gratian's *Decretum."* In *The Nature of Customary Law: Legal, Historical and Philosophical Perspectives,* edited by Amanda Perreau-Saussine and James Bernard Murphy. Cambridge: Cambridge University Press, 2007.

————. *Natural and Divine Law: Reclaiming the Tradition for Christian Ethics.* Grand Rapids: Eerdmans, 1999.

————. "Natural Right, Authority, and Power: The Theological Trajectory of Human Rights." Forthcoming in *The Journal of Law, Philosophy and Culture,* Spring 2011.

————. *Nature as Reason: A Thomistic Theory of the Natural Law.* Grand Rapids: Eerdmans, 2005.

Rawls, John. "The Law of Peoples." In *On Human Rights,* edited by Stephen Shute and Susan Hurley. New York: Basic Books, 1993.

————. *The Laws of Peoples.* Cambridge, MA: Harvard University Press, 1999.

————. *Political Liberalism.* New York: Columbia University Press, 1993.

————. *A Theory of Justice.* Cambridge, MA: Harvard University Press, 1971.

Raz, Joseph. *The Authority of Law: Essays on Law and Morality.* Oxford: Clarendon Press, 1979.

————. *Between Authority and Interpretation.* Oxford: Oxford University Press, 2009.

————. *The Morality of Freedom.* Oxford: Clarendon Press, 1986.

Reid, Charles J., Jr. *Power over the Body, Equality in the Family: Rights and Domestic Relations in Medieval Canon Law.* Grand Rapids: Eerdmans, 2004.

Reynolds, Barbara. *Fiefs and Vassals: The Medieval Evidence Reinterpreted.* Oxford: Oxford University Press, 1994.

Robertson, D. B. "Introduction." In *Love and Justice: Selections from the Shorter Writings of Reinhold Niebuhr.* Louisville: Westminster/John Knox Press, 1957.

Robertson, Geoffrey. *Crimes against Humanity: The Struggle for Global Justice.* Second edition. New York: Penguin, 2002.

Rogoff, Barbara. *The Cultural Nature of Human Development.* Oxford: Oxford University Press, 2003.

Rorty, Richard. *Consequences of Pragmatism.* Minneapolis: University of Minnesota Press, 1982.

Rosen, Lawrence. *The Anthropology of Justice: Law as Culture in Islamic Society.* Cambridge: Cambridge University Press, 1989.

————. *The Culture of Islam: Changing Aspects of Contemporary Muslim Life.* Chicago: University of Chicago Press, 2002.

————. *Law as Culture: An Invitation.* Princeton: Princeton University Press, 2006.

Rubin, Trudy. "Musharraf War on Courts Hurts Terror Fight." *Philadelphia Inquirer,* December 26, 2007.

Sahaydachcy, Antonia Bocarius. "The Marriage of Unfree Persons: Twelfth Century Decretals and Letters." In *De Jure Canonico Medii: Festschrift für Rudolf Weigand, Studia Gratiana* XXVII (1996).

Sands, Philippe. *Lawless World.* New York: Penguin, 2005.

Scalia, Antonin. "Common Law Courts in a Civil-Law System." In *A Matter of Interpretation: Federal Courts and the Law,* edited by Antonin Scalia and Amy Gutmann. Princeton: Princeton University Press, 1997.

Scalia, Antonin. "Originalism: The Lesser Evil." *University of Cincinnati Law Review* 849 (1989).

Scalia, Antonin, and Amy Gutmann. *A Matter of Interpretation: Federal Courts and the Law.* Princeton: Princeton University Press, 1997.

Sen, Amartya. *Development as Freedom.* New York: Random House, 1999.

Sengupta, Somini. "For Now, Musharraf Has Muzzled Legal Critics in Pakistan." *New York Times,* January 5, 2008.

Shklar, Judith. *The Faces of Injustice.* New Haven: Yale University Press, 1990.

————. *Ordinary Vices.* Cambridge, MA: Harvard/Belknap Press, 1984.

Shue, Henry. *Basic Rights: Subsistence, Affluence, and U.S. Foreign Policy.* Second edition. Princeton: Princeton University Press, 1996.

Bibliography

Shweder, Richard. *Why Do Men Barbecue? Recipes for Cultural Psychology.* Cambridge, MA: Harvard University Press, 2003.

Simon, Yves. *A General Theory of Authority.* Notre Dame: University of Notre Dame Press, 1962, 1980.

Slaughter, Anne-Marie. *A New World Order.* Princeton: Princeton University Press, 2004.

Southern, R. W. *Scholastic Humanism and the Unification of Europe,* Volume 1: *Foundations.* Oxford: Blackwell, 1995.

Spruyt, Hendrik. *The Sovereign State and Its Competitors.* Princeton: Princeton University Press, 1994.

Stoner, James R., Jr. *Common Law Liberty: Rethinking American Constitutionalism.* Lawrence: University Press of Kansas, 2003.

Tierney, Brian. *The Idea of Natural Rights: Studies on Natural Rights, Natural Law and Church Law, 1150-1652.* Atlanta: Scholars Press, 1997.

Tomasello, Michael. *The Cultural Origins of Human Cognition.* Cambridge, MA: Harvard University Press, 1999.

Tomasello, Michael, et al. "Understanding and Sharing Intentions: The Origins of Cultural Cognition." *Behavioral and Brain Sciences* 28 (2005): 675-735.

Tuck, Richard. *Natural Rights Theories.* Cambridge: Cambridge University Press, 1979.

Urquhart, Brian. "The UN and the Race Against Death." *The New York Review of Books* 55.11 (June 26, 2008).

van Caenegem, R. C. "Government, Law and Society." In *The Cambridge History of Medieval Political Thought, c. 350–c. 1450,* edited by J. H. Burns. Cambridge: Cambridge University Press, 1988.

———. *An Historical Introduction to Western Constitutional Law.* Cambridge: Cambridge University Press, 1995.

Vinogradoff, Paul. *Roman Law in Medieval Europe.* Second edition. Oxford: Clarendon Press, 1929.

Wallace, James. *Virtues and Vices.* Ithaca: Cornell University Press, 1978.

Walzer, Michael. *Exodus and Revolution.* New York: Basic Books, 1985.

Watson, Gerard. "Natural Law and Stoicism." In *Problems in Stoicism,* edited by A. A. Long. London: Athlone, 1971.

Weigand, Rudolf. *Die Naturrechtslehre der Legisten und Dekretisten von Irnerius bis Accursius und von Gratian bis Johannes Teutonicus.* Munich: Max Hueber, 1967.

Wickham, Chris. "Conclusion." In *The Moral World of the Law,* edited by Peter Coss. Cambridge: Cambridge University Press, 2000.

Winroth, Anders. *The Making of Gratian's Decretum.* Cambridge: Cambridge University Press, 2000.

Wolterstorff, Nicholas. *Justice: Rights and Wrongs.* Princeton: Princeton University Press, 2008.

Yoder, John Howard. *The Politics of Jesus: Vicit Angus Noster.* Second edition. Grand Rapids: Eerdmans, 1994.

Index of Proper Names

Index of Proper Names

Gustafson, James, 57n.111

Hare, Robert, 192n.43
Harkness, Sara, 217n.68
Hart, H. L. A., 9-19, 21, 24-29, 32-33, 39-
40, 65-66, 87, 136, 168, 224-25, 231n.10,
232, 255, 265, 278n.48, 279, 339-40
Hauerwas, Stanley, 308n.22
Hays, Richard, 308n.22
Hittinger, Russell, 60-61, 149n.5
Hoffmann, Stanley, 303n.14
Hollenbach, David, 148-50, 166n.17, 203,
286n.55
Holmes, Oliver Wendell, 257-58, 260
Howard, Michael, 304n.16
Hrdy, Sarah Blaffer, 192n.42
Hugh of St. Victor, 73
Hursthouse, Rosalind, 84n.29
Hyams, Paul, 338n.61

Ignatieff, Michael, 320, 326
Insole, Christopher, 55n.109, 186n.36,
239n.16
Irnerius, 46, 48

Judt, Tony, 198n.50, 300-301

Justinian, 46, 50, 72n.16, 73

Kant, Immanuel, 1-2, 321, 324, 349
Keefer, Constance, 217n.68
King, Anthony, 2n.3, 245n.18
King, Geoffrey, 254n.26

Landau, Peter, 3, 71n.14, 73n.17
Lennox, James, 85-86, 114n.59
Lepore, Jill, 327n.49
Little, Lester, 224n.1
Lloyd, G. E. R., 109
Lottin, Odon, 58n.112, 151n.7, 162n.16,
262n.37
Lowe, E. J., 86n.32
Luhmann, Niklas, 16n.32, 18

MacCormick, Neil, 2n.3, 7, 16n.32,
25n.52, 27n.53, 65-66, 145, 169-71, 175,
225, 236, 245-46, 258-59, 270n.45, 273,

276, 291n.1, 294, 297-98, 306, 317-20,
323n.40, 328, 337
MacIntyre, Alasdair, 38n.82, 84n.29,
88n.35, 101n.40, 197n.48, 333
Maritain, Jacques, 338n.62
Marmor, Andrei, 9n.14, 80, 101n.41
McDowell, John, 103-5
Meron, Theodor, 341-42
Milbank, John, 308n.22
Milsom, S. F. C., 50n.102
Morris, Christopher, 291n.1, 306n.19
Moss, Lenny, 84n.29
Murray, John Courtney, 5n.7, 6

Nederman, Cary, 48n.100, 81
Nelson, Katherine, 192n.42
Niebuhr, Reinhold, 197n.49, 227, 281,
309-12, 315
Nobles, Richard, 16n.32
Nussbaum, Martha, 182-83, 320n.33, 337

O'Connell, Mary Ellen, 295-96, 303n.15,
305n.17, 308, 343-46
O'Donovan, Oliver, 57, 125, 226-27, 230-
31, 241, 296

Padgen, Anthony, 108n.47
Parish, Steven, 111-12, 138
Pasnau, Robert, 85n.30
Patterson, Orlando, 43n.87, 44, 282n.53
Peirce, Charles, 31
Pennington, Kenneth, 42n.85, 47-48, 50,
55
Perry, Michael, 324, 326-28
Pitts, Leonard, 289-90

Rawls, John, 155-56, 166, 171-72, 196n.47,
228, 240, 319, 336-37
Raz, Joseph, 7-8, 15n.28, 17n.33, 34-40, 49,
53-54, 64-65, 75, 121n.65, 130nn.70-71,
133-34, 172n.23, 187, 189n.40, 196n.47,
199, 226, 239n.15, 240n.16, 285-86
Reid, Jr., Charles, 44n.88, 328n.52,
337n.59
Reynolds, Barbara, 301n.10
Robertson, D. B., 309n.23

Robertson, Geoffrey, 210n.63, 305n.17
Rogoff, Barbara, 216n.68
Rorty, Richard, 215
Rosen, Lawrence, 63-64, 139-40, 166n.17,
    209, 234, 261n.36
Rubin, Trudy, 209n.61

Sahaydachcy, Antonia, 44n.88
Sands, Philippe, 210n.63
Scalia, Antonin, 3n.4, 269-70
Sen, Amartya, 182
Sengupta, Somini, 209n.61
Shklar, Judith, 208, 212n.64
Shue, Henry, 157n.12
Shweder, Richard, 108-13, 138-39, 152, 160,
    201-2
Simon of Tournai, 161-62
Simon, Yves, 228n.8
Slaughter, Anne-Marie, 303n.15
Southern, R. W., 42n.85, 44n.91, 71n.14,
    224n.1
Spruyt, Hendrik, 291n.1, 301-2
Stoner, Jr., James, 172n.23, 257
Super, Charles, 217n.68

Thomas Aquinas, 42, 49, 58-61, 66-67,

70, 75, 78-79, 82, 85, 89-98, 103-5, 137,
    140, 146-47, 151-55, 163-64, 178, 186,
    227-29, 234, 236n.14, 241-43, 262-63,
    270, 306, 313-15, 337, 345
Tierney, Brian, 48n.99, 77-78, 322, 328-32,
    338n.61, 347
Tomasello, Michael, 104-6, 192n.42
Tuck, Richard, 325-26, 347

Urquhart, Brian, 214n.66, 217n.69

van Caenegem, R. C., 42n.85, 43, 45, 259-
    60, 291-92
Vinogradoff, Paul, 261n.35

Wallace, James, 84n.29, 115
Walzer, Michael, 280
Watson, Gerard, 63, 67, 205
Weigand, Rudolf, 46n.94-95, 79n.23,
    261n.35
Wickham, Chris, 16, 235
Winroth, Anders, 72n.16, 73n.19
Wolterstorff, Nicholas, 321-24, 328,
    333n.56

Yoder, John Howard, 308n.22

Index of Subjects

Adjudication, 2, 8-9, 15, 25, 30, 45-46, 50, 62, 75, 156, 169, 175, 177, 226, 230, 241, 258, 265, 272, 275-77, 279, 292, 326, 331-32, 346; constrained by existing law, 30, 62, 75, 175-76, 226-27, 241-42, 269, 275-76, 291-92; innovative elements of, 45-46, 50, 177, 229-30, 258-59, 265, 276-77; necessity for a legal system, 2, 8, 15, 25, 45-46, 156, 238-39, 326-31, 332, 346. *See also* Interpretation; Lawmaking

Authority, 3-6, 12, 17-23, 27, 42, 45-46, 48-51, 53-56, 58-60, 62, 69, 81-83, 114, 125-26, 129, 131, 143, 146, 205, 219-20, 246-48, 250-53, 255, 257-66, 269-72, 274-75, 292-93, 296-97, 299-300, 320-22, 329, 331, 337, 339-43, 347-48; and democracy, 32-33, 165-66, 172-74, 246, 256-58; contingency or arbitrariness of, 17, 19, 144-45, 170-76, 274-75, 298; distinct from dominion, 17, 46-49, 78, 135-36, 146-47, 159, 164-66, 174-75, 179-80, 186, 219-20, 225, 227, 247, 258, 266-67, 296-97, 300-302, 308-9, 328, 330, 334; distinct from order or command, 129-30, 135-36, 145, 147, 167, 179, 186, 224-25, 242, 334; political character of, 22, 32-33, 48-51, 78, 135-37, 140, 145-47, 159, 163-68, 170, 175, 179-80, 186, 189, 205, 219-20, 222-30, 232-33, 237, 239,

244-46, 266-67, 272-73, 289-92, 294-96, 298, 300-301, 303-4, 309, 317, 319, 322, 326, 330-32, 334, 339-40; reasonable character of, 19, 33-41, 45-46, 53, 131-36, 140, 144-46, 164-65, 168, 170, 175-77, 179, 186, 189, 223, 235, 245, 250, 261, 265, 270, 342. *See also* Positivism; Service conception

Autonomy, personal, 34-36, 38, 53, 186, 188, 201-2, 329; and liberal ideals, 186-88, 239-40, 285-86, 337-38; presupposes communal structures, 134-36, 187-88. *See also* Freedom

Autonomy of law, 16-17, 32-33, 139, 238

Bureaucracy, 43, 174, 224-25, 239-41, 243, 336

Capability, 96, 120, 182-85, 193, 200, 333, 335, 337

Coercive sanctions, 11-12, 15, 164, 306-8

Common good, 148-66, 179-88, 197-210, 228-34, 258-71, 280-81; as communal ideal, 148-50, 155-57, 159-63, 179-81, 185-88, 197-98, 200, 203-7, 232-33, 241, 258-59, 283, 299-300; as form of happiness, 151, 154-56, 186, 198, 229; modern views of, 147-49, 205-6, 303-4; political in character, 150, 163-64, 179-81, 198-200, 203-5, 232-34, 241, 299-300,

and cruelty, 211-14, 216-17, 349; and exploitation, 208-16

Justice, 2-4, 21, 49, 52, 75, 78, 125, 137, 147, 155-56, 171-72, 193, 201, 208-9, 224-25, 227-28, 233, 240-43, 252, 268, 273, 276, 281-83, 289-90, 294, 299, 303-4, 310-11, 316-17, 319, 334, 349

Law, types of (omitting natural order), 61-62, 75-76, 79-80, 249-50, 262; Common law, 50-51, 256-60; Customary law, 45-46, 246-48, 250-60, 339-42; Eternal law, 58-62, 69, 89-90, 96-97, 178-79, 297, 313, 343-44; Formal law, 2-23, 51-52, 61-62, 74-76, 139-41, 232-35, 243-44, 270-72; International law, 211-12, 244-45, 295-97, 303-5, 339-49; Positive (also human; written) law, 45, 51, 58, 61-62, 68-69, 74-75, 77-81, 248-55, 262, 316, 328-29

Lawgiver. *See* Lawmaking

Lawmaking, 4-10, 20-33, 42-53, 252-75, 296-97, 339-43; constraints on, 42-53, 166-77, 244-57; innovative function of, 42-53, 257-72; political in character, 144-47, 171-76, 226-27. *See also* Adjudication

Legislation. *See* Lawmaking

Marriage, 6, 44, 60, 115-28, 132-33, 187-88, 216, 231-32, 282, 284, 286-87

Nation-State, as law state, 224-25, 291-310, 317-20, 326-28. *See also* Sovereignty

Natural law, 20-22, 32, 111-12, 143-49, 310-12, 339-48; and eternal law, 59-62, 69, 89-90, 96-97, 343-44; and human nature, 4, 61-62, 68-69, 80, 83, 89-93, 99, 107, 115-17; and natural relations, 41, 48, 81-83, 92-93, 126-31; as basis for analysis, 4-6, 101-3, 113-22, 208-15; as legitimating principle, 48-51, 74-75, 122-29, 206; as ground for rhetorical persuasion, 169-78, 169, 196, 296; as rational principle, 41, 48, 60-61, 67-68,

76-81, 89-99, 100-101; mediated through conventions, 63-65, 67-69, 80-81, 100-101, 115-17, 248-50, 253-55; modern conceptions of, 41, 149, 182-84; new theory of, 66, 83, 182-84; scholastic concept of, 47-51, 60-61, 67-82, 89-97, 169, 204-6, 278, 329-30

Nature, 48-50, 58, 63-66, 72-80, 83-95, 114-17, 124-26, 247-48; Aristotelian philosophy of, 48-49, 83-88, 91-92, 114-15, 127, 206; as intelligible and purposeful, 58, 69, 72-78, 99-102, 153-54, 178-80, 332-36; as source for norms or values, 86-88, 99-102, 126-27, 137-39, 206-7, 263-64, 278. *See also* Human nature

New natural law, 66, 83, 182-84

Normal justification thesis, 37-41, 133-35

Orders of society, 148-50, 159, 179-80, 198, 267, 291

Paradigmatic concepts, 7, 35-41, 56-61, 87-88, 98-104, 116-22, 129-31, 134-35, 146-47, 203, 233, 242-43, 311-12, 365

Peremptory norms. *See Jus cogens* norms

Perfectionism, 131, 133-35, 153-55, 179-80, 199-204, 207

Political morality, 24-33, 186-89, 234, 237-41, 265-69, 276-77, 319; and common good, 156, 171-72, 203-4, 240-41, 263, 266-67; and Western liberalism, 127-28, 171-72, 186-88, 239-41, 279

Positivism, legal, 17-23, 32, 63-67, 275

Practices, xiv, xvi, 4, 6, 7-8, 10, 13, 17, 23-25, 28-29, 44, 50-51, 63, 66-70, 72, 74-76, 78-83, 98-99, 102, 105, 107-8, 105-21, 123-24, 129, 132, 136-38, 140, 144, 146, 155, 158-69, 181, 187, 189-92, 195-97, 199, 202-6, 208-10, 215-18, 221-22, 223-24, 227-28, 234, 236-37, 246-57, 259-65, 270-71, 274-75, 277-81, 285-88, 292, 297, 299-300, 305, 316, 329, 331, 338-44, 345-46, 348-50. *See also* Custom, Customary law